SOLOMON'S VINEYARD

Society of Biblical Literature

Ancient Israel and Its Literature

Number 1

SOLOMON'S VINEYARD
Literary and Linguistic Studies
in the Song of Songs

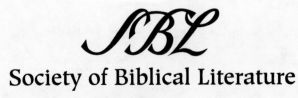

SOLOMON'S VINEYARD

Literary and Linguistic Studies in the Song of Songs

by

Scott B. Noegel

and

Gary A. Rendsburg

Society of Biblical Literature
Atlanta

SOLOMON'S VINEYARD
Literary and Linguistic Studies
in the Song of Songs

Library of Congress Cataloging-in-Publication Data

Noegel, Scott B.
Solomon's vineyard : literary and linguistic studies in the Song of Songs / by Scott B. Noegel and Gary A. Rendsburg.
p. cm. — (Society of Biblical Literature ancient Israel and its literature ; v. 1)
Includes bibliographical references and indexes.
ISBN 978-1-58983-422-4 (pbk. : alk. paper)
1. Bible. O.T. Song of Solomon—Criticism, interpretation, etc. I. Rendsburg, Gary. II. Title.
BS1485.52.N64 2009b
223'.9066—dc22 2009040646

17 16 15 14 13 12 11 10 09 5 4 3 2 1
Printed in the United States of America on acid-free, recycled paper conforming to ANSI/NISO Z39.48-1992 (R1997) and ISO 9706:1994 standards for paper permanence.

For Alan Corré—teacher, colleague, friend

דקרי אורייתא נביאי וכתובי בדיוקא

(Bavli Qiddušin 49a)

Contents

Acknowledgments ix

Abbreviations xi

Introduction 1

1. Israelian Hebrew in the Song of Songs 3

   Excursus to Chapter 1: Additional IH Features in 4QCant[b] 57

2. Alliteration as a Compositional Factor in the Song of Songs 63

3. Variation in the Poetry of the Song of Songs as a Literary Device 107

4. The Genre of the Song of Songs in the Light of Arabic Poetic Traditions 129

Conclusion 171

The Song of Songs: Translation and Notes 187

Bibliography 207

Indices
- Primary Texts 227
- Authors and Reference Works 239
- Premodern Authors 244
- Words and Phrases 245
- Languages 254
- Subjects 256
- Names 264
- Toponyms 266

Acknowledgments

There are a number of individuals who have aided our project in a variety of ways, and we take this opportunity to thank them. Several colleagues have read portions or all of the manuscript, and we have benefited greatly from their comments. These include James Monroe, Suzanne Pinckney Stetkevych, Yaroslav Stetkevych, Brannon Wheeler, Michael Weiss, and Farhat J. Ziadeh. We also thank David Carr for providing us with the written version of his talk delivered at the joint meeting of the National Association of Professors of Hebrew and the Society of Biblical Literature, in Washington, D.C., on November 20, 2006, and for allowing us to cite his work in the conclusion section of the present monograph.

The following students (either past or present) at the University of Washington served as research and/or editorial assistants: Gary Martin, Alex Jassen, Robert Vanhoff, Joseph DuWors, and Jacob Rennaker. Toward the end of our project, we profited from the work of two additional individuals. William Reed (also a student at the University of Washington) produced the indices with both alacrity and assiduousness, while the keen editorial eye of Samantha Ehrlich (a graduate of Rutgers University, now a student at Jewish Theological Seminary) reviewed the proofs one final time. We are indebted to all for their diligence.

We are grateful to Steven McKenzie (Rhodes College) for accepting our manuscript on behalf of the Society of Biblical Literature for the newly launched Ancient Israel and Its Literature series, and indeed we are especially proud to have our monograph appear as the inaugural volume therein. In addition to Professor McKenzie, we also thank Benjamin Sommer (Jewish Theological Seminary) for recommending our work.

It was a pleasure to work with the extremely professional staff at SBL, in particular, Leigh Andersen, Managing Editor, and Bob Buller, Editorial Director. The latter deserves our special appreciation for shepherding our very technical prose from typescript to book.

In dedicating this book to Alan Corré, our dear teacher, colleague, and friend, we express our appreciation for all that he has taught us over the years, for his warm and abiding friendship, and most of all for his humanity, reflected in so many ways.

Finally, we express our enduring love to our wives, Laurie Ramacci Noegel and Beth Kraemer, who make any enterprise with which we are involved a most pleasant song.

Abbreviations

AB	Anchor Bible
ABD	*The Anchor Bible Dictionary*. Edited by David Noel Freedman. 6 vols. New York: Doubleday, 1992.
AJSL	*American Journal of Semitic Languages and Literatures*
AnOr	Analecta orientalia
AOAT	Alter Orient und Altes Testament
AOS	American Oriental Series
ʿArak.	ʿArakin
AuOr	*Aula Orientalis*
b.	Babylonian Talmud
B. Bat.	Baba Batra
B. Qam.	Baba Qamma
BASOR	*Bulletin of the American Schools of Oriental Research*
BASP	*Bulletin of the American Society of Papyrologists*
BDB	Brown, F., S. R. Driver, and C. A. Briggs. *A Hebrew and English Lexicon of the Old Testament*. Oxford: Clarendon, 1907.
Ber.	Berakot
BHQ	*Biblia Hebraica Quinta*. Edited by A. Schenker. Stuttgart: Deutsche Bibelgesellschaft, 2004–.
BHT	Beiträge zur historischen Theologie
Bib	*Biblica*
BibOr	Biblica et orientalia
BMAP	Kraeling, E. G. *The Brooklyn Museum Aramaic Papyri*. New Haven: Yale University Press, 1953.
BO	*Bibliotheca Orientalis*
BRev	*Bible Review*
BSOAS	*Bulletin of the School of Oriental and African Studies*
BTB	*Biblical Theology Bulletin*
BZAW	Beihefte zur Zeitschrift für die alttestamentliche Wissenschaft

CAT	*The Cuneiform Alphabetic Texts from Ugarit, Ras Ibn Hani and Other Places*. Edited by M. Dietrich, O. Loretz, and J. Sanmartín. 2nd ed. Münster: Ugarit-Verlag, 1995.
CBQ	*Catholic Biblical Quarterly*
CBQMS	Catholic Biblical Quarterly Monograph Series
CD	Damascus Document (Cairo Genizah)
Cowley	Cowley, A. E. *Aramaic Papyri of the Fifth Century B.C.* Oxford: Clarendon, 1923.
DCH	*Dictionary of Classical Hebrew*. Edited by D. J. A. Clines. 8 vols. Sheffield: Sheffield Academic Press; Sheffield Phoenix Press, 1993–.
DJD	Discoveries in the Judaean Desert
DNWSI	Hoftijzer, J., and K. Jongeling. *Dictionary of the North-West Semitic Inscriptions.* 2 vols. Leiden: Brill, 1995.
EncIsl	*Encyclopedia of Islam*. Edited by P. J. Bearman et al. 2nd ed. 12 vols. Leiden: Brill, 1960–2005.
FAT	Forschungen zum Alten Testament
Giṭ.	Giṭṭin
HALOT	Koehler, L., W. Baumgartner, and J. J. Stamm. *The Hebrew and Aramaic Lexicon of the Old Testament*. Translated and edited under the supervision of M. E. J. Richardson. 4 vols. Leiden: Brill, 1994–99.
HAR	*Hebrew Annual Review*
HDHL	*The Historical Dictionary of the Hebrew Language: Materials for the Dictionary, Series I, 200 B.C.E.–300 C.E.* Jerusalem: Academy of the Hebrew Language, 1988 (microfiche).
HKAT	Handkommentar zum Alten Testament
HS	*Hebrew Studies*
HSM	Harvard Semitic Monographs
HSPh	*Harvard Studies in Classical Philology*
HSS	Harvard Semitic Studies
HTR	*Harvard Theological Review*
HUCA	*Hebrew Union College Annual*
ICC	International Critical Commentary
IDBSup	*Interpreter's Dictionary of the Bible: Supplementary Volume.* Edited by K. Crim. Nashville: Abingdon, 1976.
IEJ	*Israel Exploration Journal*
IH	Israelian Hebrew
IOS	*Israel Oriental Studies*
JAAR	*Journal of the American Academy of Religion*
JAL	*Journal of Arabic Literature*

JANES	*Journal of the Ancient Near Eastern Society*
JAOS	*Journal of the American Oriental Society*
JBL	*Journal of Biblical Literature*
JBQ	*Jewish Bible Quarterly*
JE	*The Jewish Encyclopedia*. Edited by Cyrus Adler and Isodore Singer. 12 vols. New York: Funk & Wagnalls, 1901–6.
JEA	*Journal of Egyptian Archaeology*
JH	Judahite Hebrew
JHS	*Journal of Hebrew Scriptures*
JJS	*Journal of Jewish Studies*
JNES	*Journal of Near Eastern Studies*
JNSL	*Journal of Northwest Semitic Languages*
JQR	*Jewish Quarterly Review*
JSOT	*Journal for the Study of the Old Testament*
JSOTSup	Journal for the Study of the Old Testament Supplement Series
JSS	*Journal of Semitic Studies*
JTS	*Journal of Theological Studies*
K	Ketiv
KAI	Donner, H., and W. Rollig. *Kanaanäische und aramäische Inschriften*. 2nd ed. 3 vols. Wiesbaden: Harrassowitz, 1966–1969.
KB	Koehler, L., and W. Baumgartner, eds. *Lexicon in Veteris Testamenti libros*. 2nd ed. Leiden: Brill, 1958.
Ketub.	Ketubbot
LBH	Late Biblical Hebrew
LXX	Septuagint
m.	Mishnah
Mak.	Makkot
Makš.	Makširin
Menaḥ.	Menaḥot
MH	Mishnaic Hebrew
MT	Masoretic Text
MUSJ	*Mélanges de l'Université Saint-Joseph*
Naz.	Nazir
NIBC	New International Bible Commentary
Nid.	Niddah
NJPS	*Tanakh: The Holy Scriptures: The New JPS Translation according to the Traditional Hebrew Text*
OED	*The Oxford English Dictionary*. Edited by J. A. Simpson and E. S. C. Weiner. Oxford: Clarendon, 1989.
ʾOhal.	ʾOhalot

OLA	Orientalia Lovaniensia Analecta
Or	*Orientalia*
ʿOr.	ʿOrlah
OTA	*Old Testament Abstracts*
Pesaḥ.	Pesaḥim
Pesiq. Rab Kah.	Pesiqta de Rab Kahana
Q	Qeri
QH	Qumran Hebrew
Qoh. Rab.	Qohelet Rabba
Roš Haš.	Roš Haššanah
SAA	State Archives of Assyria
Šabb.	Šabbat
Sanh.	Sanhedrin
SBH	Standard Biblical Hebrew
SBLDS	Society of Biblical Literature Dissertation Series
SBLMS	Society of Biblical Literature Monograph Series
SBLWAW	Society of Biblical Literature Writings from the Ancient World
ScrHier	Scripta hierosolymitana
Šeb.	Šebiʿit
Šeqal.	Šeqalim
STDJ	Studies on the Texts of the Desert of Judah
TD	*Theology Digest*
Ter.	Terumot
UF	*Ugarit-Forschungen*
ʿUq.	ʿUqṣin
UT	Gordon, C. H. *Ugaritic Textbook.* Rome: Pontifical Biblical Institute, 1965.
Vay. Rab.	Vayyiqraʾ Rabba
VT	*Vetus Testamentum*
VTSup	Supplements to Vetus Testamentum
WHJP	World History of the Jewish People
WO	*Die Welt des Orients*
y.	Jerusalem Talmud
Yad.	Yadayim
Yebam.	Yebamot
ZAH	*Zeitschrift für Althebräistik*
ZAW	*Zeitschrift für die alttestamentliche Wissenschaft*
ZBK	Zürcher Bibelkommentare
ZPE	*Zeitschrift für Papyrologie und Epigraphik*

Introduction

This monograph presents four studies on the linguistic, literary, and polemical nature of the Song of Songs, one of the most intriguing books in the biblical canon. Each of the four primary chapters stands alone in terms of its contribution to the discipline of biblical studies. At the same time, however, the four studies cohere in support of our overall argument that the Song of Songs is a sophisticated poem with a polemical purpose.

In chapter 1 we provide detailed linguistic evidence for the Israelian Hebrew (northern) dialect of the Song of Songs. Here we briefly survey the history of scholarship on the subject and lay out our methodology for identifying northern linguistic features. We then organize the data into the four traditional categories of linguistic research: phonology, morphology, syntax, and lexicon. In an excursus at the end of this chapter, we discuss an important set of variant readings found in a Qumran witness to the book, namely, 4QCant^{b}.

The focus of chapter 2 is on the poem's sophisticated use of alliteration, with particular attention to the role that alliteration plays in determining compositional choices. We begin by defining the criteria by which to determine the presence of alliteration, and we then illustrate the process by examining more than sixty examples of the device within the exquisite poetry of the Song of Songs.

Chapter 3 presents another literary device in the Song of Songs: the use of variation. The poet frequently rehearses poetic lines used earlier in the composition, but always there is a minor variation of some sort, either lexical, morphological, or syntactic. While this feature of biblical rhetorical style has been noted by M. V. Fox in his splendid treatment of the Song of Songs, we believe that our chapter carries this line of research further. To be sure, this feature of biblical literature continues to be underappreciated in the discipline of biblical studies.

In chapter 4 we turn our attention to the interpretation of the Song of Songs, a topic that has engaged scholars for generations, indeed for centuries if not millennia (witness the famous statement of Rabbi Aqiba in m. Yad. 3:5). We examine the Song in the light of its shared features with the medieval

Arabic poetic genres of *tašbīb* and *hijā'*, which we may briefly define here as invective poetry. We contextualize our observations by offering a brief overview of other ancient Near Eastern parallels that have been proposed for the Song, especially that of the Arabic *waṣf*, a genre that is largely seen as comic in purpose. After discussing the literary conventions and functions of *tašbīb* and *hijā'*, we provide the comparative evidence from the Song of Songs. This approach allows us to underscore the findings of the previous chapters, especially chapter I. In particular, the Song the Song has greater force when we realize that the invective poetry is directed at the Judahite monarchy. Similarly, we can appreciate more deeply the literary devices surveyed in chapters 2 and 3 when we see them in the light of the Song's polemic. Indeed, the poet's alliterative artistry and sophisticated use of variation serve to captivate the listener and thus draw attention away from the many double entendres in the Song (also examined in ch. 4). In turn, the subtle use of double entendres allows the poet to escape censure.

The conclusion then offers a synthetic assessment of the combined import of the four chapters, including our overall opinion on the date of the book.

At the end of the book we have placed our translation of the Song. Since many of the artistic and polemical subtleties discussed in the previous chapters are impossible to render into English, we have provided copious explanatory footnotes to make clear our interpretation of the Song.

As the informed reader no doubt recognizes, the secondary literature on the Song of Songs is enormous, and we readily admit to having cited the works of our colleagues only selectively. At the same time, we wish to state publicly how much we have benefited from a number of important commentaries, translations, and specialized studies—ranging from Marvin Pope's monumental effort (1977) to Michael Fox's expert philological treatment (1985) to Roland Murphy's fine commentary (1990) to the joint venture of Ariel Bloch and Chana Bloch (1995) and to a series of articles by Shalom Paul (1997, for example)—even if we do not cite these works in any systematic fashion.

Finally, we note that, although this book has been a joint endeavor, we feel it is important to recognize each other's primary contributions to the various parts of this project. Chapter 1 is the combined effort of both authors; chapters 2 and 3 are primarily the work of Rendsburg with contributions from Noegel; and chapter 4 is primarily Noegel's work with contributions from Rendsburg.

1
Israelian Hebrew in the Song of Songs

For more then two decades, we have been engaged in ongoing research into the question of regional dialects in ancient Hebrew. Previous scholars had theorized that regional dialects existed,[1] but in the main very little data was put forward to defend this hypothesis. Our research, presented in a series of articles and two monographs,[2] has provided (or at least we hope it has) the empirical evidence necessary to demonstrate the utility of our method and the significance of the results.[3]

The picture that emerges provides for the existence of two main geographical dialects in ancient Hebrew. The one we call Judahite Hebrew (JH), that is, the dialect of Judah. Since so much of the Bible emanates from Judah in general or Jerusalem in particular (or is written by exiles from that community), JH is the dominant dialect in the Bible. It is, for all intents and purposes, what we may call Standard Biblical Hebrew (SBH).

The second dialect we call Israelian Hebrew (IH), that is, the dialect of those regions that formed the kingdom of Israel. In reality, this is most likely a dialect cluster, incorporating a variety of dialects such as Ephraimite Hebrew, Transjordanian Hebrew, Galilean Hebrew, and so forth. Generally we do not

---

1. The clearest statements are by C. Rabin, "The Emergence of Classical Hebrew," in *The Age of the Monarchies: Culture and Society* (ed. A. Malamat and I.Ephʿal; WHJP; Jerusalem: Masada, 1979), 71–78, 293–95; idem, *A Short History of the Hebrew Language* (Jerusalem: Jewish Agency, 1973), 25–33.

2. The monographs are G. A. Rendsburg, *Linguistic Evidence for the Northern Origin of Selected Psalms* (SBLMS 43; Atlanta: Scholars Press, 1990); idem, *Israelian Hebrew in the Book of Kings* (Bethesda, Md.: CDL, 2002). The articles will be cited below as necessary.

3. The most recent and most comprehensive statement is G. A. Rendsburg, "A Comprehensive Guide to Israelian Hebrew: Grammar and Lexicon," *Orient* 38 (2003): 5–35. Almost every feature to be treated in the present study is listed in this article, but we shall refrain from constantly cross-referencing the two.

possess the quantity of data necessary to make such small distinctions, however, so we content ourselves with the umbrella term IH, recognizing it as the polar contrast to JH. Since only a minority of the Bible stems from northern Israel, this dialect is less represented in the corpus. Nevertheless, our research has shown that significant portions of the Bible are written in this dialect, ranging from about 16 to about 24 percent of the corpus, depending on how one quantifies the IH material.[4]

The most obvious place to look for IH is in the history of the northern kingdom of Israel recorded in the book of Kings; our recent monograph is devoted to presenting the data.[5] Similarly, IH may be found in the stories of the northern judges (Deborah, Gideon, Jephthah, etc.) in the book of Judges. Another clear source for IH are the northern prophets Hosea and Amos.[6] From these three basic sources for IH, one may obtain a good idea of what this dialect looked like. A long list of lexical and grammatical features can be built from this material in Kings, Judges, Hosea, and Amos.

The methodology involved in IH research is outlined in our books on the northern psalms and the Israelian material in Kings.[7] The treatment there is heavily indebted to the work of Avi Hurvitz in his attempts to identify Late Biblical Hebrew (LBH) texts. Without repeating the details here, note that the basic key words, as they are for Hurvitz, are the following: (1) "distribution"—the lexical or grammatical feature should be found exclusively, or almost exclusively, in northern texts;[8] (2) "extrabiblical sources"—the feature should have a cognate in a language used to the north of Israel, typically Ugaritic, Phoenician, or Aramaic (the Transjordanian dialects as well, but the corpus is much smaller); and (3) "opposition"—one should be able to contrast

4. See the discussion in ibid., 8–9.

5. Rendsburg, *Kings*.

6. The northern home of Hosea is accepted by all. The linguistic evidence is presented in Y. J. Yoo, "Israelian Hebrew in the Book of Hosea" (Ph.D. diss., Cornell University, 1999). The northern home of Amos was posited first by David Qimḥi in the late twelfth–early thirteenth century. For a recent monograph devoted to this view, see S. N. Rosenbaum, *Amos of Israel: A New Interpretation* (Macon, Ga.: Mercer University Press, 1990). The linguistic question is addressed in an important article by C. Rabin, "Leshonam shel ʿAmos ve-Hosheaʿ," in *ʿIyyunim be-Sefer Tre-ʿAsar* (ed. B. Z. Luria; Jerusalem: Kiryath Sepher, 1981), 117–36.

7. Rendsburg, *Psalms*, 15–16; idem, *Kings*, 18–19.

8. We realize that some may consider this point somewhat circular, but we feel that enough evidence has been garnered based on other criteria (e.g., geographical setting, subject matter) to establish the Israelian provenance of the relevant biblical texts.

the IH usage with a JH usage. Ideally, all three of these criteria should be present to establish a particular feature as an IH usage. But due to the limited nature of the evidence, this is not always possible, so occasionally only two of these criteria can be invoked. Our assumption is: if we had the total picture of ancient Hebrew and its surrounding dialects and languages, we would be able to prove the point to the extent that a linguist working in the field of dialect geography would like.[9]

Once we are able to isolate IH elements using the above methodology, the next step is to look for a "concentration" of such elements in specific texts. This naturally arises, as we have demonstrated in our previous publications. As noted above, this is an ongoing project, so some of the material that has been collected still awaits publication. In such cases, the reader is requested to consult our published work on selected biblical texts for references to IH features in other biblical texts. Using this approach, our research points to the northern dialect in the following books and chapters of the Bible: the material in Kings and Judges mentioned above; Hosea; Amos; Mic 6–7; Isa 24–27; selected psalms (the largest collections are the Asaph and Korah collections); Proverbs; Qohelet; Song of Songs; Deut 32; 2 Sam 23:1–7; Neh 9; and the blessings to the northern tribes in Gen 49 and Deut 33.[10] In addition, one must keep in mind that other compositions are presented in an Aramaizing dialect (whether they were written in the north or the south) for stylistic reasons. Here one may point most of all to Job, with a Transjordanian setting, and the Balaam story, which both has a Transjordanian setting and centers on the prophet who hailed from Aram. Other biblical texts of this nature are the narratives in the book of Genesis set in the land of Aram.[11] Furthermore, when the prophets address the foreign nations, they typically incorporate linguistic features of those countries into their speeches, again for stylistic purposes. The former technique (seen in Job, Balaam, etc.) is

---

9. Compare, e.g., the dialect atlases that have been produced for English, German, French, or Italian, based on a complete survey of the living languages today. For further reference to English regional dialectology, see below, n. 117.

10. To repeat what is stated above in n. 2, our studies will be cited below as necessary. On Hosea, see Yoo's dissertation cited above (n. 6). On Proverbs, see Y. Chen, "Israelian Hebrew in the Book of Proverbs" (Ph.D. diss., Cornell University, 2000).

11. See J. C. Greenfield, "Aramaic Studies and the Bible," in *Congress Volume: Vienna, 1980* (ed. J. A. Emerton; VTSup 32; Leiden: Brill, 1981), 129–30; G. A. Rendsburg, "Some False Leads in the Identification of Late Biblical Hebrew Texts: The Cases of Genesis 24 and 1 Samuel 2:27–36," *JBL* 121 (2002): 23–46, in particular 24–32; and idem, "Aramaic-Like Features in the Pentateuch," *HS* 47 (2006): 163–76.

called "style-switching"; the latter technique (used by the prophets) is called "addressee-switching."[12]

Three additional sources for IH need to be mentioned. The first is Mishnaic Hebrew (MH; the term Tannaitic Hebrew is preferable, but we will stick with the former term since it is in more general use), which in our view is the northern dialect of Hebrew in the Roman period.[13] As such, it has many features in common with IH (even though the IH found in the Bible, like JH, is a literary language, whereas MH represents a colloquial dialect). Even where it does not connect directly with IH, MH by itself has many isoglosses—mainly of a lexical nature—with Ugaritic and Phoenician (and, of course, with Aramaic, but this is well-recognized). Almost all of the MH material that we will cite stems from MH^1, that is, Tannaitic sources, reflecting the period when Hebrew was still spoken (up to ca. 300 C.E.), at least according to most scholars. Occasionally we will cite data from MH^2, that is, Amoraic sources, reflecting the period when Hebrew no longer was spoken (after ca. 300 C.E.), again, at least according to the standard opinion. Such cases are few, but when we do so, we assume, along with many scholars, that the lack of attestation of such words in Tannaitic sources is merely coincidental.[14]

---

12. For the former, see S. A. Kaufman, "The Classification of the North West Semitic Dialects of the Biblical Period and Some Implications Thereof," in *Proceedings of the Ninth World Congress of Jewish Studies: Panel Sessions: Hebrew and Aramaic Languages* (Jerusalem: World Congress of Jewish Studies, 1988), 54–55. For additional material on style-switching and on the device of addressee-switching, see G. A. Rendsburg, "Linguistic Variation and the 'Foreign Factor' in the Hebrew Bible," *IOS* 15 (1996): 177–90. On occasion it is difficult to determine whether style-switching or addressee-switching is at work, but both can be considered interpretative options for the evidence.

13. G. A. Rendsburg, "The Galilean Background of Mishnaic Hebrew," in *The Galilee in Late Antiquity* (ed. L. I. Levine; New York: Jewish Theological Seminary, 1992), 225–40; idem, "The Geographical and Historical Background of the Mishnaic Hebrew Lexicon," *Orient* 38 (2003): 105–15.

14. In citing MH evidence, especially lexical material, we have relied on the Historical Dictionary of the Hebrew Language project of the Academy of the Hebrew Language. In the case of MH^1 material, we have taken the time to cite the older microfiche version by fiche and plate number, using the abbreviation *HDHL* = *The Historical Dictionary of the Hebrew Language: Materials for the Dictionary, Series 1, 200 B.C.E.– 300 C.E.* (Jerusalem: Academy of the Hebrew Language, 1988). All MH materials, both MH^1 and MH^2, are to be found on the newer CD-ROM version: *Ma'agarim: The Hebrew Language Historical Dictionary Project*, CD-ROM version (Jerusalem: Academy of the Hebrew Language, 1998). Due to the nature of this latter technology, however, no specific citations can be made (page, plate, etc.), and thus we

The second additional source that requires brief comment is the Benjaminite dialect. The best source for this dialect is the prophet Jeremiah, who hailed from Anathoth in Benjamin.[15] In addition, elements of the Benjaminite dialect most likely occur in the stories of Saul and Jonathan recorded in 1 Samuel.[16] While Benjamin was part of the kingdom of Judah, this does not automatically mean that its dialect was the same as Judah's.

Benjaminite Hebrew probably was a border dialect, at times going with JH and at times going with IH. Of special interest is the opening section of Ps 80, one of the Asaph psalms:[17] after "Israel" and "Joseph" are presented in parallel in verse 2, the poet next evokes "Ephraim, Benjamin, and Manasseh" in verse 3. And while one would not want to reconstruct either Israelite history or Hebrew dialect geography based on the stories in Genesis, it is noteworthy that Benjamin and Joseph are paired as the two Rachel tribes. In short, although a thorough linguistic study still needs to be accomplished, evidence from these Benjaminite sources may be used—with all due caution—to enlarge the IH picture.

The third additional source is LBH, a stratum of the language in which one may encounter northern features. Cyrus Gordon proposed, even without full documentation, that this phenomenon is due to the reunion of Israelian

---

have refrained from citing this resource, though to be sure it was consulted throughout our research. We similarly rely on this enterprise for data concerning Qumran Hebrew (QH). Finally, note that we also include references to M. Jastrow, *A Dictionary of the Targumim, the Talmud Babli and Yerushalmi, and the Midrashic Literature* (2 vols.; London: Luzac, 1903), notwithstanding the well-known problems with this century-old work.

15. See C. Smith, "'With an Iron Pen and a Diamond Tip': Linguistic Peculiarities in the Book of Jeremiah" (Ph.D. diss., Cornell University, 2003).

16. On these chapters, along with other material that touches upon our thesis, see A. Rofé, "Ephraimite versus Deuteronomistic History," in *Storia e tradizioni di Israele: Scritti in onore di J. Alberto Soggin* (ed. D. Garrone and F. Israel; Brescia: Paideia, 1992), 221–35.

17. The northern provenance of Ps 80 was posited by the following scholars: H. Gunkel, *Die Psalmen* (HKAT 2/2; Göttingen: Vandenhoeck & Ruprecht, 1926), 353; O. Eissfeldt, "Psalm 80," in *Geschichte und Altes Testament: Albrecht Alt zum 70. Geburtstag dargebracht* (ed. W. Zimmerli; BHT 16; Tübingen: Mohr Siebeck, 1953), 65–78, repr. in O. Eissfeldt, *Kleine Schriften* (6 vols.; Tübingen: Mohr Siebeck, 1962–79), 3:221–32; idem, "Psalm 80 und Psalm 89," *WO* 3 (1964–66), 27–31, repr. in Eissfeldt, *Kleine Schriften*, 4:132–36; and H. L. Ginsberg, *The Israelian Heritage of Judaism* (New York: Jewish Theological Seminary, 1982), 31–32.

and Judahite exiles in Mesopotamia in the sixth century B.C.E.[18] Again, one must exercise caution and not rely on this "crutch" too frequently; still, the evidence suggests itself, and examples will be noted below occasionally.

With the above material as introduction, we now turn our attention to the Song of Songs. As is well known, the poem is filled both with many unique words and with lexemes or grammatical usages that many scholars have labeled as Aramaisms.[19] These two groups of items require comment, beginning with the latter. Typically, scholars have utilized the so-called Aramaisms to support a postexilic dating of the composition,[20] for it was during the Persian period, of course, that Aramaic influence over Hebrew increased. For the nonce, however, we prefer not to speak about the date of the Song of Songs; that is a subject to which we will return later. At this point, we prefer to proceed synchronically. In short, we consider these so-called Aramaisms not as true borrowings from Aramaic but rather as evidence of isoglosses shared by the language of the Song of Songs (that is, IH) and Aramaic. This approach will become clear during the presentation of the data below. Moreover, it will be bolstered by the fact that several important lexical and grammatical items demonstrate links between the language of the Song of Songs and Phoenician-Ugaritic,[21] with no recourse to Aramaic whatsoever.

As to the unique words in the Song of Songs: uniqueness does not by itself mean that a particular word is northern; a unique word could be a word that was reserved for poetry in ancient Hebrew, or it could be simply a rare word in the language. But time and again, as we shall see, these unique words or usages have cognates in Aramaic or Phoenician-Ugaritic, and/or

18. C. H. Gordon, "North Israelite Influence on Postexilic Hebrew," *IEJ* 5 (1955): 85–88. This view was accepted by E. Y. Kutscher, *A History of the Hebrew Language* (Jerusalem: Magnes, 1982), 55. On the historical issues, see now J. W. Mazurel, "De Vraag naar de Verloren Broeder: Terugkeer en herstel in de boeken Jeremia en Ezechiel" (Ph.D. diss., Universiteit van Amsterdam, 1992); we have not seen this work; rather, we rely on the abstract in *OTA* 16 (1993): 633.

19. Several dozen are included in M. Wagner, *Die lexikalischen und grammatikalischen Aramäismen im alttestamentlichen Hebräisch* (BZAW 96; Berlin: Töpelmann, 1966).

20. See, e.g., R. E. Murphy, *The Song of Songs* (Minneapolis: Fortress, 1990), 4–5, who cited R. Tournay *apud* A. Robert, *Le Cantique des Cantiques* (Paris: Gabalda, 1963), 21.

21. We follow the classifications system of H. L. Ginsberg, "The Northwest Semitic Languages," in *Patriarchs* (ed. B. Mazar; WHJP; New Brunswick, N.J.: Rutgers University Press, 1970), 102–24, 293, which places Ugaritic and Phoenician together in the "Phoenic" subgroup of Canaanite.

they are more common in MH, and/or they stand in linguistic opposition to a standard BH word that no doubt represents the JH equivalent. When these situations arise over and over, it becomes clearer and clearer that uniqueness is not uniqueness or rarity per se but rather further evidence for the IH dialect in which the book was composed.

We hasten to note that we are not the first to utilize this approach to the many unusual features in the Song of Songs. As is well known, already S. R. Driver compiled a long list of such features, with the following conclusion, quoted here *in extenso*:

> The diction of the poem exhibits several peculiarities, especially in the *uniform* use of the relative -שׁ (except in the title 1:1) for אשׁר, and in the recurrence of many words found never or rarely besides in Biblical Hebrew, but common in Aramaic, which show either that it must be a late work (post-exilic), or, if early, that it belongs to *North* Israel, where there is reason to suppose that the language spoken differed dialectally from that of Judah. The general purity and brightness of the style favour the latter alternative, which agrees well with the acquaintance shown by the author with localities of North Palestine.[22]

This northern geography of the poem is well-known and further supports the linguistic argument presented here. To list these toponyms once more (as almost every commentator on the book does), note the following: Lebanon, Gilead, Amana, Senir, Hermon, Tirzah, Mahanaim, Heshbon, Damascus, and Carmel (Heshbon is relatively south in Transjordan, but it belonged to the kingdom of Israel). In addition, the term "the Shulammite" in Song 7:1 (2x) may refer to the town of Shunem (see 1 Kgs 1:15, 2 Kgs 4:12) near Jezreel, though other meanings for this term are possible.[23] Moreover, Sharon in Song 2:1 probably refers not to the famous Sharon, that is, the southern coastal plain, but rather to a northern locale of the same name. Later Jewish sources refer to a Sharon in the Lower Galilee (see, e.g., m. Nid. 2:7; b. Nid. 21a; b. Šabb. 77a [with reference to wine], y. Yoma 5:2 [with reference to earthquakes]); no doubt this is the same Sharon that Eusebius mentions (*Onomasticon* 162.4–5) as lying between Mount Tabor and Tibe-

---

22. S. R. Driver, *An Introduction to the Literature of the Old Testament* (New York: Charles Scribner's Sons, 1920), 448–49. The two lists of truly unique items and of rare items in BH appear at the bottom of 448, notes * and †, respectively. Although many of these items are included in the listing of IH traits that follows, we refrain from citing Driver each time. The interested reader can consult Driver's list on his or her own.

23. For discussion and a survey of opinions, see M. V. Fox, *The Song of Songs and the Ancient Egyptian Love Songs* (Madison: University of Wisconsin Press, 1985), 157.

rias (to be identified with modern Khirbet Saruna in the Yavne᾿el Valley).[24] The phrase חבצלת השרון, "white-lily of the Sharon," suggests a northern setting, especially given this flower's natural home in the Galilee and on Mount Carmel (rather than in the coastal plain).[25] Furthermore, if "the Shulammite" hails from the town of Shunem, the distance between her home and Sharon in the Lower Galilee was no more than about 20 kilometers. In short, the only sure toponym in the southern part of the country (with the major exception of Jerusalem, of course) is Ein-Gedi.

But to return to linguistic issues. Driver's approach to the Song of Songs was not adopted by most scholars. Thus, for example, the two best philological commentaries in recent decades, those by Pope and Fox, took note of the theory but either discounted it (thus Pope[26]) or argued against it (thus Fox[27]). On the other hand, several contemporary scholars have followed a similar path to Driver's. Shelomo Morag provided only a brief comment: "In spite of the fact that our knowledge of ancient Hebrew dialects is rather scanty, it seems that for some books an affiliation with a certain dialect may be assumed. This is probably the case with the language of Canticles, the language of which, as suggested by S. R. Driver and other scholars, may reflect a number of northern features."[28] Yitzhak Avishur noted a large number of literary and stylistic elements common to the Song of Songs and Ugaritic poetry, which he believed proved the northern provenance of the former: "Moreover, the northern origin of most of the songs of the scroll—a problem unto itself—not only testifies to this similarity [i.e., between Ugaritic poetry and the Song of Songs], but also may be proven on the basis of this relationship."[29] And while these parallels

24. See further I. Benzinger and S. Ochser, "Sharon," *JE* 11:233–34; and Shmuel Ahituv, "Sharon, Sharoni," *᾿Enṣiqlopedya Miqra᾿it* 8 (1982): cols. 263–64. Note that the references to rabbinic texts in the *Jewish Encyclopaedia* entry are incorrect: "Yer. Yoma v. 3" should be 5:2 (as we have just noted); "Men. viii. 2" appears to mean t. Menaḥ. 9:3 (though the discussion there concerns calves, which would not point to northern Sharon per se); and "Shab. 70a" should be Šabb. 77a (again, as we have noted).

25. On the botanical identification of חבצלת and its home, see M. Zohary, *Plants of the Bible* (Cambridge: Cambridge University Press, 1982), 176. Zohary equates חבצלת with the pair שושנה/שושן, rendering both as "white lily."

26. Brief comments only in M. H. Pope, *Song of Songs* (AB 7C; Garden City, N.Y.: Doubleday, 1977), 33–34, 362.

27. Fox, *Song of Songs*, 189.

28. S. Morag, "On the Historical Validity of the Vocalization of the Hebrew Bible," *JAOS* 94 (1974): 308.

29. נראה לי גם שמוצאם הצפוני של רוב שירי המגילה, שהוא בעיה בפני עצמה, לא רק שהוא יכול להעיד על קרבה זו אלא אף להיות מוכח מזיקה זו (Y. Avishur, "Le-

are not purely linguistic, they indicate a shared literary tradition in northern Canaan.[30] Hurvitz, while not committing himself fully, noted that the northern hypothesis answers many of the problems of the language of the Song of Songs.[31] Most recently, Ian Young has argued for the northern origin of the Song of Songs, though he also gave equal or greater weight to another consideration, namely, that the poem exhibits "'Low' dialectal features that would be excluded from Standard Biblical Hebrew."[32]

The linguistic features presented below are divided into four categories: phonology, morphology, syntax, and lexicon. The items are presented in the order in which they appear in the book.[33] Taken collectively, these elements provide the "concentration" described above that enables us to conclude that the Song of Songs was composed in the northern dialect of ancient Hebrew.[34]

1.1. Phonology

1.1.1. In standard Hebrew, the proto-Semitic phoneme /ẓ/ shifts to /ṣ/, thus in words such as צל "shade," צור "rock," נצר "guard," and so on. In Aramaic,

---

Ziqa ha-Signonit ben Shir ha-Shirim ve-Sifrut ʾUgarit," *Beth Mikra* 59 (1974): 525. An earlier study, though far less comprehensive, which also accepted the "North Palestinian origin" of the Song of Songs, is W. F. Albright, "Archaic Survivals in the Text of Canticles," in *Hebrew and Semitic Studies Presented to Godfrey Rolles Driver* (ed. D. W. Thomas and W. D. McHardy; Oxford: Clarendon, 1963), 1–7 (quotation from 1).

30. In his larger, more sweeping study, Y. Avishur, *Stylistic Studies of Word-Pairs in Biblical and Ancient Semitic Literatures* (AOAT 210; Neukirchen-Vluyn: Neukirchener, 1984), noted that a number of biblical compositions, which on independent grounds are to be considered northern texts (Hosea, Ps 29, Deut 32, as well as the Song of Songs), "contain [word] pairs common to them and Ugaritic, in a high degree of concentration" (440).

31. A. Hurvitz, "Ha-Lashon ha-ʿIvrit ba-Tequfa ha-Parsit," in *Shivat Ṣiyyon: Yeme Shilton Paras* (ed. H. Tadmor and I. Ephʿal; Ha-Historiya shel ʿAm Yisraʾel; Jerusalem: Peli, 1983), 217–18.

32. I. Young, *Diversity in Pre-exilic Hebrew* (FAT 5; Tübingen: Mohr Siebeck, 1993), 157–68 (with the quotation appearing on 168).

33. The only exception is in the Morphology section, where we have placed the discussion of -של immediately after -ש, as §§1.2.1 and 1.2.2, due to the close relationship between these two forms. Normally §1.2.3 in the Morphology section would have interposed.

34. A sketch of the present study appeared recently as G. A. Rendsburg, "Israelian Hebrew in the Song of Songs," in *Biblical Hebrew in Its Northwest Semitic Setting: Typological and Historical Perspectives* (ed. S. E. Fassberg and A. Hurvitz; ScrHier 39; Jerusalem: Magnes, 2005), 315–23, though space limitations necessitated the evidence to be presented there in outline form only.

the phoneme /z̥/ shifts to /ṭ/, thus, for example, טלל "shade," טור "mountain," נטר "guard," and so forth. But four times in the Song of Songs (1:6 [2x]; 8:11, 12) the root *nẓr* "guard, watch" appears not as נצר as in standard BH but as נטר, thus creating an isogloss between the language of the Song of Songs and Aramaic.

The root נטר occurs elsewhere in BH (Lev 19:18; Jer 3:5, 12; Nah 1:2; Ps 103:9) but with the meaning "be angry." Some lexicographers relate the two roots, believing that the latter develops semantically from "guard, keep" to "keep one's anger, maintain one's wrath perpetually."[35] Others separate the two meanings altogether and assume homonymous roots.[36] But regardless of how one decides this issue, all scholars agree that the presence of נטר "guard, keep" in the Song of Songs four times represents a unique usage.[37]

At first glance it would appear that the noun מטרה, meaning both "guardhouse" (11x in Jeremiah [32:2, etc.], 2x in Nehemiah [3:25; 12:39]) and "target (for an arrow)" (1 Sam 20:20; Job 16:12; Lam 3:12), could serve as a counter to our argument. The first meaning clearly derives from the root נטר "guard," while the second meaning may also (cf. English "*keep* one's eye on the target"). How should one explain the presence of this noun in the language, especially vis-à-vis the above discussion? One approach is simply to ignore the evidence, the argument being that the noun is just that, a noun, while the usage in the Song of Songs is a verb. As stated at the end of the preceding paragraph, the verbal use of the root נטר "guard, keep" is unique to the Song of Songs.

But we might be able to work the evidence of nouns based on the root נטר into our discussion in the following way. With the meaning "guardhouse," מטרה occurs only in Jeremiah and Nehemiah. The usage in the former book may reflect the dialect of Benjamin; recall that the prophet hails from Anathoth. The presence of מטרה in Nehemiah may be explained as IH influence over LBH or, more likely, as a true Aramaism. If we wish to correlate the second meaning "target," then it is noteworthy that the earliest occurrence of this word in 1 Sam 20:20 is in the mouth of Jonathan, likewise a Benjaminite. The examples in Lamentations and Job are again Aramaisms; the spelling מטרא in Lam 3:12, with *ʾaleph*, may point in that direction.

Regardless of how the existence of מטרה "guardhouse, target" is integrated into the discussion, the main point remains. The root נטר "guard,"

35. BDB, 643; see also *HALOT*, 695.

36. KB, 613.

37. Thus not just the two standard dictionaries cited in the two previous notes but also A. Even-Shoshan, *Qonqordanṣya Ḥadasha* (Jerusalem: Kiryat Sefer, 1992), 758.

reflecting the shift of /z̥/ > /ṭ/, in the Song of Songs represents an isogloss with Aramaic.

In addition, two other examples of the /z̥/ > /ṭ/ shift occur in the Song of Songs: רהיטנו "our runners," that is, "beams, rafters," in Song 1:17Q and רהטים "tresses" in 7:6 both derive from the root רהט, the Aramaic equivalent of Hebrew רוץ "run." Discussion of these items is found below in the Lexicon section (§§1.4.3 and 1.4.31, respectively).

1.1.2. In standard Hebrew, the proto-Semitic phoneme /d̥/ also shifts to /s̥/, as in words such as ארץ "earth," רצה "desire," ביצה "egg," and so on. In Aramaic, /d̥/ shifts first to /q/ (in Old Aramaic) and then to /ʿ/ (in Imperial and Middle Aramaic); or, to state this more accurately, /d̥/ is represented by the consonants *qof* and later *ʿayin* (we do not enter here into a discussion of the actual realization of this phoneme in ancient Aramaic[38]). Thus, for example, to use only the later forms, the Aramaic equivalents of the above Hebrew nouns are ארעא "land," רעה "desire," ביעה "egg," and so forth. But in a few instances in Hebrew, the shift /d̥/ > /ʿ/ is attested. One of the best examples is the root that appears normally in Hebrew as צרר "be an enemy, adversary" but that appears in Aramaic and in a few biblical passages as ערר. Thus, Ps 9:7 ערים "enemies" occurs in a northern poem,[39] and 1 Sam 28:16 ערך "your adversary" is in the mouth of the dead Samuel (from Ephraim) as mediated through the witch of Endor (in Manasseh).[40] עריך "your enemies" (Ps 139:20) appears in a poem that we previously had not included in the northern corpus but that deserves reconsideration (to note another usage paralleled in Aramaic, see אסק from the root נסק "go up" in v. 8, the only such attestation in the Hebrew portions of the Bible; see the next paragraph as well).[41]

All of this serves as background for establishing the presence of the root רעה "desire" in Song 1:7. The verse includes a Janus parallelism where the pivot word תרעה means both "desire" (paralleling what precedes) and "shepherd" (anticipating what follows).[42] The same root, in its IH manifestation,

---

38. See the brief treatment in S. Segert, "Old Aramaic Phonology," in *Phonologies of Asia and Africa* (ed. A. S. Kaye; 2 vols.; Winona Lake, Ind.: Eisenbrauns, 1997), 1:119.

39. Rendsburg, *Psalms*, 19–27.

40. Note further that the use of ערך in 1 Sam 28:16 heightens the alliteration with the word רעך "your compatriot" in v. 17 (and note also ויקרע "and [YHWH] has torn" in the same verse also with *reš* and *ʿayin*).

41. For additional examples, using the root רעע "break" (= SBH רצץ), see S. Noegel, "Dialect and Politics in Isaiah 24–27," *AuOr* 12 (1994): 182.

42. S. B. Noegel, *Janus Parallelism in the Book of Job* (JSOTSup 223; Sheffield: Sheffield Academic Press, 1996), 154–55.

occurs in Qohelet also, in the nominal forms רעות (1:14 + 6x) and רעיון (1:17 + 2x), both meaning "desire, longing, striving." Still another word, apparently from the same root, occurs twice in Ps 139 (vv. 2, 17), namely, רע "thought" (see the previous paragraph for the proposal that Ps 139 is a northern composition).

The Janus technique works in Song 1:7 only because the dialect in which the poem was composed included the /ḍ/ > /ʿ/ shift, an isogloss shared by Aramaic and IH.

1.1.3. Typically in Hebrew the proto-Semitic phoneme /ṯ/ shifts to /š/, as in the common verbs ישׁב "sit" and שׁוב "return." But occasionally in Hebrew the phoneme /ṯ/ shifts to /t/, exactly as occurs in Aramaic (see יתב "sit," תוב "return," etc.). A clear instance of this occurs in Song 1:17 in the word ברותים "cypresses"; compare Standard Hebrew ברושׁים (2 Sam 6:5, etc.).

Other examples of this atypical sound shift occur in Judg 5:11 יתנו and 11:40 לתנות, both from the root *ṯny* "tell, repeat." The former occurs in the Song of Deborah, and the latter occurs in the story of Jephthah, both with northern settings. The verb תני "tell, repeat" occurs in Aramaic; the standard Hebrew reflex is שׁנה. It is apparent from both the Aramaic evidence and the distribution of these examples in the Bible that the /ṯ/ > /t/ shift was a feature of IH.[43]

1.1.4. Similar to the treatment of the voiceless interdental /ṯ/ in Northwest Semitic is the treatment of the voiced interdental /ḏ/. In standard Hebrew this phoneme shifts to /z/, as in זוב "flow, flux"; in Aramaic this phoneme shifts to /d/, as in דוב "flow, flux." In Song 7:10 the unusual form דובב occurs, in the extremely difficult passage דובב שׂפתי ישׁנים. Most likely the word means "flow, flux" here (note that it is parallel to הולך, another verb of motion, with reference to "wine") and thus should be considered a byform of the root זוב/דוב "flow, flux." If this is correct, and we find none of the other solutions proffered by scholars to be convincing,[44] then once more the phonology in the Song of Songs aligns with Aramaic, providing further evidence for the northern origin of the composition. Note further that the root דבב occurs in MH, albeit MH², with the meaning "flow, drip."[45] In fact, several Amoraic

43. In Transjordan, or at least in some dialects in that region, this phoneme was retained; see G. A. Rendsburg, "The Ammonite Phoneme /T̲/," *BASOR* 269 (1988): 73–79; idem, "More on Hebrew *Šibbōlet*," *JSS* 33 (1988): 255–58.

44. For a survey of opinions, see Pope, *Song of Songs*, 640. For understanding דבב as "drip, flow," see Fox, *Song of Songs*, 163.

45. Jastrow, *Dictionary*, 276. For a brief note on the range of meanings of the root דבב, including the general notion "bewegen" and the more specific connotations

sources imply that this is how the rabbis understood Song 7:10 (b. Yebam. 97a, y. Šeqal. 47a).

1.2. Morphology

1.2.1. One of the most characteristic features of the language of the Song of Songs is, as is well known, the consistent employment of the relative pronoun -שׁ (only in the superscription in Song 1:1 does the standard form אשׁר occur).[46]

The origin of the form -שׁ has been widely discussed, but one will agree with E. Y. Kutscher that "its use was common in the vernacular of Northern Palestine."[47] This conclusion is reached based on the cognate evidence and on the distribution of this form in IH texts. The cognate form אשׁ occurs in Phoenician and Ammonite.[48] In preexilic biblical texts, -שׁ is limited to northern contexts: the Song of Deborah (Judg 5:7 [2x]); the Gideon cycle (Judg 6:17; 7:12; 8:26); and the Elisha cycle (2 Kgs 6:11) (the specific form is מִשֶּׁלָּנוּ, on which see further below, §1.2.2). In exilic and postexilic times -שׁ penetrated into Judahite texts (Lam 2:15, 16; 4:9; 5:18; Jonah 1:7, 12 [again, see §1.2.2 for these attestations]; Ezra 8:20; 1 Chr 5:20; 27:27; various late psalms, etc.), though never consistently. Another northern composition of the Persian period that employs -שׁ frequently (though not in the consistent manner of the Song of Songs) is Qohelet. In addition, Ps 133, which is both northern and postexilic, employs -שׁ two times (vv. 2 and 3).[49] Finally, in MH, representing a northern dialect in postbiblical times, -שׁ is the only relative pronoun used.[50] The evidence on this point is exceedingly clear.

"feucht werden, Saft absondern," see F. G. Hüttenmeister, *Übersetzung des Talmud Yerushalmi: Sheqalim–Scheqelsteuer* (Tübingen: Mohr Siebeck, 1990), 8 n. 245.

46. For what follows, see the previous treatments in Rendsburg, *Psalms*, 91–92; idem, *Kings*, 103–4; and idem, "The Galilean Background of Mishnaic Hebrew," 228. See also Young, *Diversity in Pre-exilic Hebrew*, 163.

47. E. Y. Kutscher, *A History of the Hebrew Language* (Leiden: Brill, 1982), 32. See earlier C. F. Burney, *Notes on the Hebrew Text of the Books of Kings* (Oxford: Clarendon, 1903), 208.

48. W. R. Garr, *Dialect Geography of Syria-Palestine, 1000–586 B.C.E.* (Philadelphia: University of Pennsylvania Press, 1985), 85–86.

49. On these two aspects of Ps 133, see A. Hurvitz, *Beyn Lashon le-Lashon* (Jerusalem: Bialik, 1972), 156–60; and Rendsburg, *Psalms*, 91–93 (see especially 93 n. 12).

50. See M. H. Segal, *A Grammar of Mishnaic Hebrew* (Oxford: Clarendon, 1927), 42; idem, *Diqduq Leshon ha-Mishna* (Tel-Aviv: Devir, 1936), 57; and M. Pérez Fernández, *An Introductory Grammar of Rabbinic Hebrew* (Leiden: Brill, 1999), 50.

1.2.2. Closely related to the presence of the relative pronoun -שׁ in the Song of Songs is the use of the independent possessive pronoun -שׁל. This form occurs in Song 1:6; 8:12 שׁלי "of mine" and 3:7 שׁלשלמה "of Solomon." It occurs elsewhere in a clearly northern context, 2 Kgs 6:11 משלנו "from among us," in the Elisha cycle, and in a northern composition Qoh 8:17 בשל "in that" (or some such translation). Two further occurrences are Jonah 1:7 שלמי and 1:12 בשלי, on which see ahead. As with -שׁ discussed above (§2.1), -שׁל is standard in MH.[51] A parallel occurs in Aramaic דיל/זיל, also comprised of relative pronoun + preposition ל.

The evidence points to a northern provenience for this feature, and indeed already J. A. Montgomery and H. S. Gehman expressed the view that -שׁל is a "good N Israelite" usage.[52]

Hurvitz offered another proposal, that the example in 2 Kgs 6:11, placed in the mouth of the Aramean king, is a calque on Aramaic דיל/זיל in an attempt to capture the foreignness of the monarch's native Aramaic speech (what we called style-switching above).[53] Similarly, the presence of -בשל in Jonah may be part of the author's attempt to portray the foreign setting. Note that the first attestation, in Jonah 1:7, is in the mouth of the sailors, though admittedly the second usage, in 1:12, is in Jonah's speech. While this approach remains viable, it does not impact directly on the use of -שׁל three times in the Song of Songs; to repeat the above conclusion, this usage is further evidence for the northern origin of the poem.

1.2.3. The noun נשיקה "kiss" in Song 1:2 represents a *nomen actionis* of the *qətîlāʰ* formation, a relatively rare usage in BH. As is well known, this form is extremely common in MH,[54] which leads one to suspect that the fewer instances of this usage in BH may bespeak an IH feature.[55] A survey of the *qətîlāʰ* forms in the Bible suggests that is indeed the case.[56] The noun

---

51. Segal, *Grammar*, 43–44; idem, *Diqduq*, 46, 48; and Pérez Fernández, *Grammar of Rabbinic Hebrew*, 30–31.

52. J. A. Montgomery and H. S. Gehman, *A Critical and Exegetical Commentary on the Book of Kings* (ICC: Edinburgh: T&T Clark, 1950), 383.

53. A. Hurvitz *apud* G. A. Rendsburg, *Diglossia in Ancient Hebrew* (New Haven: American Oriental Society, 1990), 123 n. 29. See similarly I. Young, "The 'Northernisms' of the Israelite Narratives in Kings," *ZAH* 8 (1995): 65, though he concentrated on the issue of -שׁ alone (not -שׁל).

54. Segal, *Grammar*, 103–4; idem, *Diqduq*, 73–74; and Pérez Fernández, *Grammar of Rabbinic Hebrew*, 57, 59. The latter counts 130 *qətîlāʰ* nouns in MH.

55. See the earlier studies in Rendsburg, "The Galilean Background of Mishnaic Hebrew," 229; and idem, *Kings*, 56–57.

56. We have not been able to locate a bibliographic source that lists all *qətîlāʰ*

שריקה "piping, hissing" occurs in Judg 5:16, the song of Deborah set in the north, and in Jer 18:16, from the prophet who hails from Anathoth. The form חנינה "mercy" occurs in the Bible only in Jer 16:13, again within the speech of the Benjaminite prophet. Within the same general geographical domain is the Saul narrative, which attests to the form פצירה "sharpening" in 1 Sam 13:21. In the story of Elijah we encounter the word אכילה "eating" in 1 Kgs 19:8. The word נשיקה "kiss" occurs not only in Song 1:2 but also in Prov 27:6, another northern composition. The form נטישה "sneezing" occurs in Job 41:10, and the noun יגיעה "tiring" appears in Qoh 12:12; both of these books reflect northern provenance. Finally, there is the form שחיטה "slaughtering" in 2 Chr 30:17. This last form could be an example of IH influence on LBH, although we also must note that this chapter, which has no parallel in Kings, is concerned specifically with the remnant of the Israelians residing in the north during the reign of Hezekiah.

This is not to say that all nouns of the *qətîlāʰ* type automatically are to be associated with IH. There are, in fact, some *qətîlāʰ* nouns that occur in the Bible that lack connection to northern texts and contexts, including, for example, נגינה "tune" (14x), חליפה "change-of-clothing" (8x), and הליכה "way, caravan" (6x). On the other hand, note that, while these nouns are based on verbs that appear in BH, these forms are not *nomina actionis* per se. In two instances, it appears that *qətîlāʰ* forms reflect IH influence on LBH, namely, סליחה "forgiveness" (Ps 130:4; Neh 9:17; Dan 9:9) and קריאה "calling, speech" (Jonah 3:2)—though we also note that Neh 9 is a northern text, as well as a late composition, and that the author of Jonah may have included an occasional IH feature in light of the prophet's original home in Gath-hepher (see 2 Kgs 14:25). In one case, a presumably Judahite author has incorporated a *qətîlāʰ* form into his story for aural effect; see בריאה "creation" in Num 16:30, evoking the sounds of אבירם "Abiram."[57]

The evidence in the preceding paragraph is included to give as complete a picture as possible, even though most of it is less relevant to the present point. The evidence in the first paragraph in this section, by contrast, dem-

---

forms in the Bible but instead have created a list based on the following two works in particular: H. Bauer and P. Leander, *Historische Grammatik der hebräischen Sprache* (Halle: Niemeyer, 1992; repr., Hildesheim: Olms, 1991), 471; and J. L. Sagarin, *Hebrew Noun Patterns (Mishqalim)* (Atlanta: Scholars Press, 1987), 65–66. In what follows, for the sake of simplicity, we present the nouns in the feminine singular absolute form, regardless as to their specific form within the biblical text.

57. M. Garsiel, *Biblical Names: A Literary Study of Midrashic Derivations and Puns* (Ramat-Gan: Bar-Ilan University Press, 1991), 225.

onstrates the point well. The *nomen actionis* form of the *qətîlāʰ* type occurs rarely in BH, though typically in IH texts.[58]

1.2.4. The unique form איכה *ʾêkāʰ* "where" appears in Song 1:7 (2x). Closely related is the form איכה *ʾêkôʰ* "where" appearing in 2 Kgs 6:13 in the Elisha cycle (and see below for a possible additional example).[59] A century ago both BDB and Burney identified this item as a northern lexeme,[60] and more recently Rabin concurred, labeling it a "a clear northern word."[61] The cognate evidence is forthcoming from Aramaic-Syriac, where the form איכא/היכא "where" occurs.[62] As an example, note the Peshitta's use of איכא "where" in Gen 3:9.[63] Also related, as Rabin posited, is the exceedingly frequent MH form היכן "where" (212 attestations, some of which are spelled with *ʾaleph*).[64]

Rabin pointed to one additional biblical passage in his presentation.[65] In Judg 20:3 the Israelites gathered at Mizpah ask איכה נהיתה הרעה הזאת "איכה did this evil happen?" The Levite who hailed from "the mount of Ephraim" (Judg 19:1) begins his response to this question with geographical information: הגבעתה אשר לבנימין "to Gibeah of Benjamin [I and my concubine came]" (20:4). For Rabin this exchange points to an understanding of the word איכה as "where," again set in a northern context. If this interpretation is accepted, then we have another attestation of איכה "where" in northern Hebrew.

But regardless of the example of Judg 20:3, the evidence is clear that איכה (with the second syllable vocalized with either ā or ô, attested for certain in Song 1:7 (2x) and 2 Kgs 6:13, is an IH trait.

1.2.5. The form שלמה "lest" in Song 1:7 parallels Aramaic דילמא "lest." Both forms are comprised of the relative pronoun + the preposition ל + the interrogative "what" to create an independent morpheme. Most scholars aver that the former is based on the latter, most likely as a calque.[66] While some

58. See already Segal, *Grammar*, 103 (though no such statement occurs in Segal, *Diqduq*, 73–74); more recently, Pérez Fernández, *Grammar of Rabbinic Hebrew*, 57.

59. See Rendsburg, *Kings*, 104.

60. BDB, 32; and Burney, *Kings*, 209. Both spoke of a Ketiv/Qeri reading in 2 Kgs 6:13 and in Song 1:7, though neither the St. Petersburg [Leningrad] Codex nor the Aleppo Codex indicates such.

61. מלה צפונית מובהקת (Rabin, "Leshonam shel ʿAmos ve-Hosheaʿ," 123).

62. Jastrow, *Dictionary*, 1:47, 345; and J. Payne Smith, *A Compendious Syriac Dictionary* (Oxford: Clarendon, 1903), 13.

63. As noted by C. Brockelmann, *Lexicon Syriacum* (Halle: Niemeyer, 1928), 14.

64. *HDHL*, microfiche 018, plates 3573–77; and Jastrow, *Dictionary*, 1:48, 345.

65. Rabin, "Leshonam shel ʿAmos ve-Hosheaʿ," 123–24.

66. See, e.g., Hurvitz, "Ha-Lashon," 217; and Fox, *Song of Songs*, 103.

scholars view this example as evidence for the postexilic date of the Song of Songs,[67] it is equally possible (especially given the amount of data garnered herein) that this Hebrew form was an IH trait. This calque on Aramaic exemplifies how northern Israelites looked to the major political power of Aram centered in Damascus for linguistic coinage (either consciously or subconsciously). The parallel would be the manner in which many languages of the world today (Modern Hebrew included!) create calques based on English phraseology (e.g., לקחת אמבטיה "take a bath").

1.2.6. The compound preposition עד שׁ- "until" occurs repeatedly throughout the book, in Song 1:12; 2:7, 17; 3:4, 5; 4:6; 8:4 (three of these [2:7; 3:5; 8:4] are in three of the four refrains in the book; two others [2:17; 4:6] are in a repeated expression). This usage appears elsewhere in the Bible in Judg 5:7 and Ps 123:2. The former is in the Song of Deborah and thus supports the IH character of this usage. The latter is in a psalm that does not demonstrate other IH traits; but since it belongs to the Maʿalot section, which most likely comprises a late group of poems, we would explain the attestation in Ps 123:2 as a result of the union of Israelian and Judahite exiles and/or an Aramaism. Accordingly, regardless of its presence on Ps 123:2, the distribution of עד שׁ- "until" points to its being an IH feature.

In support of this position is the very common use of עד שׁ- "until" in MH.[68] In addition, Aramaic attests to the parallel construction, composed of the preposition עד and the relative particle, either the independent form די or the prefixed form ד-. The Aramaic form may mean "when, while" as well as "until" (and in fact this sense fits better in Song 1:12[69]), though obviously this often is a case of English translation, the Aramaic usage being one and the same. Examples include Dan 2:9 עד די עדנא ישתנא "until the time changes"; Dan 6:25 עד די שלטו בהון אריותא "when the lions overpowered them"; and Targum Neofiti to Gen 8:7 עד די יבשו מיא "until the waters dried," rendering Hebrew עד יבשת המים "until the drying of the waters."[70]

---

67. Again, see Murphy, *The Song of Songs*, 4 n. 10, citing Tournay *apud* Robert, *Le Cantique des Cantiques*, 21.

68. Segal, *Grammar*, 240–41; idem, *Diqduq*, 232; and Pérez Fernández, *Grammar of Rabbinic Hebrew*, 208.

69. See our translation, 191 n. g.

70. For additional examples, see M. Sokoloff, *A Dictionary of Jewish Palestinian Aramaic* (Ramat-Gan: Bar Ilan University Press, 1990), 395; and idem, *A Dictionary of Jewish Babylonian Aramaic* (Ramat-Gan: Bar Ilan University Press, 2002), 844. N.B. In citing Aramaic lexical evidence, we have utilized Jewish Aramaic evidence most systematically, culled from Sokoloff's two dictionaries. In many or most cases, we

In short, the evidence—distribution within the Bible, commonness in MH, and Aramaic cognate—converges to demonstrate that עד שׁ- "until" is a trait of IH.

1.2.7. In Song 2:13K we encounter the form לכי "to you" (Qeri: לך) in the expression קומי לכי "arise you" (or "arise yourself" or some such translation). The form includes the second feminine singular pronominal suffix -*kî* instead of the usual form -*āk*/-*ēk* (depending on the environment). The suffix -*kî* occurs in other northern texts: 2 Kgs 4:2K, 3K, 7K (2x); Ps 116:7 (2x), 19.

The first group appears in the Elisha cycle;[71] the second group occurs in a psalm replete with IH features.[72] Below we will comment on the use of -*kî* elsewhere in the Bible, but these seven attestations (eight when one includes Song 2:13K) represent sufficient grounds to label the usage an IH morpheme.[73]

The history of the form is as follows. Although absolute proof is lacking, one will assume that the proto-Semitic morpheme -*kî* was the norm in second-millennium Northwest Semitic, including Ugaritic (the orthography, of course, indicates only -*k*).[74] For the first-millennium dialects, the suffix -*kî* is attested in Aramaic, and we can be reasonably sure that this form continued in Phoenician. It appears as כי- in Imperial Aramaic[75] (examples may be found in *BMAP* 9 and in Cowley 8) and in Qumran Aramaic (Genesis Apocryphon 19:19, 20 [2x]).[76] Moreover, although many of the later dialects attest ך- or יך-,[77] the form כי- is still used, perhaps ves-

---

could have cited evidence from other dialects as well, e.g., Syriac and Samaritan Aramaic; we do so on occasion below but not in any systematic fashion.

71. Rendsburg, *Kings*, 86–87.

72. Rendsburg, *Psalms*, 83–86; and J. P. Fokkelman and G. A. Rendsburg, "נגדה נא לכל עמו (Psalm cxvi 14b, 18b)," *VT* 53 (2003): 328–36, especially 334.

73. Already Burney (*Kings*, 208) reached the same conclusion.

74. C. H. Gordon, *Ugaritic Textbook* (AnOr 38; Rome: Pontifical Biblical Institute, 1967), 36, 149.

75. S. Segert, *Altaramäische Grammatik* (Leipzig: VEB Verlag, 1975), 170–71; and P. Leander, *Laut- und Formenlehre des Ägyptisch-aramäischen* (Göteborg: Elanders, 1928), 27–32.

76. E. G. Kraeling, *The Brooklyn Museum Aramaic Papyri* (New Haven: Yale University Press, 1953), 238; A. E. Cowley, *Aramaic Papyri of the Fifth Century B.C.* (Oxford: Clarendon, 1923), 22; J. A. Fitzmyer, *The Genesis Apocryphon of Qumran Cave I* (Rome: Biblical Institute Press, 1971), 115; and B. Jongeling, C. J. Labuschagne, and A. S. van der Woude, *Aramaic Texts from Qumran* (Leiden: Brill, 1976), 91 n. 20.

77. E. Y. Kutscher, *Meḥqarim ba-ʾAramit ha-Gelilit* (Jerusalem: Hebrew University, 1969), 22 = idem, *Studies in Galilean Aramaic* (Ramat-Gan: Bar Ilan University

tigially, in Syriac.[78] For Phoenician, we can point to a Punic spelling with -כי.[79] The presence of -*kî* in IH thus creates an isogloss linking IH with Aramaic and Phoenician used to the north of Israel. All of these languages/dialects retained the proto-form. In JH, by contrast, the final long vowel -*î* was dropped; the addition of a helping vowel created the standard BH form -*āk*/-*ēk*.

The other attestations of the second feminine singular pronominal suffix -*kî* in the Bible are Jer 11:15; Pss 103:3 (2x), 4 (2x), 5; 135:9; 137:6. The presence of -*kî* in Jeremiah might be due to the local dialect of Anathoth also employing this suffix. Psalm 137:6 most likely is to be explained via the theory of the reunion of northern and southern exiles during the sixth century B.C.E., the date of this poem's composition.[80] Psalms 103 and 135 are postexilic compositions,[81] so in these cases Aramaic influence is responsible.

1.2.8. Song 2:17; 4:6 צללים "shadows" and 4:8 הררי "mountains" (in the construct state) are examples of reduplicatory plurals.[82] This term refers to the repeating of the final consonant of a singular noun based on a geminate stem. Normally, Hebrew resorts to gemination in such cases, as in עם "people," plural עמים; הר "mountain," plural הרים. But in a considerable number of instances the reduplicatory type appears.[83] The latter method of

Press, 1976), 31; and D. M. Golomb, *A Grammar of Targum Neofiti* (Chico, Calif.: Scholars Press, 1985), 48–49, 51–52.

78. C. Brockelmann, *Syrische Grammatik* (Berlin: Reuther & Reichard, 1899), 49; and T. Nöldeke, *Compendious Syriac Grammar* (London: Williams & Norgate, 1904), 46.

79. J. Friedrich and W. Röllig, *Phönizisch-punische Grammatik* (Rome: Pontifical Biblical Institute,1970), 47; and S. Segert, *A Grammar of Phoenician and Punic* (Munich: Beck, 1976), 96. The only form attested is suffixed to a noun, but one will assume that the pronominal suffix following a verb or pronoun was the same.

80. On this and other aspects of this poem see G. A. Rendsburg and S. L. Rendsburg, "Physiological and Philological Notes to Psalm 137," *JQR* 83 (1993): 385–99.

81. On Ps 103, see the detailed study of Hurvitz, *Beyn Lashon le-Lashon*, 107–52, with specific treatment of the second feminine singular pronominal suffix -*kî* on 116–19. Virtually all scholars view Ps 135 as postexilic, especially as it is constructed mainly from other biblical passages; see, e.g., A. Cohen, *The Psalms* (London: Soncino, 1945), 441.

82. See the earlier treatments in Rendsburg, *Psalms*, 40–42; idem, "Morphological Evidence for Regional Dialects in Ancient Hebrew," in *Linguistics and Biblical Hebrew* (ed. W. R. Bodine; Winona Lake, Ind.: Eisenbrauns, 1992), 84–85.

83. For the term "reduplicatory" and for the Afroasiatic background of this formation, see J. H. Greenberg, "Internal *a*-Plurals in Afroasiatic (Hamito-Semitic)," in *Afrikanistische Studien* (ed. J. Lukas; Berlin: Akademie Verlag, 1955), 198–204.

forming the plural is standard in Aramaic, as in עממין "peoples," כדדין "pitchers," and טללין "shades,"[84] and it appears in MH as well in a number of cases, such as m. Šabb. 20:4 צדדין "sides" and m. ʾOhal. 8:2 שננים "cliffs."[85] Accordingly, it is not surprising to find a goodly number of the reduplicatory plurals in the Bible appearing in northern contexts.

Judges 5, the Song of Deborah, includes two examples: עממיך "your peoples" (v. 14) and חקקי "decisions" (construct; v. 15). Numbers 23:7 הררי "mountains" (construct) is in the mouth of Balaam, the Aramean prophet. Deuteronomy 33:15 הררי "mountains" (construct) occurs in the blessing to the northern tribe of Joseph. Nehemiah 9 includes two such plurals: עממים "peoples" (v. 22) and עממי "peoples" (construct; v. 24). Psalm 36:7 הררי "mountains" (construct) occurs in a poem with a plethora of northern forms.[86] Psalms 50:10 הררי "mountains" (construct), 76:5 הררי "mountains" (construct), and 77:18 חצציך "your arrows" all appear in the Asaph collection.[87] Psalm 87:1 הררי "mountains" (construct) appears in the Korah collection.[88] Psalm 133:3 הררי "mountains" (construct) occurs in a poem that evokes Mount Hermon (v. 3) and in which several other IH features occur.[89] Proverbs 29:12 תככים "oppressions" places us in a book with a concentration of northern features. In addition, we may note the following examples: Jer 6:4 צללי "shadows" (construct); and Ezek 4:12, 4:15 גללי "pellets" (construct). The first is most likely due to the Benjaminite dialect of Jeremiah, and the second is probably due to Aramaic influence. This leaves only one occurrence

---

In light of Greenberg's study, we should view the reduplicatory plurals of geminate nouns in Hebrew as internal or broken plurals with the ־ים ending added secondarily due to *Analogiebildung*. Note the similarity between the Hebrew forms under discussion and such Afar-Saho (Cushitic) lexemes as *il* "eye," pl. *ilal*; *bōr* "cloth," pl. *bōrar*. For recent treatments, see C. V. Wallace (= C. W. Gordon), "Broken and Double Plural Formations in the Hebrew Bible" (Ph.D. diss., New York University, 1988); A. Zaborski, "Archaic Semitic in the Light of Hamito-Semitic," *ZAH* 7 (1994): 234–44, esp. 238–41; and R. R. Ratcliffe, "Defining Morphological Isoglosses: The 'Broken' Plural and Semitic Subclassification," *JNES* 57 (1998): 81–123.

84. Segert, *Altäramaische Grammatik*, 537, 546; and K. Beyer, *Die aramäischen Texte vom Toten Meer* (Göttingen: Vandenhoeck & Ruprecht, 1984), 453.

85. Segal, *Grammar*, 127; idem, *Diqduq*, 91; and Pérez Fernández, *Grammar of Rabbinic Hebrew*, 63.

86. Rendsburg, *Psalms*, 39–43.

87. Ibid., 73–81.

88. Ibid., 51–60.

89. Ibid., 91–93.

in a Judahite text, Hab 3:6 הררי "mountains" (construct), and one occurrence in a text of uncertain provenance, Deut 8:9 הרריה "her mountains."[90]

In light of the above, we conclude that the reduplicatory plural of nouns based on geminate stems is an IH feature.

1.2.9. The plural form נצנים "blossoms" in Song 2:12 is an atypical form. The singular form of the word is נצה, attested in Isa 18:5 and Job 15:33 (the latter with third masculine singular pronominal suffix: נצתו). The *-ān* ending attached to the base of this word in Song 2:12 is the same as the Aramaic ending *-ān* used to mark feminine plural nouns. Though the process of *Analogiebildung*, the common Hebrew suffix ים- was added (see similarly n. 83) to create the attested form נצנים.

There are no other instances of this morpheme *-ān* in BH, but closely related to it are several cases of the suffix *-ôn* serving the same function. The examples are as follows: עזבונים "wares" in Ezek 27 (6x), in the address to Tyre; קמשונים "weeds" in Prov 24:31, a northern text, serving as the plural of singular קמוש "weed" (Isa 34:13; Hos 9:6); and זרענים "vegetables" in Dan 1:16, an alternative plural to זרעים "vegetables" in Dan 1:12 (the singular is not attested, though no doubt the word is related to זרע "seed"), where most likely Aramaic influence is to be seen. In MH the plural of סם "spice" also takes the *-ān* ending, attested in two forms: סמנים (12x) and סממנים (11x).[91] Elsewhere among Canaanite dialects we may point to the Phoenician form אלנם "gods."

---

90. It is apposite to note that scholars have suggested that the book of Deuteronomy is a northern composition. See, among others, E. Nielsen, "Historical Perspectives and Geographical Horizons: On the Question of North-Israelite Elements in Deuteronomy," *ASTI* 11 (1977–78), 77–89; Ginsberg, *The Israelian Heritage of Judaism*, esp. 19–24; and M. Weinfeld, *Deuteronomy 1–11* (AB 5; New York: Doubleday, 1991), 44–50. For a brief discussion, see J. H. Tigay, *Deuteronomy: The JPS Torah Commentary* (Philadelphia: Jewish Publication Society, 1996), p. xxiii. A thorough investigation of this question using the linguistic evidence, especially the differentiations between IH and JH, remains a desideratum. We have pointed to an occasional northernism in Deuteronomy (see G. A. Rendsburg, "Notes on Israelian Hebrew [II]," *JNSL* 26 [2000], 33–45, esp. 35–36, 42), and yet at the same time one hesitates to claim that a significant concentration of such elements is present in the book. Until this question is settled with some certainty, for the nonce we should judge Deuteronomy to be a Judahite composition, and thus we would not include Deut 8:9 within the IH corpus.

91. *HDHL*, microfiche 067, plates 13703–4. The standard BH form סמים, by contrast, occurs only 6x in rabbinic texts. The Ben Sira–Dead Sea Scrolls material attests to only the BH form, not surprisingly (once in each corpus: Ben Sira 49:1; 11QT 3:10).

The evidence demonstrates that the *-ān/-ôn* suffix is known from Aramaic and Phoenician and occurs only in northern biblical texts or in Daniel where Aramaic influence is strongly felt. The form נצנים "blossoms" in Song 2:12, accordingly, is likely an IH feature.

1.3. Syntax

1.3.1. The "double plural" construction, in which both elements in a construct phrase are placed in the plural, is a feature of northern Hebrew.[92] Stanley Gevirtz was the first to take note of this, bringing not only biblical examples but also evidence from Phoenician, Ugaritic, and Byblos Amarna.[93] Not every construct phrase with both the *nomen regens* and the *nomen rectum* in the plural should automatically be considered a double plural. For example, the phrase בתי הקדשים in 2 Kgs 23:7 refers to the many houses of the many *qedešim*, and thus both forms are in the plural. We propose to call such instances "pseudo-double plural," because the language has no choice but to express the phrase in this manner.

By contrast, in the cases below, the true double plural is present, because either element of the construct phrase (usually the *nomen rectum*) could have been in the singular. For example, in Ps 47:10 נדיבי עמים "princes of peoples," but really "princes of the people" (note the parallel phrase עם אלהי אברהם "the people of the God of Abraham"), the *nomen rectum* is in the plural because the *nomen regens* is in the plural. Standard Hebrew expresses this differently, with the *nomen rectum* in the singular, as expected, in Num 21:18 נדיבי העם and Ps 113:8 נדיבי עמו. The same occurs in Ps 74:13 ראשי תנינים "the heads of the monsters," but really "the heads of the Tannin," because we know that there is only one multiheaded Tannin (in addition, note the singular ים "Sea" in the parallel stich; the term לויתן "Leviathan" in v. 14a; and the object pronoun "him" in the word תתננו "you give him" in v. 14b).[94] The opposite occurs in the phrase in Ps 116:9 ארצות החיים "the lands of the living," but really "the land of the living." Because the *nomen rectum* חיים is

92. See the earlier treatment in Rendsburg, *Psalms*, 35–36; idem, *Kings*, 130–31; and idem, "Israelian Hebrew Features in Genesis 49," in *Let Your Colleagues Praise You: Studies in Memory of Stanley Gevirtz 2* (ed. R. J. Ratner, L. M. Barth, M. L. Gevirtz, and B. Zuckerman; Rolling Hills Estates, Calif.: Western Academic Press, 1993) = *Maarav* 8 (1992): 168–69.

93. S. Gevirtz, "Of Syntax and Style in the 'Late Biblical Hebrew'–'Old Canaanite' Connection," *JANES* 18 (1986), 28–29; idem, "Asher in the Blessing of Jacob (Genesis xlix 20)," *VT* 37 (1987): 160.

94. See G. A. Rendsburg, "*UT* 68 and the Tell Asmar Seal," *Or* 53 (1984): 448–52.

in the plural, the *nomen regens* occurs in the plural as ארצות instead of the expected ארץ.

At times it is difficult to tell whether we have a true double plural or a pseudo-double plural; in compiling the following list, we have made the judgment that we are dealing with true double plurals.

The Song of Songs includes one certain example of the double plural syntagma: 1:17 קרות בתינו "rafters of our houses," really "rafters of our house." An additional example might be Song 8:14 הרי בשׂמים "mountains of spices," especially when compared to 2:17 הרי בתר, a difficult phrase, but one that might mean "mountains of spice" (thus the Peshitta's understanding).

[The book also includes examples of pseudo-double plurals, such as the following: (1) Song 1:7 עדרי חבריך "flocks of your friends," since the lover can have plural friends and they in turn can possess multiple flocks; (2) 1:8 משכנות הרעים "dwellings of the shepherds," because the plural shepherds can have plural tents; (3) the two instances in 4:8 מענות אריות "dens of lions" and הררי נמרים "mountains of leopards," since multiple felines inhabit the mountains; (4) 5:7 שׁמרי החמות "watchmen of the city walls," since ancient Hebrew usage shows us that the city wall (which we might consider to be singular) could be envisioned as plural, thus, for example, the expression חמות ירושלם "city walls of Jerusalem" (Jer 39:8, etc.); see similarly Ezek 26:4 (Tyre); Jer 51:12; 51:58 (Babylon); and (5) Song 7:10 שׂפתי ישׁנים "lips of those-who-sleep" (a notoriously difficult phrase, but we shall translate literally for our present purpose), since multiple sleeping individuals, each with a pair of lips, may be intended.]

In the northern psalms we have the three previously cited examples (Pss 47:10; 74:13; 116:9), along with Pss 29:1 בני אלים "sons of the gods" (= deities); 45:10 בנות מלכים "daughters of the kings" (= princesses); 77:6 שׁנות עולמים "years of eternities"; and 78:49 מלאכי רעים "messengers of evils."

A particularly striking example is 2 Kgs 15:25 בני גלעדים "sons of Gilead," that is, "Gileadites." Note how unusual this phrase is, with a toponym as the *nomen rectum* yet nevertheless in the plural. Obviously, the norm in Hebrew is represented by such expressions as בני יהודה "sons of Judah," that is, "Judahites" (2 Sam 1:18; Hos 2:2, etc.); בני דן "sons of Dan," that is, "Danites" (Judg 18:2, etc.); בני חת "sons of Heth," that is, "Hittites" (Gen 23:3, etc.); and many others.

A systematic survey of the entire Bible would no doubt uncover additional examples of the phenomenon, but the examples cited here, in our opinion, provide sufficient evidence by which to label this usage an IH feature.

1.3.2. The periphrastic genitive מטתו שלשלמה "the divan of Solomon" occurs in Song 3:7 and in no other place in the Bible. This syntagma, used especially to indicate inalienable or intrinsic possession, is well-known from Mishnaic Hebrew,[95] Aramaic,[96] and Amurru Akkadian.[97] There is no clear evidence that this usage ever penetrated southward to JH. We have a large corpus of JH texts, not only the majority of the Bible but presumably the Dead Sea Scrolls as well, and yet we have no examples from either body of material. Accordingly, the aggregate evidence points to the northern origin of this syntagma.

1.3.3. The phrase אחזי חרב "grasping the sword" in Song 3:8 is one of only two biblical examples of the passive participle used with the active voice.[98] The second example is 2 Kgs 6:9 נחתים "descending," in a story concerning Elisha and Jehoram king of Israel.[99] This usage is extremely common in MH[100] and in certain Aramaic dialects, most notably Syriac.[101] We conclude that this is an IH syntagma.

---

95. Segal, *Grammar*, 191–92; idem, *Diqduq*, 200–201; and Pérez Fernández, *Grammar of Rabbinic Hebrew*, 28, 32.

96. The most detailed treatment is M. L. Folmer, *The Aramaic Language in the Achaemenid Period: A Study in Linguistic Variation* (Leuven: Peeters, 1995), 259–325. See also W. R. Garr, "On the Alternation between Construct and *DĪ* Phrases in Biblical Aramaic," *JSS* 35 (1980): 213–31.

97. S. Izre'el, *Amurru Akkadian: A Linguistic Study* (HSS 40–41; 2 vols.; Atlanta: Scholars Press, 1991), 1:205–9.

98. In the words of Fox (*Song of Songs*, 124), the passive participle is used in Song 3:8 "instead of the active participle to show a characteristic or habitual action."

99. See further Rendsburg, *Kings*, 101–2. Note that P. Joüon ("Notes de critique textuelle [AT] 2 Rois 6,8–10," *MUSJ* 5 [1911–12]: 477) proposed emending the form to the active participle *nôḥătîm*. The *dagesh* in the *taw* of נחתים *nĕḥittîm* is problematic, but parallels exist (though admittedly not with the passive participle); see W. Chomsky, *David Kimḥi's Hebrew Grammar (Mikhlol)* (New York: Bloch, 1952), 244.

100. Segal, *Grammar*, 160–61; idem, *Diqduq*, 133–34; and Pérez Fernández, *Grammar of Rabbinic Hebrew*, 139–40. The most detailed treatment is Y. Blau, "Benoni Paʿul be-Horaʾa ʾAqtivit," *Leshonenu* 18 (5713/1953): 67–81. Blau posited two other BH examples, Neh 4:12 אסורים and Isa 46:1 נשאתיכם (see 72), but we do not find either example convincing. Without wishing to think in English, note that the former is the exact equivalent of English "girded," that is, in the passive. In the latter it is not clear whether the word refers back to the idols or to the animals (as Blau admitted); note the NJPS rendering: "The things you would carry," understanding the word in the passive sense, that is, "the carried things." But even if Blau were granted these examples, we would explain them as Aramaisms in the language of the exilic prophet and of the postexilic Nehemiah, both members of the Aramaic-speaking Babylonian Jewish community.

101. T. Nöldeke, *Kurzgefasste Syrische Grammatik* (Leipzig: Tauchnitz, 1898),

1.3.4. Song 4:9 reads אחד ענק "one strand, one bead," with a syntax of the numeral known from Aramaic[102] but not from elsewhere in the Hebrew portions of the Bible. This feature represents another isogloss shared by the dialect of the Song of Songs and Aramaic.

1.3.5. In Song 4:15 the phrase מן לבנון "from Lebanon" is an example of the preposition מן before an anarthrous noun. The norm in Hebrew calls for the *nun* of the preposition מן to assimilate before a noun without the definite article. Indeed, the Bible attests to three such examples with this very noun, that is, מלבנון, two of which are in the Song of Songs; see Ezek 27:5 and Song 4:8 (2x; the alternative usage מהלבנון occurs in 2 Chr 2:7).

The use of מן לבנון in Song 4:15, soon after the appearance of the two instances of מלבנון in 4:8, is probably the result of the poet's desire to vary his or her language, as is typical of ancient Hebrew literary style.[103] But the fact that the expression מן לבנון was available to the poet indicates that he or she was conversant in IH.

Cognate evidence and the distribution of this phenomenon in the Bible indicate that this feature is an IH trait.[104] In Aramaic, the norm is the retention of the full form מן (especially since the definite article is postpositive, not prepositive, but always with proper nouns in any case, as in our example מן לבנון). The same holds for the Deir ʿAlla dialect, where it is attested five times, such as I:3 מן מחר "on the morrow."

In the Bible, the use of מן before an anarthrous noun is well-attested, ninety-eight times, to be exact.[105] Of these ninety-eight occurrences, fifty-one are in Chronicles, and a few additional ones appear in Daniel and Nehemiah. Undoubtedly the widespread appearance of this usage in Chronicles and the other late books is due to Aramaic influence over LBH.[106]

211. See also M. L. Margolis, *A Manual of the Aramaic Language of the Babylonian Talmud* (Munich: Beck, 1910), 82.

102. See the many examples put forward by Sokoloff, *Dictionary of Jewish Palestinian Aramaic*, 187; idem, *Dictionary of Babylonian Aramaic*, 431. Note that the regular usage is the numeral חד "one" before the noun and that many of the exceptions, with חד after the noun, occur in Targumim that are rendering a Hebrew text with the numeral אחד after the noun.

103. See R. Ratner, "Morphological Variation in Biblical Hebrew Rhetoric," in Ratner et al., *Let Your Colleagues Praise You*, 143–59.

104. See already G. A. Rendsburg, "The Dialect of the Deir ʿAlla Inscription," *BO* 50 (1993): 314–15.

105. For a complete list of occurrences, see E. König, *Historisch-kritisches Lehrgebäude der hebräischen Sprache* (3 vols.; Leipzig: Hinrichs, 1895), 2:292.

106. See R. Polzin, *Late Biblical Hebrew: Toward an Historical Typology of Biblical*

But what of the earlier attestations of מן before an anarthrous noun? Although we readily admit to not being able to account for every instance of this usage in earlier parts of the Bible, a pattern is discernible. As the following listing of examples indicates, מן before an anarthrous noun almost certainly was a feature of IH.[107] Note the following: Num 23:7, in the Balaam oracles; Judg 5:20, in the Song of Deborah; 7:23 (2x), in the Gideon story; 10:11 (2x), in a story set in Gilead; 19:16, concerning the Ephraimite man traveling through Gibeah of Benjamin; 2 Kgs 15:28, in the account of Pekah king of Israel; Jer 7:7; 17:5; 25:3, 5; 44:18, 28, reflecting the Benjaminite dialect; Pss 45:9; 73:19; 116:8, all northern psalms; Prov 27:8, a northern composition; and Job 30:5; 40:6, in a work with strong Transjordanian influence.

In sum, the syntagma under discussion was a trait of IH, Aramaic, and the Deir ʿAlla dialect. Our passage in Song 4:15 is part of this picture. Under the influence of Aramaic, we aver, the usage became more common in LBH as well.

1.3.6. The phrase שִׁשִּׁים הֵמָּה מְלָכוֹת "there are sixty queens" in Song 6:8 occurs only here in the Bible, but the syntagma is very common in MH. To cite a famous example, see m. Roš Haš. 1:1 ארבעה ראשי שנה הם "there are four New Years."[108] We recognize the slight difference here—in the biblical example the independent pronoun is placed before the noun, while in the Mishnaic example it is placed after the noun—but the parallel is present nonetheless. Furthermore, Syriac provides an even closer analog to Song 6:8, as in Luke 13:14 *štā ʾēnnôn yawmîn* "there are six days" and 4 Ezra 7:101 *šabʿā ʾēnnôn yawmîn* "there are seven days," with the same word order: numeral + personal pronoun + noun.[109] This link between the language of the Song of Songs and MH, especially when coupled with the Syriac evidence, supports the conclusion that the syntagma in Song 6:8 is a northern feature.

Hebrew Prose (HSM 12; Missoula, Mont.: Scholars Press, 1976), 66; and G. A. Rendsburg, "Late Biblical Hebrew and the Date of 'P,'" *JANES* 12 (1980): 72.

107. We omit from consideration Deut 33:11, where מן is an interrogative pronoun. Also, מן הוא in Isa 18:2, 7 is not to be considered in this regard, though clearly it represents a dialectal feature of some sort (our hunch is that addressee-switching is at work here, since Cush is addressed in this pericope). For an earlier treatment, see Rendsburg, *Kings*, 132.

108. This point was noted by Fox, *Song of Songs*, 152.

109. This feature of Syriac grammar has not been noted in the literature. We are extremely grateful to Jan Joosten (Université des Sciences Humaines de Strasbourg, Faculté de Théologie Protestante) for bringing this material to our attention (oral communication, December 2001; email communication, June 2005) and for supplying us with a copy of his manuscript in progress on the subject.

1.3.7. The phrase זאת קומתך "this your stature" (or "this stature of yours") in Song 7:8 is an example of the demonstrative pronoun with irregular syntax.[110] The norm in Hebrew, of course, would call for קומתך הזאת*, that is, with the noun first, then the demonstrative pronoun following.[111] But in a handful of cases in the Bible we encounter the opposite order, with the demonstrative pronoun before the noun.

This construction appears elsewhere in the Bible in the following verses: Josh 9:12 זה לחמנו "this our bread" (or "this bread of ours"); 9:13 אלה נאדות היין "these our wineskins" (or "these wineskins of ours"); 9:13 אלה שלמותינו "these our clothes" (or "these clothes of ours"); 1 Kgs 14:14 זה היום "this day"; 2 Kgs 6:33 זאת הרעה "this evil"; Isa 23:13 זה העם "this people." These passages all occur in northern settings (see below for details), but first we present some general discussion.

Some scholars have explained these phrases as "this is your stature," "this is our bread," "this is the day," and so on. That is to say, this approach argues that the demonstrative pronoun in these cases is used not attributively as a modifier, but rather substantively as the subject of the sentence. Certainly there are such instances in the Bible, such as Pss 104:25 זה הים "this is the sea" (NJPS: "there is the sea") and 118:20 זה השער "this is the gate."

In addition, in expressions such as Exod 32:1 זה משה "this Moses," the demonstrative pronoun does not bear its usual deictic or anaphoric function, but rather a distancing function is present; that is, "the speakers take their distance from Moses."[112]

In contrast to examples such as Ps 104:25 and Exod 32:1, in the previously cited seven passages (Song 7:8, etc.), the contexts argue that the paradigm זה היום is the semantic equivalent of היום הזה, with no difference in meaning. Accordingly, we conclude that the above seven cases represent a different syntactic construction only.

This usage is well-known from both Arabic and Aramaic,[113] the latter of which is especially germane for the present enterprise. In Aramaic, this

110. For this section, see also G. A. Rendsburg, "Shimush Bilti Ragil shel Kinnuy ha-Remez ba-Miqra᾽: ῾Edut Nosefet le-᾽Ivrit Ṣefonit bi-Tqufat ha-Miqra᾽," *Shnaton* 12 (2000): 83–88; and idem, *Kings*, 38–40.

111. In this particular case, קומתך זאת*, that is, without definite article, also is possible. But usually the definite article is present on the demonstrative pronoun when the noun that it modifies is definite.

112. J. Joosten, "The Syntax of *zeh Mošeh* (Ex 32,1.23)," *ZAW* 103 (1991): 412–15, in particular 413.

113. See Z. Harris, *Development of the Canaanite Dialects* (New Haven: American Oriental Society, 1939), 69.

construction is relatively frequent (see Ezra 5:4; Dan 4:15, for examples in Biblical Aramaic); in some dialects (e.g., Syriac and Mandaic), it is the norm.[114] It also is attested in Phoenician in one or two places.[115] Furthermore, this usage occurs in MH with some frequency; see, for example, m. Ketub. 4:6; m. Naz. 3:2; 7:2.[116]

With this cognate evidence in hand, it remains to demonstrate that the above passages occur in northern contexts. The two passages from Kings occur, respectively, in the history of Jeroboam I and in the Elisha cycle. The three examples in Josh 9:12–13 provide an excellent illustration of style-switching. As the story makes clear, the Gibeonites arrived in Gibeon from afar. Of course, the story does not tell us of their exact origins, but internal evidence suggests they originated in the northern part of Canaan. The text refers to the people of Gibeon as Hivites (9:7), and from elsewhere in the Bible we learn that the Hivites lived at the base of Hermon (11:3) and in Mount Lebanon from the mountain of Baal Hermon unto Lebo-hamath (Judg 3:3). So while the exact origins of the Hivites of Gibeon alludes us, the evidence suggests a home to the north. Thus, we suggest that the author of this pericope attempted to paint the foreign atmosphere of these folk by placing in their mouth three times the syntagma under discussion. Finally, Isa 23:13 is an example of addressee-switching. This passage occurs in the prophet's address to Tyre. In addition, it makes mention of the Chaldeans and Assyrians: the former in the Bible are related to the Arameans (see Gen 22:21–22) and later become a designation for the Aramaic-speaking Neo-Babylonians; the latter also spoke Aramaic in Isaiah's time.

The sum of the evidence points to the זה היום construction, and the specific example of זאת קומתך in Song 7:8, as a northern feature. The usage is attested in Aramaic, Phoenician, and MH and in seven places in the Bible with northern settings.

---

114. See W. H. Rossell, *A Handbook of Aramaic Magical Texts* (Ringwood Borough, N.J.: Shelton College, 1953), 27; Sokoloff, *Dictionary of Jewish Palestinian Aramaic*, 53; idem, *Dictionary of Jewish Babylonian Aramaic*, 357, 361; and R. Macuch, *Handbook of Classical and Modern Mandaic* (Berlin: de Gruyter, 1965), 406–9.

115. Segert, *A Grammar of Phoenician and Punic*, 170–71.

116. Segal, *Diqduq*, 51; Pérez Fernández, *Grammar of Rabbinic Hebrew*, 23.

1.4. Lexicon[117]

1.4.1. The root נעם "good, sweet, pleasant" occurs in Song 1:16; 7:7. This is one of the clearest cases of a northern Hebrew lexeme in the Bible. But first the cognate evidence: in Phoenician נעם is the only word for "good, etc." attested,[118] while in Ugaritic *nʿm* appears quite commonly (alongside *ṭb* "good").[119] Furthermore, נעם is a fairly common element in Phoenician personal names.[120] In addition, נעמן is the Phoenician name for Adonis,[121] and the same name is borne by one of the leading Aramean characters in the Bible, the general Naaman (2 Kgs 5). All of this suggests that the root נעם was common in areas to the north of Israel, Phoenicia in particular, but perhaps Aram as well.

When we turn to the Bible, we note that at least twenty-two and perhaps as many as twenty-six of the thirty attestations of נעם are in northern contexts.[122] Its most extensive use is in the book of Proverbs (9x), and it occurs six times in northern psalms (16:6, 11; 81:3; 133:1; 141:4, 6). Job 36:11 presents another example, this time in a book that may be Israelian in origin but that, regardless of provenance, casts its speeches in a Transjordanian dialect

---

117. As readers work through the lexical data—representing the largest section of this chapter—they will notice that on occasion a particular northern feature occurs sporadically in a Judahite text (see, e.g., §§1.4.2, 1.4.4, 1.4.16). Such is to be expected, however, as may be seen from inspecting a linguistic atlas of any modern language. Note, for example, that "sup" is used for "drink" in northern England but that it also occurs in a linguistic island in Oxfordshire, a southern county; and that "poke" occurs in southern American English for "bag, sack" but that it also occurs in one small part of Oregon. For these and other examples, see the popular book by B. Bryson, *The Mother Tongue* (New York: William Morrow, 1990), 101, 111. Bryson, in turn, relies on the major linguistic atlases for such details, most importantly H. Orton, S. Sanderson, and J. Widdowson, *The Linguistic Atlas of England* (London: Croom Helm, 1978).

118. *DNWSI* 2:738–39; and C. R. Krahmalkov, *Phoenician-Punic Dictionary* (Leuven: Peeters, 2000), 330–31.

119. Gordon, *Ugaritic Textbook*, 445; and G. del Olmo Lete and J. Sanmartín, *Diccionario de la Lengua Ugarítica* (2 vols.; Barcelona: Editorial AUSA, 1996–2000), 2:314 = G. del Olmo Lete and J. Sanmartín, *A Dictionary of the Ugaritic Language* (ed. and trans. W. G. E. Watson; Leiden: Brill, 2004), 2:613–14.

120. F. L. Benz, *Personal Names in the Phoenician and Punic Inscriptions* (Rome: Biblical Institute Press, 1972), 102, 146–47, 176, 185, 362.

121. W. F. Albright, *Yahweh and the Gods of Canaan* (London: School of Oriental and African Studies, 1968), 186–87.

122. See the earlier treatments in G. A. Rendsburg, "Additional Notes on 'The Last Words of David' (2 Sam 23,1–7)," *Bib* 70 (1989): 403–8; and idem, *Psalms*, 30–31.

mixed with Aramaic features; Gen 49:15 is in Jacob's blessing to Issachar, a northern tribe; 2 Sam 23:1 appears in a short poem with a high concentration of IH elements; Isa 17:10 appears in the address to Damascus; and Ezek 32:9 appears in the address to Egypt, so style-switching is at work in these two instances. The two Song of Songs examples bring the number of northern attestations to twenty-two.

Four additional usages may be relevant as well. The two examples in David's lament over Saul and Jonathan (2 Sam 1:16, 26) are from the pen of a Judahite poet (or at least purportedly), but the setting is Gilboa and the two slain heroes are Benjaminites, factors that may have had an effect on the word choice. Finally, the two cases in Zech 11:7, 10 could be explained either as northern influences over postexilic Hebrew or as continuations of the address to Lebanon in 11:1–3. If these examples are included in our calculation, then the number is increased to twenty-six.

Our conclusion is reached quite easily: נעם "good, sweet, pleasant" was used commonly in IH and only rarely employed in the dialect of Judah.

1.4.2. The word עֶרֶשׂ "bed" occurs in Song 1:16. Six of the eight additional attestations in the Bible are in northern contexts: Deut 3:11, where the setting is Bashan; Amos 3:12; 6:4, from the pen of a northern prophet; Ps 132:2, in a northern psalm;[123] Prov 7:16, in a northern composition; and Job 7:13, again, perhaps of Israelian origin but certainly presenting nonstandard Hebrew. (The only exceptions are Pss 6:7; 41:4, but most likely the poets have chosen עֶרֶשׂ for alliterative purposes in these two verses: 6:7 בדמעתי אמסה ערשי "with my tears I drench my bed" [also עֶרֶשׂ is the B-word here for מטה]; 41:4 יהוה יסעדנו על ערש דוי "YHWH sustains him on the bed of sickness."[124]) By including the Song 1:16 occurrence, we have seven of nine attestations in northern contexts, a significant ratio.

The cognate evidence corroborates the biblical data. The word *ʿrš* is attested commonly in Ugaritic, appearing in the Kret and Aqhat stories as

123. However, the evidence of עֶרֶשׂ was not included in the treatment of this psalm in Rendsburg, *Psalms*, 87–90.

124. The use of an IH lexeme as the B-word in poetic parallelism within Judahite compositions requires further comment. Here we have in mind the same technique as noticed by G. R. Driver, "Hebrew Poetic Diction," in *Congress Volume: Copenhagen, 1953* (VTSup 1; Leiden: Brill, 1953), 26–39, concerning the use of Aramaic words (or, more accurately, Hebrew words that are more widely attested and more common in Aramaic) as B-words within poetic parallelism. In the same vein, Judahite poets would utilize Israelian lexemes as B-words in parallelism. We will notice several more examples of this phenomenon below.

well as elsewhere.[125] In Aramaic, the cognate form ערס is also very common.[126] Moreover, the word occurs in the Targumim as the translational equivalent of Hebrew מטה "bed," as in Targum Onqelos to Exod 7:28 and Targum Jonathan to 2 Sam 3:31 (in the latter passage the meaning is "bier"). See also Targum Neofiti to Gen 50:1, at the scene of Jacob's deathbed, even though the Hebrew original lacks an explicit mention of "bed" here. Similarly, Vay. Rab. 105:5 translates Amos 6:4 מטות שן "beds of ivory" as ערסין דשן פיל "beds of ivory (of elephant)."

In MH the standard word for "bed" remains מטה,[127] but a byform of ערש/ערס, namely, עריסה, appears twenty-four times.[128] We consider this increased use of our word—or at least a byform thereof—in MH to be significant (notwithstanding the presence of ערש three times in QH[129]).

We conclude as follows: Hebrew had two terms for "bed," מטה and עֶרֶשׂ. The former predominated throughout the land, north and south, while the latter was used less commonly regardless of dialect. But even though עֶרֶשׂ could be utilized by Judahite authors on occasion (viz., a few biblical passages and several Qumran texts), it was northern Israelites, both in the biblical period and in the postbiblical period, who were much more likely to employ the word in their discourse, both written and oral. The total picture, based on the distribution of the vocable in the Bible and in postbiblical texts and the cognate evidence, argues for a northern home for BH עֶרֶשׂ.

1.4.3. The word רהיטים "beams, rafters" in Song 1:17Q derives from the Aramaic root for "run." While this root appears as רוץ in Hebrew, its Aramaic equivalent is רהט. The final root letter is /ẓ/, which shifts to /ṣ/ in Hebrew and to /ṭ/ in Aramaic (see the discussion above in the Phonology section re נטר, §1.1.1). In addition, the hollow root develops a medial ה in Aramaic, paralleled in בהת "be ashamed" = Hebrew בוש. Thus the noun רהיטים means something like "runners," therefore "beams, rafters" in the context of house construction as in Song 1:17. This word appears only here in BH and provides an excellent isogloss between the northern dialect reflected in the Song of Songs and Aramaic. רהיטים "runners, beams, rafters" continues in postbibli-

125. Gordon, *Ugaritic Textbook*, 461–62; del Olmo Lete and Sanmartín, *Diccionario de la Lengua Ugarítica*, 1:90 = *A Dictionary of the Ugaritic Language*, 1:185.

126. Jastrow, *Dictionary*, 2:1121; Beyer, *Die aramäische Texte vom Toten Meer*, 665; Sokoloff, *Dictionary of Jewish Palestinian Aramaic*, 420; and idem, *Dictionary of Jewish Babylonian Aramaic*, 882.

127. *HDHL*, microfiches 064–065, plates 13145–49.

128. *HDHL*, microfiche 073, plate 14820.

129. Ibid.

cal sources, but as far as we can tell, only in MH², that is, in Amoraic sources.[130] Perhaps more relevant, because it is attested in MH¹, that is, in Tannaitic texts produced while Hebrew still was spoken, is the word רטן "runners" (in the sense of human couriers), from the same root with the ה elided, attested in t. Šabb. 5:11 (2x).[131] On the related word רהטים "tresses," see below §1.4.31.

1.4.4. The noun חוח "thorn, thornplant, bramble" occurs in Song 2:2. Three additional attestations are in northern compositions: Hos 9:6; Prov 26:9; Job 31:40. The twin attestations of 2 Kgs 14:9 = 2 Chr 25:18 are in the story of the Judahite king Amaziah, but significantly they are in the mouth of king Jehoash of Israel in his statement "The thornplant that is in Lebanon sent [word] to the cedar that is in Lebanon" (indeed this statement may imply that the חוח is a plant native to the northern reaches of Israel). The only exception in BH, then, is Isa 34:13.

Aramaic uses the noun חוחא too, though one must admit that it is not all that common in that language either.[132] The combination of the distribution of חוח in the Bible and the cognate evidence from Aramaic, slim though it may be, yields the conclusion that this lexeme is a feature of IH. Although one must be careful in establishing an exact contrast—because we cannot be sure that word X and word Y refer to the same botanical phenomenon—possibly IH חוח "thorn, thornplant, bramble" stands in contrast to JH קוץ "thorn, thornplant, bramble," more widely distributed throughout the Bible.

1.4.5. The verb קפץ in Song 2:8 is the only Piʿel of this root in the Bible and the only instance where the meaning is "jump, leap." Otherwise the verb is attested in the Qal and Niphʿal with the meaning "shut, draw together."[133] The meaning "jump, leap" is continued in MH, albeit almost always in the Qal (43 attestations, along with 1 Niphʿal and 1 Piʿel).[134] The cognate root occurs in Aramaic, in the corresponding Paʿel conjugation.[135] It is, for example, the typical Aramaic equivalent for the more common BH root נתר "jump, leap," as in Targum Neofiti to Lev 11:21, and in Pesiq. Rab Kah. 392:11, where

130. Jastrow, *Dictionary*, 2:1454.

131. *HDHL*, microfiche 083, plate 16978. The word רהיטני, a tool of some sort, attested 6x in several contexts (*HDHL*, microfiche 091, plate 18720), including woodworking (e.g., t. B. Qam. 11:15) and hairstyling (m. Mak. 3:5), is of Greek origin; see S. Krauss, *Griechische und Lateinische Lehnwörter im Talmud, Midrasch und Targum* (2 vols.; Berlin: S. Calvary, 1898–99), 2:575 (see also 1:103).

132. Jastrow, *Dictionary*, 1:431.

133. BDB, 891; KB, 845–46; and *HALOT*, 1118.

134. *HDHL*, microfiche 080, plates 16282–83.

135. Jastrow, *Dictionary*, 2:1403; Sokoloff, *Dictionary of Jewish Palestinian Aramaic*, 500; and idem, *Dictionary of Jewish Babylonian Aramaic*, 1032–33.

Aramaic קפץ is used to explain Job 37:1 ויתר. The BH, MH, and Aramaic evidence converge to confirm the northernness of קפץ "jump, leap." The contrasting JH root is the aforementioned נתר "jump, leap."

1.4.6. The noun כתל "wall" is a *hapax legomenon* in Song 2:9. It appears more commonly in Aramaic.[136] In the Targumim, for example, כתל is the regular rendering of Hebrew קיר "wall," while in the Talmud Yerushalmi we encounter the phrase משתין בכתלא "urinates against the wall" (y. Sanh. 20b [16]), said of a dog, equivalent to the BH expression משתין בקיר.

Both כתל and קיר continue in postbiblical Hebrew as words for "wall," but the distribution is telling. In MH the ratio of the former to the latter is 231:40, while in QH and Ben Sira (taken as a unit) the ratio is 1:29 (the sole attestation of כתל is in CD 12:17).[137] Furthermore, of the forty attestations of קיר in MH, many occur in biblical phrases such as קירות הבית "walls of the house" and קיר המזבח "wall of the altar" when these topics are raised in halakic discussions.

The evidence points to כתל "wall" as an IH feature. It occurs in Song 2:9, it continues as the regular word in MH, and it has a cognate in Aramaic. The contrasting JH word is קיר "wall," which is regular in BH and dominates in QH and Ben Sira.

1.4.7. Another unique noun in the poem is חרכים "lattices" in Song 2:9.[138] The word is not attested in MH^1, but it does occur several times in MH^2.[139] Obviously, this evidence from rabbinic texts is slim, but we must recall that we are dealing with a relatively rare word to begin with.

136. Jastrow, *Dictionary*, 1:627; Beyer, *Die aramäische Texte vom Toten Meer*, 611; Sokoloff, *Dictionary of Jewish Palestinian Aramaic*, 255; and idem, *Dictionary of Jewish Babylonian Aramaic*, 567.

137. *HDHL*, microfiche 054, plates 10941–45 (for כתל), microfiche 079, plates 16147–48 (for קיר).

138. The verb חרך in Prov 12:27 means "burn, scorch, singe," a meaning better attested in MH; see *HDHL*, microfiche 044, plate 8821. Thus we may conclude that חרך "burn, scorch, singe" is also an IH lexeme, and we may use this as additional evidence for the northern origin of Proverbs discussed above (with all due cognizance of the circular reasoning implied by the two halves of this argument). KB (333) state "meaning unknown," but the context is one of cooking (see צידו "his game"), so clearly חרך = "burn" > "cook, roast" here. Thus traditional Jewish exegesis as well, as noted by BDB, 355, though, oddly, they opt for "start" based on an Arabic cognate. For the proper translation of the verb, note NJPS "roast."

139. Jastrow, *Dictionary*, 1:503.

Cognate support is forthcoming from Aramaic חרך, which bears a more general meaning "window, opening."[140] It appears commonly in the Targumim to translate Hebrew חלון, thus, for example, Targum Neofiti to Gen 8:6 (margin); 26:8; Targum Jonathan to Josh 2:15, 18, 21; Judg 5:28; 1 Sam 19:12; 2 Sam 6:16. In addition, it translates other Hebrew terms; for example, Targum Neofiti uses חרך to render ארבות in Gen 7:11 (margin), and Targum Pseudo-Jonathan uses it to render מחתרת in Exod 22:1.

The pattern of rare BH noun, attestation in MH (limited though it may be, and in this case only in MH^2), and Aramaic cognate yields the conclusion that חרכים "lattices" in Song 2:9 is an IH trait.

1.4.8. Another *hapax legomenon* is סתו "winter" in Song 2:11. This noun is known from Aramaic as well.[141] For example, Targum Neofiti uses it to translate חרף in Gen 8:22, and Targum Jonathan uses it when rendering the verb תחרף in Isa 18:6. Furthermore, the *qətāl* form of the word is typical of Aramaic but not of Hebrew. Accordingly, סתו "winter" represents an isogloss between IH and Aramaic. In JH the aforenoted חרף served for "winter." Of additional interest is the existence of the MH word סתוונית "winter fruit, late fruit," attested six times in the corpus (e.g., m. Ter. 11:2);[142] this indicates that the word סתו "winter" continued to be productive in northern Hebrew during the Roman period (even if the actual word סתו is not attested in Tannaitic sources [חרף is also rare, attested only once in MH as well as once in QH[143]]).[144]

---

140. Ibid.; and Sokoloff, *Dictionary of Jewish Palestinian Aramaic*, 215.

141. Jastrow, *Dictionary*, 2:1030; and S. A. Kaufman and M. Sokoloff, *A Key-Word-in-Context Concordance to Targum Neofiti* (Baltimore: Johns Hopkins University Press, 1993), 1039.

142. *HDHL*, microfiche 068, plate 13787; and Jastrow, *Dictionary*, 2:1030.

143. *HDHL*, microfiche 044, plate 8833.

144. Young (*Diversity in Pre-exilic Hebrew*, 164) claims that "a more general confusion or interchange of sibilants is found to be characteristic of Northern sources (although not exclusively Northern sources) in the Old Testament," with the word סתו in Song 2:11 as a prime example thereof, for based on the Arabic cognate *šitāʾ* "winter," one expects the Hebrew form to appear with *śin*, not *samekh*. While it is true that /ś/ shifts to /s/ in later Aramaic, and thus one might expect to find the same shift more frequently in IH than in JH, the operative word here is *later* (Aramaic). In the period contemporary with Biblical Hebrew, one finds /ś/ retaining its value in Aramaic (see E. Lipiński, *Semitic Languages: Outline of a Comparative Grammar* [OLA 80; Leuven: Peeters, 1997], 130). Furthermore, as Young himself indicated in the above quotation, there are sufficient examples of the phenomenon in Judahite sources as well (for a fuller discussion, see Young, *Diversity in Pre-exilic Hebrew*, 187–92). We do not wish to close the door on this issue, however, and admit that the question remains

1.4.9. Yet another *hapax legomenon* is פג "unripe fig" ("young-fruit," with special reference to the fig tree, in our translation) in Song 2:13. The noun occurs in MH rather commonly (32x).[145] In Aramaic the noun is not widely used, but one may point to Targum Pseudo-Jonathan to Num 6:4, where פגא renders the *hapax legomenon* זג.[146] In addition, a denominative verb פגג "be unripe" occurs in Aramaic.[147] The evidence, especially the widespread use of our word in MH, points to the conclusion that we are dealing with an IH lexeme.

1.4.10. The noun סמדר in Song 2:13, 15; 7:13 refers to an early stage in the ripening of grapes (or perhaps to a specific type of grape, one without seeds[148]). It is attested epigraphically at Hazor,[149] and it appears four times in MH (m. ʿOr. 1:7 [2x], m. Giṭ. 3:8, Sifra Qedošim 4:1).[150] The cognate סמדר occurs in Aramaic, and while it is not widely attested,[151] its use in Targum Jonathan to Isa 18:5 to translate Hebrew גמל is noteworthy (see further below). Given the many biblical contexts in which wine and grapes play a major role,[152] it is striking that this word is not used elsewhere in BH. While this could be a coincidence, most likely it is due to the fact that the majority of the Bible stems from Judah, where presumably סמדר was not part of the native vocabulary. We conclude that it is an IH lexeme and that its JH equivalent is the previously cited גמל in Isa 18:5.

---

open and deserves a full treatment. The "database" for such an inquiry already is in place; see J. Blau, *On Pseudo-Corrections in Some Semitic Languages* (Jerusalem: Israel Academy of Sciences and Humanities, 1970), 114–25 ("Appendix A: Irregular Spellings of *Samekh* and *Śîn* in Biblical Hebrew"). All of this to explain why we have not included this (potential) feature in the Phonology section above.

145. *HDHL*, microfiche 074, plate 15054.

146. See Jastrow, *Dictionary*, 2:1132.

147. Sokoloff, *Dictionary of Jewish Palestinian Aramaic*, 424.

148. For this view, see M. Altbauer, "ʿOd ʿal Semadar she-ʿal Qanqan me-Ḥaṣor," in *Zalman Shazar Volume = Eretz Israel* 10 (Jerusalem: Israel Exploration Society, 1971), 64–66. We use "in bud" in our translation (see 194, 204) simply for convenience, given the context.

149. Hoftijzer and Jongeling, *Dictionary of the North-West Semitic Inscriptions*, 2:791.

150. *HDHL*, microfiche 067, plate 13690; and Jastrow, *Dictionary*, 2:998.

151. See Jastrow, *Dictionary*, 2:998.

152. See J. M. Sasson, "The Blood of Grapes: Viticulture and Intoxication in the Hebrew Bible," in *Drinking in Ancient Societies: History and Culture of Drinks in the Ancient Near East* (ed. L. Milano; Padua: Sargon, 1994), 399–419.

1.4.11. The adjective ערב "sweet, pleasing" occurs in Song 2:14 and again only in Prov 20:17.[153] This distribution points to a northern home for this usage.[154] The Song of Songs passage קולך ערב "your voice is sweet" contrasts with the Judahite equivalent יפה קול "beautiful of voice" in Ezek 33:32.

The MH evidence supports this conclusion, for the adjective ערב "sweet, pleasing" appears sixteen times in Tannaitic texts, such as in the common expression שמן ערב "sweet oil" (m. Demai 1:3, etc.).[155] A strikingly similar usage to Song 2:14 is m. ʿArak. 2:3 קולו ערב "its voice is sweet," said of a reed flute (in contrast to a metal one). In addition, the cognate עריב "sweet, pleasing" occurs in Aramaic, for example, in the phrase הוה ערב להון "it was pleasing to them" in Qoh. Rab. 2b (10).[156]

1.4.12. The noun שׁוק "street" in Song 3:2 appears elsewhere in the Bible only in northern compositions: Prov 7:8; Qoh 12:4, 5. The cognate in Aramaic is the common word for "street" in that language, though it possesses a wider range of meanings ("quarter, district, outside place, public square, market, marketplace, etc.").[157] In the Targumim, שׁוק is the standard correspondence of Hebrew חוץ in both its meanings "outside" and "street," as in Targum Neofiti to Gen 39:12, 15, 18; Exod 21:19; Deut 24:11; Targum Jonathan to 2 Sam 22:43; 1 Kgs 20:34; Targum to Prov 7:12, and so forth. The evidence indicates that שׁוק "street" is a feature of IH, in contrast to the aforementioned JH term חוץ "street, outside."[158]

153. BDB, 787; KB, 733; and *HALOT*, 879.

154. It is quite possible that the root ערב "be pleasing" in general is an IH feature. The verb appears mainly in IH texts, that is, if we include two Jeremiah passages representing the border Benjaminite dialect, though there are still some JH usages. Of the former, note Hos 9:4; Prov 3:24; 13:19, along with Jer 6:20; 31:26; of the latter, note Ezek 16:37; Mal 3:4; Ps 104:34. In MH^1, however, the verb ערב "be pleasing" is not attested, though it does appear in MH^2 and in Aramaic; see Jastrow, *Dictionary*, 2:1110; and Sokoloff, *Dictionary of Jewish Palestinian Aramaic*, 417. This evidence could be interpreted to claim that not only the adjectival form but the root in general was a feature of IH; thus Chen, *Israelian Hebrew in the Book of Proverbs*, 51–52. But regardless of how one weighs the evidence of the verb, we are on solid ground when concluding that the adjectival form ערב "pleasant" was a component of the IH lexicon.

155. *HDHL*, microfiche 072, plate 14757–14758; see also Jastrow, *Dictionary*, 2:1110–11.

156. Sokoloff, *Dictionary of Jewish Palestinian Aramaic*, 419.

157. Sokoloff, *Dictionary of Jewish Palestinian Aramaic*, 542; idem, *Dictionary of Jewish Babylonian Aramaic*, 1123–24.

158. See Chen, *Israelian Hebrew in the Book of Proverbs*, 77.

1.4.13. The verb גלשׁ in Song 4:1; 6:5 has caused difficulty for translators and commentators alike, but, fortunately, the fine study by S. S. Tuell points us in the proper direction.[159] The cognate *glṯ* is attested four times in Ugaritic, three times in meteorological or cosmological contexts (and once in a broken context in a difficult text (*CAT* 1.8:II:13). As a verb, it appears in *CAT* 1.92:5 *tglṯ thmt*, meaning something like "the ocean swells." As a noun it occurs in *CAT* 1.101:7 in the description of Baal *rišh bglṯ bšmm*, a difficult phrase but perhaps something like "his head in the swelling/flowing in the sky," referring to the flowing clouds probably; and in a familiar text in the Baal cycle *CAT* 1.4:V:7) *yʿdn ʿdn ṯkt bglṯ*, "(Baal) makes luxuriant the ship on the waves" (the passage is difficult, other translations are possible,[160] but this one is serviceable for the nonce).

The contexts of Ugaritic *glṯ* accord well with the meaning of גלשׁ in postbiblical Hebrew, though the sole attestation is in MH², namely, b. Pesaḥ. 37b, where it refers to boiling or bubbling water. Apparently the word was borrowed into Jewish Palestinian Aramaic, for it occurs there as גלשׁ (if it were a natural Aramaic development, we would expect גלת* with the shift of /ṯ/ > /t/), also with the meaning "boil over" (y. Pesaḥ. 31a [50]), but with reference to "a type of hair arrangement" as well, most likely wavy hair (Shemot Rabba 23b [28]).[161] The total picture—taking the Ugaritic, MH², and Aramaic attestations into account—suggests a meaning such as "wave motion." Tuell rightly asked, "Yet how can the meaning of גלשׁ be deduced from *glṯ* if … *glṯ* means 'wave'? The setting of the Song is pastoral, not nautical!" and then provided the following response to his query: "The answer lies in the motion of the animals. A densely packed herd, viewed from a distance, seems to move downhill with a rippling, wavelike motion.… The point of the simile now becomes clear: the beloved's hair is wavy.… The Hebrew text, then, should be translated, Your hair is like a flock of goats, flowing in waves from (Mount) Gilead."[162] In addition, we note that the poet's selection of גלשׁ allowed him to create a delightful alliteration with גלעד "Gilead" (on which see more below, ch. 2, at Song 4:1, as well as the section on Song 6:5–6, 8–9).

---

159. S. S. Tuell, "A Riddle Resolved by an Enigma: Hebrew גלשׁ and Ugaritic *glṯ*," *JBL* 112 (1993): 99–104.

160. See, e.g., M. Smith, "The Baal Cycle," in *Ugaritic Narrative Poetry* (ed. S. B. Parker; SBLWAW 9; Atlanta: Scholars Press, 1997), 129 and 171 n. 121.

161. Sokoloff, *Dictionary of Jewish Palestinian Aramaic*, 131.

162. Tuell, "A Riddle Resolved," 103. In our translation (see 196, 201), we use an adaptation of Tuell's rendering.

Back to the main point of this chapter: the attestation of גלשׁ in the Song of Songs, Ugaritic, MH (albeit MH²), and Aramaic points to the northern nature of this word.

1.4.14. The root קצב "cut, chop, shear" appears in Song 4:2, in the feminine plural passive participle form in the phrase כעדר הקצובות "like a flock of shorn-ones." The verb is used again in the Bible only in 2 Kgs 6:6, in the Elisha cycle, with reference to wood (the exact action is uncertain: possibilities include the breaking off of a branch, the cutting of a stick, or the chopping of a piece of wood). This distribution suggests that we may be dealing here with an IH lexical feature.[163] Support for this conclusion comes from the more frequent use of the verb קצב in MH. It occurs seventeen times in the corpus (12x in the Qal, 5x in the Piʿel), with a variety of meanings, not only "cut" but also "decide, determine."[164] In addition, the noun קצב serves as the common MH word for "butcher."[165]

The derived noun קצב occurs in 1 Kgs 6:25; 7:37, with the meaning shape, no doubt the result of semantic extension from something cut. These passages occur in the description of the construction of the temple, a section of the Bible in which one finds a good number of Phoenicianisms (see, most prominently, the month names Ziv, Bul, and Ethanim, along with the word ירח "month"; see also 1 Kgs 6:1, 37–38; 8:2). While a complete study of 1 Kgs 6–8 remains a desideratum, based on the evidence collected from a surface reading of the material, we suggest that these chapters were composed by Phoenician scribes who accompanied the Phoenician architects and craftsmen engaged by Solomon for his major construction project. Although the context is not perfectly clear, the root קצב occurs in one Punic text, *KAI* 145:9.[166] The evidence is not overwhelming, but we would conclude that our root was characteristic of Phoenician as well.

The root קצב also occurs in Aramaic, more commonly as the word for "butcher"[167] but occasionally as a verb as well. The Samaritan Targum, for example, uses קצב to render the Hebrew verb בתר in Gen 15:10 (2x; in addi-

163. Rendsburg, *Kings*, 99.

164. *HDHL*, microfiche 080, plates 16284–85; see also Jastrow, *Dictionary*, 2:1404.

165. *HDHL*, microfiche 080, plate 16285; see also Jastrow, *Dictionary*, 2:1404.

166. Scholars disagree as to whether the specific form עקצב is a noun ("cut stone" or "statue" or the like) or a verb (that is, "cut") in this text. For discussion, see *DNWSI* 2:1021.

167. Jastrow, *Dictionary*, 2:1404; Sokoloff, *Dictionary of Jewish Palestinian Aramaic*, 500; and idem, *Dictionary of Jewish Babylonian Aramaic*, 1033. The word also occurs once in Palmyrene, though subject to varying interpretations; both "butcher"

tion to which occurs the noun form קצוב "piece" as the equivalent to the Hebrew noun בתר in this verse).[168]

The sum of this evidence is, as noted above, that the root קצב, in both verbal and nominal forms, is an IH lexical trait.[169]

1.4.15. The verb שׁור appears in Song 4:8 in the stich תשורי מראשׁ אמנה. There is some uncertainty concerning the meaning of the verb in this context, but the parallelism with תבואי "come" suggests a verb of motion.[170] A fitting cognate occurs in Syriac, where the verb שׁור is the common word for "leap, bound, spring, jump," used of humans as well as animals.[171] (However, the Peshitta uses תעברין to render תשורי in Song 4:8.) Thus we would translate the phrase as "bound from the summit of Amana." This meaning for שׁור is to be found in one other place in the Bible, also a northern text, namely, Hos 13:7 כנמר על דרך אשור "as a leopard on the path I will pounce."[172] The distribution of this verb, along with the Syriac cognate evidence, points to our conclusion: שׁור "leap, bound, spring, jump" is an IH lexical feature.

In addition, note that the word choice most likely was governed by the desire for alliteration between the verb שׁור "bound" and the following word ראשׁ "head, summit" (see further in ch. 2, on Song 4:8).

1.4.16. The noun נפת "honey" in Song 4:11 appears elsewhere in the Bible predominantly in northern texts, specifically Prov 5:3; 24:13; 27:7. Psalm 19:11 is the only Judahite text that uses this word, as the B-word for דבשׁ in the famous expression נפת צופים. It is important to note that דבשׁ also appears in Proverbs (16:24; 24:13; 25:16, 27) and the Song of Songs (4:11; 5:1), so the claim is not that נפת was used in total contrast to דבשׁ in northern Hebrew but rather that the two terms coexisted in this dialect.[173] This was

---

and "sacrificial victim" are possible. See D. R. Hillers and E. Cussini, *Palmyrene Aramaic Texts* (Baltimore: Johns Hopkins University Press, 1996), 407.

168. A. Tal, *A Dictionary of Samaritan Aramaic* (2 vols.; Leiden: Brill, 2000), 1:791–92.

169. The sole remaining instance of this root in BH, namely, in the phrase קצבי הרים "extremities of the mountains" in Jonah 2:7, is most likely from the same root but with a very specific meaning. Accordingly, one should not attempt to relate this usage to the present discussion. In any case, the text is a poem, where rare and unusual lexemes may be expected.

170. See Fox, *Song of Songs*, 135.

171. Payne Smith, *Compendious Syriac Dictionary*, 568.

172. See I. Eitan, "Biblical Studies," *HUCA* 14 (1939): 4–5.

173. Indeed, the form of דבשׁ, akin to that of an Aramaic segholate, suggests that it (along with a few other Hebrew words of "rustic semantics") originated in a dialect other than Jerusalemite Hebrew, after which it spread throughout all dialects of the

not the case in JH, where דבשׁ alone was used (again with the one exception of Ps 19:11, though for poetic purposes), as is indicated by its wide distribution throughout the corpus.

Cognates of נפת "honey" occur in Ugaritic and Phoenician/Punic, to the total exclusion of cognates to דבשׁ. In Ugaritic *nbt* appears commonly.[174] Admittedly, the evidence from Phoenician/Punic is rather meager, and the sole instance in *KAI* 76B:8 (a Punic inscription) appears in an imperfectly understood text. Nevertheless, since this inscription mentions a variety of foodstuffs (fruit, bread, etc.), there is little doubt that נפת means "honey" here.[175] The evidence from the Bible and from elsewhere in Northwest Semitic suggests that נפת "honey" is an IH lexical feature.[176]

1.4.17. The noun מגד "choice-fruit" in Song 4:13, 16 (in both cases in the plural, the latter with pronominal suffix) occurs elsewhere in the Bible only in Deut 33:13–16, where it occurs five times in the blessing to Joseph. This distribution alone would suggest that מגד "choice-fruit" is a characteristic of IH. The presence of an Aramaic cognate מגד with meanings "precious ware, costly gift, etc." as well as "choice-fruit"[177] solidifies this conclusion.

1.4.18. The verb ארה "pluck" occurs in Song 5:1 and again only in Ps 80:13: למה פרצת גדריה וארוה כל עברי דרך "why did you breach its walls, so that every passerby could pluck it." This psalm is one of the best exemplars of an Israelian composition in the Bible: as we mentioned in the introduction to this chapter, it refers to Joseph, Ephraim, Benjamin, and Manasseh (vv. 2–3); the phrase ארזי אל "cedars of God" (or "lofty cedars") in verse 11 most likely refers to the cedars of Lebanon; several IH linguistic features occur in the

---

Hebrew language. See J. L. Malone, "Wave Theory, Rule Ordering and Hebrew-Aramaic Segolation," *JAOS* 91 (1971): 44–66, esp. 56–57 (with the term "rustic semantics" used on 56).

174. Gordon, *Ugaritic Textbook*, 441.

175. Thus, e.g., *KAI* 2:93–94. See also the brief entry in *DNWSI* 2:749; as well as Krahmalkov, *Phoenician-Punic Dictionary*, 333.

176. See already Chen, *Israelian Hebrew in the Book of Proverbs*, 61.

177. For Aramaic מגד, see Jastrow, *Dictionary*, 2:726, with the meaning "precious ware" as well as "fine fruit"; and Sokoloff, *Dictionary of Jewish Palestinian Aramaic*, 289, with the form מגדנין meaning "precious goods." See also Syriac מגדא "costly gift" in Brockelmann, *Lexicon Syriacum*, 373; though Payne Smith (*Compendious Syriac Dictionary*, 249) offers the translation "some sort of fruit" for this word.

poem;[178] and it is part of the Asaph collection for which a northern origin has been posited by a number of scholars.[179]

In addition, the verb ארה "pluck" occurs in MH (m. Šeb. 1:2; t. B. Bat. 4:9 [2x]),[180] where it stands in contrast to the total absence of the verb in other texts, most prominently the Dead Sea Scrolls and Ben Sira. The biblical and postbiblical evidence reveals that this item is another lexical feature of IH.

1.4.19. Another unique vocable in the book is קוצות "(hair)locks" in Song 5:2, 11. This word also continues in MH, though again in a very limited way; the two attestations, in similar texts, are t. Naz. 4:7 and Sifre Bemidbar 22.[181] Again we can assume that the word was rare even in the northern dialect; in addition, we must keep in mind that the subject of hairlocks is not a common one. Finally, note that a cognate occurs in Syriac; it is used in the Peshitta not only here in Song 5:2, 11 but in Ezek 44:20 as well to translate Hebrew פרע "long hair."[182] Accordingly, קוצות "(hair)locks" should be added to our list of northern features in the Song of Songs.

1.4.20. Another rare word occurring in Song 5:2 is רסיסים "droplets." It derives from the root רסס "drip, moisten, sprinkle," known from Aramaic and Syriac.[183] A verb from this root appears in Ezek 46:14, most likely a true Aramaism in the book of the exilic prophet. The cognate noun occurs in Aramaic as well, attested as a plural רסיסין "droplets."[184] This form is the standard rendering in the Targumim for Hebrew רביבים "droplets," as in Targum Onqelos, Targum Neofiti, and Fragment Targum to Deut 32:2, Targum Jonathan to Jer 3:3; 14:22. Similarly, the verb רסס "drip, moisten, sprinkle" is used in the Targumim to render several Hebrew equivalents, for example, Samaritan Targum to Deut 32:2 for Hebrew ערף, Targum to Prov 3:20 for Hebrew רעף, Targum to Prov 7:17 for Hebrew נוף II. The evidence demonstrates that

---

178. Rendsburg, *Psalms*, 79.

179. See, most importantly, M. J. Buss, "The Psalms of Asaph and Korah," *JBL* 82 (1963): 382–92, in particular 384. H. P. Nasuti (*Tradition History and the Psalms of Asaph* [SBLDS 88; Atlanta: Scholars Press, 1988]) never stated explicitly that the Asaph group is of northern origin, but he used the term "Ephraimite tradition stream."

180. *HDHL*, microfiche 025, plate 4932.

181. *HDHL*, microfiche 079, plate 16144.

182. Payne Smith, *Compendious Syriac Dictionary*, 497; and Brockelmann, *Lexicon Syriacum*, 656.

183. Jastrow, *Dictionary*, 2:1484–85; Sokoloff, *Dictionary of Jewish Babylonian Aramaic*, 1089; and Payne Smith, *Compendious Syriac Dictionary*, 544.

184. Jastrow, *Dictionary*, 2:1484; and Sokoloff, *Dictionary of Jewish Palestinian Aramaic*, 527.

רסיסים "droplets" was an IH lexical item,[185] with the JH equivalent being רביבים "droplets."

1.4.21. The word טנף "soil" in Song 5:3 is a *hapax legomenon*.[186] The word appears more commonly in MH, occurring fourteen times in both the Piʿel (e.g., t. Šabb. 16:19) and Nitpaʿel (e.g., m. Makš. 4:5).[187] In addition, the noun טנפת "spoiled produce" appears three times (e.g., m. B. Bat. 6:2). The cognate טנף "soil" occurs in Aramaic, in the corresponding Paʿel and ʾItpaʿal forms.[188] Examples from the Targumim include Targum Pseudo-Jonathan to Num 35:33 to render Hebrew חנף (2x), Deut 21:23 to render Hebrew טמא, Targum to Lam 4:14 to render Hebrew גאל, and in Targum Neofiti marginal gloss to Gen 34:31, referring to the defilement of Dinah, as part of a very large expansion of the original Hebrew text. The pattern of rare word in BH, common word in MH, and Aramaic cognate, as we have argued in this chapter, points to the northernness of this root. The JH equivalent(s) of טנף "soil" would be any or all of the above items (חנף, טמא, גאל, etc.).

1.4.22. The unique noun מלאת "pool" in Song 5:12 is a paradigm example of an ancient Hebrew word whose meaning was recovered by a modern scholar doing basic manuscript research. We refer to E. Y. Kutscher's discovery that מלאת occurs in Bereshit Rabba 95 (in Aramaic) with the meaning "place of water-drawing," or more simply "pool," a connotation that fits the context of Song 5:12 perfectly.[189] This is a small amount of evidence, but we consider it sufficient grounds by which to identify this word as an IH lexeme.

1.4.23. BH has two nouns for "moon." The more common is ירח distributed throughout the Bible; the less common is לבנה, occurring only in Isa 24:23; 30:26; Song 6:10. The first of these appears in a section of Isaiah (chs. 24–27) that, notwithstanding its placement in an overall Judahite composition, contains a high concentration of dialect features in the service of

185. The homonym רסיסים "fragments" in Amos 6:11 is also an IH feature, though it is not relevant for the present discussion. Note its sole occurrence in a northern book, the continued life of the root רסס "break, crush" in MH (*HDHL*, microfiche 083, plate 17092–17093; Jastrow, *Dictionary*, 2:1484), and the Aramaic cognate רסס with the same meaning (Jastrow, *Dictionary*, 2:1484–85).

186. F. E. Greenspahn, *Hapax Legomena in Biblical Hebrew* (Chico, Calif.: Scholars Press, 1984), 120.

187. *HDHL*, microfiche 046, plate 9243; and Jastrow, *Dictionary*, 1:541.

188. Jastrow, *Dictionary*, 1:541.

189. E. Y. Kutscher, *Studies in Galilean Aramaic* (Ramat-Gan: Bar-Ilan University, 1976), 33.

producing style-switching.[190] The second, we admit, appears in a Judahite text devoid of IH traits—though we hasten to add that Isa 30:26 occurs within the context of the prophet's oracles to the foreign nations, even if this particular passage addresses "Zion" and "Jerusalem" (see v. 19). In light of the general context here, one wonders whether the author selected לבנה intentionally for the purposes of dialectal expression. When we add the attestation in Song 6:10 to this picture, we note that at least two of the three (if not all three) occurrences of this word are in northern texts or in texts with style-switching and/or addressee-switching at work.

The evidence of postbiblical Hebrew is most important. The more common BH word ירח appears four times in Ben Sira and once in QH but never in MH.[191] By contrast, the less common BH word לבנה is the only one used in MH, where it is attested fifty-five times.[192] This pattern supports the view that לבנה "moon" is the northern equivalent of southern ירח "moon."

In this case, the cognate evidence is of no use, since all the languages to the north of Israel use ירח for "moon" (thus Ugaritic, Phoenician, and Aramaic).[193] We must assume that לבנה "moon" was used in a small subscribed area within Northwest Semitic, but that small area must have been the very region in which IH (or at least one subdialect thereof) and later MH were used.

1.4.24. Similarly, BH has two nouns for "sun." The more common is שמש, of course, appearing throughout the corpus. The less common is חמה, occurring in the same three passages as לבנה "moon" (see immediately above), as well as in Ps 19:7 and Job 30:28.

Psalm 19 has not been discussed until this point, so note the following details.[194] Scholars have noted that Ps 19 divides into two parts: verses 2–7 appear to be an adaptation of a Canaanite solar hymn, while verses 8–15 focus on more traditional Israelite concerns (Torah, fear of Yahweh, etc.). Three IH features appear in the former section: (1) the root חוה "tell" in verse 3, attested otherwise only in Job (5x); (2) the lexeme מלה "word" in verse 5,

---

190. Noegel, "Dialect and Politics in Isaiah 24–27," 177–92, with reference to לבנה on 182.

191. *HDHL*, microfiche 049, plate 9896.

192. *HDHL*, microfiche 058, plates 11749–50.

193. Gordon, *Ugaritic Textbook*, 414; del Olmo Lete and Sanmartín, *Diccionario de la Lengua Ugarítica*, 2:536 = *A Dictionary of the Ugaritic Language*, 2:979–980; *DNWSI* 1:469; Krahmalkov, *Phoenician-Punic Dictionary*, 215; Sokoloff, *Dictionary of Jewish Palestinian Aramaic*, 245; and idem, *Dictionary of Jewish Babylonian Aramaic*, 542.

194. See already G. A. Rendsburg *apud* Noegel, "Dialect and Politics in Isaiah 24–27," 183 n. 45.

attested elsewhere mainly in northern texts, especially Job; and (3) the use of חמה for "sun." Such IH features are lacking in the latter half of the poem. In light of this evidence, we can refine the above statement and claim that the solar hymn section of Ps 19 stems from northern Canaan and not from the region of Judah.

Accordingly, the distribution of חמה in the Bible is four times in IH texts and only once in JH texts (namely, Isa 30:26). This pattern points to a northern provenience for this word.

The evidence of postbiblical Hebrew is again very important. In the corpus formed by Ben Sira and QH, the data are thirty-four times שׁמשׁ (12x in Ben Sira, 22x in the Dead Sea Scrolls) versus once חמה (in Ben Sira). In Tannaitic texts, the data are 207 times חמה versus 114 times שׁמשׁ.[195] Thus, while שׁמשׁ continues to be used in MH, the dominant form for "sun" is חמה.

Once more, the cognate evidence does not assist us, because Ugaritic *špš* and Phoenician and Aramaic שמש are the attested forms,[196] and nowhere does a cognate of חמה occur. Thus, as was the case with לבנה "moon" above, we must assume that חמה "sun" was used in a relatively restricted area but that this area was the region in which IH (or at least one subdialect thereof) and later MH were used.

1.4.25–26. The two lexical elements in אבי הנחל "fruit of the palm tree" in Song 6:11 both should be considered IH features. אב "fruit" occurs again only in Job 8:12 in a Transjordanian setting. It appears in MH, albeit in only a single passage, t. ʿUq. 2:11 (2x).[197] The Aramaic cognate, attested in two forms, אבא and אנבא, is slightly better attested.[198] It is used, for example, in Targum Onqelos to Gen 4:3 and in Targum Jonathan to 2 Kgs 19:29 to render Hebrew פרי "fruit" and in Targum to Job 31:12 to render Hebrew תבואה "produce."

---

195. *HDHL*, microfiche 043, plates 8630–34 (for חמה), and microfiche 088, plates 18025–28 (for שׁמשׁ).

196. Gordon, *Ugaritic Textbook*, 493–94; del Olmo Lete and Sanmartín, *Diccionario de la Lengua Ugarítica*, 2:449–450 = *A Dictionary of the Ugaritic Language*, 2:836–838; *DNWSI* 2:1168–69; Krahmalkov, *Phoenician-Punic Dictionary*, 472; Sokoloff, *Dictionary of Jewish Palestinian Aramaic*, 558–59; and idem, *Dictionary of Jewish Babylonian Aramaic*, 1136.

197. *HDHL*, microfiche 013, plate 2332. See also Jastrow, *Dictionary*, 1:2, where it is defined as "young shoots of a tree."

198. For Biblical Aramaic, see BDB, 1078; KB, 1047; and *HALOT*, 1817. For Jewish Babylonian Aramaic, see Sokoloff, *Dictionary of Babylonian Aramaic*, 73; and Jastrow, *Dictionary*, 1:44, 80.

In Ugaritic *ib* appears once in the meaning of "fruit," in *CAT* 1.19:I:31 (earlier publications of the tablet indicated a break immediately after *ib*, so this reading was not certain, but see now the new collation in *CAT* indicating not only a word divider after *ib* but also the next word *krmm* "groves, vineyards").[199] In addition, *ib* "fruit" is most likely the second element in the fused name of the Ugaritic lunar goddess *nkl wib* "Nikkal-and-Ib" (*CAT* 1.24:1), split into *ib* and *nkl* in parallel lines of poetry (*CAT* 1.24:17–18).[200]

The meaning "palm tree" for נחל (and not "wadi") was demonstrated by Shelomo Morag, with Num 24:6, in the mouth of Balaam in a Transjordanian setting, as the only other attestation of this word.[201] We have no Northwest Semitic evidence to assist us in this particular case (the best known cognate is Arabic *nḫl* "palm tree," which is not relevant to our enterprise, since Arabic falls outside the Northwest Semitic arena). Nevertheless, from the distribution of נחל "palm tree" in the Bible, limited to the oracles of Balaam and the book of Song of Songs, we may conclude that the word was an IH lexical trait. To be sure, it was not a word that a Judahite would have selected in his or her speech or writing.

The evidence points to a northern origin for the two words individually, in which case we also may suggest that the two-word construct phrase אבי הנחל "fruit of the palm tree" is a northern idiom.[202]

1.4.27. The noun פעם "foot" in Song 7:2 is an IH feature, in contrast to JH רגל "foot."[203] This is the only word for "foot" in both Phoenician and Ugaritic (the latter actually *pʿn*).[204] Indeed, H. L. Ginsberg already sug-

199. See M. Dietrich, O. Loretz, and J. Sanmartín, *The Cuneiform Alphabetic Texts from Ugarit, Ras Ibn Hani and Other Places* (Münster: Ugarit-Verlag, 1995), 56. Notwithstanding the difficulty in reading this line, previous scholars affirmed the existence of *ib* "fruit" in *CAT* 1.19:I:31. See W. L. Michel, *Job in the Light of Northwest Semitic* (BibOr 42; Rome: Biblical Institute Press, 1987), 1:190 and the bibliography cited in n. 74.

200. Gordon, *Ugaritic Textbook*, 348. See also del Olmo Lete and Sanmartín, *Diccionario de la Lengua Ugarítica*, 1:2 = *A Dictionary of the Ugaritic Language*, 1:4–5, where the entry *ib* may be found, though the authors are less sure that the common word for "fruit" underlies the divine name Ib.

201. S. Morag, "Rovede Qadmut: ʿIyyunim Leshoniyim be-Mishle Bilʿam," *Tarbiz* 50 (1980–81): 14–16.

202. We have elected to use "produce of the palm tree" in our translation (see 202), in order to distinguish between אב "produce" and פרי "fruit."

203. See the earlier treatment in Rendsburg, *Psalms*, 66–67.

204. For Phoenician, see *DNWSI* 2:928–929; and Krahmalkov, *Phoenician-Punic Dictionary*, 404. For Ugaritic, see Gordon, *Ugaritic Textbook*, 469; and del Olmo Lete

gested that פעם is a lexical feature distinguishing the Phoenic group from the Hebraic group.[205]

The distribution of פעם "foot" in the Bible is as follows: 2 Kgs 19:24 = Isa 37:25; Isa 26:6; Pss 58:11; 140:5. The first of these occurs in Isaiah's speech placed in the mouth of Sennacherib, so we would explain this passage as an example of style-switching. Mesopotamian invaders are consistently depicted in the Bible as coming from the north (Isa 14:31; Jer 1:13; 6:22; Ezek 1:4; 26:7; etc.). Moreover, the context portrays Sennacherib boasting about his conquest of Lebanon and its mountains and cedars (2 Kgs 19:23 = Isa 37:24). Within such a setting, we can explain Isaiah's use of a non-Judahite lexeme when portraying the speech of the Assyrian king. Isaiah 26:6 returns us to Isa 24–27, with its large number of dialect features employed to produce style-switching (see above).[206] The last two occurrences listed above are in northern psalms.

The three criteria are met in this case: we have Ugaritic and Phoenician evidence, the presence of פעם "foot" in other northern texts, and a contrast with JH רגל. The picture that emerges indicates that פעם "foot" is an IH trait.

1.4.28. The noun אמן "artisan, craftsman" occurs in Song 7:2 and only here in the Bible in this form. The byform אמון occurs in Prov 8:30, another northern composition.[207] The latter form may occur in Jer 52:15, which would dovetail nicely with Jeremiah's use of this nominal form in two other

---

and Sanmartín, *Diccionario de la Lengua Ugarítica*, 2:342 = *A Dictionary of the Ugaritic Language*, 2:660.

205. Ginsberg, "The Northwest Semitic Languages," 105.

206. Noegel, "Dialect and Politics in Isaiah 24–27," 177–92, with reference to פעם "foot" on 184.

207. On this word, see A. Hurvitz, "Le-Diyyuqo shel ha-Munaḥ אמון be-Sefer Mishle 8:30," in *Ha-Miqra᾽ bi-Re᾽i Mefarshav: Sefer Zikkaron le-Sarah Qamin* (*The Bible in the Light of Its Interpreters: Sarah Kamin Memorial Volume*) (ed. S. Japhet; Jerusalem: Magnes, 1994), 647–50. Actually, as Hurvitz pointed out, the word אמון means both "artisan" and "foster-parent" in Prov 8:30, where it serves as the pivot word in a Janus parallelism. For another recent treatment of this word, see V. A. Hurowitz, "Nursling, Advisor, Architect? אמון and the Role of Wisdom in Proverbs 8, 22–31," *Bib* 80 (1999): 391–400. Hurowitz argues that "nursling" is the most appropriate meaning of אמון in Prov 8:30, though he adds that "it is slightly possible that other interpretations are legitimate secondary meanings, on the level of intentional wordplays and double entendres" (400). For the sake of bibliographic completeness, we also add the following references: M. V. Fox, "᾽*amon* Again," *JBL* 115 (1996): 699–702 (with a thorough review of the literature, both ancient and modern, and with a conclusion that the word means "being raised"); and B. J. Schwartz and A. Focht, "אמון—Constantly," *ZAH* 14 (2001): 43–49 (with a conclusion as per the title of the article).

places: בחון "assayer" in 6:27 and עשׁוק "oppressor" in 22:3[208] (though many scholars assume a byform of המון "multitude" in Jer 52:15 based on the context, the craftsmen having been exiled at an earlier time, according to 2 Kgs 24:14). The JH equivalent is the standard BH word חרשׁ "artisan, craftsman."

Though אמן "artisan, craftsman" is rare in BH, it is the regular MH word with this designation (typically with plene spelling אומן), occurring eighty-six times (versus 19 for חרשׁ).[209] In the roughly contemporary Qumran texts composed in JH, the opposite may be seen: חרשׁ occurs six times; אומן appears not at all (though it does occur once in Ben Sira 7:22). Furthermore, the word אומן "artisan, craftsman" is productive in MH, as indicated by the common abstract noun אומנות "skill, handiwork, etc." (attested 68x).[210]

The cognate אומן "artisan, craftsman" is also the standard word in Aramaic (Official, Nabatean, Palmyrean, Samaritan, Jewish, Syriac, etc.).[211] For example, the Peshitta uses אומן to translate Hebrew חרשׁ in Gen 4:22 and Exod 28:11, as well as elsewhere;[212] see also Samaritan Targum to Deut 27:15 (variant) to render Hebrew חרשׁ, Targum Neofiti to Gen 4:22 to render Hebrew חרשׁ, and Targum Onqelos and Targum Neofiti to Exod 26:1 to render Hebrew חשׁב.

Finally, it is important to note the single attestation of this word in Phoenician, specifically in *KAI* 178:2–3, an inscription in Latin letters from Leptis Magna, Tripolitana. This short inscription reads FELIOTH IADEM SY ROGATE YMMANNAI "the handiwork [lit. the work of the hands] of Rogate the artisan," with the last word equivalent to Hebrew אומן. "Die Form des Wortes ist noch nicht sicher erklärt, doch dürfte es mit grosser Wahrscheinlichkeit zu hebr … zu stellen sein."[213]

---

208. On these forms and their connection to MH, see M. Bar-Asher, "ʾAḥduta ha-Hisṭorit shel ha-Lashon ha-ʿIvrit u-Meḥqar Leshon Ḥakhamim," *Meḥqarim ba-Lashon* 1 (1985): 93–94.

209. *HDHL*, microfiche 021, plates 4039–41 (see also Jastrow, *Dictionary*, 1:27). For חרשׁ, see *HDHL*, microfiche 044, plate 8852.

210. *HDHL*, microfiche 021, plates 4041–42; see also Jastrow, *Dictionary*, 1:27.

211. *DNWSI* 1:71–72; Jastrow, *Dictionary*, 1:27; Sokoloff, *Dictionary of Jewish Palestinian Aramaic*, 40; idem, *Dictionary of Jewish Babylonian Aramaic*, 90; Payne Smith, *Compendious Syriac Dictionary*, 6; and Tal, *Dictionary of Samaritan Aramaic*, 1:42.

212. As noted by Driver, *Introduction*, 448; BDB, 53; and Brockelmann, *Lexicon Syriacum*, 25.

213. Donner and Röllig, *Kanaanäische und aramäische Inschriften*, 2:165. See also Krahmalkov, *Phoenician-Punic Dictionary*, 60.

Once more, several lines of evidence (BH distribution, MH commonness, Aramaic and Phoenician cognates) converge to affirm the northernness of אמן "artisan, craftsman."[214]

1.4.29. The form מזג "mixed wine" is a *hapax legomenon* in Song 7:3. The root occurs much more frequently in MH: forty-six times as a verb (including the verbal noun מזיגה "mixing" 6x) and eight times as the noun מזג.[215] In addition, it has a cognate in Aramaic מזג.[216]

Closely related to מזג is the alternative form מסך "mixed wine" (the latter with two voiceless consonants, corresponding to the two voiced consonants of the former), appearing in Ps 75:9, an Asaph poem. This form has an exact cognate in Ugaritic *msk*.[217] Another variant form ממסך "mixed wine" appears in Isa 65:11 and Prov 23:30. The latter passage occurs in one of the most Phoenicianizing of all chapters in Proverbs. The former passage was written during the exilic or early postexilic period, but we need not rely on the mixing of northern and southern exiles in Mesopotamia. Far more important is the manner in which the prophet utilizes ממסך in this verse, attributing "mixed wine" to the pagan cults of Gad "Fortune" and Meni "Destiny."[218]

A verb מסך "mix" also exists in BH, and its distribution also points to a northern home. Two of the attestations, Prov 9:2 and 5, are in a section of Proverbs replete with IH features. Isaiah 19:14 occurs in the oracle against Egypt, so a Phoenicianism is not unexpected here (addressee-switching with Egypt often involves Phoenician forms, probably the result of the traditional relationship between Egypt and Phoenicia [especially Byblos]). Psalm 102:10 occurs in an exilic poem, so the theory of the reunion of the exiles can be advanced to explain this usage. In addition, we may note the alliteration in this verse, with five of its seven words possessing a *kaf* and a sixth one includ-

214. Discussion of Hebrew אמן "artisan, craftsman" almost always elicits discussion of Akkadian *ummiānu* with the same range of meanings. Since our chapter is limited to presenting the evidence from within Northwest Semitic, however, we do not extend the discussion to other branches within the Semitic family. Needless to say, many of the lexemes treated herein have cognates in other branches of Semitic, though once again, our approach here is to focus on the Northwest Semitic evidence.

215. *HDHL*, microfiche 061, plates 12337–39.

216. Jastrow, *Dictionary*, 2:753; and Beyer, *Die aramäischen Texte vom Toten Meer*, 621.

217. Gordon, *Ugaritic Textbook*, 435; del Olmo Lete and Sanmartín, *Diccionario de la Lengua Ugarítica*, 2:295 = *A Dictionary of the Ugaritic Language*, 2:582.

218. J. P. Brown, "The Mediterranean Vocabulary of the Vine," *VT* 19 (1969): 153; and idem, *Israel and Hellas* (3 vols.; BZAW 231, 276, 299; Berlin: de Gruyter, 1995–2001), 1:143.

ing a *qof*—thus the poet may have chosen the root מסך here specifically for the aural effect. Only Isa 5:22 occurs in a decidedly Judahite context, though note that מסך is used as the B-word in parallelism with שׁתה "drink."[219]

Of further import is the presence of Greek *misge*, Latin *misce*, both meaning "mix." While typically one assumes a direction of Semitic to Greek when the two languages (language families) share vocables, according to Saul Levin this "is the most readily provable case of an IE verb borrowed by Semitic."[220] Accordingly, we propose the following scenario: the word entered Northwest Semitic from a Mediterranean source—most likely this will explain the variants מזג (with voiced consonants) and מסך (with voiceless consonants)—and it became part of the vocabulary of the more internationally oriented regions such as Ugarit, the kingdom of Israel, and Aram (and almost undoubtedly the Phoenician city-states as well, though it is not attested in Phoenician-Punic).[221] But because the kingdom of Judah was more geographically isolated and insulated, the word did not become part of the everyday vocabulary of JH. A poet such as Isaiah could utilize the word as the B-word in poetic parallelism (Isa 5:22), and he could evoke it for the style-switching effect (Isa 19:14), but by and large it remained an IH vocable.

All of this evidence converges to demonstrate that מזג "mixed wine" in Song 7:3, along with the related root מסך (two nominal forms and the verb), belonged to the IH vocabulary, without finding a secure home in the JH lexicon.

1.4.30. The verbal root סוג II "fence, border" occurs only in Song 7:3. All other attestations of the root are סוג I "turn back."[222] The root is used in Aramaic commonly and produces the common Aramaic noun סיג "fence."[223] This form translates a series of Hebrew nouns in the Targumim, for example, Targum Pseudo-Jonathan to Num 22:25 rendering קיר, Targum Neofiti to Num 22:24 rendering גדר, and Targum Neofiti to Deut 22:8 rendering מעקה.

---

219. Again, see Driver, "Hebrew Poetic Diction."

220. S. Levin, *Semitic and Indo-European I: The Principal Etymologies* (Current Issues in Linguistic Theory 129; Amsterdam: Benjamins, 1995), 237–39 (the quotation is from 237).

221. For general discussion on "mixed drinks," see Brown, *Israel and Hellas*, 142–43.

222. BDB, 690–91; KB, 650–51; and *HALOT*, 744–45. The first of these dictionaries suggested the Pilpel form in Isa 17:11 as another attestation of סוג II "fence" (with *śin* instead of *samekh*), but the context calls for a meaning such as "grow" (parallel to פרח "blossom").

223. Jastrow, *Dictionary*, 2:961, 978; Sokoloff, *Dictionary of Jewish Palestinian Aramaic*, 369, 373–74; and Beyer, *Die aramäischen Texte vom Toten Meer*, 644.

The same noun appears in MH, where it is attested eighteen times.[224] As we have seen in so many parallel instances above, the data yield the conclusion that סוג II "fence, border" was an element of IH. The contrasting JH term is גדר "fence," well-distributed through the corpus.

1.4.31. Above we discussed the word רהיטנו "our runners," that is, "beams, rafters," derived from the root for "run" (see §1.4.3). A related word רהטים appears in Song 7:6, where long, flowing hair must be intended; perhaps the meaning "tresses" is most appropriate. It is quite easy to see how the root "run" can develop into this meaning as well. This lexeme appears nowhere else in the Bible and should be considered another feature of IH.

The word רהטים "tresses" is a homonym of the word רהטים "water troughs" attested in Gen 30:38, 41; Exod 2:16. Scholars divide on the source of this root. If it derives from the same root as the Aramaic for "run," with a semantic development from "runners" to "water troughs," which is perfectly possible, then it needs to be related to our discussion. Most striking is the fact that the two Genesis passages occur in the Jacob and Laban story, which is a repository for Aramaic usages, as part of a stylistic device to portray the setting in the land of Aram.[225] Of course, this would not work for the land of Midian portrayed in Exod 2:16, though the setting there is also in a foreign land.[226] The other approach is to assume that רהטים "water troughs" derives from a separate root altogether, the best candidate being *rhṭ* occurring in Arabic with the meaning "collect," thus a place where water is collected. Regardless of how this issue is decided, we can aver that רהטים "tresses" derives from רהט "run," a root that bridged Aramaic and IH, and thus should be included in our list of northern features in the Song of Songs.

1.5. Summary

The twenty grammatical and thirty-one lexical items delineated above demonstrate that the Song of Songs is a northern composition.[227] In identifying

---

224. *HDHL*, microfiche 067, plate 13615.

225. See Greenfield, "Aramaic Studies and the Bible," 129–30; Rendsburg, "Linguistic Variation," 182–83; and idem, "Aramaic-Like Features in the Pentateuch."

226. We also note the intertextuality between Exod 2:16 and Gen 30:38, 41, with the author of the former wishing to direct the reader's attention to the last time an eligible Israelite bachelor encountered females and flocks in a foreign land.

227. Note that two other lexemes were included in Rendsburg, "Israelian Hebrew in the Song of Songs," but that we have elected not to include these items in the present study. The two items are (1) the verb רפד "spread out, support, refresh" in Song 2:5, along with the noun רפידה "support" (for a piece of furniture) in Song 3:10; and

a particular feature as northern, one often must make judgments. In a few instances we have noted that the supporting evidence is not great, but we have judged the feature to be an IH trait nonetheless. In other cases, for particular reasons, we have elected to exclude an item from the list. For example, the word סנסנים "date-palm panicles" in Song 7:9 is another unique word in the poem, indeed it is a *hapax legomenon*, and it is attested in Aramaic too, but its uniqueness and this cognate usage are not enough to mark it as an IH feature. It must have been a rare and technical term throughout Hebrew (and Aramaic), regardless of dialect, perhaps an Akkadianism (see *sinsinnu/sissinnu* in Akkadian) known to only the educated elite (compare Latin words and expressions in English).

Of course, one might argue that words such as פג "unripe fig" and סמדר (referring to an early stage in the ripening of grapes) are additional examples of technical words, but we have opted to include them in the list of IH lexical features. We have done so because in these cases the evidence is clear. The former, for example, occurs frequently in MH, it appears in Aramaic as an independent lexeme, and a denominative verb פגג "be unripe" exists in Aramaic. Similarly, the latter occurs in MH, in Aramaic, and in a Hazor epigraph, in addition to which we are able to postulate a JH equivalent גמל in Isa 18:5.

So we repeat the above statement: in identifying IH elements one must make judgments, but the aggregate weight of the evidence—fifty-one features in our counting, in a brief poem of only eight chapters—should serve as a counter to the potential critique of any particular item on the list that another scholar might have excluded for lack of supporting evidence.

As noted in the introduction to this chapter, those who have posited a late date for the composition of the Song of Songs have used much of the same evidence adduced above. That is to say, many of the features, admittedly a majority of them, are supported by evidence from Aramaic and MH. These two factors also could point to identifying a feature as an element of LBH;

(2) the noun חלאים "jewels" in Song 7:2. In both cases, identification of these lexical items as IH features must rely solely on the distribution of these words in the Bible. The verbal root רפד occurs elsewhere in Job 17:13; 41:22; while variant (singular) forms of חלאים occur elsewhere in Hos 2:15; Prov 25:12. There is, however, no cognate data for these words, nor is there any continuation of these items in later Hebrew texts. One can note בית הרפד in Lachish Letter 4:5, which might suggest that the root רפד was productive in JH, but since this phrase is a toponym (see also ארפד and רפידים), one should be cautious in building an argument therefrom. For comment on the phrase, see S. Ahituv, *Ha-Ketav ve-ha-Miktav* (Jerusalem: Bialik, 2005), 68. On חלאים, see Yoo, *Israelian Hebrew in the Book of Hosea*, 51–52; and Chen, *Israelian Hebrew in the Book of Proverbs*, 189.

in fact, this approach underlies the methodology employed by Hurvitz and others. But a control is present that allows us to see these Aramaic and MH parallels not as signs of lateness but as indications of northernness. We refer to those features that are paralleled by Phoenician (and Ugaritic) but not by Aramaic. Here we have in mind such characteristics as the relative pronoun -שׁ (§1.2.1), the "double plural" construction (§1.3.6), the root נעם "good, sweet, pleasant" (§1.4.1), the verb גלשׁ (§1.4.14), the noun נפת "honey" (§1.4.16), and the noun פעם "foot" (§1.4.27). Most of these, it should be noted, are very basic elements (a notable exception is גלשׁ, of course). Once this picture begins to emerge, one can add to this arsenal of information those items that occur in MH but not in Aramaic. Here, most importantly, one can count לבנה "moon" (§1.4.23) and חמה "sun" (§1.4.24), as well as several additional items, such as the usage represented by ששים המה מלכות "there are sixty queens" (§1.3.5), the verb ארה "pluck" (§1.4.18), and so forth.

In other words, if the evidence were backed in the great majority of cases only by Aramaic and/or MH, then certainly one would have to conclude that the linguistic indicators point to a late date of composition. Such has been the emphasis by most commentators on the Song of Songs.[228] But to look at this material only, and not at the other items summarized in the above paragraph, is to look at only half of the picture.[229] The totality of the evidence, as realized long ago by Driver, is that the Song of Songs was composed in the northern part of ancient Israel.[230]

This does not mean that the book could not have been written in postexilic times. It is possible that a text could be both northern and late: an exemplar of such may be found in the Bible in Neh 9.[231] Of course, Neh 9 is written in prose, and it is therefore easier to judge the lateness of the chapter. Because the Song of Songs is a work of poetry, the discriminants between SBH and LBH are more difficult to detect. In fact, among the dozens of LBH traits that have been identified by Hurvitz and others in their study of the diachronic development of BH, only one occurs within the poetry of the Song

228. See, for example, Fox, *Song of Songs*, 189.

229. In like fashion, one might wish to argue that many of so-called Aramaisms in the Song of Songs are due to the poetic language of the book. Here we have in mind, once more, Driver's "Hebrew Poetic Diction." But the same arguments that hold for seeing these items as indications of northernness and not lateness (that is, the presence of Phoenician parallels, etc.) could be adduced to counter this approach as well.

230. In theory, the author could be a Judahite who couched the poem in Israelian Hebrew, though this would be difficult to substantiate.

231. See G. A. Rendsburg, "The Northern Origin of Nehemiah 9," *Bib* 72 (1991): 348–66.

of Songs. That example, of course, is the crucial lexical item פרדס "pleasure-garden" in Song 4:13, considered by most scholars to be a Persian loanword and about which we have said nothing until now. We shall return to this very important point in the conclusion, when we will summarize and synthesize the results of the individual chapters that comprise this monograph. For now, we are content to conclude, as the evidence adduced herein demonstrates, that the Song of Songs is a northern composition.

Excursus to Chapter 1
Additional IH Features in 4QCant^b

As the contents of chapter 1 make clear, our focus has been on the Masoretic Text (MT) of the Song of Songs: we have not engaged in any text-critical procedures that might affect our analysis. We relegate such matters to this excursus.

In an important article, Ian Young called attention to a series of "Aramaisms" in 4QCant^b (covering Song 2:9–3:2; 3:5, 9–11; 4:1b–3, 8–11a, 14–5:1) representing different readings from those preserved in MT.[1] In what follows, we comment on these linguistic traits (the rubrics below [appearing in italics] are Young's) from the vantage point of our inquiry into IH. When a particular feature appears also in MT, and thus has been commented upon in our chapter 1 above, we include a cross-reference to that section. Following Young's lead, we will withhold discussion of the significance of these elements for our research until the data have been presented.

1. מן *"from" unassimilated.* As noted above (§1.3.5), the phrase מן לבנון "from Lebanon" in Song 4:15 is an example of the preposition מן before an anarthrous noun. This feature is known from Aramaic especially, and it also occurs in IH and in the Deir ʿAlla dialect.

4QCant^b attests to seven (!) additional cases of this phenomenon, as follows:

---

1. I. Young, "Notes on the Language of 4QCant^b," *JJS* 52 (2001): 122–31. The quotation marks around the word "Aramaisms" are Young's usage (see 122), a usage with which we agree. Young built on the foundation laid by E. Tov in his preliminary study of the Song of Songs Dead Sea Scrolls fragments: "Three Manuscripts (Abbreviated Texts?) of Canticles from Qumran Cave 4," *JJS* 46 (1995): 88–111 (see 99–100 for a convenient listing of the features in 4QCant^b that Tov attributes to Aramaic influence). While Young's article was in press, the official publication of the Qumran Song of Songs material appeared: E. Tov, "Canticles," in *Qumran Cave 4.XI: Psalms to Chronicles* (ed. E. Ulrich et al.; DJD XVI; Oxford: Clarendon, 2000), 195–220 (again, see 209 for the relevant chart concerning Aramaic influence), though Young informs us that he had opportunity to see this material in advance, courtesy of Tov.

4:8 מן לבנון corresponding to MT מלבנון (first occurrence thereof)
4:8 מן לבנון corresponding to MT מלבנון (second occurrence thereof)
4:8 מן ראשי corresponding to MT מראש (first occurrence thereof)
4:8 מן הררי corresponding to MT מהררי
4:10 מן יין corresponding to MT מיין
4:10 מן כל corresponding to MT מכל
4:16 מן ג[דיו] corresponding to MT מגדיו פרי (reanalyzed as if it were "from his fortune" apparently)

By contrast, there are only two cases of the SBH usage, corresponding to MT of the Song of Songs: ממענות in 4:8 and מעיניך in 4:9 (the latter damaged, but the reading seems likely).

As Young pointed out, "4QCant^b and the MT thus present mirror images of each other in this feature."[2] According to his count, the MT of the Song of Songs includes twenty-five cases of assimilated *nun* versus only the one instance of unassimilated *nun* (at 4:15, see above), while in 4QCant^b we encounter only two cases of the former versus seven cases of the latter.

2. הררי *"mountains" (plural construct)*. Above (§1.2.7) we treated the presence of הררי in Song 4:8, along with a second instance of the reduplicated plural of a geminate noun צללים in Song 2:17; 4:6. This feature is an element of Aramaic, and it is well-attested in IH texts.

4QCant^b agrees with MT in reading הררי at Song 4:8, but it also reads הררי at Song 2:17, in contrast to MT, which has the standard form הרי in this verse. The third example of "mountains" in the plural construct in the Song of Songs occurs in 8:14, where MT has הרי, but this verse is wanting in 4QCant^b, and thus no comparison can be made.

The data reveal that while MT is inconsistent on this point—using the standard form twice and the dialectal form once (at 4:8)—4QCant^b is consistent in using only the latter in the two instances (2:17; 4:8).

3. *Aramaic phonology* טללים *"shadows."* As noted above (§1.1.1), the shift of /ẓ/ > /ṭ/ occurs in the Song of Songs in several places: in the root נטר "guard" in Song 1:6 (2x); 8:11, 12 and in the vocables רהיטים "beams" in 1:17Q and רהטים "tresses" in 7:6. This represents a phonological feature of Aramaic, which to our mind was present in IH as well.

This trait does not occur consistently in MT of the Song of Songs, however, as the noun form צללים "shadows" (Song 2:17; 4:6) demonstrates. In

2. Young, "Notes on the Language of 4QCant^b," 123.

4QCant^{b} 2:17, however, the reading is טללים (4:6 is not preserved in the Qumran text), providing another instance of this usage.

4. *Masculine plural noun with* nun. This trait is not attested in MT of the Song of Songs, though it does occur elsewhere in the Bible sporadically, as well as in Aramaic, Moabite, the Deir ʿAlla dialect, and MH.[3]

One instance of this features occurs in 4QCant^{b}: בשׂמין "spices" in 4:10. In the Bible, one finds the masculine plural suffix ין- most frequently in the book of Job (15x), where it functions as part of the style-switching technique employed by the author.[4] In addition, note the following examples in northern contexts: Judg 5:10 מדין "saddle-cloths" (?), in the Song of Deborah; 1 Kgs 11:33 צדנין "Sidonians," in the mouth of the prophet Ahijah from Shiloh in the territory of Ephraim; and Prov 31:3 מלכין "kings," in a section of the Bible stemming from Massa. Also of relevance may be 2 Kgs 11:13 רצין "outrunners," where the perspective of Athaliah (an Israelian princess on the throne of Judah) may be represented (if so, this would be a very subtle rhetorical device). Finally, note Ezek 26:18 אין "islands," in connection with Tyre; although standard Phoenician used ים-, at least one dialect, that of Arslan Tash, used ין-, so style-switching may be at work here.

5. את *in 4QCant^{b} 4:8*. The issue under discussion here is more complicated than the items presented above. The form אתי occurs twice in Song 4:8, and in both cases the Masoretic reading is אִתִּי "with me." The LXX, the Vulgate, and the Peshitta understood these consonants as derived from the verb אתה (אתי) "come."[5]

By contrast, 4QCant^{b} reads את, without the additional *yod*. E. Tov explained the Qumran orthography as a hypercorrection of an original אתי. That is to say, at one point the text before the Qumran scribe read אתי (as per MT), which the scribe understood as the second-person feminine independent pronoun (as in Aramaic; for the biblical evidence, see below), and thus he altered the form to the SBH pronoun את.

Young accepted this analysis as possible, but he also proposed an alternative: "It is not impossible that the verse was meant to be understood originally as: 'You from Lebanon, O bride, you from Lebanon, you come.' Such a translation would not seriously affect the poetic structure of the bicolon."[6]

---

3. For previous discussion, see Rendsburg, "The Dialect of the Deir ʿAlla Inscription," 311.

4. Kaufman, "The Classification of the North West Semitic Dialects of the Biblical Period and Some Implications Thereof," 54–55.

5. See P. B. Dirksen, "Canticles," in *General Introduction and Megilloth*, *BHQ* 18:61*.

6. Young, "Notes on the Language of 4QCant^{b}," 126.

Young continued, "Of importance for our current discussion is the observation that in this case 4QCant^b seems to be going against the trend of the other linguistic variants we have discussed. That is, 4QCant^b presents us with a standard Hebrew form, whereas the consonants of the MT could be interpreted as an Aramaic form."[7]

6. *Geographical Name* אומנון. The MT of Song 4:8 presents the form אמנה for this toponym. 4QCant^b, by contrast, provides an alternate form אומנון. On the one hand, the use of an alternate geographical term should not be deemed as noteworthy a linguistic trait as the other elements included in this study. On the other hand, a clue provided by Young suggests that this form is indeed significant. I refer to the Akkadian transcription of Amanah as ^kur*am-ma-na-nu*, with a second *nun*,[8] exactly as in the form attested in 4QCant^b.[9] Most likely, this form reached the Akkadian scribes via Aramaic speakers (exiles, vassals, etc.), and we therefore suggest that it represents an Aramaic form, in contrast to the Hebrew/Canaanite form אמנה. If it appears in a Hebrew text such as 4QCant^b, then it similarly must have reached the Israelites via Aramaic mediation. As the Bible makes clear, the Israelites in more regular contact with Arameans were obviously the people of northern Israel. Accordingly, if our analysis here is correct, we may aver that אומנון in 4QCant^b represents another isogloss linking IH and Aramaic.[10]

---

7. Ibid.

8. For attestations, see S. Parpola, *Neo-Assyrian Toponyms* (Neukirchen-Vluyn: Kevelaer, Butzon & Bercker, 1970), 16. See the discussion in N. Na'aman, "Two Notes on the Monolith Inscription of Shalmaneser III from Kurkh," *Tel-Aviv* 3 (1976): 98 n. 20; and M. Cogan, "…From the Peak of Amanah," *IEJ* 34 (1984): 255–59. The orthography with double *m*, resulting in a normalization of Ammananu, is problematic, but parallels occur elsewhere; see G. A. Rendsburg, "Baasha of Ammon," *JANES* 20 (1991): 58–59.

9. Young, "Notes on the Language of 4QCant^b," 127. Young did not, however, comment on the point that we are making here. Instead, he focused more on the two *waws* in אומנון, understanding the first as representing an *o*-vowel, influenced by the following labial consonant *mem*, and understanding the second as also representing an *o*-vowel, patterned after the first *o* (vowel harmony).

10. For another instance of the use of a toponym in IH research, see Rendsburg, *Psalms*, 35, re Sirion in Ps 29:6. As we learn from Deut 3:9, this was the Phoenician designation for Hermon, which most likely penetrated into IH but not into JH.

The Significance of These Variations

Young began his interpretation of the above data as follows: "In regard to the linguistic variations we have discussed, either 4QCant[b] represents a revision of the original linguistic form preserved in the MT, or the MT represents a revision of the original linguistic form preserved in 4QCant[b]."[11] He then continued, "It could be argued that since the linguistic variations of 4QCant[b] discussed above mostly relate to the addition of Aramaic, or at least later Hebrew, forms in comparison to the MT, that this proves that 4QCant[b] represents a text form later than the MT."[12] This argument is bolstered by the paradigm example of 1QIsa[a] vis-à-vis MT Isaiah, with the former representing an updated text, as demonstrated by E. Y. Kutscher in his classic study.[13]

The picture, however, is not that simple, for as Young commented, "especially in the case of the Song of Songs, the opposite process is equally plausible: a scribe corrects the language of the text toward a more classical form of Biblical Hebrew."[14] That is to say, unlike the case of Isaiah, whose MT version has only a limited number of nonstandard forms, especially when compared to the complete Isaiah scroll from Qumran, given the plethora of nonstandard forms in the Song of Songs, even in MT, a good case can be made for the Dead Sea Scrolls manuscript representing the more original form.

We are in essential agreement with Young's position, though in line with our approach in this study, we would change the framework of the discussion from "updating," "Aramaisms," and the like to the question of regional dialectal variation. For the present authors, the linguistic profile of 4QCant[b] provides additional evidence for the claim that the Song of Songs is a northern composition. We make no attempt to determine which of the two text-types that have reached us is the more original, for in our estimation it matters not. IH features abound in the Masoretic version, while the Qumran text supplies still more features. Some of these (nos. 1–3 above) are attested already in MT, with 4QCant[b] simply providing more examples of these elements. In two cases (nos. 4 and 6 above), 4QCant[b] contributes additional examples to our line of research, one of which (no. 4) is known from other Israelian texts, with the other (no. 6) presenting something altogether new.

---

11. Young, "Notes on the Language of 4QCant[b]," 127.
12. Ibid., 128.
13. E. Y. Kutscher, *The Language and Linguistic Background of the Isaiah Scroll (1QIsa[a])* (Leiden: Brill, 1974).
14. Young, "Notes on the Language of 4QCant[b]," 129.

The one remaining case, the issue of whether to read את or אתי in Song 4:8 and of how to interpret the matter (no. 5 above), remains the most complicated of the points discussed herein. Tov's approach is probably the correct one, and indeed to some extent it bolsters the view that 4QCant^b—or rather the text on which it is based—is the more original, or shall we say (without making judgment) equally original. That is to say, if the scribe of 4QCant^b changed an original אתי to את, in an attempt to replace the dialectal form with the SBH form, then one is justified in accepting the additional dialect features in the Dead Sea Scroll text as original.

In short, as maintained in the summary section of chapter 1, the linguistic profile of MT of the Song of Songs demonstrates that the poem is an Israelian composition, while 4QCant^b provides additional valuable information in support of that conclusion.

2

Alliteration as a Compositional Factor in the Song of Songs

One of the striking features of Hebrew poetry is the frequent use of alliteration. Although this technique is duly noted and described in standard treatments of Hebrew poetry,[1] we believe that the presence of alliteration in biblical Hebrew literature has been greatly underestimated.[2] True, alliteration in ancient Hebrew poetry is not as omnipresent as alliteration in such diverse poetic traditions as Old English, Old German, Old Hungarian, and Somali, to name but several.[3] Nevertheless, as we hope to demonstrate in this essay, allit-

1. See, for example, W. G. E. Watson, *Classical Hebrew Poetry: A Guide to Its Techniques* (JSOTSup 26; Sheffield: JSOT Press, 1986), 225–28.

2. We use the term "biblical Hebrew literature" here quite consciously. The present essay focuses on poetry in general and the Song of Songs in particular, but we believe that alliteration is also very prominent in biblical prose literature. Rendsburg has spoken publicly on this issue on a number of occasions (e.g., Leiden University in January 2000, Johns Hopkins University in February 2000, Jewish Theological Seminary in October 2002); he invites the interested reader to request the handout distributed at these lectures. Noegel has addressed alliteration within the larger context of wordplay in general in several lectures, most prominently "Pungent Puns with a Punitive Punch: Contextualizing Ancient Near Eastern Word Play," delivered at the American Oriental Society plenary session on wordplay, San Diego, March 2004. Both scholars are preparing monographs on these respective subjects; for a foretaste of one of these, see S. B. Noegel, "'Word Play' in Qohelet," *JHS* 7 (2007). Toward the end of our research, the following book came to our attention, with an approach very similar to the one that we are employing herein: T. P. McCreesh, *Biblical Sound and Sense: Poetic Sound Patterns in Proverbs 10–29* (JSOTSup 128; Sheffield: Sheffield Academic Press, 1991).

3. The presence of alliteration in both Old English and Old German verse, which clearly is part of a common Anglo-Saxon poetic tradition, is well-known to readers of such classic pieces as *Beowulf*. For the broader picture in Indo-European in general, see V. N. Toporov, "Die Urspringe der indoeuropäischen Poetik," *Poetica* 13 (1981):

eration serves as a significant compositional factor in biblical poetry. While our focus in this chapter remains the relatively short book of the Song of Songs, we hasten to add that our conclusions can be extended to other biblical books as well—and not only poetic texts, but prose compositions as well.[4]

From the outset it is important to define the term "alliteration."[5] The dictionary definition typically refers to a string of words whose *initial* sound is the same,[6] and indeed this is what one finds in the poetic traditions referred to above (the Anglo-Saxon in particular, as exemplified by Old English and Old German). In dealing with poetry composed in Biblical Hebrew, we opt to expand the term to refer to the collocation of the same or similar consonants in two or more words in close proximity to each other.[7] (We limit the term "assonance" to refer to the effect created by like-sounding vowels.[8] Given the

---

189–251; and C. Watkins, *How to Kill a Dragon: Aspects of Indo-European Poetics* (Oxford: Oxford University Press, 1995), 179–93. The Old Hungarian (Magyar) material was brought to the attention of biblical scholars by I. Gábor, *Der hebräische Urrhythmus* (Giessen: Töpelmann, 1929); see also the review essay by O. S. Rankin, "Alliteration in Hebrew Poetry," *JTS* 31 (1930): 285–91. For the Somali tradition, see B. W. Andrzejewski and I. M. Lewis, *Somali Poetry: An Introduction* (Oxford: Clarendon, 1964), 42–46.

4. For a survey of examples in prose, see G. A. Rendsburg, "Alliteration in the Exodus Narrative," in *Birkat Shalom: Studies in the Bible, Ancient Near Eastern Literature, and Postbiblical Judaism Presented to Shalom M. Paul on the Occasion of His Seventieth Birthday* (ed. C. Cohen et al.; Winona Lake, Ind.: Eisenbrauns, 2008), 83–100.

5. For a different approach, see McCreesh, *Biblical Sound and Sense*, 27–28.

6. P. G. Adams, "Alliteration," in *The New Princeton Encyclopedia of Poetry and Poetics* (ed. A. Preminger and T. V. F. Brogan; Princeton: Princeton University Press, 1993), 36–38.

7. For a discussion on the effect of consonant sounds in biblical poetry, very much in line with what we describe here, though with attention to parallelism, see A. Berlin, *The Dynamics of Biblical Parallelism* (Bloomington: Indiana University Press, 1985), 103–26. In addition, one gains a native appreciation of what constitutes sound play by looking at Mic 1:10–16, in which many of the place names are echoed in like-sounding words. Note, for example, the alliterations between שפיר and עריה בשת in v. 11, between צאנן and לא יצאה (and probably also האצל) in v. 11, and between לכיש and רכש in v. 13. For discussion, see F. I. Andersen and D. N. Freedman, *Micah* (AB 24E; New York: Doubleday, 2000), 212–14; and M. Garsiel, *Biblical Names: A Literary Study of Midrashic Derivations* (Ramat-Gan: Bar-Ilan University Press, 1991), 109.

8. In line with the remarks of P. G. Adams, "Assonance," in Preminger and Brogan, *The New Princeton Encyclopedia*, 102–4.

linguistic structure of Semitic words, based on roots comprised generally of three consonants, assonance will be far less common, though not altogether absent,[9] in contrast to the much more common use of alliteration.) While one can marvel at the ability of the poets in the aforementioned literary traditions (Old English, Somali, etc.) to commence each word of a poetic line with the same sound, the biblical poets had a greater flexibility in their employment of the device. First of all, to state the obvious, alliteration is not a requirement for each line or stich. Furthermore, in line with what we stated above, when an ancient Israelite poet elected to employ the device, he or she was not restricted to words beginning with the same consonant. Instead, the poets enjoyed greater freedom in creating the acoustic effect, using two or three identical consonants, two or three similar consonants, or any combination thereof; with the evocative sounds presented either in the same order or in scrambled fashion; with the sound effect placed in either the same verse or in adjacent verses; with the option of highlighting just two crucial words in the poetry or of creating a veritable cluster of alliterative words; and so on.

The above description of alliteration in biblical Hebrew poetry is best demonstrated by a typical example. Of the literally hundreds of passages that may be selected, we present the following stich from Ps 55:9:

מרוח סעה מסער From the sweeping wind, from the storm.

The expression "same or similar sounds" in the above paragraph may be illustrated by these three words. Same or identical sounds are, of course, easy to identify. The *mem* and *reš* that occur in מרוח and מסער represent, of course, the same sounds. The *samekh* and *ʿayin* that occur in סעה and מסער are again the same sounds. Since the letters *ʿayin* and *ḥet* each represent two consonants in Hebrew (/ʿ/ and /ġ/ for the former; /ḥ/ and /ḫ/ for the latter),[10] whenever these letters appear in an alliterative string we will note exactly

9. A good example is the use of רֹעֶה "shepherding" in Gen 37:2 and תֹּעֶה "wandering" in Gen 37:15, both predicated of Joseph. On the function of these two words in the narrative, see J. P. Fokkelman, "Genesis 37 and 38 at the Interface of Structural Analysis and Hermeneutics," in *Literary Structures and Rhetorical Strategies in the Hebrew Bible* (ed. L. J. de Regt, J. de Waard, and J. P. Fokkelman; Assen: Van Gorcum, 1996), 157.

10. For details, see J. Blau, *On Polyphony in Biblical Hebrew* (Proceedings of the Israel Academy of Sciences and Humanities 6/2; Jerusalem: Israel Academy of Sciences and Humanities, 1982). For a basic treatment, see G. A. Rendsburg, "Ancient Hebrew Phonology," in *Phonologies of Asia and Africa* (ed. A. S. Kaye; 2 vols.; Winona Lake, Ind.: Eisenbrauns, 1997), 1:65–83, especially 71–72.

which consonants are involved. In the above example, as far as we are able to determine (through the use of Arabic and Ugaritic cognates), the ʿ*ayin* in both סעה and סער represents /ʿ/. Accordingly, the consonants are the same. On the other hand, even if one of the two consonants were /ǵ/, the alliteration would still work because the pharyngeal fricative /ʿ/ and the velar fricative /ǵ/ are similar. The employment of like-sounding consonants in an alliterative chain permits us to see still one more link in the three words cited from Ps 55:9. The *ḥet* in רוח and the ʿ*ayin* in the two words סעה and סער also alliterate because both /ḥ/ and /ʿ/ are pharyngeal fricatives. Furthermore, when we realize that סעה in Ps 55:9 is a *hapax legomenon*, we understand the conscious lexical choice made by the ancient Israelite poet. Finally, we may note that the two *samekhs* in this stich create an onomatopoetic effect, as the reader hears the sound of the wind whistling in these words.[11]

The fact that writers could employ not only identical sounds but also similar sounds to produce alliteration means that, as the above example illustrates, some basic knowledge of phonology is required in order to follow the data that we will present in support of each example.[12] Sometimes voiced and voiceless counterparts will alliterate with one another (e.g., /b/ *bet* and /p/ *pe*). Sometimes the nasals (/m/ *mem* and /n/ *nun*) and the liquids (the rolled /r/ *reš* and the lateral /l/ *lamed*) will alliterate with each other, including across these groups (thus, e.g., *nun* and *lamed*). Finally, certain consonants can be employed in a variety of ways. For example, the lateral /ś/ *śin* is most like the lateral /l/ *lamed*, but it also can be used in alliterative chains with the sibilants /s/ *samekh*, /z/ *zayin*, and /š/ *šin*.

As we work through the instances of alliteration in the Song of Songs, we will see a wide variety of examples. The common thread throughout all these examples is the poet's employment of identical or similar sounds to create an auditory experience befitting of a literature with an oral/aural quality, that is,

---

11. For a parallel to this effect in an Egyptian text, note Pyramid Text, Utterance 253, §275: *šw sšw sw šw sšw sw* "O Shu, lift him up! O Shu, lift him up!" with its invocation of Shu, the god of air. See C. T. Hodge, "Ritual and Writing: An Inquiry into the Origin of the Egyptian Script," in *Linguistics and Anthropology: In Honor of C. F. Voegelin* (ed. M. D. Kinkade, K. L. Hale, and O. Werner; Lisse: Peter de Ridder Press, 1975), 15; reprinted in: S. B. Noegel and A. S. Kaye, eds., *Afroasiatic Linguistics, Semitics, and Egyptology: Selected Writings of Carleton T. Hodge* (Bethesda, Md.: CDL, 2004), 215. The standard English translation is R. O. Faulkner, *The Ancient Egyptian Pyramid Texts* (Oxford: Clarendon, 1969), 63.

12. For a general introduction to the subject, see Rendsburg, "Ancient Hebrew Phonology," 65–83.

one that was intended to be read aloud by a single reader before a listening audience.[13]

Naturally, we are not the first to recognize the importance of alliteration in the understanding of Hebrew poetry. As noted above, one finds mention of the device in standard works on Hebrew poetry. We desist from a complete survey of the secondary literature, but we do wish to mention two important studies on alliteration, one by Baruch Margalit and the other by Lawrence Boadt. Margalit's work deals not with Hebrew poetry per se but rather with the closely related Ugaritic poetic corpus.[14] We do not accept all of Margalit's examples nor his interpretation of much of the Ugaritic literary corpus,[15] but he is absolutely correct in noting the role of alliteration as a compositional factor in the creation of Ugaritic literature. Margalit enjoys using the term "alliterative exigency," or in Latin *alliterationis causa*, to describe this technique, and below we shall use the same terms at times. Simply stated, Margalit's view is that we can explain "the selection of uncommon words and forms, as well as choices made between synonymous alternatives, as creative responses by the poet and his tradition to the demands of alliterative poetry."[16] Of the many passages put forward by Margalit to demonstrate the point, we select the following bicolon (*CAT* 1.14: I:10–11 [Kret Epic]) as illustrative of alliteration in Ugaritic poetry.[17]

krt ḥtkn rš	Kret, his progeny is ruined,
krt grdš mknt	Kret, destroyed is (his) place.

13. One need only recall that the common verb קרא means both "read" and "call," that is, to pronounce something aloud. See also the important passage in Isa 29:18, where the deaf is mentioned as one excluded from the reading process. And of course unto the present day the oral reading of the Torah remains the centerpiece of the synagogue service.

14. B. Margalit, "Alliteration in Ugaritic Poetry: Its Role in Composition and Analysis," *UF* 11 (1979): 537–57; and idem, "Alliteration in Ugaritic Poetry: Its Role in Composition and Analysis (Part II)," *JNSL* 8 (1980): 57–80.

15. We do not wish to enter into a full critique of Margalit's work here. Suffice to say that many of his reconstructions of Ugaritic texts remain problematic.

16. Margalit, "Alliteration in Ugaritic Poetry (Part II)," 58.

17. For a more recent effort to collect examples of alliteration in Ugaritic poetry, see W. G. E. Watson, "Puns Ugaritic Newly Surveyed," in *Puns and Pundits: Word in the Hebrew Bible and Ancient Near Eastern Literature* (ed. S. B. Noegel; Bethesda, Md.: CDL, 2000), 117–34.

The *-n* ending in the form *ḥtkn* "his offspring" is attested elsewhere in Ugaritic, but it is unusual nonetheless since we expect the typical *-h* ending for "his." But as Margalit pointed out, the poet used this pronominal suffix to capture the alliteration with *mknt* in the next line. This is borne out by a comparison with *CAT* 1.14: I: 21–23:

yʿn ḥtkh krt	Kret sees his progeny,
yʿn ḥtkh rš	He sees his progeny ruined,
mid grdš tbth	His dwelling greatly destroyed.

In these lines we have the normal form *ḥtkh* instead of *ḥtkn* and the word *tbth* "his dwelling" instead of *mknt*.

Margalit further noted that the rare word *grdš* "destroyed" was chosen in the B-line of the above couplet due to the presence of *rš* "ruined" in the A-line (especially in light of the fact that other words were available to the Ugaritic bard, e.g., *ʾbd*, *kly*, *mḫṣ*, *ṣmt*,[18] not to mention others known from Hebrew though not attested in Ugaritic, viz., *hrs*, *ḫrb*, *šmd*, etc.[19]). In addition, Margalit recognized the alliteration created between *-rd-* in *grdš* and *-rt* in *krt*. One can go further on this last point, however, and note that all of *krt* alliterates with the first three letters in *grdš*, since /k/ is the voiceless equivalent of /g/ just as /t/ is the voiceless equivalent of /d/. Moreover, one should note how the word order is changed from "Kret-subject-verb" in the A-line to "Kret-verb-subject" in the B-line (in both lines "Kret" is in *casus pendens*). This procedure allows *grdš* to follow *krt* immediately. True, it thereby distances *mknt* from *ḥtkn*, but it is possible that the poet desired to juxtapose *krt* and *grdš*, because here the sounds are not exactly equivalent but rather, as just noted, the voiced and voiceless correspondents of each other (Margalit calls this "partial alliteration" as opposed to complete "alliteration").

Only a very small amount of research by a few scholars has applied Margalit's approach to biblical poetry. The single scholar most directly indebted to

18. Most scholars emend *itdb* in the preceding line 8 to *itbd*, from the root *ʾbd* "perish," especially in light of line 24, where *yitbd* occurs; see, e.g., E. L. Greenstein, "Kirta," in Parker, *Ugaritic Narrative Poetry*, 42 n. 2. We are not totally convinced, however, since the presence of the root אדב "be sick, languish" in 1 Sam 2:33 must be countenanced. Greenspahn, *Hapax Legomena in Biblical Hebrew*, 102 n. 11, noted the possible correlation of the Ugaritic and the Hebrew, even though he doubted the existence of the root *ʾdb* in the former.

19. The root *ḫrb* is attested in Ugaritic, but only with the meaning "dry," not as "devastate"; see Olmo Lete and Sanmartín, *Diccionario de la Lengua Ugarítica*, 1:197 = *A Dictionary of the Ugaritic Language*, 1:403.

Margalit's work is Boadt, whose article on Second Isaiah is filled with valuable insights.[20] Of the numerous passages discussed by Boadt, we present Isa 41:24 as a prime example.

הן אתם מאין	Behold, you are less than nothing,
ופעלכם מאפע	Your work is less than nil;
תועבה יבחר בכם	One who chooses you is an abomination.

In this verse one encounters the *hapax legomenon* אפע, which based on the context and the parallelism can be determined to mean "nothingness" or "nil" (note that it is parallel to אין). Why was this exceedingly rare word chosen? Boadt's response, which not only took note of the stylistic feature but also countered the oft-repeated proposal to emend the word to אפס, was as follows: "the lack of *samekhs* in this line, and the strong *ʿayin* alliteration potential may have suggested to the poet a rarer form of the word that meant the same as *ʾepes*."[21]

Boadt is undoubtedly correct, though one can go even further and note that it is not the *ʿayin* alone that creates alliteration in this verse but the combination of letters *pe* and *ʿayin*. Note that the previous word is פעלכם "your work," with both *pe* and *ʿayin* in the same order. Furthermore, the following stich reads תועבה יבחר בכם "one who chooses you is an abomination" and contains additional alliterative chains. The word תועבה includes *ʿayin* and *bet*, the latter being the voiced equivalent of *pe*; the word יבחר has both *bet* and *ḥet*, the former again the voiced equivalent of *pe* and the latter the voiceless equivalent of *ʿayin*; even the final word בכם includes the *bet* and a velar *kaf* pronounced deep in the mouth approaching the throat. All of this goes to show that the *hapax legomenon* אפע in Isa 41:24 was chosen for good reason, to produce the alliteration so characteristic of ancient Hebrew poetry.[22]

---

20. L. Boadt, "Intentional Alliteration in Second Isaiah," *CBQ* 45 (1983): 353–63.

21. Ibid., 360.

22. We note that Boadt has retained his interest in alliteration in biblical literature, as evidenced by his comment on Jer 50:33–38 incorporated by Alice Ogden Bellis into her recent article on these verses. Boadt espied the following cluster of words with *reš* and *bet*: ריב יריב את ריבם "he will indeed champion their cause" (v. 34), חרב "sword" (5x in vv. 35–37), גבוריה "her heroes" (v. 36), רכבו "its chariotry" (v. 37), ערב "motley crowd" (v. 37), and חרב "drought" (v. 38). See L. Boadt *apud* A. O. Bellis, "The New Exodus in Jeremiah 50:33–38," in *Imagery and Imagination in Biblical Literature: Essays in Honor of Aloysius Fitzgerald, F.S.C.* (ed. L. Boadt and M. S. Smith; CBQMS 32; Washington: Catholic Biblical Association of America, 2001), 168 and n. 15.

The three passages discussed above, one from Ugaritic and two from the Bible, exemplify the use of alliteration by the ancient bards. We could multiply such examples at will, but at this point it is time to turn our attention to the many instances of alliteration in the Song of Songs. We shall present each example with brief comments on the specific sounds evoked. We also shall note, in line with Margalit's observation, and as the above passages illustrate, how frequently rare words, including *hapax legomena*,[23] have been selected by the poet for the specific purpose of producing or enhancing the alliteration.

Finally, before proceeding to the Song of Songs, let us note that we use the term alliteration in a relatively specific and restricted sense; that is to say, we generally do not include in our study examples such as the following: (1) sound play on personal names (e.g., Exod 2:10; Mic 1:14; etc.); (2) set phrases such as תהו ובהו (Gen 1:2; Jer 4:23), הוד והדר (Ps 21:6, etc.), and so on; (3) instances where the same root appears in different forms (e.g., Isa 7:9; Jer 48:15; etc.); and (4) examples of cognate accusative (legion in the Bible).[24] We will include a few examples of these kinds of sound play in our study, especially when they support the main alliteration under investigation, but by and large we have in mind the kind of alliteration described and illustrated above, with altogether different vocables evoking the sounds of each other.

Song 1:1

שיר השירים אשר לשלמה

The song of songs, which is Solomon's.

We begin with the superscription of the book. Most scholars believe that this line is a later addition to the poem and/or that the presence of the relative pronoun אשר, as opposed to the shorter form -שׁ, which occurs otherwise in the book, is an indication of a prosaic hand typical of a superscription. These viewpoints notwithstanding, we note that the use of אשר here enhances the alliteration of this line. Note that the *šin* and *reš* in this form echo the same

23. On the finding that *hapax legomena* are indeed rare words in the lexicon of the language, and not common words which by chance are attested only once, see Greenspahn, *Hapax Legomena in Biblical Hebrew*, 31–46.

24. Some of these usages fall within the category of paronomasia, at least as far as the term is commonly used by scholars. The standard treatment remains I. M. Casanowicz, "Paronomasia in the Old Testament" (Ph.D. diss.; Johns Hopkins University, 1892).

two consonants that occur in the two previous words (the singular and plural forms of שׁיר "song") and that they further alliterate with the *lamed-šin-lamed* sequence that begins the next word, לשׁלמה "to Solomon."[25] This latter connection is due to the fact that /l/ and /r/ are both dental liquids and/or they share the phonetic quality of resonance.[26]

Song 1:2

ישׁקני מנשׁיקות פיהו
May he kiss me with the kisses of his mouth.

Our first example from the poetry of the Song of Songs is an instance of paronomasia, for the two alliterative words derive from the same root, namely, נשׁק "kiss." Nevertheless, our poet has gone beyond the bounds of simple paronomasia, because he has completed the alliteration in a very artistic manner. We refer to the fact that whereas the noun form (in the plural) נשׁיקות "kisses" contains all three root letters, the prefix-conjugation (PC) verb form derived from a פ"נ root does not, thus (without the suffix) ישׁק "may he kiss." To compensate for the assimilation of the *nun* in the form ישׁק, the poet has included the pronominal suffix -ני "me," thereby restoring the "lost" *nun*. While it is true that this suffix is common in the poem (1:4 [2x], 6 [3x], etc.)—and the alternative form אותי never occurs (see, however, the fourfold use of אתכם in the refrain in 2:7; 3:5; 5:8; 8:4)—nevertheless we believe that the poet has set the stage for alliteration by introducing the "lost" *nun* in the suffix of ישׁקני to evoke the same three consonantal sounds as the following word נשׁיקות.

The use of the pronominal suffix -ני serving as the direct object is even more noteworthy when one realizes that normally the verb נשׁק "kiss" governs the preposition -ל. This is clearly the case in prose texts (19x with -ל, 3x with pronominal suffix or with את [Gen 33:4; 1 Sam 10:1; 20:41]); though admittedly in poetic texts the evidence is less clear (Prov 7:13; Job 31:27 use -ל; Ps 2:12 is too difficult a passage to use as evidence, since it is not clear that

25. In translating the preposition -ל here as "to," we are merely following standard convention. In truth, however, the preposition is ambiguous, on which see further in ch. 4, pp. 140–41, in the discussion of *hijāʾ* poetry.

26. We cannot be more specific on this issue, because of the uncertainty over the exact realization of the consonant *reš* in ancient Hebrew, and indeed in ancient Semitic and Afroasiatic in general. For discussion, see E. Lipiński, *Semitic Languages: Outline of a Comparative Grammar* (Leuven: Peeters, 1997), 132–133 (and see also 135 for examples of the interchange between /l/ and /r/ within Semitic).

the meaning "kiss" is present here; Prov 24:26 may not indicate an object at all, since שפתים "lips" may be the mechanism by which one kisses, not the object of the kiss; thus only in Hos 13:2; Song 1:2; 8:1 does the verb נשק "kiss" unambiguously govern the direct object).

Song 1:3–4

לריח שמניך טובים
שמן תורק שמך ...
משכני אחריך נרוצה ...
נגילה ונשׂמחה בך ...
מישרים אהבוך

To the scent of your good oils,
"*Turaq* oil" is your name. …
Draw me, after you let us run. …
Let us be glad and let us rejoice in you. …
(More than) smooth-wine, they love you.

The word תורק remains one of the most obscure in the Bible. It would be splendid if we were able to explain its presence in our verse—regardless of what it might mean—*alliterationis causa*, but there is no similar string of consonants in close proximity. We have, therefore, nothing new to offer on this word.

We may, however, point to a series of alliterative words in these two verses, centered around the letters *šin* and *mem*. We begin with the obvious, the manner in which the repeated word שמן "oil" (in plural form with pronominal suffix in the first stich, in singular form in the second stich) echoes in the word שם "name" at the end of the second stich. It is as if the poet is expressing the notion that the male lover's very name is so akin to goodly oil, that the former is contained within the latter.

Next we may admire the manner in which the poet begins verse 4 with the word משכני "draw me," a perfect anagram of the word שמניך "your oils" in verse 3. Later in verse 4 appears the word נשׂמחה "let us rejoice," with the *mem* and *nun* echoing the same sounds in the former two words, and with *śin* capturing the sibilant quality of *šin*, albeit with a different point of articulation.

Finally, the poet's penchant for alliteration led to the selection of the word מישרים "smooth-wine."[27] A better-known synonym for יין "wine" is the

27. On the evidence for this word meaning "smooth wine," including the cognate

lexeme תירוש "new wine," probably from the same nominal stem, but this form would not continue the alliterative string in these verses to the same extent as the much rarer word מישרים. By using this noun, the *mem-šin* link of the aforenoted words is maintained—plus the *reš* and second *mem* in מישרים serve to create an additional nexus with the *mem* and the *nun* in the words שמן, משכני, and נשמחה.

Song 1:6

אל תראוני שאני שחרחרת
ששזפתני השמש
בני אמי נחרו בי

Do not look at me, that I am dark,
That the sun has glared at me;
The sons of my mother were angry at me.

Two common Hebrew roots occur in these two stichs, though each occurs in an uncommon form. The form שחרחרת is the only *qәtaltōl* of the root שחר "dark, black" in the Bible,[28] while נחרו is one of only three instances of the Niphʿal form of the root חרה "be angry." The reduplication in the former word allows for the reader to hear the sequence *ḥet-reš* three times in this verse. In addition, the consonant *šin* occurs six times in the first two stichs,[29] with one of the six provided by the rare verb שזף "glare" (it is attested only twice elsewhere, in Job 20:9; 28:7).

Song 1:7

איכה תרביץ בצהרים
Where do you cause-(them)-to-lie-down at noon?

The two alliterative words in this stich are standard items in the Hebrew lexis. The Hiphʿil of רבץ "lie down > cause to lie down" occurs in other shep-

---

forms Ugaritic *mrṯ* and Aramaic מירת, "wine (of some sort)," with metathesis (as frequently happens when a *reš* or *lamed* is present in the word), see Fox, *Song of Songs*, 98–99.

28. For discussion, see A. Brenner, *Colour Terms in the Old Testament* (JSOTSup 21; Sheffield: JSOT Press, 1982), 121.

29. See already Fox, *Song of Songs*, 102.

herding contexts (Isa 13:20; Jer 33:12; Ezek 34:15; Ps 23:2), and, of course, צהרים "noon" is a standard term. Furthermore, the latter word almost always occurs with the preposition ב-, thus, "at noon" (12x, versus only three cases of צהרים not preceded by ב-). But notwithstanding these standard usages, we still can appreciate the manner in which the poet has juxtaposed the two words תרביץ and בצהרים, with all three root letters of the former appearing in the latter in anagrammatic fashion.

Song 1:9

לססתי ברכבי פרעה
דמיתיך רעיתי

To a mare in pharaoh's chariotry,
I liken you, my darling.

The word רעיתי "my darling" is a key word in the Song of Songs, appearing nine times. In this verse, the first time that we encounter the word, we note the alliteration with פרעה "pharaoh." Both words include *reš* and *ʿayin*, in that order. Moreover, this verse follows upon 1:7–8 in which occurs the root רעה "shepherd" three times, specifically תרעה "you shepherd" (as a PC verb) in 1:7, רעי "shepherd" (as an imperative) in 1:8, and רעים "shepherds" (plural noun) in 1:8. Naturally, the root occurs elsewhere in the book, but always in the metaphorical usage in a well-known phrase, such as הרעה בשׁ ושנים "he who shepherds among the lilies" in 2:16; 6:3 (similarly in 4:5; 6:2). Only here in 1:7–8 do we have reference to actual shepherds and actual shepherding of flocks. The net result is a continual string of *reš-ʿayin* words in three successive verses.

Much has been written about the suffix on ססתי "mare" (certainly not "my mare"); most likely it is a rare instance of the archaic absolute form with the retention of the genitive ending *-i*, here lengthened to *-î*. Noteworthy for our present enterprise is its use in this verse alongside two other instances of the syllable *-tî-*, within דמיתיך "I liken you" and at the end of רעיתי "my darling."

Song 1:10–11

נאוו לחייך בתרים
צווארך בחרוזים:
תורי זהב נעשׂה לך

Your cheeks are lovely with circlets,
Your neck with strings-of-beads.
Circlets of gold we will make for you.

As the male lover continues his first speech, he describes the jewelry adorning his beloved. The related expressions בתרים "with circlets" and תורי זהב "circlets of gold" provide alliteration, obvious through the use of the shared word תור "circlet" (the first time in absolute plural, the second time in construct plural), but enhanced by the inclusion of the preposition -ב "with" in the first instance, the sound of which repeats in the word זהב "gold."

Furthermore, the sounds of the last word in verse 10, בחרוזים "with strings-of-beads," are echoed in the first phrase of verse 11, תורי זהב "circlets of gold." Once more, note how the presence of the preposition -ב "with" in בחרוזים "with strings-of-beads" provides the additional consonantal link found in תורי זהב "circlets of gold." Thus, the *bet*, *reš*, and *zayin* in בחרוזים all appear in תורי זהב, while the pharyngeal *ḥet* of חרוזים "strings-of-beads" is approximated by the laryngeal *he* in זהב "gold."

Song 1:12

נרדי נתן ריחו
My nard gives-forth its scent.

The *nun* and *reš* that commence the word נרד "nard" occur at the head of the next two words in this stich: נתן "give" with initial *nun*, and ריח "scent" with initial *reš*. In addition the voiced dental *dalet* in נרד finds its voiceless counterpart in the *taw* in the following word נתן, thereby adding secondary support to the alliterative chain. In line with the process described in the introduction to this chapter, note that a rare word—נרד occurs only three times in the Bible, all in the Song of Songs—is used to produce alliteration (see also Song 4:13–14 below). In short, the three words in this stich work together to create the alliteration.

Song 1:15–16

עיניך יונים
הנך יפה דודי אף נעים
אף ערשׂנו רעננה

Your eyes are doves.
Behold you are beautiful, my beloved,

indeed pleasant,
Indeed our couch is verdant.

Three words that occur only once in the Song of Songs are collocated in verse 16 for acoustic effect. They are נעים "pleasant," ערשׂנו "our couch," and רעננה "verdant." Note that the first word has *nun* and *ʿayin*; the second word has *ʿayin*, *reš*, and *nun*; and the third word has *reš*, *ʿayin*, *nun*, and *nun* again. Again we note how the addition of a pronominal suffix serves to enhance the alliteration, in this case, the suffix נו- "our" attached to ערשׂ "couch," thus allowing all three words to include both *nun* and *ʿayin*. In the first two words, the letter *ʿayin* represents the phoneme /ʿ/ (as opposed to /ǵ/), as the Ugaritic cognates *nʿm* and *ʿrš* demonstrate; unfortunately there is no etymon for Hebrew רענן in all of Semitic, so no judgment is possible for this word.

Moreover, the sounds of these words are anticipated in the last stich of verse 15, with the *ʿayin* and *nun* in עיניך "your eyes." In addition, the *nun* and *kaf* in this word reverberate in the same last two consonants of הנך "behold you."

Song 1:17 (reading with qeri)

קרות בתינו ארזים
רהיטנו ברותים

The rafters of our house are cedars,
Our runners are cypresses.

The following words share a series of consonants: קרות has *reš* and *taw*, בתינו has *bet* and *taw*, רהיטנו has *reš* and *ṭet* (the latter the emphatic dental, which corresponds closely to the voiceless dental *taw* appearing in the other words), and ברותים has *bet*, *reš*, and *taw* representing the sum of the sounds in the three preceding words. It is noteworthy that ברותים "cypresses" is a dialectal variant of the standard form ברושים (2 Sam 6:5, etc.). The PS consonant /ṯ/ (which must be assumed for this word, based on the two variant forms [there are no cognates in Ugaritic, Arabic, etc.]) shifted to *š* in standard Hebrew but to *t* in the northern dialect represented in the Song of Songs (see ch. 1, §1.1.3). This dialectal form allows for the alliteration to work much more efficiently. The same is true for the rare word רהיטנו "our runners," which most likely was employed *alliterationis causa*.

In addition, we may note how two key words in verses 16 and 17 function together to create another alliterative link. The forms ערשׂנו "our couch" and ארזים "cedars" share four same or similar sounds, in matching order. Pharyngeal *ʿayin* and laryngeal *ʾaleph* appear at the start of each word, next follows *reš* in each form, then come the sibilant sounds *śin* and *zayin* respectively, and finally the nasals *nun* and *mem* occur.

Song 2:1–3

אני חבצלת השרון ...
כתפוח בעצי היער ...
בצלו חמדתי וישבתי

I am a daffodil of the Sharon …
As an apricot-tree among the trees of the forest …
In his shade I delight and I sit.

The above three stichs begin the first three lines of poetry spoken by the female lover in chapter 2. The interposing verse 2:2 is spoken by the male lover. She begins her words by comparing herself to the חבצלת flower, to be identified with the asphodel, whence the more common English designation daffodil.[30] This term is exceedingly rare in the Bible, appearing only here and in Isa 35:1. The four main consonants of this floral term are echoed in the first four consonants in the third stich reproduced above: בצלו ח-. Less striking, but also at hand, is the alliteration in the first two words of the second stich presented above: כתפוח בעצי. Four of the letters of חבצלת, namely, *ḥet*, *bet*, *ṣade*, and *taw*, appear in scrambled fashion in these two words. As noted above, these phrases are interrupted by the voice of the male lover in 2:2, but as the listener focuses on the voice of the female lover, as if it were a continuous flow, he or she admires the acoustic effect produced by the poet.

30. The identification is based on the phonetic resemblance, Hebrew *ḥăbaṣṣelet* (cf. also Akkadian *ḫabaṣillatu* [*CAD* 8 (Ḫ), s.v.], with a slightly different meaning "reed shoot," though note that both the asphodel and the reed are characterized by their height) = Greek *asphodelos*, Latin *asphodelus*/*asphodilus*, English *asphodel*. Through a series of mutations, not all reconstructable, the latter term resulted in the more common form *daffodil* (see the *OED* for details). Note the correspondence of consonants between the Hebrew and Greek forms: Hebrew *ḥ* not represented in the Greek (is the Akkadian form borrowed from West Semitic?), Hebrew *b* = Greek *ph*, Hebrew *ṣ* = Greek *s*, Hebrew *l* = Greek *l*, Hebrew *t* = Greek *d*. The metathesis is likely due to the presence of /l/ in these forms. Bibliography: G. Dalman, "Die Blume *ḥabaṣṣelet* der Bibel," in *Vom Alten Testament: Karl Marti zum siebzigsten Geburtstage gewidmet* (ed. K. Budde; BZAW 41; Giessen: Töpelmann, 1925), 62–68; and O. Keel, *Das Hohelied* (ZBK, AT 18; Zürich: Theologischer Verlag Zürich, 1986), 79.

Song 2:4, 8

ודגלו עלי אהבה ...
מדלג על ההרים

And his glance toward me is love ...
Bounding over the mountains.

These two stichs are relatively distant from each other, with verses 5–7 separating them. Yet given the abundance of alliteration in the Song of Songs, we are justified in recognizing even relatively long-distance examples such as the present one. This is especially the case when we note that the two key words are either unique or rare: (1) this is the only instance of דגל "glance" in the Bible (in all other instances דגל = "standard, banner");[31] and (2) the verb דלג "leap, bound" is limited to but five poetic passages in the corpus. Enhancing the nexus is the presence of the preposition על in both passages.[32]

We also note here—and this point will be relevant to all other examples of alliteration produced by words at a larger-than-usual distance from one another (see, e.g., the root מלא in Song 5:12,14)—that the individual performer of this poem, who presumably held the text in his or her hand, would gain a visual imprinting of these words. That is to say, his or her eye could still see ודגלו in verse 4 when encountering מדלג in verse 8 (unless, of course, there was a column break at this particular point).

Song 2:9

הנה זה עומד אחר כתלנו
משגיח מן החלנות
מציץ מן החרכים

Behold, he stands behind our wall,
Gazing through the windows,
Peering through the lattices.

31. For discussion, see the references in *DCH* 2:625.

32. Was the scribe of 4QCant[b] attempting to introduce an additional long-distance alliteration when he wrote המדלגה at Song 2:14 for MT המדרגה? Was this done consciously? subconsciously?

The *hapax legomenon* חרכים "lattices" is a classic example of a rare or unique word employed by the poet for the purposes of alliteration. The sequence of letters *ḥet-reš-kaf* occurs in the first line of this tristich, at the junction of the words אחר כתלנו "behind our wall." No doubt the poet reached deep into the recesses of the Hebrew lexis to accomplish this sound play.

SONG 2:13

התאנה חנטה פגיה
והגפנים סמדר נתנו ריח

The fig-tree perfumes its young-fruit,
And the vines in bud, they give forth fragrance.

Two alliterations are present in this couplet. First, the *hapax legomenon* פג "young-fruit" is echoed in the following word גפנים "vines," with the *pe-gimel* sequence reversed as *gimel-pe*. Moreover, the specific form of the former, פגיה "its young-fruit," with the pronominal suffix with *he*, finds a further echo in the specific form of the latter, הגפנים "the vines," with the definite article formed with *he*.

The second alliteration is produced by the string of words with both dental and nasal consonants: תאנה "fig" with *taw* and *nun*; חנטה "perfumes" with *nun* and *ṭet*; סמדר "bud" with *mem* and *dalet* (and note, of course, that this word is another rare vocable in BH, occurring only three times, all in the Song of Songs [2:13, 15; 7:13]); and נתנו "gives forth" with *nun*, *taw*, and again *nun*. A special link among these words occurs between the word חנטה "perfumes" and the phrase נתנו ריח "gives forth fragrance," meaning essentially the same thing, with the string of *ḥet-nun-ṭet* in the former echoed in the *nun-taw-nun-ḥet* in the latter. The *ḥet* in these two words represent the same phoneme, the pharyngeal fricative /ḥ/.

SONG 2:13–15

והגפנים סמדר נתנו ריח ...
בסתר המדרגה ...
וכרמנו סמדר

And the vines in bud, they give forth fragrance. ...
in the covert of the cliff ...
and our vineyards in bud.

Above we noted that the rare word סמדר "bud" is limited to three attestations in the Song of Songs. Two of the occurrences are in close proximity, in 2:13 (in the female lover's imagination of her male lover's words) and in 2:15 (uncertain speaker, though most likely in the voice of the female once more). In between these two attestations is the construct phrase בסתר המדרגה "in the covert of the cliff."

The first of these words, that is, בסתר "in the covert of," occurs commonly in the Bible, yet it is noteworthy how nicely this term alliterates with the rare סמדר. Note specifically the following: both words have *samekh* and *reš*; the former has the voiceless dental plosive *taw* corresponding to the voiced dental plosive *dalet* in the latter, while the remaining two consonants, *bet* in the former and *mem* in the latter, are labials.

Even more striking is the manner in which the second word in the phrase, namely, המדרגה "the cliff," includes the string of letters *mem-dalet-reš*, exactly as appears in the word סמדר. Once more we take note of the rareness of the alliterating lexemes. We already have commented on סמדר twice; it remains to point out that מדרגה "cliff" occurs only here and in Ezek 38:20.[33]

Song 3:1

על משכבי בלילות
בקשתי את שאהבה נפשי
בקשתיו ולא מצאתיו

On my couch at night,
I sought him whom my inner-being loves,
I sought him, but I did not find him.

A key word in this tristich, obvious through its repetition, is בקשתי(ו) "I sought (him)" in the second and third stichs. The sounds of this word are anticipated in the first stich of the verse in the word משכבי "my couch." Both words have *bet* and *šin*, while the *qof* in בקשתי(ו) is the voiceless emphatic velar plosive corresponding to the simple voiceless velar plosive *kaf* present in משכבי.

33. Verse 14 also includes paronomasia produced by the threefold use of the root ראה "see" (the relevant Hebrew lines are not reproduced here), in the words הראיני "show me," מַרְאַיִךְ "your visage," and מַרְאֵיךְ "your visage" (with a slightly different form).

Song 3:2

אקומה נא ואסובבה בעיר
בשוקים וברחבות
אבקשה את שאהבה נפשי
בקשתיו ולא מצאתיו

Let me arise, please, and let me roam the city,
In the streets and in the piazzas,
Let me seek whom my inner-being loves;
I sought him, but I did not find him.

As was the case in 3:1, so too in the following verse: the key verbal root בקש "seek" appears twice, and in anticipation thereof the poet again has evoked its sounds in a preceding word. This time the word is a rare one, namely, שוקים "streets," the plural of שוק "street," which appears elsewhere only in Prov 7:8; Qoh 12:4, 5. The combination of *šin* and *qof* from the singular would have been sufficient for the alliteration to work with בקש. However, note that the form שוקים appears in the plural, adding two labials, *waw* and *mem*, both of which resemble the labial *bet* in בקש. But even more striking is the manner in which the word occurs with the prefixed preposition -ב, thereby allowing all three root letters of בקש "seek" to occur as an anagram in בשוקים "in the streets."

Song 3:6

מי זאת עלה מן המדבר
כתימרות עשן
מקטרת מור ולבונה
מכל אבקת רוכל

Who is this coming up from the wilderness,
As columns of smoke;
Redolent with myrrh and frankincense,
With every powder of the merchant.

The key alliteration in this verse is between the rare word תימרות "columns" (it appears elsewhere only in Joel 3:3), especially with the prefixed preposition -כ, and the form מקטרת "redolent," the only Puʿal form of the verb קטר attested in the Bible. Note the match of consonants: the voiceless velar plosive *kaf* corresponds to the emphatic velar plosive *qof*; the *ṭet* and the *taw* in מקטרת echo the two *taws* in תימרות; and each word has *mem* and *reš*.

But additional words in the verse assist this central alliteration. For example, even a common word such as מדבר "wilderness" evokes the sounds of the two key words, with *mem* and *reš* once more, along with the voiced dental *dalet* tallying with the dentals *taw* and *ṭet*. Similarly, מור "myrrh" delivers *mem* and *reš* in yet another vocable. Moreover, all three words in the fourth stich lend aid. מכל "with every" includes *mem* and *kaf*, along with the liquid *lamed* resembling the liquid *reš* of the other words noted thus far. אבקת "powder" presents a *qof* and a *taw*, as in מקטרת, and adds to the mix a labial *bet* to elicit the sound of the labial *mem*. Finally, רוכל provides the voiceless velar plosive *kaf* between the two liquid consonants *reš* and *lamed*. Regarding the frequency of these words, we may note that, while the term אבק "powder" is more common in BH, occurring six times, the feminine form אבקה* appears only here, with its construct form אבקת providing the *taw* to enhance the alliteration. That is to say, while the more common masculine form would have worked to some extent, the poet's choice of the feminine form, undoubtedly a much rarer lexeme in the language, and with its construct form providing even greater acoustic effect, was clearly intentional.

Song 3:6, 8

מכל אבקת רוכל ...
איש חרבו על ירכו

With every powder of the merchant. ...
Each-man, his sword on his thigh.

The three consonants of the word רוכל "merchant," discussed in the previous section, find another echo two verses later in the expression על ירכו "on his thigh." The exact three consonants are used, in anagrammatic fashion. In addition, assonance between the two enhances the aural link. Note that the vowels of רוכל are *ô* and *ē* and that the main vowels of the dominant word ירכו in the expression על ירכו are *ē* and *ô*. The expression על ירכו "on his thigh" is not unique—it appears in Gen 32:31; Exod 32:27 as well, the latter in fact with the verbatim wording of Song 3:8—and its presence at this point in the poem is very much in order, yet we still may delight in the poet's selection of these words within close proximity to the term רוכל "merchant."

Song 3:6, 9

מקטרת מור ולבונה ...
מעצי הלבנון

Redolent with myrrh and frankincense …
From the trees of the Lebanon.

These stichs are separated by several verses, yet one nevertheless appreciates the clear likeness of sound between the words לבונה "frankincense" in verse 6 and לבנון "Lebanon" in verse 9. Because the latter word is a common toponym in the book (appearing six times), one might wish to argue that wherever לבונה "frankincense" occurs in the Song of Songs, it would appear in close proximity to לבנון "Lebanon." But such is not the case, since there are entire chapters in which לבנון "Lebanon" does not occur (Song 1–2; 6; 8). Accordingly, we find it striking that the two occurrences of לבונה "frankincense" are within "earshot" of לבנון "Lebanon." The first of these occurs here, in the scene describing the arrival of Solomon and his entourage. We will deal with the second case below, at Song 4:14–15.

Song 3:8

כלם אחזי חרב
מלמדי מלחמה

All of them, grasping the sword,
Trained in battle.

Three of the five words in the first half of verse 8 share the consonants *lamed* and *mem*: כלם "all of them," מלמדי "trained," and מלחמה "battle." In fact, the latter two words each have two *mem*s, making the collocation of these sounds even more perceptible.

Song 3:9–10

אפריון עשה לו המלך שלמה ...
רפידתו זהב ...
תוכו רצוף אהבה

The king Solomon made himself a palanquin …
Its support of gold …
Its interior arranged/burning with leather/love.

In the description of Solomon's palanquin in these two verses, the listener hears three uncommon words with the same pair of consonants, *pe* and *reš*. The word אפריון is a *hapax legomenon* in the Bible of uncertain etymology, though most likely it derives from the same source as English "palanquin" (see the conclusion). As discussed in chapter 1 (n. 227), the root רפד "support" is relatively rare in the Bible, occurring only four times, and the noun רפידה "support" (for a piece of furniture) occurs only here. Finally, רצוף, which bears two meanings in this passage, is also a unique word. With the meaning "arranged" it most likely is related to the words רצפה (occurring seven times in the Bible) and מרצפת (attested only in 2 Kgs 16:17); with the meaning "burning" it is related to the nouns רצפה (Isa 6:6) and רצפים (1 Kgs 19:6), referring to "glowing stone" or "hot coals." As an aside, we note that both meanings of רצוף are echoed in the similarly bivalent word at the end of the stich: אהבה bears not only its usual meaning "love" (appropriate for the Song of Songs in general) but also the atypical meaning "leather" (fitting for a description of Solomon's palanquin, in line with all the other materials listed).[34] In sum, we stand in admiration of the ancient poet who was able to offer the three alliterative words—אפריון, רפידתו, and רצוף (the last with double meaning[35])—united by the sounds *pe* and *reš*, in relative propinquity.

Song 3:9–11

אפריון עשׂה לו המלך שׁלמה ...
בנות ציון צאינה וראינה

The king Solomon made himself a palanquin ...
Go out and see, O daughters of Zion.

The young women addressed throughout the poem typically are called בנות ירושלם "daughters of Jerusalem" (1:5; 2:7; 3:5, 10; 5:8, 16; 8:4). Only here

34. G. R. Driver, "Hebrew Notes on 'Song of Songs' and 'Lamentations,'" in *Festschrift, Alfred Bertholet zum 80. Geburtstag gewidmet von Kollegen und Freunden* (ed. W. Baumgartner; Tübingen: Mohr Siebeck, 1950), 135; and D. Grossberg, "Canticles 3:10 in the Light of a Homeric Analogue and Biblical Poetics," *BTB* 11 (1981): 124–32.

35. As we shall see in ch. 4, p. 157, a third sense is present, namely, "arranged in an alliance" (see translation, n. 22).

in the poem are they referred to as בנות ציון "daughters of Zion." In fact, this is the only mention of ציון "Zion" in the Song of Songs. This word choice may be explained on two accounts.

First, the poet used the *hapax legomenon* אפריון "palanquin" in verse 10. Both it and the word ציון "Zion" in verse 11 end in the syllable *-yôn*. The acoustic effect continues, moreover, into the next verse, 4:1, in the form יונים "doves," which commences with the same set of sounds *yôn-*. Thus, we have a case of assonance alongside alliteration.

Second, the feminine plural imperative verb צאינה "go out" and the toponym ציון "Zion," occurring in the same stich in verse 11, share the two consonants *ṣade* and *nun*.

In addition, we may note another instance of assonance. The expected feminine plural imperative of the root יצא "go out," which is both a I-*y* verb and a III-ʾ verb—in which case one would expect the characteristics of the former to dominate—would be צֶאנָה. But the form appears as צְאֶינָה, as if it were a III-*y* verb from a metaplastic root צאה*, with its vowel pattern conforming to the following form רְאֶינָה "see," the proper feminine plural imperative of the root ראה.

Song 4:1

הנך יפה רעיתי הנך יפה
עיניך יונים
מבעד לצמתך
שׂערך כעדר העזים
שׁגלשׁו מהר הגלעד

Behold you are beautiful, my darling,
behold you are beautiful,
Your eyes are doves,
Behind your braids;
Your hair is like a flock of goats,
That flow down from Mount Gilead.

A series of sound effects is operative in this verse. We begin by noting that all three words in the stich שׂערך כעדר העזים "your hair is like a flock of goats" include the letter ʿ*ayin*. For שׂער "hair" and עז "goat," we can be sure that the same phoneme is involved, namely, /ʿ/. We cannot be sure of the phoneme present in the noun עדר "flock." The dictionaries attempt a connection with the Hebrew root עדר "be lacking," with an Arabic cognate *ġdr* (that is, the word "flock" is a semantic extension derived from those animals who lag or stray behind),[36] but the association is not convincing. Of course, even if this etymology were proven to be sound, the alliteration still would work, since /ʿ/ and /ǵ/ are pronounced similarly, the former a pharyngeal fricative, the latter a velar fricative.

Regardless of this issue, there is much more that binds the three words in this stich than this one sound. The last three consonants of שׂערך "your hair" are rehearsed in the following word כעדר "like a flock," while the two consonants of the base word עז "goat," namely, /ʿ/ + sibilant, echo the first two sounds of שׂערך "your hair." The result is a neatly constructed alliterative stich.

In addition, one may note that the word עיניך "your eyes," occurring in the first half of the verse, also includes *ʿayin* and *kaf*, as in both שׂערך "your hair" and כעדר "like a flock," and that the *nun* of עיניך serves to complete the aural effect with its likeness to *reš* in the two other words. Furthermore, רעיתי "my darling" provides the conjunction of *reš* and *ʿayin* as in both שׂער "hair" and עדר "flock."

The final stich in this verse employs the *hapax legomenon* גלשׁ "flow down" (on which see above §1.4.14). There can be little doubt that the poet selected this verb in conjunction with the toponym גלעד "Gilead" *alliteratio-nis causa*. We also note that the last three consonants of גלעד "Gilead" evoke the same sounds as עדר "flock." Both contain *ʿayin* and *dalet*, with the *lamed* of the former and the *reš* of the latter providing the third match.

Finally, linking three separate stichs in the verse is the combination of *ʿayin* and *dalet*, in that order in all three cases, in the words בעד "behind," עדר "flock," and גלעד "Gilead."

Song 4:1–2

שׁגלשׁו מהר הגלעד ...
שׁכלם מתאימות
ושׁכלה אין בהם

That flow down from Mount Gilead. …
All of whom are twinned,
And none of them bereaved.

All readers of the Song of Songs have noticed the paronomasia present in the forms שׁכלם "all of whom" and שׁכלה "bereaved" in verse 2.[37] What has

---

36. BDB, 727; and KB, 684–85.

37. See, e.g, Berlin, *The Dynamics of Biblical Parallelism*, 110.

not been noticed until now is that the three consonants *šin-kaf-lamed* in these two words resonate in the unique verb גלש "flow down" in the last stich of the previous verse. The *lamed* and *šin* in this word match perfectly, while *gimel* is the voiced counterpart of the voiceless velar plosive *kaf*. Above we noted that the poet chose גלש "flow down" *alliterationis causa*. We now can go one step further in noting that the verb גלש "flow down" was chosen for two reasons: not only because of its aural nexus with גלעד "Gilead," but also because of its reverberation in שכלם "all of whom" and שכלה "bereaved."

Song 4:2–3

שניך כעדר הקצובות ...
כחוט השני שפתתיך

Your teeth are like a flock of shorn-ones ...
Like a thread of scarlet are your lips.

This is the only occurrence of the word שני "scarlet" in the Song of Songs. Its appearance in close proximity to the word שניך "your teeth," with the same sequence of letters *šin-nun-yod*, cannot be coincidental.

Song 4:3

ומדבריך נאוה
כפלח הרמון רקתך
מבעד לצמתך

And your mouth is lovely;
Like a slice of pomegranate is your cheek,
Behind your braids.

The use of מדבר for "mouth" in this passage is unique in the Bible. Can we explain its employment here due to alliterative exigency? We note the presence of מדבר "wilderness" in 3:6, though the distance between the two homonyms is greater than one would expect for sound play to be effective.[38] Accordingly, we prefer to look at the other words in the same verse and thus note the following resonances: *mem* and *reš* in מדבר "mouth" with *mem*

38. See below, however, for the second use of מדבר "wilderness" at Song 8:5, with alliteration with the following word מתרפקת "leaning."

and *reš* in רמון "pomegranate"; and *mem*, *dalet*, and *bet* in מדבר with *mem*, *bet*, and *dalet* in מבעד "behind" (in addition to which the *reš* of the former and the *ʿayin* of the latter complete the alliteration as secondary correspondences).

Song 4:4

בנוי לתלפיות
אלף המגן תלוי עליו
כל שלטי הגבורים

Built to the heights;
A thousand shields hang upon it,
All the weapons of the heroes.

The *hapax legomenon* תלפיות "heights" has received much attention over the years. The most recent treatment is Rendsburg's elucidation of the term from the Semitic root *lpy* "be high," thus producing a nominal form meaning "heights."[39] The poet selected this rare verb from the Hebrew lexicon *alliterationis causa*. Note the following aural reverberations: *lamed* and *pe* in תלפיות "heights" with the same two consonants in אלף "thousand"; *taw*, *lamed*, and *yod* in תלפיות with the same three consonants in תלוי "hang"; and *lamed* and *taw* in תלפיות with *lamed* and *ṭet* in שלטי "weapons of."

Song 4:8–9

אתי מלבנון תבואי ...
לבבתני אחתי כלה
לבבתני באחת מעיניך

With me, from Lebanon come. …
You entice me, my sister, (my) bride,
You entice me with but one of your eyes.

The form לבבתני "you entice me" is heard twice in verse 9. These two usages represent the only attestations of the verb לבב "entice," denominative from the common noun לב "heart," in the history of ancient Hebrew.[40]

39. G. A. Rendsburg, "*Talpiyyôt* (Song 4:4)," *JNSL* 20 (1994): 13–19.

40. The Nipḥʿal in Job 11:12 means something else, probably "gain understand-

Clearly the poet's word choice was guided by the presence of לבנון "Lebanon" in the previous verse. The addition of the first common singular pronominal object suffix -ני "me" to the verb לבב "entice" enhances the alliteration. The listener to the poem hears *lamed*, *bet*, and *nun* in both forms. Moreover, one of the two consonants is repeated in each of the forms: *nun* in לבנון "Lebanon" and *bet* in לבבתני "you entice me."

Song 4:8

תשורי מראש אמנה
מראש שׂניר וחרמון

Bound from the summit of Amana,
From the summit of Senir and Hermon.

Above (§1.4.15) we noted that the verb שׁור "jump, leap, bound, pounce" occurs in only two places in the Bible, here and in Hos 13:7, thus permitting the conclusion that we are dealing with an IH lexeme. We now go one step further in recognizing why the poet selected this rare verb. The two main consonants in שׁור "bound," namely, *šin* and *reš*, are heard in the next word ראשׁ "head, summit," in reverse order. The word ראשׁ "head, summit" occurs again in the next stich, along with the toponym שׂניר "Senir." The *śin* and *reš* in the latter form serve to augment the alliteration with שׁור "bound."

Song 4:8

תשורי מראש אמנה
מראש שׂניר וחרמון
ממענות אריות
מהררי הנמרים

Bound from the summit of Amana,
From the summit of Senir and Hermon,
From the dens of lions,
From the mountains of leopards.

---

ing." The Piʿel in 2 Sam 13:6, 8 is denominative from לבבה cake," thus, "bake a cake." The attestations in rabbinic literature carry still other connotations, such as "encourage, strengthen"; see Jastrow, *Dictionary*, 2:687.

Eight of the ten words in this half-verse include a *reš*. To count in a different fashion, there are nine instances of *reš* in this half-verse (since the reduplicatory plural form הררי [see §1.2.8] includes this phoneme twice). The alliteration is self-evident, in addition to which we may note that the constant use of /r/ evokes the sound produced by large felines; compare, by way of parallel, English *roar* (and its Germanic cognates), "probably of imitative origin" (thus *OED*).

Song 4:8–9

ממענות אריות ...
לבבתיני באחד מעיניך
באחד ענק מצורניך

From the dens of the lions ...
You entice me with but one of your eyes,
With but one strand from your necklace.

The noun ענק "strand" is a rare noun in Hebrew (the two other attestations are Judg 8:26; Prov 1:9; note its absence from the list of about a dozen jewelry items in the famous passage of Isa 3:18–21). It is evoked here by our poet to alliterate with the common noun (plus pronominal suffix) עיניך "your eyes." Assuming that ענק is related to Arabic *ʿunq* "neck,"[41] we may conclude that the *ʿayin* in the two alliterative words represents the same phoneme, namely, /ʿ/, the pharyngeal fricative. The two *nun*s match exactly, of course, and the final consonants are both velars, the voiced /k/ and the emphatic /q/, respectively.

Also of alliterative service is the prepositional phrase ממענות "from the dens of" in 4:8, whose *mem-ʿayin-nun* string anticipates the same string in מעיניך "of your eyes" in 4:9. Based on the Old South Arabian cognate *mʿn* "dwelling,"[42] we conclude that the *ʿayin* of Hebrew מעון ~ מעונה (both masculine and feminine forms are attested) represents /ʿ/, and thus the phoneme in this word matches that of the previous two nouns, as noted above.

---

41. In which case there is also a remarkable wordplay at work here, on which see Fox, *Song of Songs*, 136.

42. A. F. L. Beeston, M. A. Ghul, W. W. Müller, and J. Ryckmans, *Sabaic Dictionary/Dictionnaire Sabéen* (Leuven: Peeters, 1982), 23; and J. C. Biella, *Dictionary of Old South Arabic: Sabaean Dialect* (HSS 25; Chico, Calif.: Scholars Press, 1982), 359

Song 4:11

נפת תטפנה שׂפתותיך
Your lips drip honey.

This three-word passage is a stunning example of the device under consideration. The three consonants in the initial word, נפת "honey," are rehearsed in the next word תטפנה "drip," which also includes an additional dental sound in *ṭet*. The combination of *pe* and two dentals (*taw* and *ṭet*) in the word תטפנה "drip" is then echoed in the following word שׂפתותיך "your lips," with *pe* and two *taws*. It is noteworthy that in this passage נפת "honey" appears in the A-line, with the more common synonym דבשׁ "honey" occurring in the B-line. One expects the opposite, since there is a tendency in Hebrew poetry for the more common word to appear in the A-line, with the rarer word in the B-line. In fact, this is exactly what occurs in the two other instances in the Bible in which these two words for "honey" are collocated: דבשׁ precedes נפת in both Ps 19:11 and Prov 24:13. Accordingly, we conclude that the ordering of the word pair in our verse is intentional, allowing for נפת "honey" to commence an alliterative chain.

Song 4:11, 13

וריח שׂלמתיך כריח לבנון ...
שׁלחיך פרדס רמונים

And the scent of your clothes is like the scent of Lebanon. …
Your shoots are an orchard of pomegranates.

The noun שְׁלָחַיִךְ is either a rare or a unique usage in the Bible, depending on its meaning in this passage. We have elected to render the word as "your shoots," understanding it as a byform of the base noun of שְׁלֻחוֹתֶיהָ "her shoots" in Isa 16:8, in which case the usage is unique. Alternatively, שְׁלָחַיִךְ could mean "your water channels," attested elsewhere in Neh 3:15 as שֶׁלַח and in MH.[43] In either case, we assume that the noun is based on the verbal root שׁלח "send." According to our understanding, the semantic development is "that which is sent forth" > "shoot (of a plant)." But regardless of what it means here (and the option of polysemy needs to be considered in any case), the poet employed this word to evoke the sounds heard slightly earlier (in

43. See Fox, *Song of Songs*, 137, for discussion.

4:11, with the intervening 4:12, a relatively short verse), namely, the letters that bridge the expression ריח שלמתיך "the scent of your clothes." The *ḥet*, *śin*, and *lamed* in this phrase correspond to the *šin*, *lamed*, and *ḥet* in שלחיך "your shoots." Note that both *ḥet*s are the phoneme /ḥ/, as can be determined from the cognate Ugaritic evidence in which both *šlḥ* "send" and *rḥ* "wind, breath" are attested.

Song 4:12

גן נעול אחתי כלה
גל נעול מעין חתום

A locked garden is my sister, (my) bride;
A locked fountain, a sealed spring.

All commentators on the Song of Songs have noticed the collocation of the two nouns גן "garden" and גל "fountain." The latter is a unique usage in the Bible, employed here by the poet *alliterationis causa*. Additional links solidify the aural quality of this verse. Note that the repeated word נעול "locked" provides both a *nun* to alliterate with גן "garden" and a *lamed* to alliterate with גל "fountain." Furthermore, the word גל "fountain" follows כלה "bride," presenting another nexus: both words have *lamed* preceded by a velar consonant, the voiceless *kaf* in the case of כלה "bride," and the voiced *gimel* in the case of גל "fountain."

Song 4:13–14

שלחיך פרדס רמונים
עם פרי מגדים
כפרים עם נרדים ...
נרד וכרכם ...
מר ואהלות

Your shoots are an orchard of pomegranates,
With fruit of choice-fruits;
Henna with nard. ...
Nard and saffron ...
Myrrh and aloes.

As is well known, the noun פרדס "orchard" in verse 13 is a rare noun in the Bible. The poet's selection of this word may be explained by the requirements of alliterative exigency. The word begins with *pe* and *reš*, the same two consonants that occur in the words פרי "fruit" and כפרים "henna." Note that these sounds are evenly distributed in the verse, with one set in each stich. Furthermore, the *reš* and *dalet* in פרדס is rehearsed in נרדים "nard" (plural form) later in verse 13 and in נרד "nard" (singular form) in verse 14.

Second, an entire series of words here includes the pair of consonants *reš* and *mem*: רמונים "pomegranates," כפרים "henna," נרדים "nard" (plural form), כרכם "saffron," and מר "myrrh." Two of these, כפרים "henna" and כרכם "saffron," share a third common consonant, namely, *kaf*.

Song 4:14

קנה וקנמון
Cane and cinnamon

The happy circumstance that the two English words "cane" and "cinnamon" match the Hebrew forms of these words affords us the opportunity to reproduce the Hebrew alliteration in English (though only to an extent, since the original hard *c* /k/ in the word *cinnamon* has softened to /s/). These two words are relatively rare in Hebrew; only here in the Bible has the author collocated the two to produce the paronomasia (akin to the examples תהו ובהו and הוד והדר cited above).[44]

Song 4:14–15

עם כל עצי לבונה ...
ונזלים מן לבנון

With all trees of frankincense …
And streams from Lebanon.

As noted above (see at Song 3:6, 9), לבונה "frankincense" occurs twice in the Song of Songs, and in both cases it appears in close proximity to the toponym לבנון "Lebanon." In this second instance, in addition to producing the alliteration once more, the poet incorporates a delightful wordplay. A common expression in the Bible is the phrase עצי (ה)לבנון "trees of (the) Lebanon" (as in Song 3:9; 2 Chr 2:7; see also Ezra 3:7 and of course numer-

44. The author of Exod 30:23 includes both words in the same passage, but the alliterative effect is minimal.

ous other passages that refer to the trees of Lebanon). In this passage the poet uses the atypical expression עצי לבונה "trees of frankincense," evoking the sounds of the standard phrase but opting instead to collocate עצי "trees of" with לבונה "frankincense."

Song 5:1–2

אכלתי יערי עם דבשי ...
אכלו רעים ...
אני ישנה ולבי ער ...
פתחי לי אחתי רעיתי

I have eaten my honeycomb with my honey. …
Eat, friends! …
I am asleep, but my heart is awake. …
Open for me, my sister, my darling.

The two verses excerpted here are separated by a *setuma* paragraph break,[45] yet there are clear thematic and alliterative links bridging these passages. The alliterative nexus, our main concern at present, centers on the consonants ʿ*ayin* and *reš* found in the following words: יערי "my honeycomb," רעים "friends," ער "awake," and רעתי "my darling."

Song 5:2–6

פתחי לי אחתי רעיתי ...
פשטתי את כתנתי ...
איככה אטנפם ...
קמתי אני לפתח לדודי
וידי נטפו מור ...
על כפות המנעול
פתחתי אני לדודי ...
נפשי יצאה בדברו

Open for me, my sister, my darling. …
I have removed my tunic. …

45. Thus in the Leningrad Codex. The Cambridge manuscript has a *petuḥa*; while the Aleppo Codex is missing the leaves following Song 3:11. See the convenient chart in Dirksen, "Canticles," 9*.

How shall I soil them? …
I arose to open for my beloved,
And my hands dripped myrrh …
On the handles of the lock.
I opened for my beloved …
My inner-being went out when he spoke.

These verses provide a long series of alliterations focusing most of all on the anagrammatic roots טנף "soil" and נטף "flow." The former is a *hapax legomenon*, so that once more we may assume that the poet selected this verb for the reason of alliteration. The combination of *pe* and *ṭet* in these two verbs is echoed in the following words: פתחי "open" in 5:2, with *pe* and *taw*; פשטתי "I have removed" in 5:3, with *pe*, *ṭet*, and *taw*; לפתח "to open" in 5:5, with *pe* and *taw*; כפות "handles" in 5:5, with *pe* and *taw*; and פתחתי "I opened" in 5:6, with *pe* and two *taws*. In addition, the two anagrammatic verbs noted above also contain both *nun* and *ṭet*, the sounds of which are heard in כתנתי "my tunic" in 5:3, with *nun* and two *taws*. Finally, the two main verbs present *nun* and *pe*, which appear once again in the word נפשי "my inner-being" in 5:6. The end result is a long series of words within the female lover's dream sequence with an arresting aural effect.

Song 5:7–10

נשׂאו את רדידי מעלי …
אם תמצאו את דודי …
מה דודך מדוד …
מה דודך מדוד …
דודי צח ואדום

They lifted my shawl from upon me. …
If you find my beloved …
How is your beloved more so than other beloveds? …
How is your beloved more so than other beloveds? …
My beloved is radiant and red.

The word רדיד "shawl" in Song 5:7 is a rare word in the Bible; it occurs only here and in Isa 3:23. The word דוד "beloved" is exceedingly common in the Song of Songs, occurring thirty-seven times (in addition to which there are six occurrences of the abstract noun דודים "love"), so to some extent it would be impossible not to alliterate the words רדיד and דוד within the poem. We note the following two points, however: (1) the next verse, 5:8, is the only one of the four iterations of the refrain that includes the word דוד "beloved"; and (2) verses 8–10 contain the greatest concentration of דוד in the Song of Songs, with six repetitions of the word within the three verses. The closest competitor, in fact, is 5:4–6, with four attestations of דוד within the three verses (and note also the two cases of יד "hand," one in v. 4 and one in v. 5). Since this passage occurs just before the alliteration under discussion here, one could broaden the picture and note that Song 5:4–10 includes ten cases of דוד "beloved," plus two cases of יד "hand," and thus one can understand why the poet selected the rare word רדיד "shawl" at specifically this juncture.

Song 5:11, 13

שחרות כעורב ...
נטפות מור עבר

Black as the raven ...
Dripping (with) flowing myrrh.

These two stichs are separated by seven other stichs (four in v. 12, and the first three in v. 13), but because they are part of the female lover's description of her beloved, the alliteration present in them functions effectively. Furthermore, we must keep in mind that the poet was restricted by the order of the body parts in this *waṣf* stanza, moving from top to bottom, with the first phrase above describing the hair and the second phrase used to portray the lips.

The reverberating words are עורב "raven" and עבר "flowing," with the same three consonants in anagrammatic order. The *ʿayin* in these two words is most likely the same phoneme, namely, /ʿ/. This is clearly the case with the verb עבר "pass," as indicated by Ugaritic *ʿrb* "enter" and the like. The case of עורב "raven" is more complicated. From the Arabic cognate *ǵurāb*, one would assume that the phoneme represented by *ʿayin* is /ǵ/, but most likely this is a secondary development, with original /ʿ/ having shifted to /ǵ/ before /r/, exactly as occurred in the Arabic verb *ǵaraba* "leave, depart," nominal forms *ǵarb* "west," *maǵrib* "place of sunset, west," cognate to the previously mentioned Ugaritic *ʿrb* "enter." Support for this conclusion is forthcoming from the Septuagint rendering of the proper noun עורב as Ωρηβ (Judg 7:25, etc.); if the Hebrew phoneme present in this word were /ǵ/, one would expect the Septuagint rendering to begin with the letter *gamma*.[46] In addition, note that

46. For discussion, though with a different opinion, see Blau, *On Polyphony in Biblical Hebrew*, 18–19.

the vowel pattern of the two words is the same—*ḥolem* and *ṣere*—so that assonance is present as well.

Song 5:11–13

שחרות כעורב ...
רחצות בחלב ...
לחיו כערוגת הבשׂם
מגדלות מרקחים

Black as the raven ...
Washed in milk ...
His cheeks are like a bed of spices,
Towers of perfumes.

These four stichs provide another string of alliterative words operating at the beginning of this *waṣf*, notwithstanding some intervening passages indicated by the ellipses.[47] The key sounds are the consonants *ḥet* and *reš*, to be found in שחרות "black," רחצות "washed," and מרקחים "perfumes," along with the like-sounding pair of *ḥet* and *lamed* in חלב "milk" and לחיו "his cheeks." In addition, the similar pair of *ʿayin* and *reš* is present in the two words עורב "raven" and ערוגת "bed of (spices)," both of which, perhaps not coincidentally, are preceded by prefixed -כ "like." The result is a cluster of words repeating the same or similar sounds.

In all five of these cases, the letter *ḥet* represents the phoneme /ḥ/, as the following selected etyma demonstrate: Arabic *šaḥara* "blacken with soot," *šuḥḥār* "soot"; Ugaritic *rḥṣ* "wash"; Ugaritic *rqḥ* "perfume, ointment"; Ugaritic *ḥlb* "milk"; and Ugaritic *lḥm* "cheeks," Arabic *laḥy* "jawbone." As to the two words with *ʿayin*: as noted above the phoneme in עורב "raven" is most likely /ʿ/; and if ערוגה "garden bed" is related to Arabic *ʿarağa* "ascend," based on the notion that a garden bed is created on raised soil, then the *ʿayin* in this word also represents /ʿ/.

Song 5:10, 13–14

דגול מרבבה ...
מגדלות מרקחים ...
ידיו גלילי זהב

47. For more on the *waṣf* in the Song of Songs, see chapters 3 and 4.

More dazzling than a myriad …
Towers of perfumes …
His hands are bracelets of gold.

As in the above examples, again there is some distance separating the relevant phrases, but once more we take note that all three are united by their presence in this cohesive stanza, as it proceeds from general introduction to cheeks to hands (with other material intervening). The word דגול is a rare word (three out of the four attestations of this root occur in the Song of Songs; the other is in Ps 20:6); the meaning "dazzling" that we have assigned to it is from context and is based on a presumed connection with Akkadian *dagālu* "see," thus something special to be seen or witnessed. The three root letters of this word appear in anagrammatic fashion in the word מגדלות "towers." Finally, the reader is treated to the string of *dalet-gimel-lamed*, the original order of these consonants in the word דגול in the first two words of the third stich presented above, ידיו גלילי "his hands are bracelets of (gold)" (with a *waw* interposed, though with an extra *lamed* to boot).

Song 5:12, 14

רחצות בחלב ישבות על מלאת ...
ידיו גלילי זהב ממלאים בתרשיש

Washed in milk, sitting by the pool …
His hands are bracelets of gold, inlaid with beryl.

A verse intercedes between these two passages, so that the like-sounding words are not in immediate proximity to one another. As with the above examples, however, we assume that the sound play would have been grasped by the listeners of the Song of Songs. The two operative words in this passage are מלאת "pool" and ממלאים "inlaid." The former is a unique word in the Bible, so once more we may assume that alliterative exigency explains its presence at this point in the composition. Since both derive from the same root, מלא "fill," technically this is an instance of paronomasia (as defined above).

Song 5:14

מעיו עשת שן
מעלפת ספירים

His loins are a block of ivory,
Studded with sapphires.

The form מעלפת "studded" represents an uncommon usage in BH. The root עלף usually means "be faint, be weak." The closest usage to our passage is Gen 38:14, where ותתעלף means "she covered herself."[48] We opt to translate מעלפת as "studded," not "covered," because one should not envision a block of ivory covered with sapphires, which would defeat the purpose of using ivory, but rather one studded with sapphires. Attention to the sounds surrounding this word explains the bard's choice of מעלפת in this context. The words מעיו "his loins" and עשת "block" in the previous stich provide the consonants *mem*, *ʿayin*, and *taw*, which appear as well in מעלפת "studded." We also may note an echo of ממלאים "inlaid," of similar semantic range, earlier in the verse. Apart from the shared preformative *mem* of the Puʿal participle in both forms, the roots have the following aural links: both have *lamed*; the *ʾaleph* of the one evokes the *ʿayin* of the other; and the *mem* of the one root and the *pe* of the other root are both labials.

Song 5:14–15

מעיו עשת שן ...
שוקיו עמודי שש

His loins are a block of ivory. …
His calves are pillars of marble.

In the previous section we concentrated on the rareness of the lexeme מעלפת "studded," with the observation that its occurrence can be explained in part by the presence of the word עשת "block" in the same verse. But in truth עשת "block" is also an unusual lexical item. It occurs only here in the Bible, though note the expression ברזל עשות "massed iron" (?) in Ezek 27:19. In postbiblical texts it occurs in the Copper Scroll 3Q15:i:5 and in MH with reference to "blocks" or "bars" of metal.[49] A further look at Song 5:14 explains the presence of עשת, especially in conjunction with the first stich in the following verse, for once more we see the workings of alliteration. The first stich reproduced above includes one *mem*, two *ʿayin*s, and two *šin*s, along with the voiceless dental *taw*. The second stich presented here includes one *mem*, one *ʿayin*, and three *šin*s, along with the voiced dental *dalet*.

48. Note, incidentally, that the presence of ותתעלף in Gen 38:14 is also due to alliterative exigency. The immediately preceding word is צעיף "scarf."

49. See J. K. Lefkovits, *The Copper Scroll (3Q15): A Revaluation* (STDJ 25; Leiden: Brill, 2000), 61.

Song 6:2

לערוגות הבשׂם
לרעות בגנים

To the beds of spices,
To graze in the gardens.

These two short phrases, juxtaposed to each other, include a series of aural correspondences. The first three letters of לערוגות "to the beds," namely, *lamed*, *ʿayin*, and *reš*, are rehearsed in anagrammatic fashion in the first three letters of לרעות "to graze." The *gimel* in לערוגות is repeated in בגנים "in the gardens"; and the *taw* at the end of לערוגות occurs at the end of לרעות as well. Finally, the *bet* and the *mem* in בשׂם "spices" are echoed in the word בגנים "in the gardens."

Song 6:2, 4–5

דודי ירד לגנו ...
אימה כנדגלות
הסבי עיניך מנגדי

My beloved went down to his garden. ...
Awesome as the luminaries.
Turn your eyes from before me.

The word at the end of verse 4 is not the typical Hebrew word כוכבים "stars" but rather a poetic term נדגלות, which we have rendered "luminaries."[50] The poet no doubt shows his or her lexical prowess with this word choice, but in addition one may note the alliteration that is produced. The sounds of this rare word are anticipated two verses earlier—the intervening verse 3 is quite short—in the word לגנו "to his garden" along with the preceding letter *dalet* at the end of ירד "went down." Note that the first four letters of נדגלות "luminaries" occur in this sequence of letters -ד לגנ-. Moreover, the first three consonants of נדגלות "luminaries" are rehearsed in the next stich, at the beginning of verse 5, in the word מנגדי "from before me."

---

50. For discussion of this word, see S. D. Goitein, "Ayumma Kannidgalot" (Song of Songs VI. 10): 'Splendid Like the Brilliant Stars,'" *JSS* 10 (1965): 220–21; and R. Gordis, "The Root דגל in the Song of Songs," *JBL* 88 (1969): 203–4.

SONG 6:5–6, 8–9

שגלשו מן הגלעד ...
שכלם מתאימות
ושכלה אין בהם ...
ושמנים פילגשים ...
ופילגשים ויהללוה

That flow down from the Gilead. …
All of whom are twinned,
And none of them bereaved. …
And eighty concubines …
And concubines, and they praise her.

The alliteration treated above at 4:1–2 occurs in 6:5–6 as well; there is no need to repeat that discussion here. Noteworthy in the present instance, however, is the continuation of the same sounds in the word פילגשים "concubines" used twice, in verses 8 and 9. The intervening verse 7 is, as we saw in similar cases above, a relatively short verse. The three consonants of the rare verb גלש "flow down" appear as in anagrammatic fashion in the middle of the word פילגשים "concubines." Note that this latter word is limited in the Song of Songs to these two attestations.

SONG 6:10–11

אימה כנדגלות
אל גנת אגוז ירדתי

Awesome as the luminaries.
To the walnut garden I went down.

The word נדגלות "luminaries," discussed two sections above, occurs a few verses later as well, at 6:10. Once more alliteration is present, and once more the key word is גן "garden." In this case we find the feminine form in the construct, thus, גנת, with the preceding consonant being *lamed* in the preposition אל "to." The result is the string of letters ל גנת-, all of which occur in נדגלות "luminaries."

SONG 7:1–2

מה תחזו בשולמית
כמחלת המחנים ...
חמוקי ירכיך כמו חלאים

How you gaze at the Shulammite,
Like a dance of the two-camps. …
The curves of your thighs are like ornaments.

These stichs are characterized by the combination of *mem* and *ḥet*, in the phrase מה תחזו (joined by a *maqqef*) "how you gaze," and in the words מחלת "dance of," המחנים "the two-camps," חמוקי "curves of," and חלאים "ornaments." Two of these words, in fact, share three consonants: note not only the *mem* and *ḥet*, but also the *lamed*, in מחלת "dance of" and חלאים "ornaments." Moreover, two of these words are rare in Biblical Hebrew: חמוקי(ם) "curves" is unique (the root occurs twice elsewhere, as a verb, in Song 5:6 and Jer 31:22); and חלאים "ornaments" is the only plural form of a rare noun attested in two other passages in variant forms, Hos 2:15 חליה, Prov 25:12 חלי (see ch. 1, n. 227). Once again the poet has employed rare words for the sake of alliteration.

Where such can be determined, the *ḥet* in these words represents etymological /ḥ/. The cognates Ugaritic *ḥdy* "see, gaze" and Arabic *ḥaly* "ornament" provide evidence for two of our words. The phoneme present in מחנים "two-camps" is established through the transcription of the place name מחנים "Mahanaim" in both Egyptian *ma-ḥa*$_2$*–n-ma*$_4$ (Shishak list no. 22) and Greek Μααναιμ (Septuagint to 1 Chr 6:65, etc.), Μαναιμ (Septuagint to Josh 13:26, etc.).[51] For the other two lexemes, as far as we know, there are no cognates.

SONG 7:3

שררך אגן הסהר
אל יחסר המזג
בטנך ערמת חטים
סוגה בשושנים

51. Occasionally the Septuagint renders מחנים "Mahanaim" as a common noun παρεμβολή "encampment" (e.g., Gen 32:3). Blau, *On Polyphony in Biblical Hebrew*, 55, listed the Proto-Semitic root of our word as *ḥny*, but we are unaware of any etyma that would substantiate this claim, unless he had in mind Arabic *ḥanā* "bend, curve, twist, turn."

Your vulva is a bowl of the crescent,
Let it not lack mixed-wine;
Your "stomach" is a heap of wheat,
Bordered with lilies.

This verse includes two unusual lexical items. The first is the noun סהר "crescent" (though it may simply be another term for "moon," without referring to a specific phase). This word choice clearly was governed by presence of the verbal root חסר "lack" in the next stich. The phonetic correspondences are quite obvious and require no elucidation here.

The second atypical lexical item is the form סוגה "bordered"; indeed, this is the only occurrence of the root סוג "fence, border" in BH (see further at ch. 1, §1.4.30). We assume that the poet selected this word because of the presence of the noun מזג "mixed-wine" earlier in the verse. Note that both words have *gimel* and that the *samekh* in סוגה is the voiceless equivalent of the voiced sibilant *zayin* in מזג. Furthermore, the letter that precedes סוגה is *mem*, at the end of the word חטים "wheat," thus supplying the final link with the word מזג "mixed-wine."

Song 7:8–9

זאת קומתך דמתה לתמר ...
אמרתי אעלה בתמר

This your stature resembles a palm-tree. ...
I said, "I will ascend the palm-tree."

The words in the first line are linked by the letters *mem* and *taw*, occurring in that order in קומתך "your stature" and in דמתה "resembles," and in reverse order in תמר "palm-tree." All three of these words are part of the standard Hebrew lexicon, but note that the first of these has a synonym in the word גובה "height, stature." The poet's choice of קומה "stature," especially in the construct form yielding -קומת, enhanced the alliteration. The word תמר "palm-tree" is repeated in the second line reproduced above, and the same three consonants appear in the verb form אמרתי "I said." Once more, we are dealing with common lexemes in the language, but still we can admire the poet's alliterative artistry.

Song 7:13

נשכימה לכרמים
נראה אם פרחה הגפן
פתח הסמדר
הנצו הרמונים

Let us arise-early to the vineyards,
Let us see if the vine has bloomed,
(If) the bud has opened,
(If) the pomegranates have blossomed.

Three words, all related to the vineyard scene portrayed here, include the consonants *reš* and *mem*: כרמים "vineyards," סמדר "bud," and רמונים "pomegranates." The second of these, one should recall, is a rare word in the Bible, attested only in the Song of Songs, in this verse and at 2:13, 15. We also may note that נראה "let us see" includes *nun* and *reš* to bolster the sound effect.

Song 7:13–14

שם אתן את דדי לך
הדודאים נתנו ריח ...
דודי צפנתי לך

There I will give my love to you.
The mandrakes give forth scent. ...
My beloved, I have hidden (them) for you.

An obvious alliterative sequence occurs in these stichs with the words דדי "my love," דודאים "mandrakes," and דודי "my beloved." In fact, quite probably, either (1) mandrakes were called in Hebrew by the term דודאים because the plant was believed to have aphrodisiacal power, or (2) the plant was called דודאים for whatever reason any name is attached to any plant (or any thing, for that matter) and thence came to be considered an aphrodisiac because its name evoked the sounds of the poetic word for "love."

Song 8:1–2 (with 7:11)

אני לדודי ועלי תשוקתו ...
אמצאך בחוץ אשקך ...
אשקך מיין הרקח

I am my beloved's, and towards me is his urge. …
I would find you in the street, I would kiss you. …
I would ply you with spiced wine.

In 8:1–2 the poet incorporates an alliteration known from other biblical texts. We refer to the use of the roots נשק "kiss" and שקה "ply, give drink" (see, e.g., Gen 29:10–11).[52] Because both are weak roots, the wordplay between them is even more striking, since all that remains in many of these verbal forms is *šin* and *qof*. In the present instance, the alliteration is anticipated, albeit at long range, by the use of תשוקתו "his urge" in 7:11.

Song 8:5

מי זאת עלה מן המדבר
מתרפקת על דודה

Who is this coming up from the wilderness,
Leaning on her beloved.

The verbal root רפק "lean, support," used here in the Hitpaʿel, is a *hapax legomenon* in the Bible.[53] This is another instance of the poet using a rare word to produce the alliterative result. The string of letters *mem-taw-reš-pe* at the beginning of the word מתרפקת matches very closely the consonants in the noun מדבר "wilderness." Both have *mem* and *reš*, while the voiceless consonants *taw* and *pe* in the former correspond to the voiced equivalents *dalet* and *reš* in the latter. In addition, while there is nothing atypical about the verb עלה in the first stich and the preposition על in the second stich, the *ʿayin-lamed* combination in these two words creates still another aural link in the passage.

Song 8:13–14

חברים מקשיבים לקולך …
ברח דודי

52. See S. B. Noegel, "Drinking Feasts and Deceptive Feats: Jacob and Laban's Double Talk," in Noegel, *Puns and Pundits*, 173–74.

53. Greenspahn, *Hapax Legomena in Biblical Hebrew*, 159.

Friends attend to your voice. …
Flee, my beloved.

The two alliterative words in these passages are common in Hebrew, yet they are rare in the Song of Songs. חברים "friends" occurs only here and in 1:7, while this is the only attestation of the verb ברח "flee" in the book. The two *ḥets* represent the same phoneme, namely, /ḥ/; note the Ugaritic cognates *ḥbr* "friend" and *brḥ* "flee."

As should be clear by now, the Song of Songs is a veritable tapestry of alliteration. Nearly every one of its passages shines with alliterative artistry. As we have seen, time and again the poet selected rare and uncommon words for the purpose of achieving an aural effect, with the goal of enhancing the oral presentation of the poem. Moreover, as we shall demonstrate in the next two chapters, the poet's creative abilities relied upon a much wider and well-developed arsenal of poetic techniques that makes the Song of Songs one of the finest literary achievements of ancient Israel.

3
Variation in the Poetry of the Song of Songs as a Literary Device

The previous chapter was devoted to the literary device of alliteration, with numerous examples in the Song of Songs, all serving to enhance the orality of the poetic reading. The present chapter focuses on a different literary device, variation within the poetry. Once more, however, the oral nature of ancient literature serves as the background for appreciating the importance of this device. If we can imagine a group of ancient Israelites assembled to hear the Song of Songs read (sung?) aloud—in whatever setting one might envision[1]—we may rightly ask: how does one continue to engage the attention of the gathered throng as the poetry proceeds through its eight chapters? Given the superb poetry involved in this particular case, and the alluring and engaging subject matter, one might argue that not much is needed beyond the surface reading of the text—a point to which we readily admit—and yet the human mind does require exercise to stay tuned at all times. It is our belief that the writers of ancient literature intentionally varied their language, where possible, specifically to engage the listener and to demand his or her absolute attention when the text was read aloud.[2] We will illustrate this notion with the poetry of the Song of Songs below, though again we need to note that the intentional use of variation is to be found in all biblical genres and compositions.

To present what are probably the most extreme examples, we invite the reader to work carefully through Num 1; 7; and 29 and to take note of the exceedingly minor changes in the wordings for each tribe (in the first two

1. For one such imagined setting, see R. Alter, *The Art of Biblical Narrative* (New York: Basic, 1981), 90–91. Note that Alter's subject here is repetition and that he pays attention to variation within the repetition.

2. For a discussion of some relevance to our topic, see Watson, *Classical Hebrew Poetry*, 64. The discussion centers on "retroactive reading," a term coined by semioticians to describe what the listener to a poem must do as he or she absorbs the poetry.

chapters) or for each day of Sukkot (in the third chapter). For example, note the inclusion of the word פקדיו between the words אבתם and במספר in Num 1:22; the lack of a *lamed* in the expression בני נפתלי at the beginning of 1:42; the presence of the verb הקריב in 7:18–19; and the uses of ונסכיהם in 29:19 and ונסכיה in 29:31—all of which depart from the standard parallel wordings in these litanies.

A survey of *The New Princeton Encyclopedia of Poetry and Poetics* reveals that there is no special term for the device studied here. The most relevant items in this standard reference work are "repetend" and "variation." The former is defined by Marianne Shapiro as follows: "usually denotes the irregular recurrence of a word, phrase, or line in a poem (unlike a regular *refrain* [q.v.]), or a partial rather than complete r."[3] The implication here is that repetends typically include the same wording, though at varying intervals (and thus are not the same as a refrain), whereas the passages that we will survey below are characterized by different language. The latter term, therefore, might appear to be more promising, but it too describes something slightly different. T. V. F. Brogan wrote as follows: "More generally, v. is often held to be a desirable characteristic of structure which sustains reader interest."[4] The cases of variation surveyed herein, however, are not tied to the structure of the Song of Songs per se (though we will study the four iterations of the refrain[5] below) but rather surface at any given moment in the composition.

Accordingly, we elect to coin a new term for our device: "polyprosopon." Repeated lines in the Song of Songs present many faces, which we believe the ancient listeners of the poem would grasp as the composition was read aloud to them, notwithstanding the distance between passages at times.[6]

We base our neologism on the term "polyptoton," defined as either "a rhetorical figure consisting in the repetition of a word in different cases or

---

3. M. Shapiro, "Repetition," in Preminger and Brogan, *The New Princeton Encyclopedia*, 1036.

4. T. V. F. Brogan, "Variation," in Preminger and Brogan, *The New Princeton Encyclopedia*, 1341. For a more detailed study, see C. S. Brown, "Theme and Variations as a Literary Form," *Yearbook of Comparative and General Literature* 27 (1978): 35–43.

5. Technically speaking, the four passages in Song 2:7; 3:5; 5:8; 8:4 are not refrains, since they do not occur at regular intervals (see above) and reflect different language (except for the first two passages, which are identical; see below), but we retain this time-honored label nonetheless.

6. We take this opportunity to thank Terry Brogan for a very informative email exchange, July 2005.

inflexions *in the same sentence*,"[7] or "related to the varieties of simple word-repetition or iteration, which in Cl. rhet. are treated under the genus of *ploce* (q.v.), is another class of figures which repeat a word or words by varying their word-class (part of speech) or by giving different forms of the same root or stem."[8] Some of the examples given above from the book of Numbers, such as ונסכיהם in 29:19 and ונסכיה in 29:31, would qualify as examples of polyptoton, or as very close approximations thereto, and a fine survey of this rhetorical device in the Bible was presented by R. J. Ratner,[9] but the kind of variation that we will present below from the Song of Songs is of a different order. As intimated above and as will become apparent below, in our examples: (1) the passages typically do not occur in close proximity to one another, and (2) the differences frequently are in the realm of syntax, word order, and lexis (not just morphology).[10] In short, one could say that polyprosopon functions on the large scale of the composition in similar fashion to the way that polyptoton operates on the small scale: both incorporate variation into the language of the poetry (or prose).

One additional point requires our attention before moving to a presentation of the evidence. The question arises: To what extent would a listener to the Song of Songs realize that a verse in, say, chapter 7 repeats with variation a passage heard earlier in chapter 4, or with even greater distance, that a verse in chapter 8 changes ever so slightly a passage heard earlier in chapter 2 (see below for two cases of each scenario). To present one of those specific instances here, we wish to know, for example, whether or not someone listening to the text of the Song of Songs in its entirety could recall, upon hearing ברח דודי ודמה לך לצבי או לעפר האילים על הרי בשׂמים in 8:14, the last line of the poem, that previously he or she had heard the words סב דמה לך דודי לצבי או לעפר האילים על הרי בתר in 2:17, relatively near the start of the composition. While we have no empirical evidence to judge this question, we are led to answer in the affirmative—if for no other reason than the internal evidence of the Song of Songs itself, that is to say, the manner in which these variations appear throughout the composition.

The question of the memorability of biblical poetry was studied by Ziony Zevit, but he was more interested in the retention of words over a short span,

7. *OED*, emphasis added.

8. T. V. F. Brogan, "Polyptoton," in Preminger and Brogan, *The New Princeton Encyclopedia*, 967–68 (the quotation is from the head of the entry on 967).

9. R. J. Ratner, "Morphological Variation in Biblical Hebrew Rhetoric," in Ratner et al., *Let Your Colleagues Praise You*, 143–59.

10. For an example of lexical substitution noticed by a previous scholar, see Alter, *The Art of Biblical Narrative*, 91.

in order to understand the listener's processing of parallelism and word pairs, for example.[11] Zevit quoted a well-known article by Eric Wanner entitled "The Parser's Window," which states:

> Although estimates of short term memory capacity disagree—there are no estimates of the capacity of immediate memory which would even remotely suggest that the human listener can hold in mind (say) the entire fifteen to twenty-five words of a modestly complicated spoken sentence. Perhaps the simplest way to appreciate this fact is to notice that there are many sentences which we understand without difficulty in ordinary conversation but which we could not possibly repeat back word for word upon hearing.[12]

No one can argue with this statement, based as it is on modern psycholinguistic studies, but we also note that the subjects of the studies cited by Wanner (along with other scientists summarized by Zevit) were by and large, if not all, individuals whose culture is characterized by the written word, Western Europeans, Americans, and the like—and who were listening, as Wanner implies, to ordinary conversation.

Would the conclusions of the studies cited by Wanner be true if the subjects were stage actors, people attuned to presenting the written word in oral performance? Would the conclusions of these studies be the same if the subjects were Somali or Ethiopian peasants engaged with literature, and not with mere conversation? We mention these two groups specifically for good reason. First, as B. W. Andrzejewski and I. M. Lewis noted in their research into Somali poetry readings, the poets and reciters (who may be one and the same at times) are able to commit to memory exceedingly long compositions:

> Unaided by writing they learn long poems by heart and some have repertoires which are too great to be exhausted even by several evenings of continuous recitation. Moreover, some of them are endowed with such powers of memory that they can learn a poem by heart after hearing it only once, which is quite astonishing, even allowing for the fact that poems are chanted very slowly, and important lines are sometimes repeated. The reciters are not only capable of acquiring a wide repertoire but can store it in their memories for many years, sometimes for their lifetime. We have met

11. Z. Zevit, "Cognitive Theory and the Memorability of Biblical Poetry," in Ratner et al., *Let Your Colleagues Praise You*, 199–212.

12. E. Wanner, "The Parser's Window," in *The Cognitive Representation of Speech* (ed. T. Myers, J. Laver, and J. Anderson; Amsterdam: North-Holland, 1981), 211 (cited by Zevit on 202).

> poets who at a ripe age could still remember many poems which they learnt in their early youth.[13]

Furthermore, it is not only the poets/reciters who have this ability: in public gatherings the listeners to the poems often will correct the reciter if he makes a mistake. In the words of Andrzejewski and Lewis, "moreover, among the audience there are often people who already know by heart the particular poem, having learnt it from another source. Heated disputes sometimes arise between a reciter and his audience concerning the purity of his version."[14]

Second, we include here a story that Wolf Leslau related to one of us [G.A.R.] several years ago. While doing his fieldwork in the 1950s, Leslau recorded a story recounted by a Gurage storyteller; he later published this text in one of his dozens of books on Ethiopian languages, and then he proudly returned to the same village about ten years later, with book in hand, to show his informants his accomplishment. The locals asked Leslau to read from the book, and when he reached a particular passage in the story, the villagers corrected Leslau and told him that he must be mistaken. Leslau reported that when he returned to Los Angeles to check his tape recording and his notes, he realized that indeed—no surprise—the villagers were correct: Leslau had transcribed the tape incorrectly at this point.

In like fashion, we all know stories of Yemenite Jews (or may know such people personally) who can correct others in their reading of Torah and other texts from memory. We also suspect that there are Iranians who know large portions of the Persian poetic corpus by heart—and no doubt similarly Russian peasants with their Puskhin and Irish farmers with their Yeats. Perhaps the closest analogy in our own society are young children, who know when their parents have erred in reading them a bedtime story. We realize that we are mixing apples and oranges here, and we repeat that we have no real empirical evidence on which to base our judgment, but rather only anecdotal tales to tell. Nevertheless, we suspect that in a culture such as ancient Israel, which to our mind placed a primacy on its national literature, listeners to classical texts could appreciate the variation that we find in these texts. Yes, they would realize that אני לדודי ודודי לי הרעה בשושנים in 6:3 varies the earlier language of דודי לי ואני לו הרעה בשושנים in 2:16 (to cite another example to be studied below).

As was the case with the chapter on alliteration above, so too here: we believe that variation in biblical literature deserves a systematic study. Until

---

13. B. W. Andrzejewski and I. M. Lewis, *Somali Poetry: An Introduction* (Oxford: Clarendon, 1964), 45.

14. Ibid., 46.

such can be produced, however, we content ourselves with a survey of examples from the Song of Songs, to which we now turn our attention.[15]

SONG 1:15 AND 4:1

Song 1:15: הנך יפה רעיתי הנך יפה עיניך יונים
Behold you are beautiful, my darling,
Behold you are beautiful, your eyes are doves.

Song 4:1: הנך יפה רעיתי הנך יפה עיניך יונים מבעד לצמתך
Behold you are beautiful, my darling,
Behold you are beautiful, your eyes are doves,
behind your braids.

The simple statement in 1:15 is expanded in 4:1 with the addition of the expression מבעד לצמתך "behind your braids." The variation is noteworthy unto itself, but we also note how the different wordings enhance the alliteration in each passage.[16] As indicated in chapter 2, the ʿ*ayin* and *nun* in עיניך "your eyes" in 1:15 are echoed in the following verse, in which appear the words נעים "delightful," ערשׂנו "our couch," and רעננה "verdant," all of which have the same two consonants. Had the phrase מבעד לצמתך been inter-

15. We hasten to add that Michael Fox already deduced many of these examples in his excellent book; see Fox, *Song of Songs*, 209–15 (referring to them as "repetends," incidentally). Fox's objective was different, though: he utilized these parallel passages as an argument in favor of the unity of the Song of Songs, a point with which we wholeheartedly agree (see further below, conclusion, pp. 172–73). He paid less attention to the variations present in the repeated passages (though naturally he noted such), and thus our treatment herein has a different focus altogether than Fox's contribution. Only at the end of our research did the work of R. Kessler, *Some Poetical and Structural Features of the Song of Songs* (Leeds University Oriental Society Monograph Series 8; Leeds: Leeds University, 1957), come to our attention. We have not been able to consult this work, but a fine summary of it appears in Pope, *Song of Songs*, 48–50. Kessler's list of examples, which he called "distant repetitions," is essentially the same as ours. Finally, for a much smaller number of examples, see J. B. White, *A Study of the Language of Love in the Song of Songs and Ancient Egyptian Poetry* (SBLDS 38; Missoula, Mont.: Scholars Press, 1978), 29 (see especially the chart). Again, as with Fox, neither Kessler (apparently) nor White used the approach that we are taking in this chapter.

16. For the same observation regarding *Beowulf*, see W. K. Wimsatt, *The Verbal Icon: Studies in the Meaning of Poetry* (Lexington: University of Kentucky Press, 1954), 190.

posed, the alliteration still would have been present, but at a greater distance (notwithstanding examples of long-range alliterations presented in ch. 2). Similarly, the inclusion of the phrase מבעד לצמתך in 4:1 allows for three consecutive stichs to contain words with ʿ*ayin* and *dalet*: בעד "behind," עדר "flock," and גלעד "Gilead."

SONG 2:5 AND 5:8

Song 2:5 כי חולת אהבה אני
For I am sick with love.

Song 5:8 שחולת אהבה אני
That I am sick with love.

The two phrases vary only in the use of different coordinating conjunctions: the former uses כי, which we have translated as "for," while the latter utilizes -שׁ, which we have rendered as "that."

SONG 2:6 AND 8:3

Song 2:6 שׂמאלו תחת לראשי
His left-hand is beneath my head.

Song 8:3 שׂמאלו תחת ראשי
His left-hand is under my head.

The difference between these stichs is the use or nonuse of the prefixed preposition -ל following the preposition תחת (note our renderings "beneath" and "under," used to highlight the variation; see further the translation, n. af). No difference in meaning is present; the change is simply for the sake of variation. We further note that this is one of only two or three instances of the compound preposition -תחת ל in the Bible. The only true parallel occurs in 2 Chr 4:3, in the expression תחת לו "beneath it" (in place of the standard form תחתיו), in addition to which note the form -אל תחת ל in Ezek 10:3. (We consider the form -מתחת ל, attested thirteen times in the Bible [Gen 1:7, etc.], to be a different preposition altogether, standard in its own right.) In light of the rarity of the preposition -תחת ל in the Bible, we suspect that listeners to the Song of Songs would notice this linguistic oddity at 2:6, only to be treated to a smile when the reader reached 8:3 near poem's end, with the correct usage now in place.

SONG 2:7; 3:5; 5:8; AND 8:4

Song 2:7
השבעתי אתכם בנות ירושלם
בצבאות או באילות השדה
אם תעירו ואם תעוררו את האהבה
עד שתחפץ
I adjure you, O daughters of Jerusalem,
By the gazelles, or by the hinds of the field;
Do not rouse, and do not arouse love,
Until it desires.

Song 3:5
השבעתי אתכם בנות ירושלם
בצבאות או באילות השדה
אם תעירו ואם תעוררו את האהבה
עד שתחפץ
I adjure you, O daughters of Jerusalem,
By the gazelles, or by the hinds of the field;
Do not rouse, and do not arouse love,
Until it desires.

Song 5:8
השבעתי אתכם בנות ירושלם
אם תמצאו את דודי
מה תגידו לו
שחולת אהבה אני
I adjure you, O daughters of Jerusalem,
If you find my beloved,
What will you tell him? (or: Do not tell him,)
That I am sick with love?

Song 8:4
השבעתי אתכם בנות ירושלם
מה תעירו ומה תעררו את האהבה
עד שתחפץ
I adjure you, O daughters of Jerusalem,
Do not rouse, and do not arouse love,
Until it desires.

These four verses are the refrain that repeat throughout the Song of Songs. The first two instances, 2:7 and 3:5, are exactly the same—word for word, grapheme for grapheme, accent mark for accent mark.[17]

---

17. We take note of the same graphemes and accent marks, because in other

We will return to the third example, at 5:8, in a moment, but first we wish to treat the fourth refrain at 8:4. Here we notice two changes: (1) the second stich invoking the gazelles and the hinds is omitted, and (2) the negative particle has been changed from אם to מה, the latter a relatively rare usage in Hebrew, though common elsewhere in Semitic (cf. Arabic *mā*) as well as further afield in Afroasiatic (cf. Egyptian *m*).

Of the four verses, the most divergent is 5:8, the third of the instances. The command not to arouse love—the centerpiece of the refrain in the three other occurrences—is omitted in this iteration, with a different thought incorporated in its stead. (To repeat what was noted in ch. 2, pp. 95–96, this new thought allows the use of the word דוד "beloved" in order to enhance the alliteration.) Apart from this major change, however, there is also a much more technical variation in 5:8. The author plays with his audience at this point, in particular at the start of the second stich, which also begins with אם, but in this case the particle bears its usual meaning "if"—that is, it does not function as the negative particle, as it does in 2:7 and 3:5. Which is to say, only as the listeners hear the second word in the second stich, or perhaps the second stich in its entirety, is their expectation countered—as they come to realize that אם has a different function altogether and thus the refrain says something totally different in this instance.[18] We further note that the third stich of 5:8 begins with מה, which most likely functions here in its normal manner as the interrogative "what?" (It is also possible to understand מה as the negative particle "not" in this passage, though in light of what we state in the next paragraph, we are inclined to see the standard usage here.) In short, the two relevant particles function in 5:8 in their normal "prosaic" manners.

When we now look at 8:4 once more, we recall that in the final occurrence of the refrain, the negative particle is altered from אם (see 2:7 and 3:5) to מה, as noted above. The astute listener will realize at this point that he or

---

cases of verbatim repetition in the Bible, we have noted that sometimes the spelling is changed (viz., a *mater lectionis* is either added or deleted) or the Masora includes a different set of accent marks. Such is not the case here, though, as Song 2:7 and 3:5 have not the slightest difference. On the other hand, see the end of this section for a discussion of the variant orthography of one of the words repeated in 8:4.

18. The technical name for this technique is *antanaclasis*, on which see Brogan, "Polyptoton," 968. The standard treatment of this device in the Bible remains A. R. Ceresko, "The Function of Antanaclasis (*mṣʾ* 'to find' // *mṣʾ* 'to reach, overtake, grasp') in Hebrew Poetry, Especially in the Book of Qoheleth," *CBQ* 44 (1982): 551–69. Antanaclasis is also treated in the following articles: J. M. Sasson, "Wordplay in the O.T.," *IDBSup*, 970; E. L. Greenstein, "Wordplay, Hebrew," *ABD* 6:969; and S. B. Noegel, "'Word Play' in Qohelet," *JHS* 7 (2007): 4, 21–23.

she heard the two forms together during the last recitation of the refrain, at 5:8, though in that passage the two lexemes functioned in their most typical fashion, as "if" and "what?" respectively. Here in 8:4 מה functions in a very atypical way, serving to express the notion "not."[19] One can only marvel at the poet who toyed with his or her audience in this fashion, especially that segment of the ancient Israelite consumers of poetry who could appreciate this deft maneuver.

In addition, two minor points are worth noting. First, we note that when the root עור returns in 8:4 (that is, after its absence in 5:8) in its two forms, Hiphʿil תעירו and Polel תעררו, the second of these appears with variant spelling, since earlier the spelling תעוררו (2:7; 3:5) was used. Naturally, this would be a visual device, for only the oral reader holding the text would behold this minor difference. Second, we observe that the return of the Polel form עור > ערר in 8:4 is echoed in 8:5 תחת התפוח עוררתיך "under the apricot-tree I aroused you." This represents the only instance beyond the refrain of the Song of Songs in which the Hiphʿil or Polel form of this verb is used (Qal forms occur in 4:16 [feminine singular imperative] and 5:2 [masculine singular stative participle]).

Song 2:9, 17; 8:14

Song 2:9 דומה דודי לצבי או לעפר האילים
My beloved is like a gazelle, or a fawn of the hinds.

Song 2:17 סב דמה לך דודי לצבי או לעפר האילים
על הרי בתר
Turn, liken yourself, my beloved, to a gazelle,
or to a fawn of the hinds,
Upon the mountains of cleavage.

Song 8:14 ברח דודי ודמה לך לצבי או לעפר האילים
על הרי בשׂמים
Flee, my beloved, and liken yourself to a gazelle,
or to a fawn of the hinds,
Upon the mountains of spices.

---

19. See *DCH*, 162; and A. Bloch and C. Bloch, *The Song of Songs* (New York: Random House, 1995), 211. For a brief comment in line with the variation presented here, see Bloch and Bloch, *The Song of Songs*, 183.

Three times in the Song of Songs the female lover compares (using the verb דמה "liken, be similar") her lover to a gazelle or a fawn of the hinds. The simple statement appears in 2:9, after which the poetry presents the lover stationed outside of the house looking in through the windows.

Song 2:17 and 8:14 more closely parallel each other, as in these two passages the verb דמה occurs in the imperative and in each case is preceded by another verb in the imperative. Polyprosopon is seen most clearly by comparing the wording of these two verses. (1) In 2:17 the first verb is סב "turn," while in 8:14 the first verb is ברח "flee." (2) In 2:17 the two verbs appear in asyndetic parataxis, with the word דודי "my beloved" following, while in 8:14 the two imperatives are separated by the insertion of the word דודי "my beloved" between them. (3) The enigmatic phrase על הרי בתר "on the mountains of cleavage" (one of many possible meanings) occurs in 2:17, whereas the wording in 8:14 is על הרי בשׂמים "on the mountains of spices."

Song 2:16; 6:3; and 7:11

Song 2:16 דודי לי ואני לו
הרעה בשושנים
My beloved is mine, and I am his,
Grazing among the lilies.

Song 6:3 אני לדודי ודודי לי
הרעה בשושנים
I am my beloved's, and my beloved is mine,
Grazing among the lilies.

Song 7:11 אני לדודי
ועלי תשוקתו
I am my beloved's,
And toward me is his urge.

All three passages are spoken by the female lover, obviously. The first two bear the greatest resemblance; in fact, their B-lines are exactly the same. We note the variation, however, in the respective A-lines. Song 2:16 reads דודי לי ואני לו "my beloved is mine, and I am his," while 6:3 reads אני לדודי ודודי לי "I am my beloved's, and my beloved is mine." Note how (1) the order of the two phrases is reversed: in the former the female voice leads with "my beloved," while in the latter she leads with "I"; and (2) the former uses the pronoun form in the phrase ואני לו "and I am his," while the latter utilizes the noun form in the wording אני לדודי "I am my beloved's," thereby repeating the word דודי "my beloved" in this line.

In the third instance once more the female voice leads with אני לדודי "I am my beloved's," but in this passage there is no parallel phrase; instead, the poet has the female lover express an even more intimate sentiment with the words ועלי תשוקתו "and toward me is his urge." Even in this most divergent expression, however, we notice further use of variation. The reader presumably expected the phrase ודודי לי "and my beloved is mine" to follow at this point, with noun + pronoun-suffix before preposition + pronoun-suffix. But in fact the poet changes the syntax in the phrase ועלי תשוקתו "and toward me is his urge," with preposition + pronoun-suffix preceding noun + pronoun-suffix. This example truly tests the listener's capacity to comprehend the text, but such, we would argue, is the very essence of poetry. One recalls the famous statement of Vladimir Nabokov, who, when asked what he found enthralling about the two very dissimilar disciplines in which he was active (lepidoptery and literature), responded: "the beauty of science and the precision of poetry."[20]

SONG 3:1, 2; 5:6

Song 3:1
בקשתי את שאהבה נפשי
בקשתיו ולא מצאתיו
I sought whom my inner-being loves,
I sought him, but I did not find him.

Song 3:2
אבקשה את שאהבה נפשי
בקשתיו ולא מצאתיו
Let me seek whom my inner-being loves;
I sought him, but I did not find him.

Song 5:6
בקשתיהו ולא מצאתיהו
קראתיו ולא ענני
I sought him, but I did not find him,
I called him, but he did not answer me.

20. We have not been able to find these exact words attributed to Nabokov, but such was the lore at Cornell University, at which institution the present authors were previously associated. We have found the following statements, however: "the passion of science and the patience of poetry" and "the precision of poetry and the excitement of pure science." See B. Osimo, "Nabokov's Selftranslations: Interpretation Problems and Solutions in Lolita's Russian Version," *Sign Systems Studies* 27 (1999): 215–33, available at http://www.ut.ee/SOSE/sss/articles/osimo_27.htm.

Once more we have a threefold cord, and once more all three passages are spoken by the female lover. The first two occur in consecutive verses; one notes that the B-lines in these two passages are identical, whereas the A-lines differ: in 3:1 the A-line is in the past tense (SC, or suffix-conjugation), while in 3:2 the A-line is in the subjunctive/future (a form of the PC, or prefix-conjugation)—matching the different larger settings of these two verses.

In the third case, we note an even greater incidence of variation. In 5:6, a morphological alteration occurs, with the archaic third masculine singular pronominal suffix יהו- replacing the standard form יו- (occurring in both 3:1 and 3:2), on both verbs "I sought him" and "I did not find him." In addition, in the first two usages, the key phrase בקשתיו ולא מצאתיו "I sought him, but I did not find him" concludes both verses. In 5:6, by contrast, the poet adds an additional stich, one with added impact: קראתיו ולא ענני "I called him, but he did not answer me." We learn at this point that the female lover not only sought her beloved, which could have been or might have been done silently, simply by walking the city streets, but indeed she cried out to him, presumably calling his name, but that this effort too was for naught, for, in the stark final words: ולא ענני "but he did not answer me."

Song 3:3 and 5:7

Song 3:3 מצאוני השמרים
הסבבים בעיר
את שאהבה נפשי ראיתם
The watchmen found me,
They who go-about the city;
"He whom my inner-being loves, did you see (him)?"

Song 5:7 מצאוני השמרים הסבבים בעיר
הכוני פצעוני
The watchmen found me, they who go-about the city,
They struck me, they wounded me.

The two verses begin with the identical wording, though in this case we note a difference in the punctuation. In 3:3 the four words are spread over two small stichs, with *zaqef qaton* on השמרים and *ʾatnaḥ* on בעיר. The passage continues in an innocent or at least neutral fashion as the female lover simply asks the watchmen if they have seen her beloved. In 5:7, by contrast, the first four words are combined into one stich, with *tipḥa* on בעיר, so that already the reader is aware that something different is transpiring. The careful reader's instinct is confirmed when the verse continues with the very jarring statement that the watchmen struck the female lover and injured her (and, as the verse continues, mistreated her by removing her shawl from upon her). Naturally, we know very little about the oral reading tradition before the Masoretes created the system of accent/punctuation marks, but we believe that already in antiquity the individual trained in the Miqraʾ—that is, the proper oral reading of a skeletal written text—knew how to intone the text in distinct manners such as indicated and illustrated above.[21]

Song 4:1 and 6:5

Song 4:1 שׂערך כעדר העזים
שׂגלשׂו מהר גלעד
Your hair is like a flock of goats,
That flow down from Mount Gilead.

Song 6:5 שׂערך כעדר העזים
שׂגלשׂו מן הגלעד
Your hair is like a flock of goats,
That flow down from the Gilead.

With these two passages we move to a discussion of the *waṣf* poems.[22] Four times the physical features of the female lover are described, twice by her beloved (4:1–5 and 6:5–7), then once by her female companions (7:2–6) and then again by her beloved (7:8–10). The first two are very similar, especially since both begin with the hair and proceed downward, to either the breasts (4:5) or the cheeks (6:7). The third is the most different, (1) because it is spoken by a different character (or better, a set of characters), and (2) because it proceeds from bottom to top, in line with the setting of this *waṣf*, that is, the female lover as dancer, with an initial focus on her feet. The fourth is the least developed of these descriptions, as it focuses almost solely on the breasts (7:8–9), with but a quick nod to the nose and the palate (7:9–10).

A comparison of the parallel lines in these *waṣf* poems reveals that polyprosopon is at work. In the lines above, we note that the A-lines are identical but that the B-lines include a morphological change cum lexical omission. In 4:1 the prepositional phrase is מהר גלעד "from Mount Gilead," while in

21. For more on this topic, see S. Levin, "The 'Qeri' as the Primary Text of the Hebrew Bible," *General Linguistics* 35 (1995): 181–223.

22. Technically we already have entered this realm, since 4:1 discussed above begins the first *waṣf*.

6:5 we read מן הגלעד "from the Gilead." In the first instance, the form of the preposition is prefixed -מ, the noun הר "mountain" is included, and the toponym גלעד "Gilead" occurs without the definite article. In the second usage, the preposition occurs as the independent form מן, the noun הר "mountain" is absent, and the toponym הגלעד "the Gilead" occurs with the definite article. We have reflected the second and third of these differences in our translation (one cannot vary the English to indicate the different forms of "from").

These are all minor differences, but they serve as evidence of the extent to which the poet would go to vary the language of the composition. We also note that the expression הר גלעד in 4:1 is the only attestation of this usage in the Bible; in all other cases, the definite article is present: הר הגלעד (Gen 31:21, 23, 25; Deut 3:12; Judg 7:3). Poetry is less inclined to use the definite article, but nevertheless one wonders if the poet has not created the expression—notwithstanding its grammaticality (cf. ארץ גלעד three times in the Bible)—in order to distinguish the usage in 4:1 from that in 6:5 in one more minor way.

Song 4:2 and 6:6

Song 4:2 שניך כעדר הקצובות
שעלו מן הרחצה
Your teeth are like a flock of shorn-ones,
Who come up from the washing.

Song 6:6 שניך כעדר הרחלים
שעלו מן הרחצה
Your teeth are like a flock of ewes,
Who come up from the washing.

The parallel couplets are the same, letter for letter, word for word, and accent mark for accent mark, save for the difference between הקצובות "the shorn-ones" in 4:2 and הרחלים "the ewes" in 6:6.

Song 4:4 and 7:5

Song 4:4 כמגדל דויד צוארך
Like the tower of David is your neck.

Song 7:5 צוארך כמגדל השן
Your neck is like the tower of ivory.

The description of the neck of the female lover appears in the first and third of the *waṣf* poems. In both cases the neck is compared to a tower, though in the first case it is מגדל דויד "the tower of David," and in the second passage it is מגדל השן "the tower of ivory." In addition, in 4:4 the word order is simile followed by body part, while in 7:5 the word order is body part followed by simile.

Song 4:5 and 7:4

Song 4:5 שְׁני שדיך כשְׁני עפרים
תְּאוֹמֵי צביה
הרועים בשושנים
Your two breasts are like two fawns,
Twins of a doe,
Grazing among the lilies.

Song 7:4 שְׁני שדיך כשְׁני עפרים
תָּאֳמֵי צביה
Your two breasts are like two fawns,
Twins of a doe.

The first description of the breasts includes an additional line, portraying the fawns as grazing among the lilies. The second description lacks this line. If we compare the words that are present in the two passages, we note an exceedingly minor difference of a morphological nature: in 4:5 the plural (dual?) construct form is תְּאוֹמֵי, while in 7:4 we encounter the form תָּאֳמֵי.[23] The difference is about as minor as one could find in Hebrew, yet once more

23. The only grammar that treats this issue is H. Bauer and P. Leander, *Historische Grammatik der hebräischen Sprache* (Halle: Niemeyer, 1922), 535. Bauer and Leander proposed that the form תְּאוֹמֵי is the more original, on the assumption that the second vowel is a long vowel (and of course note the absolute form), with תָּאֳמֵי arising via *Analogiebildung* patterned after nouns with a short vowel in the second syllable. And while their nod to Akkadian *tuʾāmu* no longer can be used to support their argument—for the proper Akkadian form is *tūʾamu* (though note the alternative forms *tuʾīmu, tuʾû* [Neo-Assyrian])—the general argument still holds. For the Akkadian forms, see *CAD* [T], 443–44; and J. Black, A. George, and N. Postgate, *A Concise Dictionary of Akkadian* (Wiesbaden: Harrassowitz, 2000), 408.

it serves the literary purpose of attuning the listeners' ears to the nuances of the text.[24]

Song 5:2 and Other Similar Tags

In Song 5:2 the female lover imagines her beloved addressing her as follows: אחתי רעיתי יונתי תמתי "my sister, my darling, my dove, my perfect-one." Attention to the manner in which the male lover addresses his love reveals that only here are four terms strung together. The commonest usage is the one-word expression רעיתי "my darling" (1:9, 15; 2:2; 4:1, 7; 6:4). The second commonest usage is the two-word expression אחתי כלה "my sister, O bride"; indeed it becomes quite repetitive at a specific section of the Song of Songs (4:9, 10, 12; 5:1). Other usages are רעיתי יפתי "my darling, my beautiful" (2:10, 13), יונתי "my dove" (2:14), and יונתי תמתי "my dove, my perfect-one (6:9).

The first point to notice is the manner in which these phrases vary as one proceeds through the poem—but only to an extent. We agree with those scholars who have noted that the female voice uses much more expressive and varied language throughout the composition, with the male voice more limited in both its passion and its range.[25] The use of רעיתי יפתי "my darling, my beautiful" in 2:10, 13 in a passage with verbatim repetition (or nearly so; see below) is one indication of this. The series with אחתי כלה "my sister, O bride" used four times in quick succession at the end of chapter 4 and in the first verse of chapter 5 (see above) is another such indication.

In light of this evidence, the words imagined by the female lover in 5:2 are striking: she presents her beloved as saying אחתי רעיתי יונתי תמתי "my sister, my darling, my dove, my perfect-one," the only case of four tags placed together (indeed, the only case with more than two tags; there are none with three). Her passion leads her to envision him speaking in this manner, though as the attentive reader knows, the male lover never speaks in such fashion.

Finally, we note that she is the one who introduces the word תמתי "my perfect-one" at this juncture; it is not a term that the male lover has used in addressing her. And even though the male lover is not present in the dream

24. Incidentally, in the only two other instances of this word in the Bible, we encounter another example of polyptoton. Compare Gen 25:24 והנה תומם בבטנה (said of Rebekah) and 38:27 והנה תאומים בבטנה (said of Tamar). Clearly this noun was subject to morphological variation in ancient Hebrew, and the authors of the biblical texts seized the opportunity for full literary effect.

25. Noted in a number of essays in A. Brenner, ed., *A Feminist Companion to the Song of Songs* (Sheffield: JSOT Press, 1993).

scene in 5:2–6, quite remarkably he "hears" this word, for in his last reference to his love in 6:9, he indeed does use more creative language with the two-word expression יונתי תמתי "my dove, my perfect-one"—though it is not his creativity per se, since she spoke the words first as the second half of her four-word string in 5:2. If we look at these two words individually, we note the following: the male lover takes the one term that he has used least of all, namely, יונתי "my dove," heard previously only in 2:14—and there, most strikingly, in a context that calls for an actual dove!—and he adjoins to it the one word that he has not used to this point at all but that he "heard" from the mouth of his female lover, namely, תמתי "my perfect-one."[26] The last point to note in regard to this phrase is that the Masora uses the same punctuation marks—*munaḥ* and *zaqef qaton*—on this phrase in both 5:2 and 6:9. Once more, we believe that the oral presenter of these lines in antiquity would have intoned them in like fashion, thereby guiding the listeners to grasp the connection between the two passages.[27]

Song 5:13 and 6:2

Song 5:13 לחיו כערוגת הבשׂם
His cheeks are like a bed of spices.

Song 6:2 דודי ירד לגנו
לערוגות הבשׂם
My beloved went down to his garden,
To the beds of spices.

The settings of these two passages are quite different, so a general comparison cannot be made. We take note, however, of the presence of the morphological distinction between singular ערוגת הבשׂם "a bed of spices" in 5:13 and plural ערוגות הבשׂם "beds of spices" in 6:2 (our inclusion of "the" in the translation above is due only to the necessities of English). Once more the listener is invited to pay attention to the details, in this final instance of variation in our text.

---

26. This practice in the Song of Songs may be compared to the similar practice of oneupmanship in Job, in which the individual speakers continually reference one another, adopting and reworking what the other has said, often with profound subtlety. See Noegel, *Janus Parallelism in the Book of Job*, 131–35.

27. For another example of the same set of Masoretic marks serving to link two phrases at some distance to each other, see G. A. Rendsburg, "Hebrew Philological Notes (II)," *HS* 42 (2001): 191.

IDENTICAL PASSAGES

We do not mean to imply that there are no instances of verbatim repetition. We have identified the following four examples in the Song of Songs.[28] In addition to the identical wording of these passages, note that in all four cases the Masoretic punctuation is identical too.

Song 2:10 = 2:13 קומי לך רעיתי יפתי ולכי לך
Arise, my darling, my beautiful, and go forth.

Song 2:17 = 4:6 עד שׁיפוח היום
ונסו הצללים
Until the day(-wind) blows,
And the shadows flee.[29]

Song 3:6 = 8:5 מי זאת עלה מן המדבר
Who is this coming up from the wilderness.[30]

Song 4:3 = 6:7 כפלח הרמון רקתך
מבעד לצמתך

---

28. A fifth instance might be Song 1:8 = 6:1 היפה בנשׁים "O most beautiful among women," for even though this is only a two-word phrase, the expression does stand as its own stich in both verses. Nevertheless, due to its shortness, we elect to omit this passage from consideration in this section.

29. One notes that 4QCant[b] reads הטללים at 2:17 (see above, Excursus to Chapter 1), and thus one may wonder if this witness to the Song of Songs included variation in this particular instance. Recall, however, that this Dead Sea Scrolls manuscript skips from 4:3 to 4:8, with a *vacat* at this point (that is to say, the manuscript is intact here), and thus we do not possess Song 4:6 in 4QCant[b]. For the text, see Tov, "Canticles," 214.

30. Given the textual remains of the Song of Songs from Qumran, one might expect 3:6 to be extant, but such is not the case. Note the following: (1) 4QCant[a] includes a tiny fragment with 3:4–5 and a larger one with 3:7–4:6, but with no remains of 3:6; (2) notwithstanding the very fragmentary nature of 4QCant[b] frag. 2 i, with only a few letters attested at the ends of the lines, enough remains to allow the conclusion that 3:6–8 was not part of this manuscript; and (3) 4QCant[c] includes a few letters of 3:7–8 only. In short, we have no Qumran evidence by which to determine the shape of Song 3:6, and of course the same holds for 8:5 as well. For the texts, see Tov, "Canticles," 199–200, 213, 219.

Like a slice of pomegranate is your cheek,
Behind your braids.[31]

It is not easy to determine why these specific passages are identical, though two possible explanations come to mind. First, one could argue that this divergence from the norm of polyprosopon also keeps the hearers on their toes. That is to say, listeners to the Song of Songs, accustomed to variation as they proceed through the poetry, now must be attuned to verbatim repetition as well. Thus, these instances of verbatim repetition provide a certain stability that lends even greater effectiveness to the variation surveyed above.

On the other hand, we might argue that even in the four cases of 2:10 = 2:13, 2:17 = 4:6, 3:6 = 8:5, and 4:3 = 6:7, there is some evidence of variation. For instance, in the first example, we note that the Ketiv of 2:13 reads לכי for the second word, while the Qeri provides the reading לך. There is no reason to assume a scribal error here (under the influence of לכי "go" later in the verse); it is very possible if not probable that the Ketiv preserves the original form here, especially when one recalls that the Ketiv represents an IH feature (see above ch. 1, at §1.2.7). While this cannot be proven,[32] if it is correct, then 2:10 and 13 are not identical but instead present morphological variants in the two passages. In addition, note that the passage cited above appears as the second half of each verse, with different beginnings to 2:10 and 13.

If we look at the next two examples, we note that the opposite occurs: the verses begin in identical fashion but then diverge. Thus, 2:17 and 4:6 commence with the couplet presented above (that is, through the *ʾatnaḥ* in both verses), but then the verses continue with different wordings. The second half of 2:17, in fact, has its own parallels in 2:9 and 8:14, which is where the variation is to be seen (see above).

Similarly, in the third example, we note that 3:6 and 8:5 both begin with the stich presented above, but then they too diverge with different wordings. Interestingly, however, the language of 8:5 includes the word מתרפקת "leaning," which provides a long-range echo of the word מקטרת "redolent" (see also the latter's alliterative partner כתימרות "as columns," as studied above, ch. 2, pp. 81–82). In other words, the poet began the two verses in identical

31. In this case, we note that 4QCant[b] reads ומבעד לצמתך "and behind your braids," with an additional -ו (see Tov, "Canticles," 214), but alas we do not possess Song 6:7 with which to compare.

32. It would be very convenient for our argument if 4QCant[b], with its higher usage of IH features, used לכי in this passage, but it does not. Instead, the reading לך occurs; see Tov, "Canticles," 210.

fashion and then attempted to rehearse the same sounds as the two passages went their separate ways.

Concerning the fourth example above, we note that 4:3 is actually the second half of that verse (that is, the couplet follows the ʾ*atnaḥ*) but that 6:7 stands alone as its own verse. Perhaps this is enough of a difference that somehow would be noted by the listeners, assuming that the oral reader emphasized pauses in some fashion.

If these four examples are understood as polyprosoponic variation in their own right, even though not on a par with the technique surveyed in the main body of this chapter, we arrive at a position in which no passages in the Song of Songs are exact duplicates of each other (except, that is, for the first two instances of the refrain, for which see above).

Regardless of how these identical passages are to be analyzed, we believe that we have uncovered a rhetorical device in Hebrew poetry that hitherto has not been recognized or, at the very least, has not been appreciated. We may add this feature to the panoply of literary techniques that the ancient Hebrew poets utilized in crafting their exquisite compositions.

4
The Genre of the Song of Songs in the Light of Arabic Poetic Traditions*

Regarding the numerous and varied interpretations of the Song of Songs, J. William Whedbee remarked: "Perhaps no book in the Bible offers a greater diversity of readings than the Song of Songs."[1] Indeed, the Song has nearly as many interpretations as it does interpreters. This is not a phenomenon of more recent times, for already in antiquity diverse hermeneutic strategies fueled the debate over whether the poem should enter the canon of sacred scripture. Had not Rabbi Aqiba held out in favor of accepting the poem as an allegory (see m. Yad. 3:5), in contrast to those who read it as a sensual love poem,[2] the Song might have remained but an obscure reference in postbiblical Jewish texts.[3]

---

* We would like to thank Prof. James T. Monroe of the University of California at Berkeley, Prof. Suzanne Pinckney Stetkevych of Indiana University, and Prof. Farhat Ziadeh of the University of Washington for their insightful comments on a previous draft of this essay.

1. J. W. Whedbee, "Paradox and Parody in the Song of Solomon: Towards a Comic Reading of the Most Sublime Song," in Brenner, *A Feminist Companion to the Song of Songs*, 266. For a useful and brief synopsis of the various interpretive strategies applied to the Song, see R. Gordis, "The Song of Songs," in *Mordecai M. Kaplan: Jubilee Volume on the Occasion of His Seventieth Birthday* (ed. M. Davis; New York: Jewish Theological Seminary of America, 1953), 281–325, repr. in Gordis, *Poets, Prophets, and Sages: Essays in Biblical Interpretation* (Bloomington: Indiana University Press, 1971), 351–98.

2. See the similar attempt by J.-P. Audet ("The Meaning of the Canticle of Canticles," *TD* 5 [1957]: 88–92) to "de-eroticize" the Song of Songs.

3. Still, it is important to note that the allegorical interpretation of the Song cannot be traced back before 70 C.E. See R. Kimelman, "Rabbi Yohanan and Origen on the Song of Songs: A Third-Century Jewish Disputation," *HTR* 73 (1980): 567–95. In Christian circles, the exegesis of the Song as historical allegory is rare before

Since Aqiba's time, the discovery of ancient Near Eastern texts has provided scholars with a wealth of new comparative material. Among the most rewarding advances have come from comparisons with bedouin and classical Arabic poetry. In particular, one Arabic form has yielded numerous similarities with the biblical Song in style and imagery, namely, the Syrian *waṣf* (literally "description"), whose primary feature is a detailed and elaborate physical description of the poem's male and female characters.[4] Typically targeted for this comparison are Song 4:1–7; 5:10–16; 6:4–7; and 7:2–8.

The Arabic analogs were the focus of scholarly attention during the late nineteenth and early twentieth centuries,[5] but with the accumulation of Mesopotamian, Ugaritic, Egyptian, and even Indian[6] materials in the latter half

---

the time of Nicolas de Lyra (ca. 1270–1349), who himself was heavily influenced by Jewish sources, in particular the work of Rashi. See P. S. Alexander, "The Song of Songs as Historical Allegory: Notes on the Development of an Exegetical Tradition," in *Targumic and Cognate Studies: Essays in Honour of Martin McNamara* (ed. K. J. Cathcart and M. Maher; JSOTSup 230; Sheffield: Sheffield Academic Press, 1996), 14–29. Nevertheless, as Alexander noted, the presence of the Song of Songs at Qumran suggests that "the book was being read allegorically, since it is hardly conceivable, given the religious outlook of the group behind the Scrolls, that they would have read the text literally" (15 n. 3).

4. See J. G. Wetzstein, "Die syrische Dreschtafel," *Zeitschrift für Ethnologie* 5 (1873): 270–302; and R. Gordis, "A Wedding Song for Solomon," *JBL* 63 (1944): 264.

5. Wetzstein, "Die syrische Dreschtafel," pp. 270–302.

6. For Mesopotamia, see T. J. Meek, "Babylonian Parallels to the Song of Songs," *JBL* 43 (1924): 245–52; T. J. Meek, "Canticles and the Tammuz Cult," *AJSL* 39 (1922): 1–14; and T. J. Meek, *The Song of Songs and the Fertility Cult: Symposium of the Oriental Club of Philadelphia* (Philadelphia: n.p., 1924), 48–79.

For Ugarit, see H. G. May, "Some Cosmic Connotations of *Mayim Rabbîm*, 'Many Waters,'" *JBL* 74 (1955): 9–21; K. N. Schoville, "The Impact of the Ras Shamra Texts on the Study of the Song of Songs" (Ph.D. diss.; University of Wisconsin, 1969); and especially the outstanding survey by M. H. Pope, *Song of Songs* (AB 7C; Garden City, N.Y.: Doubleday, 1977), 89–229. See also more recently W. Tyloch, "Ugaritic Poems and the Song of Songs," in *Šulmu IV: Everyday Life in the Ancient Near East: Papers Presented at the International Conferance Poznań, 19–22 September, 1989* (ed. J. Zablocka and S. Zawadski; Historia 182; Poznań: Uniwersytet im Adama Mickiewicza w Poznaniu, 1993), 295–301; W. G. E. Watson, "Some Ancient Near Eastern Parallels to the Song of Songs," in *Words Remembered, Texts Renewed: Essays in Honour of John F. A. Sawyer* (ed. J. Davies, G. Harvey, and W. G. E. Watson; JSOTSup 195; Sheffield: Sheffield Academic Press 1995), 253–71.

For Egypt, see Fox, *Song of Songs*; and S. Israelit-Groll, "Ostracon Nash 12 and Chapter 5 of Song of Songs," in *Proceedings of the Tenth World Congress of Jewish*

of the twentieth century, scholars turned their attention to these sources for parallels with the Song of Songs.[7] Most of this information was incorporated by Marvin Pope into his magisterial commentary, with its view of the Song as a cultic hymn.[8]

More recently, scholars have renewed an interest in the *waṣf*, which has led them to discuss the Song's possible comic aspects,[9] in particular the way it employs description to an almost absurd degree as a form of baroque and subtle sarcasm. According to this view, one senses the sarcasm, for example, when the male lover compares his beloved's neck to "the tower of David" (4:4) or her nose to "the tower of Lebanon facing Damascus" (7:5).[10] While these comparisons have come under fire recently from certain quarters,[11] the larger hermeneutical problem faced by *waṣf* comparativists is the need to explain the non-*waṣf* sections of the Song. Such is done by appealing to theories of

---

Studies: Jerusalem, August 16–24, 1989: Division A: The Bible and Its World (Jerusalem: World Union of Jewish Studies, 1990), 131–35.

For India, see A. Mariaselvan, *The Song of Songs and Ancient Tamil Love Poems: Poetry and Symbolism* (Rome: Pontifical Biblical Institute, 1988).

7. See, e.g., J. M. Sasson, "On M. H. Pope's *Song of Songs* [AB 7C]," *Maarav* 1 (1978–79): 177–96; J. S. Cooper, "New Cuneiform Parallels to the Song of Songs," *JBL* 90 (1971): 157–62; D. O. Edzard, "Zur Ritualtafel der sog. 'Love Lyrics,'" in *Language, Literature, and History: Philological and Historical Studies Presented to Erica Reiner* (ed. F. Rochberg-Halton; New Haven: American Oriental Society, 1987), 57–69. On the rituals that address sexual jealousy, see G. Leick, *Sex and Eroticism in Mesopotamian Literature* (London: Routledge, 1994), 239–46. See also M. Nissinen, "Love Lyrics of Nabû and Tašmetu: An Assyrian Song of Songs," in *"Und Mose schrieb dieses Lied auf": Studien zum Alten Testament und zum Alten Orient: Festschrift für Oswald Loretz zur Vollendung seines 70. Lebensjahres* (ed. M. Dietrich and I. Kottsieper; AOAT 250; Münster: Ugarit-Verlag, 1998), 585–634.

8. Pope, *Song of Songs*.

9. A. Brenner, "'Come Back, Come Back the Shulammite' (Song of Songs 7.1–10): A Parody of the *Waṣf* Genre," in *On Humor and the Comic in the Hebrew Bible* (ed. Y. T. Radday and A. Brenner; JSOTSup 92; Bible and Literature Series 23; Sheffield: Almond, 1990); Whedbee, "Paradox and Parody," 266–78; and M. H. Segal, "Song of Songs," *VT* 12 (1962): 480; repr. in idem, *The Pentateuch, Its Composition and Its Authorship and Other Biblical Studies* (Jerusalem: Magnes, 1967), 230–31.

10. See also Segal, "Song of Songs," 480; repr. in idem, *Pentateuch*, 230–31.

11. See P. Trible, "Depatriarchalizing in Biblical Interpretation," *JAAR* 41 (1973): 42–45; Ilana Pardes, *Countertraditions in the Bible: A Feminist Approach* (Cambridge: Harvard University Press, 1992), 118–43; and M. Falk, "The *waṣf*," in Brenner, *A Feminist Companion to the Song of Songs*, 225–33.

multiple editors and sources, for which no textual verification exists.[12] Nevertheless, the insights into the sarcastic tone of the Song, brought to light by the comparisons with *waṣf* sections of poems, remain defensible.[13] Moreover, comparisons to Arabic poetry have led some scholars to propose new anthropological models for understanding the Song, based on modern bedouin societies in which poems of desire can represent an alternative discourse among female members of the community.[14]

These and other similarities between the Song of Songs and Arabic poetry demonstrate how literary features and styles often cross geographic and temporal boundaries. Indeed, many of the poetic images and devices familiar to Arab bedouin and classical poets can be found in the Bible and in other ancient Near Eastern literature.[15] Still, the full gamut of interpretive approaches briefly outlined above confirms Whedbee's remark that "no book in the Bible offers a greater diversity of readings."[16] For this reason, before adding to what is obviously already a long list of exegetical approaches, we should note that some of the numerous and varied interpretations are not necessarily mutually exclusive. Rather, they depend to some extent upon the Song's interpretive community and upon the historical period in which one reads the poem.[17] It is, in the words of Magne Sæbø, "a multileveled literary

12. R. E. Murphy, "The Unity of the Song of Songs," *VT* 29 (1979): 436–43. For an examination of possible poetic units in the Song, see F. Landsberger, "Poetic Units within the Song of Songs," *JBL* 73 (1954): 203–16.

13. Whedbee, "Paradox and Parody," 266–78.

14. See, e.g., the social anthropological study of D. Bergant, "'My Beloved Is Mine and I Am His' (Song 2:16)," *Semeia* 68 (1996): 23–40. On the Song as an alternative female discourse, see D. M. Carr, "Gender and the Shaping of Desire in the Song of Songs," *JBL* 119 (2000): 233–48. For a sobering critique of the difficulties in applying anthropological models to ancient Israel, see J. K. Chance, "The Anthropology of Honor and Shame: Culture, Values and Practice," *Semeia* 68 (1996): 143–44.

15. See Watson, *Classical Hebrew Poetry*, *passim*.

16. Whedbee, "Paradox and Parody," 266.

17. See S. Bakon, "Song of Songs," *JBQ* 22 (1994): 211–20; and much earlier the following remark by L. Waterman, "The Rôle of Solomon in the Song of Songs," *JBL* 44 (1925): 187: "A fertilty cult liturgy reduced to folk poetry and reinterpreted by a political *motif*, that was later partly obscured by a divergent national ideal, would seem to satisfy and explain Solomon's connection to the poem." For an exhaustive treatment of how different historical circumstances and contexts can influence the interpretive strategies of different faith communities (with special attention to the Song of Songs), see G. D. Martin, "Textual Histories of Early Jewish Writings: Multivalencies vs. the Quest for 'The Original'" (Ph.D. diss.; University of Washington, 2007).

composition."[18] The Song's interpretive history, therefore, allows us to see in the Song not only an erotic love poem but also cultic references of a bygone age, an allegory in praise of God's love, and elements of sarcastic humor.

Our focus, however, will not be on the Song's complete interpretive history but rather only on the proposed parallels to Arabic literature (e.g., *waṣf* poems). In particular, this study will augment this previous work by offering a new interpretive framework for the Song based on hitherto unrecognized Arabic parallels, specifically, the genres of *tašbīb* and *hijāʾ*. Our reason for treating them together (along with other terms) will be made clear below.

Tašbīb and Hijāʾ

Tašbīb is essentially poetry of praise, though it also can disgrace. While its elaborate descriptions of the woman's charms qualify it as a devotional expression of love, its often erotic, if not explicitly sexual, language, especially when directed at another man's wife or sister, marks it as a provocative insult on the woman's character, and by extension, on the woman's husband and kinsmen. When the object of flattery is the wife or wives of a ruling caliph, the poem is tantamount to a political invective.

A related genre is that of *hijāʾ*, which is most easily defined as a poetry of "lampooning" or "invective."[19] Poems of this genre, unlike the *tašbīb*, antedate the medieval era and typically, like those of the *tašbīb* and *waṣf* types (the latter is often a subset of *hijāʾ*),[20] teem with sarcastic flattery and elab-

---

18. M. Sæbø, "On the Canonicity of the Song of Songs," in *Texts, Temples, and Traditions: A Tribute to Menahem Haran* (ed. M. V. Fox et al.; Winona Lake, Ind.: Eisenbrauns, 1996), 272. Though Sæbø's comment addresses the levels of compositional, not necessarily interpretive, history.

19. C. Pellat, "*Hijāʾ*," *EncIsl* 3:352–55; and S. P. Stetkevych, *Abū Tammām and the Poetics of the ʿAbbasid Age* (Studies in Arabic Literature 13; Leiden: Brill, 1991), 14. Work on the *hijāʾ* genre has been undertaken by several prominent scholars since the nineteenth century and has continued with some lapse until the present day. See also A. el Tayib, "Pre-Islamic Poetry," in *Arabic Literature to the End of the Umayyad Period* (ed. A. F. L. Beeston et al.; Cambridge: Cambridge University Press, 1983), 73–81.

20. G. J. van Gelder, *The Bad and the Ugly: Attitudes towards Invective Poetry (Hijāʾ) in Classical Arabic Literature* (Leiden: Brill, 1988), 65. In pre-Islamic poetry, love is dealt with almost exclusively by way of the *nasīb* or *qaṣīda*. See G. Schoeler, "Bashshār b. Burd, Abū ʾl-ʿAtāhiyah, Abū Nīwās," in *ʿAbbasid Belles-Lettres: Arabic Literature 750–1258* (ed. J. Ashtiany et al.; Cambridge History of Arabic Literature; Cambridge: Cambridge University Press, 1990), 281; and Tayib, "Pre-Islamic Poetry," 93–104.

orate descriptions. The difference between *hijāʾ* and *tašbīb* may be seen as one of degree: the *hijāʾ* is usually the more lewd and openly crass of the two. Whereas a *tašbīb* may function in the right context to stain a person's character, a *hijāʾ* invariably does. Nevertheless, the two can overlap considerably in conception and purpose, for both can ridicule a ruler by flattering his wife or betrothed.[21] Geert Jan van Gelder observes:

> *Hijāʾ* and love poetry are not always as clearly opposite as they seem: the description of female charms (*tashbīb*) was not rarely interpreted as a form of invective by the indignant husbands, brothers, and other relatives; an interpretation that was often intended by the poet himself.[22]

Tašbīb and *hijāʾ* poems also have much in common with later *ghazal* compositions, or "boasting love poems" (*tašbīb* and *ghazal* are often used synonymously).[23] Sometimes described as "He said, she said" poems because of their male-female dialogues, *ghazal* compositions are free-standing poems (unlike the *tašbīb*) and tend to be shorter than *tašbīb* poems. Another term often appearing as a synonym for a *tašbīb* or *ghazal* is *nasīb*, "panegyric erotic prelude,"[24] though strictly speaking the *nasīb* is a much older poetic form and represents only the opening erotic verses of a *tašbīb* or *ghazal*.[25]

---

21. J. T. Monroe, "The Strip-Tease That Was Blamed on Abū Bakr's Naughty Son: Was Father Being Shamed, or Was the Poet Having Fun? (Ibn Quzmān's *Zajal* No. 133)," in *Homoeroticism in Classical Arabic Literature* (ed. J. W. Wright and E. K. Rowson; New York: Columbia University Press, 1997), 102: "A more subtle form of *hijāʾ* in the Umayyad period praised women in order to put their menfolk to shame," with citation of van Gelder, *The Bad and the Ugly*, 55. See also H. Javadi, *Satire in Persian Literature* (Rutherford, N.J.: Fairleigh Dickinson University Press, 1988), 198–219.

22. Van Gelder, *The Bad and The Ugly*, 105.

23. See, e.g., A. Hamori, "Love Poetry (*Ghazal*)," in Ashtiany et al., *ʿAbbasid Belles-Lettres*, 202–18; A. Bausani, "*Ghazal*," *EncIsl* 2:1028–36; J. A. Hayward, "*Madiḥ, madḥ*," *EncIsl* 5:958; and Tayib, "Pre-Islamic Poetry," 56–67.

24. Note the remark by Bausani, "*ghazal*," 978: "The meaning of *nasīb* is rarely defined by medieval scholars, nor can the semantic relation between the terms *nasīb* and *ghazal* be established with precision."

25. The *nasīb* is also often nostalgic and recalls past encampments; it is also much older than the *ghazal*, since it is the only form of Arabic love poetry preserved from pre-Islamic times. See R. Jacobi, "*Nasīb*," *EncIsl* 7:978–83. The *nasīb* also opens a *qaṣīda*, or "descriptive polythematic ode," as well. For an in-depth study on the complexities of the *nasīb*, see M. A. Sells, "Guises of the *Ghūl*: Dissembling Simile

It is important to recognize here a certain degree of flexibility with regard to the usage of these terms, for as we continue our comparative look at the biblical Song, we shall find a great deal of overlap between and among these interrelated genres. In addition, as we shall see, when viewed collectively, the various genres provide a more holistic interpretive framework into which to place the Song. Nevertheless, the focus of this chapter will be not on the Song's relation to Arabic "love poetry" generally but rather its similarity to "love poems" that are employed as invectives, specifically to those poems labeled *tašbīb* and *hijāʾ*. It is these genres that convey what medieval Arab scholars called *taʾkīd aḏ-ḏamm bimā yušbih al-madḥ* "emphasizing blame through what resembles praise."[26]

In terms of language and poetic features, Arabic invective poems, especially those of the *hijāʾ* type, are often composed in a colloquial dialect lending them a "street-talk" flavor that adds poignancy to the poem's overall function.[27] In addition, both *tašbīb* and *hijāʾ* exploit the full range of stock motifs found in a number of other classical genres. Thus, in invective poetry one finds the frequent mention of wine, song, vineyards, gardens, orchards, towers, fortifications, walls, military equipment, and comparisons to palm trees and animals, usually gazelles, horses, and lions. In addition, the poet not only praises his lover but frequently describes the laudation of his lover by maidens and nobles. In *hijāʾ* poems specifically, one also finds topics of familial injustice, usually in the form of complaints of overgrazing by other members of the tribe, though at times more serious matters such as incest and other sexual aberrations.

Another motif found in *tašbīb* and *hijāʾ* poems is that of unrequited love. The poet or character must endure the cruelty of the lover's avoidance usually with total submission.[28] The poet, captured by the woman's gaze

---

and Semantic Overflow in the Classical *Nasīb*," in *Reorientations: Arabic and Persian Poetry* (ed. S. P. Stetkevych; Bloomington: Indiana University Press, 1994), 130–64.

26. Van Gelder, *The Bad and The Ugly*, 113.

27. For this feature in the poems of Ibn Quzmān, see van Gelder, *The Bad and the Ugly*, 8. On the mixture of classical and street language in the poems of Archilochus, see H. D. Rankin, *Archilochus of Paros* (Park Ridge, N.J.: Noyes, 1977), 36–46, 58, 65, 86.

28. For the social and cultural aspects behind such poems, see L. Abū-Lughod, "Shifting Politics in Bedouin Love Poetry," in *Language and the Politics of Emotion* (ed. C. A. Lutz and L. Abū-Lughod; Cambridge: Cambridge University Press, 1990). The genre known as an ʿUdhrī *Ghazal* might also shed light on the theme of unrequited love in the biblical Song. On the characteristics of this genre, see Hamori, "Love Poetry (*Ghazal*)," 205–7.

(often through a veil), frequently describes this love as an intoxicating wine. Sometimes, the lover, whose teeth, hair, eyes, skin, and body are described elaborately and erotically with reference to precious metals, spices, and ivory, expresses his desires in the form of a dream. Afterwards there sometimes follows a scene praising the military prowess and troops of the ruler.

Invective poems were not taken lightly by ruling caliphs. They could land poets in prison, who sometimes were punished by flogging and even by death.[29] Their lofty praise, whether exaggerated or not, disgraced their subjects by way of name calling, giving detailed descriptions of someone's physical form (*ḫalq*, which is tantamount to a *waṣf*), especially of their beauty (*jamāl*), the mention of a well-shaped body (*baṣta*), and/or statements infringing the character (*ḫuluq*) of someone.[30] Ambiguity, therefore, was essential to the *tašbīb* and *hijā*ʾ, because it allowed poets to escape censure. This ambiguity could come in the form of "hyperbolic description" (*al-ifrāṭ fī ʿal-ṣifa*), as Ibn al-Muʿtazz (d. 908) noted in his *Kitāb al-Badī*ʿ (*Book of the New Style*),[31] or by way of subtle allusions and puns. Whether to underscore an invective's ambiguity or to lend impact to its more ribald aspects, some poets even opened their invectives with staightforward erotic praise, as Ibn al-Rīmī informs us: "Don't you see that before *hijā*ʾ poems, at their beginning I let *nasīb* precede."[32]

The poet's use of *nasīb* as an erotic prelude to invective is worthy of comment. We have mentioned above how previous scholars have compared the Song with the Arab poet's employment of the *waṣf* "description," but technically speaking, the *waṣf* does not constitute a "genre" of Arabic poetry. Rather (much like its synonym *naʿt* "qualification"[33]), it is a term that describes a poetic feature, or the way in which certain genres of poetry proceed, such as the *nasīb*. This does not negate the value of previous comparisons to the *waṣf*, but it does suggest the need for a more holistic appreciation of the poetic genres into which the *waṣf* is incorporated. Since *waṣf* is a feature of the *nasīb*, and since the *nasīb* is often employed to open *tašbīb* and *hijā*ʾ poems,[34] our

29. S. A. Bonebakker, "Religious Prejudice against Poetry in Early Islam," *Medievalia et Humanistica: Studies in Medieval & Renaissance Culture* 7 (1976): 77–99, especially 84 (though also 85, 87–88). See also M. M. Badawi, "The Function of Rhetoric in Medieval Arabic Poetry: Abū Tammām's Ode on Amorium," *JAL* 9 (1978): 45.

30. Van Gelder, *The Bad and the Ugly*, 61.

31. Ibid., 60.

32. From his *Minhāj*, 351. Translation by van Gelder, *The Bad and the Ugly*, 105.

33. G. Troupeau, "*Naʿt*" *EncIsl* 7:1034.

34. Especially after the ninth century C.E. See Hamori, "Love Poetry (*Ghazal*)," 207.

comparison of the biblical Song of Songs to invective poetry also must consider the characteristics of the *nasīb*.

It is in this light that we turn briefly to the work of Michael Sells,[35] whose work on the *nasīb* has fostered a new appreciation for its poetic subtleties. In particular, he has shown how the sophisticated use of simile in the *nasīb* can produce meaning on both individual and communal planes by compounding the simile's metonymic associations.

> The [simile's] link is not one of similarity, but of metonymy, in particular, the synecdoche variety of metonymic association, a part used to express the whole.... It is at the intersection of the logic of similarity and the logic of association that meaning overflows.[36]

The collective use of similes in the *nasīb* allows the poet to produce meaning on multiple levels. On one level, the similes paint an erotic portrait of the beloved. On another, the simile's cumulative web of metonymy conjures mythic, religious, and political associations that push the poem's interpretation beyond its surface reading. In this way, Sells observes, "The union of lover and beloved that is the point of the departure for the *nasīb* is a microcosm of the union of the differing tribes."[37] As we shall demonstrate shortly, Sells's observation applies equally to the biblical Song, whose descriptive erotic similes similarly speak on individual and communal/tribal levels.

The Song of Songs as an Ancient Invective

Even a cursory look at the Song of Songs will illustrate its similarity to the genres of *tašbīb* and *hijā*ʾ. The biblical book shares not only numerous themes, images, and motifs with the Arabic poetry under consideration here, but, as we shall argue below, a common purpose as well. Though the biblical Song and the Arabic invective genres functioned in very different cultural matrices, the conservative nature of Islamic poetry,[38] along with the successful identification of certain sections of the Song with the *waṣf*, encourages our comparison. Indeed, one of the earliest scholars to work on *hijā*ʾ poetry, Ignaz Goldziher (not surprisingly, since so much of modern Arabic studies

35. Sells, "Guises of the *Ghūl*," 130–64.

36. Ibid., 156.

37. Ibid., 137.

38. For ancient Near Eastern features in ninth-century Islamic poetry, see S. Sperl, "Islamic Kingship and Arabic Panegyric Poetry in the Early 9th Century," *JAL* 8 (1977): 20–35, especially 21, 23–25.

begins with his work), already saw links to the Bible, although not with the Song of Songs.[39] Moreover, there is evidence that a similar "invective genre of praise" was known elsewhere in the Mediterranean world as early as the seventh century B.C.E. James Monroe observed:

> The technique of compromising a man's honour by composing love poems to his womenfolk is very ancient in the shame-oriented cultures of the Mediterranean, as may be concluded from the story (whether true or not, it was universally known in Antiquity) of the Greek poet Archilochus, who was born in the first half of the seventh century B.C., and Neobulé, daughter of Lycambes and Amphimedo.[40]

Like the medieval *tašbīb* and *hijāʾ* poets, Archilochus too composed his invectives in the colloquial dialect.[41] Moreover, as Walter Burkert has demonstrated, Archilochus probably had Near Eastern sources at his disposal.[42] Thus, it is possible, if not likely, that an invective genre of praise existed in the ancient Near East as well, even though clear examples thereof have hitherto not been identified.[43]

---

39. See I. Goldziher, *Abhandlungen zur arabischen Philologie* (2 vols.; Leiden: Brill, 1896), 1:42. In the first chapter, entitled, "Über die Vorgeschichte der Higaʾ-Poesie," (1–105), the great Arabist drew an etymological analogy with the cognate root הגה "murmur, utter an incantation" in Biblical Hebrew.

40. Monroe, "The Strip-Tease," 109. Early Greek and Pre-Islamic poetry share many other features as well, e.g., several mythopoetic symbols. See S. P. Stetkevych, "Intoxication and Immorality: Wine and Associated Imagery in Al-Maʿarri's Garden," in *Literature East and West, Critical Pilgrimages: Studies in the Arabic Literary Tradition* (ed. J. W. Wright and E. K. Rowson; Austin: University of Texas, 1989), 210–32, especially 222–25.

41. See Rankin, *Archilochus of Paros*, 36–46, 61–65.

42. W. Burkert, *The Orientalizing Revolution: Near Eastern Influence on Greek Culture in the Early Archaic Age* (Cambridge: Harvard University Press, 1992), 121–23. See also M. L. West, "Some Oriental Motifs in Archilochus," *ZPE* 102 (1994): 1–5; and W. L. Moran, "An Assyriological Gloss on the New Archilochos Fragment," *HSPh* 82 (1978): 17–19.

43. Though this essay concentrates on the Song of Songs, we invite scholars of Egyptian and Mesopotamian poetry, especially love poetry, to investigate whether or not those compositions also contain comedic or satirical traits. Egyptian erotic poetry seems particularly promising in this regard. See, e.g., J. A. Omlin, *Der Papyrus 55001 und seine satirische-erotischen Zeichnungen und Inschriften* (Catalogo del Museo Egizio di Torino 3; Turin: Edizioni d'Arte Fratelli Pozo, 1973). The Egyptian mythological material also can carry political invective. See already J. Spiegel, *Die Erzählung von Streite des Horus und Seth in Pap. Beatty I als Literaturwerk* (Leipziger

We find additional justification for comparing the Song of Songs to Arabic invective poetry by looking at the Song's interpretive history. In particular, it is interesting to note that in his treatise *De divisione philosophiae*, Domingo González, Archdeacon of Segovia and dignitary in the cathedral of Toledo (ca. 1400 C.E.), pointed to the biblical Song of Songs as an illustration of poetic comedy/satire into which the poet himself does not enter.[44] When we consider also that Averroes, in his paraphrase of Aristotle's *Poetics*, rendered the Greek word κωμωδέω "comedy" as *hijāʾ*, it is possible that as early as the fifteenth century[45] the Song of Songs was interpreted, at least by some, as an invective.[46] Moreover, it is now clear that Hebrew poets of an even earlier period, such as Todros Abulafia (1247–1306), also composed invectives of the *hijāʾ* type.[47] Such observations, therefore, allow us to close

---

Ägyptologische Studien, 9; Glückstadt: Augustin, 1937), 68–70. For possible Mesopotamian counterparts we note the presence of insults between the goddess Ishtar of Babylon and her rival Zarpanitum over the privilege of serving the god Marduk in an Old Akkadian love incantation. See J. G. Westenholz and A. Westenholz, "Help for Rejected Suitors: The Old Akkadian Love Incantation: MAD V 8," *Or* 46 (1977): 214 (see also 213 n. 25 for the citation of additional Akkadian literature in which one finds unflattering remarks mingled into love lyrics). Finally, see also Nissinen, "Love Lyrics of Nabû and Tašmetu." One also might examine the royal inscriptions of Sennacherib, where scatological references are made at the enemy's expense (a common feature in Arabic invective literature). See E. Frahm, "Humor in assyrischen Königsinschriften," in *Intellectual Life in the Ancient Near East: Papers Presented at the 43rd Rencontre assyriologique internationale, Prague, July 1–5, 1996* (ed. J. Prosecky; Prague: Academy of Sciences of the Czech Republic, Oriental Institute, 1998), 147–62, especially 159.

44. Noted by E. J. Webber, "Comedy and Satire in Hispano-Arabic Spain," *Hispanic Review* 26 (1958): 7.

45. Contra B. Lewalski, *Paradise Lost and the Rhetoric of Literary Forms* (Princeton: Princeton University Press, 1987), 20, who suggested that Cornelius à Lapide living in the eighteenth century was the first to recognize the comical aspects of the Song of Songs.

46. A fruitful avenue of research might be to compare the invective genres treated herein with the midrashic interpretive approach known as הגדות של דופי, which was designed "to malign or mock the teachings or teachers of Scripture" (see b. Sanh. 99b), as well as the opposite exegetical genre of praise known as הגדות משבחות. On these exegetical genres, and for the quote above, see briefly, Michael Fishbane, "Orally Write Therefore Aurally Right," in *The Quest for Contrext and Meaning: Studies in Biblical Intertextuality in Honor of James A. Sanders* (ed. C. A. Evans and S. Talmon; Leiden: Brill, 1997), 545.

47. Though probably influenced by the Arabic models. See A. Sáenz-Badil-

the gap of centuries between the earliest forms of Greek and Arabic invective and the composition of the Song of Songs.[48]

Two interrelated questions naturally arise: Who in ancient Israel might have been responsible for the invective poem? To whom might the criticism have been addressed? One does not have to look far to realize that Solomon is mentioned by name repeatedly in the Song of Songs, that the northern kingdom established its independence upon the death of this monarch, with the prime cause being the king's heavy taxation system, and that the dialect of the composition reflects Israelian Hebrew (see ch. 1). All of this adds up to the Song of Songs bearing not only its primary reading as exquisite love poetry but the secondary reading of *hijāʾ* or *tašbīb* poetry as well. In what follows, we lay out the similarities, point by point. As to the important question of when the poem may have been composed, and who might be the object of the invective, we leave this matter aside for the moment, reserving such discussion for the conclusion.

Flattering the Ruler and His Wife or Wives

With these comparisons in mind, we now move to the Song's specific features that mark it as an early form of invective. We begin with the Song's central characters. In keeping with the Arabic invectives, which flatter women associated with the royal household, Song 7:2 gains a facile interpretation, as the poet states explicitly that the object of his praise is the daughter of nobility: מה יפו פעמיך בנעלים בת נדיב "How beautiful are your feet in sandals, O daughter of the noble!"[49]

Naturally, the Song also should refer to the ruler, and we find such a statement at the very outset, in Song 1:1: שיר השירים אשר לשלמה. Due to the flexibility of the preposition -ל, this line has been read in at least three ways: "the Song of Songs, which is by Solomon," "the Song of Songs, which is for Solomon," and "the Song of Songs, concerning Solomon." [50] It is this last

---

los, "Hebrew Invective Poetry: The Debate between Todros Abulafia and Phinehas Halevi," *Prooftexts* 16 (1996): 49–73.

48. With Pope, *Song of Songs*, 27, we find it difficult to date the poem precisely; needless to say, the opinions of scholars on this matter run the gamut. For further discussion, see our conclusion below.

49. Segal, "Song of Songs," 482 (repr. in idem, *The Pentateuch*, 232), remarks: "Contrary to her isolated picture as a shepherdess or keeper of vineyards (i 8, 6 [*sic*]), the damsel appears throughout the Song as the daughter of affluent parents living in considerable comfort."

50. Support for the last of these options comes from the similar superscriptions

reading that best fits the Song's interpretation as an invective against Solomon, and by extension, the tribe of Judah. Given the reliance of *tašbīb* and *hijāʾ* on ambiguity, we also should consider the possibility that the incipit was intended to be a polysemous disclaimer; if pressed whether the poem was directed at Solomon, the poet could say "no." Alternatively, if added by a later editor, the incipit's ambiguity could represent a deliberate attempt to capture and/or diffuse the import of the Song's invective target.

In addition, there are other passages that refer to Solomon; see especially Song 1:5; 3:7, 9, 11; 8:11, 12. Indeed, one might use this line of reasoning to argue in defense of MT at Song 1:5. Many scholars opt to emend the final word of this verse to שַׂלְמָה "Salmah" (a fitting parallel to Kedar),[51] but in light of the requirements of *tašbīb* and *hijāʾ*, we would posit that the poet sought to introduce the name of Solomon at the earliest instance (after the superscription, that is).

Elaborate Descriptions and Exaggerated Flattery

Sarcastic flattery is a standard feature of both *tašbīb* and *hijāʾ* poetry. To illustrate, we turn first to the Andalusian poet Abī ʿĀmir Ibn Šuhayd (992–1035):

> I remember a woman looking out from under the fold of her veil,
> whom a caller summoned to God and to do good.
>
> She advanced with her child, seeking a place in which to be joined to
> piety and devotion.
>
> Thus she walked proudly like a gazelle fondling its young, expressing
> concern for a gazelle in the height of youth.
>
> She came to us walking with a stately gait, yet she alighted in a valley
> full of lions.
>
> She grew frightened from concern for her little one, so I called out:
> "You there, do not be afraid!"

---

to the Ugaritic poems. See, e.g., *CAT* 1.14:1 [*lk*]*rt*, 1.16:1 [*l*]*krt*, meaning "about Kret" or "concerning Kret," and not "by Kret" or "for Kret"; and *CAT* 1.6:1 *lbʿl*, which can only mean "about Baʿal" or "concerning Baʿal."

51. See, e.g., Pope, *Song of Songs*, 320, and the list of earlier scholars noted there.

> Immediately she turned away, and the musk from her hem left upon
> the ground a trail like the back of a serpent.[52]

According to Monroe, in Ibn Duhayd's *Risalāt at-Tawābiʿ wal-zawābiʿ*, the poem "is introduced as a 'scandalous' or 'obscene' (*mujūn*) piece of poetry.[53] Since there is nothing inherently obscene in the poem itself, the obscenity must be taken to reside in the poet's intention to provoke scandal by dishonoring the lady, thereby shaming her menfolk."[54]

The Greek poet Archilochus (seventh century B.C.E.) employed a similar double-edged flattery when describing how he engaged in sex with his betrothed's (i.e., Neobulé) younger sister while making several uncompromising remarks about Neobulé. The poem forced her father Lycambes to break off the engagement and to commit suicide.[55] The poem is reproduced here in part.

> O daughter of highborn Amphimedo,
> I replied, of the widely remembered
> Amphimedo now in the rich earth dead.
>
> There are, do you know, so many pleasures
> For young men to choose from
> Among the skills of the delicious goddess …
>
> I shall climb the wall and come to the gate.
> You'll not say no, Sweetheart, to this?
> I shall come no farther than the garden grass.
> Neobulé I have forgotten, believe me, do.
> Any man who wants her may have her.
> Aiai! She's past her day, ripening rotten.
>
> The petals of her flower are all brown.
> The grace that first she had is shot.
> Don't you agree that she looks like a boy?

---

52. Translation by Monroe, "The Strip-Tease," 108.

53. Strictly speaking, unlike a *hijāʾ*, a *mujūn* is an obscene poem devoid of any political intent.

54. Monroe, "The Strip-Tease," 108.

55. A. Lesky, *A History of Greek Literature* (trans. J. Willis and C. Heer; New York: Crowell, 1966), 111–12. On the historicity of this suicide, see Rankin, *Archilochus of Paros*, 19–20.

A woman like that would drive me crazy.
She would get herself a job as a scarecrow.
I'd as soon hump her as [kiss a goat's butt] …
I said no more, but took her hand,
Laid her down in a thousand flowers,
And put my soft wool cloak around her.

I slid my arm under her neck
To still the fear in her eyes,
For she was trembling like a fawn,

Touched her hot breasts with light fingers,
Spraddled her neatly and pressed
Against her fine, hard, bared crotch.
I caressed the beauty of her body
And came in a sudden white spurt
While I was stroking her hair.[56]

Those who see the Song of Songs as representative of the Arabic *waṣf* genre already have pointed to several instances of satirical praise.[57] A few examples will suffice, though many more could be cited.

1:9 To a mare in pharaoh's chariotry, I liken you, my darling.
4:1 Your hair is like a flock of goats that flow down from Mount Gilead.
4:4 Like the tower of David is your neck.
4:5 Your two breasts are like two fawns, twins of a doe.
7:5 Your neck is like the tower of ivory.… your nose is like the tower of Lebanon, looking toward Damascus.
7:8 This your stature is likened to a palm-tree, and your breasts, to clusters.
8:10 I am a wall, and my breasts are like towers.

---

56. Translation by G. Davenport, *Archilochus, Sappho, Alkman: Three Lyric Poets of the Late Greek Bronze Age* (Berekley and Los Angeles: University of California Press, 1980), 22–24. For an edition of the Greek text, see Rankin, *Archilochus of Paros*, 69–71.

57. References to exaggerated flattery were noticed already by Waterman, "The Rôle of Solomon in the Song of Songs," 171–87, especially 180.

Such ironic praise,[58] exaggerated or not, accords with what the Arab invective poets saw as their aim. According to van Gelder, the poet's goal is achieved when he mentions "the physical and moral qualities of women (*ḫalq al-niṣaʾ wa-aḫlāyahunna*) and the various circumstances of his love for them."[59] Elaborate physical descriptions also appear in Song 4:1–7; 6:4–7; 7:2–10 (said of the woman) and 5:10–15 (said of the man).

Erotic Imagery

Another important feature of *tašbīb* and *hijāʾ* poems (as also the *nasīb*) is the use of erotic imagery. The poet invites the reader to play the voyeur and to delight in the physical beauty of a gorgeous woman (or handsome man), who is usually the wife, beloved, or lover of the ruler. Ubaydallāh ibn Qays Ar-Ruqayyāt, for example, boasts of his night of love with Umm al-Banīn, the daughter-in-law of the ruling caliph ʿAbd al-Malik (r. 685–705).

> When I enjoyed her, and her mouth, the sweetest part of her, inclined towards me,
>
> I sipped the liquor of her lips until I'd taken an initial draught, and then I whiled away the night, by giving her the liquor of my lips to drink.
>
> I spent the night in highest spirits, bedded down with her, while she delighted me, and I delighted her.[60]

Note similarly how Archilochus employed both euphemistic (e.g., "I shall climb the wall and come to the gate")[61] and explicit language (e.g., "Spraddled her neatly and pressed against her fine, hard, bared crotch") in the Greek invective quoted above. Rankin remarked:

---

58. Praising with the intention of blaming is a standard characteristic of literary irony. See e.g., D. C. Muecke, *The Compass of Irony* (London: Methuen, 1969), 61.

59. Van Gelder, *The Bad and the Ugly*, 65.

60. Ibid., 14.

61. Euphemistic erotic language is common also in ancient Near Eastern love poetry. See, e.g., J. G. Westenholz, "Metaphorical Language in the Poetry of Love in the Ancient Near East," in *La circulation des biens, des personnes et des idées dans le Proche-Orient ancien: Actes de la XXXVIIIe rencontre assyriologique internationale (Paris, 8–10 juillet 1991)* (ed. D. Charpin and F. Joannès; Paris: Editions Recherche sur les Civilisations, 1992), 383.

> His imputations are severe enough in themselves; but couched in the metaphors of the contemporary gutter which he has metamorphosed into vivid satire, their import must have been of virulent intensity which we can only with difficulty grasp millennia later.[62]

We have drawn attention to the erotic imagery in the biblical Song above, as others have done so before us.[63] For the sake of completeness, however, we include below a few of the more obvious examples.

2:3 In his shade I delight and I sit, and his fruit is sweet to my palate.
4:16 Awake, north(-wind), come, south(-wind), Blow upon my garden, may its spices stream; may my beloved come to his garden, and may he eat of the fruit of its choice-fruits.
5:5 I arose to open for my beloved, and my hands dripped myrrh, and my fingers, flowing myrrh, on the handles of the lock.
7:1 Return, return, O Shulammite, return, return, that we may gaze at you.[64]
7:3 Your vulva is a bowl of the crescent, let it not lack mixed-wine.[65]
7:8–10 This your stature is likened to a palm-tree, and your breasts, to clusters. I said, "I will ascend the palm-tree, I shall grasp its fronds"; and may your breasts be like clusters of the vine, and the scent of your nose like apricots. And your palate is like good wine.

Unrequited Love

Within the catena of sexual innuendo in *tašbīb* and *hijāʾ* poetry one encounters the theme of unrequited love. The reader is titilated but frustrated by the lover's unfulfilled and continually interrupted advances. To cite an Arabic example, we turn to the longing of ʿAbdallāh ibn ʿUmar Al-ʿArjī (d. 738):

---

62. Rankin, *Archilochus of Paros*, 65.

63. See, e.g., Edward Ullendorff, "The Bawdy Bible," *BSOAS* 42 (1979): 447–48; D. Lys, "Notes sur le Cantique," in *Congress Volume: Rome, 1968* (ed. G. W. Anderson et al.; VTSup 17; Leiden: Brill, 1969), 170–78; Pope, *Song of Songs, passim*; and S. M. Paul, "A Lover's Garden of Verse: Literal and Metaphorical Imagery in Ancient Near Eastern Love Poetry," in *Tehillah le-Moshe: Biblical and Judaic Studies in Honor of Moshe Greenberg* (ed. M. Cogan, B. L. Eichler, and J. H. Tigay; Winona Lake, Ind.: Eisenbrauns, 1997), 99–110.

64. On this verse and its use of חזה "gaze," see Ullendorff, "The Bawdy Bible," 448.

65. Ibid.

> Turn toward me, and greet me, Jabra; why this avoidance just as you're departing?
>
> Of itself, the latter is separation enough for you and me. Why this too? Know what separation is.[66]

As commentators have noted, the theme of unrequited love dominates in the Song of Songs. Several lines describe the frustrated tryst: "O my dove, in the crannies of the rock, in the covert of the cliff, show me your visage" (2:14); "on my couch at night, I sought whom my inner-being loves; I sought him, but I did not find him" (3:1); "I opened for my beloved, and my beloved turned away, passed" (5:6); and "to where has your beloved gone, O most beautiful among women, to where has your beloved turned?" (6:1).

In a Dream

The lovers' inability to meet face to face is what induced Abraham Ibn Ezra (1089–1164) to aver that the verse "I am asleep, but my heart is awake" (Song 5:2) describes the woman's desire as cast in a dream. This passage is reminiscent of the pre-Islamic and later *nasīb* poems in which the author describes the night "vision" of his beloved.[67] Since Arabic invective poems often incurred the wrath of the ruler at whom the poem was directed, the poet had to select his words carefully, being cautious to remain subtle and to provide charming disclaimers. Couching his night of love in the form of a dream provided the bard with just the required escape hatch. In the aforecited poem by Ar-Ruqayyāt, for example, the poet claims to have had sex with the daughter-in-law of the caliph, but only in his dreams.

> She came to visit me in sleep; this poem I said, the time that I was given her in dreams.
>
> When I enjoyed her, and her mouth, the sweetest part of her, inclined towards me.

66. Translation by Monroe, "The Strip-Tease," 103.

67. Later medieval scholars reinterpreted the "vision" as a dream, but it apparently was originally conceived of as an otherworldy apparition. See Jacobi, "*Nasīb*," 979.

I sipped the liquor of her lips until I'd taken an initial draught, and then I whiled away the night, by giving her the liquor of my lips to drink.

I spent the night in highest spirits, bedded down with her, while she delighted me, and I delighted her.

She kept me wide awake, the while I slept, but now, the place to which she sped is far removed from me.[68]

Metaphors of Choice

Virtually every stock classical motif employed by the classical Arabic literati can be found in the Song of Songs: the woman's gaze through a veil; singing; love as a potent wine; lists describing the lover's physical features; erotic references to luxury goods;[69] and the metaphorical use of vineyards, gardens, orchards, the wind, the seasons, walls, towers, fortifications, military accoutrements, palm trees, and animals. We have seen some of these metaphors at work already in the poem by Abī ʿĀmir Ibn Šuhayd. Read also the words of Al-ʿArjī (d. 738), again in praise of Jabra al-Maḫzūmīya, the wife of the caliph Muḥammad Ibn Hišām (r. 724–743):

For love of you, and I would hold your avoidance sacred at times, yet does an impassioned lover enjoy a sacred pledge?

She glanced with the pupil of a fawn-bearing gazelle; one fond of tender shoots whose growth is fresh,

Whose cares are redoubled by a tender fawn whose languor slows its pace …

She is like a palm tree, laden down with dates, rising high on top of a sand dune, bending down its heavily-laden branch.

She walks with the gait of one deeply intoxicated, who trails his garment, when wine has snatched away almost all his senses.

68. Translation by Monroe, "The Strip-Tease," 104–5.

69. A list is a well-known tool of the satirist. See, e.g., W. V. Wortley, "Some Rabelaisian Satiric Techniques," *Satire News Letter* 5.1 (1967): 8–15.

It is a castle in which dwelt a girl of tender youth, before whose ancestry Glory falls short.

She is radiantly beautiful, while her forefathers and their radiant noble wives raise her to a lofty rank.

From her female elders, she inherited virtue, along with the memorable good deeds they performed of old,

Yet, when ice and snow together lashed the thorny trees, while the region remained rainless,

And the north wind overpowered the area's garments, and the date faded to yellow,

The sharp edge of winter did not trouble her, nor was a curtain raised for her to go out and earn her living.[70]

Compare this with the repeated mention of vineyards, orchards, and gardens in the Song of Songs.[71]

1:6 The sons of my mother were angry at me, they set me as keeper of the vineyards, (but) my own vineyard I have not kept.
1:14 A cluster of henna is my beloved to me, from the vineyards of Ein Gedi.
2:13 The fig-tree perfumes its young-fruit, and the vines in bud, they give forth fragrance.
2:15 Catch us the foxes, the little foxes, ruining the vineyards, and our vineyards in bud.
4:12 A locked garden is my sister, (my) bride, a locked fountain, a sealed spring.
4:13 Your shoots are an orchard of pomegranates, with fruit of choice-fruits; henna with nard.

70. Translation by Monroe, "The Strip-Tease That Was Blamed on Abū Bakr's Naughty Son," p. 104.

71. The repeated mention of vineyards might also suggest a metaphorical reference to the House of Israel (e.g., Isa 5:1–10). See Paul, "A Lover's Garden of Verse." On such double entendres, see below.

4:15 A spring of the gardens, a well of living water, and streams from Lebanon.
4:16 May my beloved come to his garden, and may he eat of the fruit of its choice-fruits.
5:1 I have come to my garden, my sister, (my) bride.
5:13 His cheeks are like a bed of spices.
6:2 My beloved went down to his garden, to the beds of spices; to graze in the gardens, and to gather lilies.
6:11 To the walnut garden I went down, to see the produce of the palm-tree, to see whether the vine blooms, whether the pomegranates blossom.
7:13 Let us arise-early to the vineyards, let us see if the vine has bloomed, (if) the bud has opened, (if) the pomegranates have blossomed.
8:11–12 Solomon had a vineyard in Baal-hamon; he gave the vineyard to the keepers.... My own vineyard is before me.
8:13 O you who sits in the garden.

The repeated and elaborate metaphorical comparisons to fauna that we find in the poems of Ibn Duhayd and Al-ʿArjī also appear in the biblical Song.

2:7 = 3:5 I adjure you, O daughters of Jerusalem, by the gazelles, or by the hinds of the field.
2:9 My beloved is-like a gazelle, or a fawn of the hinds.
2:15 Catch us the foxes, the little foxes.
2:17 Turn, liken yourself, my beloved, to a gazelle, or to a fawn of the hinds.
4:1–2 (≈ 6:5–6) Your eyes are doves, behind your braids; your hair is like a flock of goats, that flow down from Mount Gilead. Your teeth are like a flock of shorn-ones.
4:5 (≈ 7:4) Your two breasts are like two fawns, twins of a doe.
4:8 From the dens of lions, from the mountains of leopards.
5:11 His locks are curled, black as the raven.
5:12 His eyes are like doves.
6:9 One is my dove.
8:14 Flee, my beloved, and liken yourself to a gazelle, or to a fawn of the hinds.

And the following passages, which evoke military language, albeit within the context of love poetry:

1:9 To a mare in pharaoh's chariotry, I liken you, my darling.
3:7–8 Behold the litter of Solomon, sixty heroes surround it, from among the heroes of Israel. All of them, grasping the sword, trained in battle, each-man, his sword on his thigh, for fear of the night.
4:4 Like the tower of David is your neck, built to the heights; a thousand shields hang upon it, all the weapons of the heroes.
6:4 You are beautiful, my darling, like Tirzah, comely as Jerusalem, awesome as the luminaries.[72]
6:12 I do not know, my inner-being sets me, the chariots of Amminadab.
7:5 Your neck is like the tower of ivory.... your nose is like the tower of Lebanon, looking towards Damascus.
8:9 If she is a wall, will we build upon her a silver turret?
8:10 I am a wall, and my breasts are like towers.

Drinking and eating, but especially the consumption of wine, are favorite subjects of *tašbīb* and *hijāʾ* poets. See, for example, how Ar-Ruqayyāt (d. 704) uses the metaphor of wine in his description of his lover's lips:

> When I enjoyed her, and her mouth, the sweetest part of her, inclined towards me,
>
> I sipped the liquor of her lips until I'd taken an initial draught, and then I whiled away the night, by giving her the liquor of my lips to drink.

Witness also the intoxicating words of Abū Nuwās (d. 810):

> Hey, pour me some wine, and let me know it is wine; don't pour in secret when it can be done openly!
>
> A pleasant life is getting drunk time after time; if this goes on for a long time, then time will become too short.

72. We include this verse in the list, due to the reference to the capital cities of the kingdoms of Israel and Judah, both of which would have been well-fortified. On the difficult expression at the end of this verse, see Goitein, "Ayumma Kannidgalot (Song of Songs VI.10) 'Splendid like the Brilliant Stars,'" 220–21; and Gordis, "The Root דגל in the Song of Songs," 203–4.

It is a disadvantage to find me sober; the advantage lies in drunkenness that staggers me.[73]

The author of the Song of Songs reveals his own oenophilic penchant with a series of passages interlaced throughout the composition:[74]

1:2 May he kiss me with the kisses of his mouth, for your love is better than wine.
1:4 Let us be glad and let us rejoice in you, let us recall your love more than wine, (more than) smooth-wine, they love you.
2:4 He brought me to the house of wine, and his glance toward me is love.
4:10 How better than wine is your love.
5:1 I have plucked my myrrh with my spice, I have eaten my honeycomb with my honey, I have drunk my wine with my milk; eat, friends! Drink! and be-drunk with love!
7:10 And your palate is like good wine, coursing to my beloved as smooth-wine; fluxing (on) the lips of those-who-sleep.
8:2 I would ply you with spiced wine, with the juice of my pomegranate.

Sometimes the poet compares his lover to precious spices, metals, ivory, and alabaster. Ibn Quzmān, for example, delivers his homoerotic *tašbīb* in this way:

Let me love the one who is as sweet as sugar;
Do you know whom? The son of *agellīd* Abū Bakr,[75]
Who has a little mouth more fragrant than ambergris.
And little teeth like pearls on a string,
Hence it is only fair that [the mouth] be called "ambergris-like,"
And "pearly," insofar as its [teeth] are strung …

To be serious, do you know what now disturbs me?
Why, the white of his shank, above its stained part! Spare me!
The very moment I saw it, it overwhelmed me;
You'd swear it was the underground product of a mine,

73. Monroe, "The Strip-Tease," 111.

74. For eating and drinking as sexual metaphors in the Bible, see Paul, "A Lover's Garden of Verse," 106 n. 44.

75. The term *agellīd* is Berber for "prince."

For you could see his shank white and tender, up above,
While its [lower] half was gilded with *jaʿfarī* [gold].[76]

As with the Greek and Arabic invectives, we also find references in the Song of Songs to exotic commodities, such as spices, ivory, and precious metals:

4:13–14 Henna with nard. Nard and saffron, cane and cinnamon, with all trees of frankincense; myrrh and aloes, with all heads of spices.
4:16 Blow upon my garden, may its spices stream.
5:1 I have plucked my myrrh with my spice.
5:13 His cheeks are like a bed of spices, towers of perfumes; his lips are lilies, dripping (with) flowing myrrh.
5:14–15 His hands are bracelets of gold, inlaid with beryl; his loins are a block of ivory, studded with sapphires. His calves are pillars of marble, supported on pedestals of bullion.

The last citation is particularly interesting for its description of the beloved's legs: "his loins are a block of ivory, studded with sapphires. His calves are pillars of marble, supported on pedestals of bullion" (5:14–15). Monroe suggested that the mention of gilding in connection with legs (thighs, etc.) in the Arabic poems may be a poetic reference to "the well-known Berber custom of staining the hands, feet, and limbs, and other parts of the body with henna … as a means of protection against harmful influences, particularly, the evil eye and the jinn."[77] Not only does henna appear in the Song of Songs (7:12), but as Ibn Ezra long ago espied, the line "turn your eyes from before me, for they dazzle me" (6:5), which occurs shortly after the description of the man's thighs (5:14–15), may constitute a reference to the evil eye.

Praise by Others

One of the *hijāʾ* compositions of Al-ʿArjī (d. 738) praises the wife of his caliph by including others' praise of her: "She is radiantly beautiful, while her forefathers and their radiant noble wives raise her to a lofty rank."[78] The Song of Songs similarly incorporates the praise by others:

---

76. Monroe, "The Strip-Tease," 96.

77. Ibid., 98. See also E. Westermarck, *Ritual and Belief in Morocco* (2 vols.; London: Macmillan, 1926), 1:310, 443, 516, 540, 582; 2:92.

78. Monroe, "The Strip-Tease," 104.

1:3–4 Therefore the maidens love you.... (More than) smooth-wine, they love you.
6:9 Daughters see her, and they extol her, queens and concubines, and they praise her.

Familial Injustice

Suzanne Stetkevych noted that in a tribal society, the Arabic *hijāʾ* often focuses on cases of injustice that kinsmen have shown the poet, because the poem's underlying motive "is self-affirmation by means of the denial of the other."[79] One injustice common to the genre is that of the overgrazing of one's pasture land by another tribe, usually one with close kinship ties.[80] Another theme is incest,[81] and by extension other sexual deviations such as adultery, prostitution, and pederasty, the expression of which is enhanced by casting the object of the poet's indictment in an inverted sex role.[82] Regarding a *hijāʾ* by Jawwās al-Ḍabbīʾ, in which the poet taints the name of woman of another tribe, Stetkevych remarked:

> The accusation of incest carries with it the concept of inbred viciousness and depravity, a heritage of baseness which is passed down genetically and genealogically that is precisely antithetical to the ancestry of noble stallions and well-bred mares ... and to the legacy of virtue and honor that they have left to their offspring.[83]

Analogous to the theme of over-grazing in Arabic *hijāʾ* poems is the double-edged meaning of רעה "graze" in the Song of Songs. Elsewhere in the Bible the word רעה "graze" is used to refer to kings who shepherd their subjects like flocks (e.g., Isa 63:11; Ezek 34:2; Nah 3:18). By extension, the "flocks" represent royal subjects (see Isa 13:14; Ezek 36:38; Ps 107:41; etc.). Important for our purpose, however, is that the word רעה "graze" often can mean "devastate" (e.g., Jer 6:3; 50:19; Ezek 34:14; Mic 5:5; 7:14). Therefore, given the word's double sense, it is possible to read the following passages as references to the king devastating the land of his subjects (i.e., his flocks):

---

79. Stetkevych, *Abū Tammām and the Poetics of the ʿAbbasid Age*, 335. This is expressly stated in Abū Tammām Ḥabīb ibn Aws al-Tāʾī, *Dīwān al-Ḥamāsah* (Clāhūr: Al-Maktabah al-Salafīyah, 1979), 607.

80. Stetkevych, *Abū Tammām and the Poetics of the ʿAbbasid Age*, 336.

81. Ibid., 342.

82. Ibid., 340, 345.

83. Ibid., 342.

1:7 Tell me, O whom my inner-being loves, where do you shepherd [רעה]? Where do you cause-(them)-to-lie-down at noon? Lest I become like one-who-veils,[84] beside the flocks of your friends.[85]

2:16 (≈ 6:3) My beloved is mine, and I am his, grazing [רעה] among the lilies.[86]

Though Ibn Ezra saw the Song as functioning within a different allegorical framework, he nevertheless astutely paraphrased the latter verse: "But I am like a lily in the valley for every passerby to trample on, and I am afraid the Egyptians will destroy me."

The topic of incest that we find in the classical Greek and medieval Arabic invectives may explain the numerous references to the male lover's beloved as both sister and bride, a point over which exegetes have struggled for centuries.[87]

---

84. If J. A. Emerton is correct in understanding עטיה as "picks lice," instead of "one-who-veils," then we have an additional insult. See J. A. Emerton, "Lice or a Veil in the Song of Songs 1:7," in *Understanding Poets and Prophets: Essays in Honour of George Wishart Anderson* (ed. A. G. Auld; JSOTSup 152; Sheffield: JSOT Press, 1993), 127–40. Various scholars have argued for "strays" here, but Fox (*Song of Songs*, 103) is correct in his rejection of this proposal.

85. On the wordplay in this verse, see S. B. Noegel, *Janus Parallelism in the Book of Job* (JSOTSup 223; Sheffield: Sheffield Academic Press, 1996), 154–55.

86. See also ibid., 154.

87. While we agree that the surface reading of "brother" and "sister" reflects the close relationship between the male and female lovers (see Fox, *Song of Songs*, 136), we would suggest that the implication of incest is present as well. Note that scholars have reconstructed the marriage of David and Abigail as one between siblings (see J. D. Levenson and B. Halpern, "The Political Import of David's Marriages," *JBL* 99 [1980]: 507–18, in particular 511); that the story of Amnon and Tamar (half-siblings) in 2 Sam 13 implies that David's two children could be married without difficulty (see v. 13 especially); and that the marriage of Abraham and Sarah (also half-siblings) is most likely a literary reflection of the above two relationships (see G. A. Rendsburg, "Biblical Literature as Politics: The Case of Genesis," in *Religion and Politics in the Ancient Near East* [ed. A. Berlin; Bethesda, Md.: University Press of Maryland, 1996], 47–70, in particular 66–67). One also wonders if additional incest (mother-son, in fact) lies behind the statements in 1 Kgs 15:2 (Abijam was the son of Maacah, daughter of Absalom), 15:8 (Asa was the son of Abijam), and 15:10 (Asa was also the son of Maacah, daughter of Absalom). Thus I. W. Provan, *1 and 2 Kings* (NIBC; Peabody, Mass.: Hendrickson, 1995), 126; though see the counter to this view by M. Cogan, *1 Kings* (AB 10; New York: Doubleday, 2000), 397. Given such a history, one can imagine the desire by the author of the Song of Songs to convey the subtle message of

4:9 You entice me, my sister, (my) bride, you entice me with but one of your eyes.
4:10 How beautiful is your love, my sister, (my) bride.
4:12 A locked garden is my sister, (my) bride.
5:1 I have come to my garden, my sister, (my) bride.
5:2 Open for me, my sister, my darling, my dove, my perfect-one!
8:1 Who would give you as a brother to me, one-who-sucked the breasts of my mother; I would find you in the street, I would kiss you.

It is clear that these verses concern sexual love and not platonic love, because in Song 1:6 the woman confesses: "The sons of my mother were angry at me, they set me as keeper of the vineyards, (but) my own vineyard I have not kept," an expression that Shalom Paul has shown must mean: "My mother's sons quarreled with me, they made me guard (my) chastity, but I have not kept chaste."[88]

Comparing the *hijā*ʾ to the *nasīb*, Stetkevych remarks:

> In the *nasīb* the mistress is usually described as both clothed and enclosed. Although occasionally bearing a cheek or dropping a veil, she is usually fully dressed and shut off in the *khidr* (women's quarters) or *hawdaj* (camel litter). She is either unattainable or irretrievable. The robes, gowns, veils, curtains, and tent-skirts constitute barriers between the pact-lover and his delight, barriers that guarantee the honor, modesty, and purity of his beloved. In *hijā*ʾ, the garments are invariably rent, the veils inevitably slip. The pure, veiled, and protected (and here unavailable) woman of the *nasīb* is (at least hypothetically) stripped bare and disgraced.[89]

Compare this statement with the passage in Song 5:3: "I have removed my tunic, how shall I put it on? I have washed my feet, how shall I soil them?"; and more to the point, Song 5:7: "The watchmen found me, they who go-about the city, they struck me, they wounded me; they lifted my shawl from upon me, the watchmen of the city-walls."

---

incest in his invective composition. For the historical reality of brother-sister marriages in ancient Egypt, see the classic study by J. Černy, "Consanguineous Marriages in Pharaonic Egypt," *JEA* 40 (1954): 23–29.

88. Paul, "A Lover's Garden of Verse," 110.

89. Stetkevych, *Abū Tammām and the Poetics of the ʿAbbasid Age*, 339.

Inverted Gender Roles

In line with the subversion of sexual (and thus social) mores in Arabic invectives is the subtle inversion of gender roles in the Song, as noted first by S. D. Goitein[90] and developed more thoroughly by Phyllis Trible.[91] M. Pope commented: "With regard to the Song of Songs she [Trible] is certainly correct in recognizing the equal and even dominant role of the female and the absence of male chauvinism or patriarchalism."[92] Whedbee similarly noted: "This paradoxical reversal of roles provides an occasion for the use of parody and travesty."[93] Song 2:9 illustrates the trend well. It describes the male lover as looking through the lattices in expectation of his lover. The biblical motif typically portrays a woman gazing through a window (or performing some action through a window).[94] See, for example, Rahab (Josh 2:15), Sisera's mother (Judg 5:28), Michal (1 Sam 19:12; 2 Sam 6:16), Jezebel (2 Kgs 9:30), and Lady Wisdom (Prov 7:6).[95] In all these cases a "male" world perceives a woman inside the house looking out through the window at action below. In Song 2:9, by contrast, we gain the female view, in line with the dominant perspective of the book: the woman is still on the inside (in line with Near Eastern ideas about "kept" women[96]), but in this case we are treated to her male lover looking in through the window from the outside.

Moreover, Carol Meyers has observed several other instances of "the reversal of conventional gender typing,"[97] including the Song's frequent association of military, architectural, and animal imagery in conjunction with the female, the mention of the king's captivation by the woman or her tresses (Song 7:6), and the atypical repeated reference to the "mother's house" (3:4; 8:2). In societies with clearly defined and socially mandated gender roles, gender hierarchy typically is commensurate with, and entrenched by,

90. S. D. Goitein, "The Song of Songs: A Female Composition" [Hebrew original, 1957], in Brenner, *A Feminist Companion to the Song of Songs*, 58–66, especially 59.

91. Trible, "Depatriarchalizing in Biblical Interpretation."

92. Pope, *Song of Songs*, 210.

93. Whedbee, "Paradox and Parody," 269.

94. The only case of a man at the window is Abimelech in Gen 26:8.

95. See also Tob 3:11. Akkadian examples also are known. See, e.g., "Kilili looking from the window," in Nissinen, "Love Lyrics of Nabû and Tašmetu" 610, and other examples at 603 n. 82.

96. Captured and introduced to a general audience in the portrayal of Princess Jasmine in the Disney animated feature *Aladdin* (1992). When Jasmine wishes to leave the palace, she needs to do so in disguise, lest she violate the social order.

97. C. L. Meyers, "Gender Imagery in the Song of Songs," *HAR* 10 (1986): 218.

the social hierarchy. In medieval Islam, as well as in ancient Greece and the ancient Near East, the social hierarchy was dominated by men, and women were expected to fulfill their gender expectations by being passive, both sexually and socially. Any reversal of this social order, by passive men or non-passive women, was seen as a violation of the code. The presence of a similar social code in ancient Israel allows us to see the Song's reversal of gender roles as another feature of invective.

Additional Double-Edged Meanings: The Case of "Lovers" as "Allies"

Sometimes an invective's metaphors can be obvious and direct, and at other times they can assume subtler forms.[98] As we have seen in the Arabic invectives, description (in both *waṣf* and *nasīb*) can communicate on two planes: an individual (and often sexual) plane; and a communal (often religious or political) plane. A close look at the language of the biblical Song reveals a similar bifurcation of meaning. We have seen this already in the Song's use of the verb רעה "graze," with an additional connotation suggesting the king's "devastation" of his subjects. This pun, however, is only one among many that the poet employs in order to achieve his or her invective. Take, for example, the word אהב "love," which occurs eighteen times in the Song. Clearly, on the surface, its use in the Song suggests human love, yet we should not forget that the same word can connote the bond of political allies.[99] See, for example, 1 Kgs 5:15, in which Hiram king of Tyre is called David's אהב "ally," and Judg 5:31, in which אהביו "his [Yahweh's] allies" is the antonymic parallel to איביך "your enemies." On occasion, we believe that the same sense can be found in the word דוד "beloved" (see Song 5:8 below, for example).

The terms אח "brother" and אחות "sister," which appear throughout the Song, also can mean "allies." The use of אח "brother" in Ps 133 as a metaphorical reference to the united monarchy is a well-known prooftext,[100] but others could be cited (e.g., 1 Kgs 9:13; Jer 3:7; Ezek 16:45). Similarly, in

98. See Badawi, "The Function of Rhetoric in Medieval Arabic Poetry."

99. W. L. Moran, "The Ancient Near Eastern Background of the Love of God in Deuteronomy," *CBQ* 25 (1963): 77–87, repr. in Moran, *The Most Magic Word: Essays on Babylonian and Biblical Literature* (CBQMS 35; Washington, D.C.: Catholic Biblical Association, 2002), 170–81. See also L. Stadelmann, *Love and Politics: A New Commentary on the Song of Songs* (New York: Paulist, 1992), 16, 23, who sees אהב as a "key word" in the Song, and as a "technical term expressing the covenant relationship between the house of David and the Jewish community" (23).

100. A. Berlin, "On the Interpretation of Psalm 133," in *Directions in Biblical Hebrew Poetry* (ed. E. Follis; Sheffield: JSOT Press, 1987), 141–47. For the use of the

Ezek 23:1–6, the prophet metaphorically employs the word אחות "sister" to describe Samaria's relationship to Jerusalem, who went whoring after מאהביו "her lovers," that is, the Assyrians. The Song's use of אח and אחות as "allies," therefore, especially when contextualized within the theme of incest as discussed above, produces a range of political interpretive possibilities.

Moreover, the word רע "friend," which also occurs frequently in the Song, likewise can mean "ally."[101] See, for example, Lam 1:2, in which the poet cries out concerning Jerusalem: כל רעיה בגדו בה "all of her friends have betrayed her."[102] Similarly, as several passages below will illustrate, the feminine form רעיה, which we have translated "darling" in this work, can bear the connotation "ally," too. Also in the same semantic field is the word חבר "friend," which likewise can signify "ally" (see, e.g., 8:13 below).

The word כלה "bride, daughter-in-law" also occurs in figurative contexts describing cities and regions. Hosea uses it when referring to the nation of Israel, which strayed by seeking the support of foreign powers (Hos 4:14), and Isaiah uses it of Zion (Isa 49:18). The political connotations of this word, therefore, permit us to read Song 4:8 "With me, from Lebanon, (my) bride, with me, from Lebanon, come," as a veiled reference to Israel (see also Song 4:9–12; 5:1).

In this regard we similarly note the double meaning of the word "daughter," especially in the construction x-בת. Here too we may cite many biblical passages in which the word "daughter" means "villages"; see, for example, Num 21:25 בחשבון ובכל בנותיה "in Heshbon and in all of its villages," and many others.[103] The possibility that the Song of Songs employed the word "daughter" in this way was astutely comprehended by Ibn Ezra, who by way of a comparison with Ezek 26:61 noted: "some say that the daughters of Jerusalem signify the nations of the world." Athalya Brenner suggested that the second part of this verse alludes to Rabbah and that it therefore constitutes

term "brothers" in Chronicles, see Gary N. Knoppers, "'Yhwh Is Not with Israel': Alliances as a *Topos* in Chronicles," *CBQ* 58 (1996): 601–26, especially 621–23.

101. See P. Kalluveettil, *Declaration and Covenant: A Comprehensive Review of Covenant Formulae from the Old Testament and the Ancient Near East* (AnBib 88; Rome: Biblical Institute Press, 1982), 101.

102. Note the alliteration between אהביה "her allies" and איבים "foes." Perhaps we also should compare the expression "friend of the king" in 1 Kgs 4:5; 1 Chr 27:33 and "friend of David" in 2 Sam 15:37; 16:16.

103. See, e.g., Num 32:42; Josh 15:45, 47; Isa 47:1; Ezek 16:27. A similar usage appears in the Assyrian Prophecy to Esarhaddon, in which a "noisy daughter" (DUMU.MÍ *ḫuburtu*) is used for "rebellious vassal." See S. Parpola, *Assyrian Prophecies* (SAA 9; Helsinki: Helsinki University Press, 1997), 16.

another critical assessment of the Shulammite woman in accordance with the *waṣf* convention: "Heshbon and Rabbah do not invoke aesthetic pleasure elsewhere in the Hebrew Bible: fear and loathing, yes, like the emotions displayed towards the Amorites, Moabites, Ammonites and especially their sexual habits."[104]

A greater appreciation for the poem's allusive (political) language forces us to reconsider the overall import of the Song and to translate the poem's pertinent lines as follows.

1:6 The sons of my mother [i.e., my brothers/allies] were angry at me, they set me as keeper of the vineyards, (but) my own vineyard I have not kept.
1:7: Tell me, O whom my inner-being loves [i.e., my ally], where do you desire/shepherd? … Lest I become like one-who-veils, beside the flocks of your friends [i.e., allies].
1:9 To a mare in pharaoh's chariotry, I liken you, my darling [i.e., my ally].
2:2 Like a lily among the brambles, so is my darling [i.e., ally] among the daughters [i.e., vassals].
2:4 He brought me to the house of wine, and his glance toward me is love [i.e., alliance].
2:5 (see 5:8) Support me with raisin-cakes, spread me among the apricots, for I am sick with [~of this] love [i.e., alliance].
2:7 = 3:5 (see also 8:4) I adjure you, O daughters [i.e., vassals] of Jerusalem, by the gazelles, or by the hinds of the field; do not rouse, and do not arouse love [i.e., an alliance], until it desires.
3:1 On my couch at night, I sought whom my inner-being loves [i.e., my ally]; I sought him, but I did not find him.
3:9–11 The king Solomon made himself a palanquin, from the trees of Lebanon. Its pillars he made of silver, its support of gold, its riding-seat of purple; its interior arranged/burning with leather/love [i.e., arranged in an alliance], from [~by] the daughters [i.e. vassals] of Jerusalem. Go out and see, O daughters [i.e., vassals] of Zion, the king Solomon; with the crown (with) which his mother crowned him, on the day of his wedding.

104. A. Brenner, "A Note on *Bat-Rabbîm* (Song of Songs VII 5)," *VT* 42 (1992): 115.

4:7–8 All of you is beautiful, my darling [i.e., ally]; and there is no blemish in you. With me, from Lebanon, (my) bride [i.e., nation], with me, from Lebanon, come.

5:7–8 The watchmen found me, they who go-about the city, they struck me, they wounded me; they lifted my shawl from upon me, the watchmen of the city-walls. I adjure you, O daughters [i.e., vassals] of Jerusalem; if you find my beloved [i.e., ally], what will you tell him, that I am sick with [~of this] love [i.e., alliance].

6:9 Daughters [i.e., vassals] see her, and they extol her, queens and concubines, and they praise her.

7:2 How beautiful are your feet in sandals, O daughter [i.e., vassal] of the noble!

8:1 Who would give you as a brother [i.e., ally] to me.

8:6–7 Set me as a seal upon your heart, as a seal upon your arm; for love [i.e., an alliance] is as strong as death, passion as fierce as Sheol; its darts are darts of fire, the intensest-flame. Great waters cannot quench love [i.e., an alliance], and rivers cannot swill it away; if one would give all the wealth of his house for love [i.e., an alliance], they surely would mock him.

8:8 We have a sister [i.e., ally], a little-one, and she has no breasts; what shall we do for our sister [i.e., our ally], on the day when she is spoken for?[105]

8:13 O you who sits in the garden, friends [i.e., allies] attend to your voice, let me hear you.

As Ibn al-Muʿtazz discussed in his *Kitāb al-Badīʿ*, "allusion" (*kināya*) and "insinuation" (*taʿrid*) are useful devices in invective poems.[106] One way to employ such features was through ambiguity and punning.[107] Archilochus

105. See Ibn Ezra, who comments: כשיעלו ישראל אז יאמרו זה לזה אחות לנו קטנה והם ב׳ שבטים וחצי שאלו גלו בתחלה "When Israel goes up they shall say one to another, 'We have a little sister,' which are the two tribes and a half, for they were exiled first" (8:8).

106. Van Gelder, *The Bad and the Ugly*, 60.

107. Badawi, "The Function of Rhetoric in Medieval Arabic Poetry." For the formative role of literary features in shaping the morphological structure of early Arabic poetry, see F. Ziadeh, "Prosody and the Initial Formation of Classical Arabic," *JAOS* 106 (1986): 333–38.

too employed puns and paronomasia in his iambic[108] invectives, as Rankin noted: "Archilochus, can be seen in these pieces also as a brilliant and unscrupulous manipulator of street language's obscene metaphor and allusion."[109] We already have seen the Song's punning use of the terms "lover," "friend," "brother," "sister," "daughter," "bride," and "graze," as well as a host of sexually charged agricultural and viticultural metaphors. Nevertheless, the Song of Song's use of punning is more extensive.[110]

Moshe Garsiel, for example, has shown how the poem frequently puns on the name Solomon found in Song 1:1, 5 and elsewhere.[111] The element שַׁלְּמָה in Song 1:7, "Lest I become like one-who-veils, beside the flocks of your friends," hints at the name Solomon, as does the feminine epithet שולמית in 7:1: "Return, return, O Shulammite, return, return, that we may gaze[112] at you. How you gaze at the Shulammite, Like a dance of the two-camps." In fact, assuming (with almost all scholars) that שולמית refers to a female from the town of Shunem (Josh 19:18; 1 Sam 28:4; 2 Kgs 4:8), we gain further understanding as to why the poet employed the (dialectal?) form שולמית instead of the expected שונמית (1 Kgs 1:3, etc.; 2 Kgs 4:12, etc.).[113] The punning effect is reinforced by the name Solomon itself, which follows closely in 8:11. The final pun on Solomon's name appears in Song 8:10, where the lover proclaims: "I am a wall, and my breasts are like towers; thus I have become in his eyes, as one who finds goodwill," with the final word in our translation rendering Hebrew שלום. The first pun in 1:7 bolsters the invective by allusively connecting a straying "ally" with "Solomon." The final pun in 8:10 alludes to Solomon vis-à-vis the word "goodwill" (or "peace") and suggests Solomon's approach to military policy, as if to say, "one becomes an ally of Solomon if well-forti-

108. C. Miralles and J. Pórtulas, *Archilocus and the Iambic Poetry* (Rome: Ateneo, 1983), 16–17.

109. Rankin, *Archilochus of Paros*, 65; see also 90 for references to paronomasia.

110. See also Noegel, *Janus Parallelism in the Book of Job*, 12, 30, 33, 34, 154.

111. See Moshe Garsiel, "Puns upon Names: Subtle Colophons in the Bible," *JBQ* 23 (1995): 187. Leroy Waterman ("דודי in the Song of Songs," 105, 107) suggested that the Hebrew דודי also plays on the house of David and Solomon. For punning on caliphs' names in Arabic poetry, see Badawi, "The Function of Rhetoric in Medieval Arabic Poetry," 54.

112. On the sexual use of the verb חזה "gaze" here, see Ullendorff, "The Bawdy Bible," 448.

113. As is well known, שונם appears in Eusebius as Σουλήμ, and the name lives on until today in the name of the Arab village Solem/Solam. For discussion, see Y. Elitzur, *Ancient Place Names in the Holy Land* (Jerusalem: Magnes; Winona Lake, Ind.: Eisenbrauns, 2004), 235.

fied." The pun in Song 7:1 subtly connects Solomon and Jerusalem[114] to the Shulammite, who is described in rather baroque terms in 7:1–6.[115]

The Song similarly references Solomon's other name ידידיה "Beloved of Yah" (2 Sam 12:25),[116] by way of the repeated forms דודי "my beloved" and דדיך "your love" (see, e.g., Song 1:4; 2:9, 17). These allusions to Solomon's name, like the others, serve to remind the reader of the poet's hidden target.

The poem also shames the woman in Song 2:13: "The fig-tree perfumes its young-fruit, and the vines in bud, they give forth fragrance; arise, my darling [i.e., my ally], my beautiful, and go forth." Of importance here are the terms for fig (both תאנה and פג), which have both political[117] and sexual overtones (see b. Ber. 40a; Bereshit Rabba 15:7). Archilochus, too, employed a comparison to figs as an allusion to sex (though such is quite common in world literature).[118] Such sexual innuendos are underscored by the Song's references to the woman as a גן נעול "locked garden," גל נעול "locked fountain," and מעין חתום "sealed spring" (all in 4:12), expressions that elsewhere in ancient Near Eastern literature suggest issues of chastity.[119] Also pertinent here is the poet's comparison of the lover to Pharaoh's mares (1:9), which may be interpreted as a slanderous comment on the woman's purity.[120] See Jer 5:7–9; 13:27, for example, where horses and horse imagery are employed to

---

114. Ibn Ezra understood the Shulammite as someone from Jerusalem.

115. Note the remark of Brenner, "Come Back, Come Back the Shulammite," 265: "The dancer is, frankly, fat, her belly in dance motion is big and quivering, such like an unstable mound of wheat. She looks comical; her body inspires pithy comments.... Together with the rest of her body, her breasts move fast, much like frolicking fawns. This is titillating, but might look ludicrous as well. At any rate, it is a good pretext as any to laugh, aloud if through a seemingly respectable metaphor, at the woman's charms."

116. Garsiel, "Puns on Names," 187.

117. As slander, that is; see Robert Gordis, *The Book of Job: Commentary, New Translation, and Special Studies* (New York: Jewish Theological Seminary, 1978), 203.

118. Rankin, *Archilochus of Paros*, 65.

119. T. Abusch, "Gilgamesh's Request and Siduri's Denial," in *The Tablet and the Scroll: Near Eastern Studies in Honor of William W. Hallo* (ed. M. E. Cohen, D. C. Snell, and D. B. Weisberg; Bethesda, Md.: CDL, 1993), 13; and Paul, "A Lover's Garden of Verse," 105.

120. A. Cooper and B. R. Goldstein, "Exodus and *Maṣṣôt* in History and Tradition," *Maarav* 8 (1992): 26, suggested that in the light of 1 Kgs 9:15–19, which associates the northern rebellion against Solomonic policies with the liberation from Egypt, the mention of the "mares of Pharaoh" in Song 1:9 may be an intertextual reference to the exodus. Thus, we may understand the passage: "I have likened you ... to the mares of Pharaoh (i.e., which drowned in the sea)."

describe whores. Compare also the political invective of Ezekiel concerning Samaria's "sister" Oholibah (i.e., Jerusalem):

> So the Babylonians came to her for lovemaking and defiled her with their whoring; and she defiled herself with them until she turned from them in disgust. She flaunted her harlotries and exposed her nakedness, and I turned from her in disgust, as I had turned disgusted from her sister. But she whored still more, remembering how in her youth she had played the whore in Egypt; she lusted for concubinage with them, whose members were like those of assess and whose organs were like those of stallions. (Ezek 23:17–21 NJPS)

Other puns in the Song have a decidely more direct political purpose. Translators typically render the repeated verse "I adjure you, O daughters [i.e., vassals] of Jerusalem, by the צבאות and אילות of the field" (2:7; 3:5), as referencing "gazelles" and "hinds." The words in question, however, may be puns on royal titles, as we find elsewhere in the Bible where "gazelles," "rams," and other fauna can represent "rulers" or "nobles." See, for example, the use of אילים "rams" in Exod 15:15 and Ezek 17:13 to mean "rulers"; the singular איל "ram" in Dan 8:3; Ezek 34:17 with the same connotation; and צבי "gazelle, beauty" used of the crown prince in 2 Sam 1:19 (a meaning attested also at Ugarit[121]). Alternatively, the term צבאות could suggest Solomon's military complex (see, e.g., Judg 8:6; Isa 34:2).

Moreover, Maimonides, in his *Epistle to Yemen*, cited an observation found in b. Ketub. 111a that treats the phrase השבעתי אתכם "I adjure you" as meaning "I adjure you not to rebel against your ruler."[122] Paraphrased, therefore, we may read the repeated passage as a scathing innuendo: "I adjure you not to rebel against your ruler, O vassals of Jerusalem, by the nobles/military and leaders of the field; do not rouse, and do not arouse an alliance, until it desires (2:7; 3:5 [see also 8:4, with the middle line omitted]).[123] Underscoring the invective dimension of this verse is the expression עד שתחפץ "until it

121. *CAT* 1.15:IV:7 *ṯmnym ẓbyy* "my eighty gazelles (sc. chiefs)."

122. The sages and Maimonides used this interpretation in reference to the Jews in exile. See A. Halkin and D. Hartman, *Crisis and Leadership: Epistles of Maimonides* (Philadelphia: Jewish Publication Society, 1985), 148 n. 275.

123. The gender of these lexemes notwithstanding, unless again a gender role reversal is present. Cf. the Septuagint rendering: ἐν δυνάμεσι καὶ ἐν ἰσχύσεσι τοῦ ἀγροῦ "by the powers and strength of the field." If we add to this a possible nuance of the term צבאות as suggested by the term הנשים הצבאות "the women who served" (?), with whom Eli's sons were having sexual relations (1 Sam 2:22), the term צבאות "gazelles, nobles" takes on a decidedly polemical flavor.

desires," which veils another sexual innuendo. The verb חפץ suggests sexual desire (e.g., Gen 34:19; Deut 21:14; Esth 2:14) and in one instance refers to the erect penis: Job 40:17 יחפץ זנבו כמו ארז "his penis [lit. tail] is erect like a cedar," spoken of the hippopotamus.[124]

In line with the sexual and political reading is the verse, "Catch us the foxes, the little foxes, ruining the vineyards, and our vineyards in bud" (2:15). Of particular importance (and difficulty) is the identity of the "foxes." If we rely solely on a literal reading of the text, they are understood as marauding "foxes" ruining a vineyard. If we read the passage for its sexual overtones, however, the verse "represents the imagery of the deflowering of the young girl."[125] However, there is more, for the innuendo works on a political level as well. Since the "vine" appears frequently in the Bible as a metaphor for Israel (e.g., Isa 5:1–10; Ezek 34:23; Ps 80:2), the passage also alludes to the enemies of Israel.[126] Within the context of an invective, therefore, these foxes represent Judahites who reap the financial benefit of the vineyards of northern Israel.[127] Possible support for reading the garden as a reference to northern viticultural land comes from Song 6:2: "My beloved went down to his garden, to the beds of spices, to graze in the gardens and to gather lilies," employing the verb ירד "go down" (does this lexeme also contain a sexual nuance? cf. colloquial English), used elsewhere for the trip from Jerusalem.[128] Such combined

124. The dictionaries (BDB, 342–43; KB, 321; *HALOT*, 339–40) distinguish two verbal roots, with Job 40:17 as the sole usage of the second root. The standard meaning "desire" is related to Arabic *ḥafiẓa* "preserve, protect, be mindful," while the usage in Job 40:17 is associated with Arabic *ḫafaḍa* "make lower, decrease, reduce." Frankly, we are not convinced by either of these connections, especially the latter, since Arabic *ḫafaḍa* bears the opposite connotation of חפץ "be erect" in Job 40:17. With no evidence to the contrary, we would derive חפץ "be erect" in Job 40:17 from the same root as חפץ "desire."

125. Ullendorff, "The Bawdy Bible," 448.

126. Thus A. Robert and R. Tournay, *Le Cantique des cantiques: Traduction et commentaire* (Paris: Librarie Lecoffre, 1963), 15. It also may be that שועלים "foxes" plays on משעול "hollow way, narrow road," attested in Num 22:24 in the expression משעול הכרמים "from the vineyard roads," though we admit to not being able to see the function of such a wordplay.

127. Note also that Ezek 13:4 uses the term "foxes" metaphorically to refer to prophets.

128. A similar echo of northern dissatisfaction may be seen in Song 6:5: "avert your eyes from me, for they overwhelm me." As Ibn Ezra noted, the semantic range of the verb רהב "overwhelm" suggests that we read the verse as meaning "are too strong for me, or have taken away my power and my command."

sexual and political allusions, known from elsewhere in the Bible,[129] may have helped the poet to avoid any repercussions by veiling the object of criticism.

Political Interpretation

The Arabic (*tašbīb* and *hijāʾ*) and early Greek parallels illustrate how elaborate praise of a ruler's wife could function on an individual plane to shame a ruler and on a communal one to shame a tribe or city. Such a "love poem," however, could not have contained the invective, much less the political impact, were it not for a social context that made such insults transparent. Our proposal to interpret the Song of Songs as an invective of similar type, therefore, is possible only if a similar social context can be demonstrated for ancient Israel.

The character and conception of female chastity in Near Eastern societies has been the focus of study by social and cultural anthropologists for some time,[130] who have seen it as "associated with institutionalized conceptions of male power and status that constitute gender-based categories of 'honor' and 'shame.'"[131] As Dianne Bergant explained:

> Where sexuality is an expression of competition and superiority among men, the fruitfulness of women becomes a resource to protect. This has resulted in male dominance over women. Violating the enclosure of a man's home is comparable to breaching the boundaries of his land. Should a man cross the line of sexual etiquette, he might be in a position to enhance his own status by this challenge to the honor of another.[132]

---

129. One may cite, for example, a similar double-edged "flattery" of Judah in Gen 49:8–12, which combines a promotion of the tribe of Judah with a critique of his sexual escapades in Gen 38. See G. A. Rendsburg, *The Redaction of Genesis* (Winona Lake, Ind.: Eisenbrauns, 1986), 84; and David Biale, "The God with Breasts: El Shaddai in the Bible," *History of Religions* 21 (1982): 251.

130. M. J. Giovannini, "Female Chastity Code in the Circum-Mediterranean: Comparative Perspectives," in *Honor and Shame and the Unity of the Mediterranean* (ed. D. D. Gilmore; Washington, D.C.: American Anthropological Society, 1987), 61–74; and Bergant, "My Beloved Is Mine," 33.

131. Bergant, "My Beloved Is Mine," 33.

132. Ibid. According to Bergant, "The general tenor of the Song of Songs throws into question most of the characteristics associated with the notions of honor and shame. There is no underlying concern for male power and status, and consequently, there is no interest in controlling what might threaten it.… The patriarchal concern for safeguarding the chastity of the woman for the sake of progeny is not evident here" (36). Thus, for her, the Song is somewhat of an anomaly defying easy categorization

While some anthropologists have cautioned biblicists to recognize the heterogeneity of ancient cultures and the relationship between normative values and actual practice,[133] the general confines of our current understanding of shame and honor in ancient Israel is not in dispute.

More recently, anthropological approaches have begun to elucidate the ways in which conceptions of individual shame and dishonor are tied, if not transmuted, to the larger covenantal system that governed both the political and religious obligations of Israel. Saul Olyan explained:

> Though scholars have paid little attention to the place of honor and shame in covenant dynamics, honor and shame were clearly components of a larger complex of ideas related to covenant, a complex characterized by notions of recipriocity. Just as covenant love and covenant loyalty were reciprocal, even between suzerain and vassal, so was honor in a covenant setting.[134]

Olyan's observation provides an insight into how the Song of Songs might have functioned as an invective. By utilizing allusive and polysemous lan-

---

according to the expected protocols of honor/shame. However, the focus of her essay is on how social anthropology can shed light on the personal relationship between the figures (and thus gender issues) in the poem, not on how the poem might have functioned within an honor/shame society. Moreover, in his critique of Bergant's essay, Chance ("The Anthropology of Honor and Shame," 143) asked: "Why does this poetry deviate from the expectations of the model? One possible answer is to construe the poems as a protest against—or an assertion of disaffection with—a system of gender relations that severely restricts the expression of female sexuality." Carr ("Gender and the Shaping of Desire") has attempted to address this issue by viewing the Song as an expression of alternative female discourse. Our analysis of the poem as an invective addresses this issue by situating the deviation within the discourse of social and political discontent.

133. See, e.g., Chance, "The Anthropology of Honor and Shame," especially 148. Chance's criticism and the questions he raised take for granted that the love expressed in the Song (as argued by Bergant, "My Beloved Is Mine") is never indecent and, thus, never a breach of sexual etiquette. G. M. Kressel ("An Anthropologist's Response to the Use of Social Science Models in Biblical Studies," *Semeia* 68 [1996]: 153–60) also based his criticism on Bergant's analysis and used her understanding of the Song's language to explain how the Song entered the biblical canon. In Kressel's words, "The canonical status of the Song revealed an authentic facet of life, another normative facet of a people (the biblical Hebrews) that couldn't be concealed" (153). Had Bergant's analysis taken into consideration the Song's allusive and indecent language, both Chance and Kressel's analyses might have come to different conclusions.

134. Saul M. Olyan, "Honor, Shame, and Covenant Relations," *JBL* 155 (1996): 201–18.

guage, the poet shamed Solomon and his rule, and by extension, his political and theological (covenantal) relationships.

Reasons for such rebuke are not difficult to find in the Bible. The issues raised against Solomon, namely, excesses in taxation, corvée, wives, and the like, are all well known and may be reflected in the Song. Since 1 Kgs 11:1–3 reprimands the leader who gathers too many wives, it therefore cannot be truly praiseworthy to say of Solomon that he has "sixty queens, eighty concubines, and maidens without number" (Song 6:8). Indeed, as Whedbee observes: "The poet satirizes Solomon as an ostentatious king whose image as a master of a great harem is undercut."[135]

The Song's portrayal of Solomon is indeed noteworthy. He is mentioned in connection with laziness (e.g., sitting on his divan [1:12], litter [3:7], or palanquin [3:9])[136] and with his mother (3:11), who is credited with the responsibility for his kingship. The Song also portrays his excess near the end of the poem:

> Solomon had a vineyard in Baal-hamon; he gave the vineyard to the keepers, each brings for his fruit, a thousand (pieces of) silver. My own vineyard is before me; the thousand is for you, Solomon, and two-hundred to keepers of his fruit. (8:11–12)

Interestingly, the Targum interpreted these verses as referring to the northern kingdom of Israel, which was required to pay a thousand pieces of silver, and the southern kingdom of Judah, which was required to pay only two hundred. Ibn Ezra also saw a political reference in this passage as he noted: "The meaning is, he [Solomon] was the cause of the division of the kingdom, and he gave his sons possession of only two of the twelve parts, namely Judah and Benjamin." Consequently, he equated the passage "each must bring for its fruit a thousand (pieces of) silver" with "Jeroboam, the son of Nebat, who had the tenth part." The policy of forced labor that Solomon imposed on Israel (1 Kgs 5:27–30) may be reflected in this passage, as well as in Song 1:6: "they set me as keeper of the vineyards."

Similarly, in light of 1 Kgs 5:27–32; 9:19; 10:21–22, which record Solomon's levy, building program, and interest in Lebanon's timber resources, passages such as Song 3:9; 4:6 gain new understanding: the former with specific reference to the wood of Lebanon, the latter with geographical details about the region. Such an interpretation lends support to reading Song 7:6 "a king is held captive by (your) 'runners' [i.e., tresses]" as an allusion to Solo-

135. Whedbee, "Paradox and Parody," 276.

136. Compare the similar portrait of David on his couch in 2 Sam 11:2.

mon's indebtedness to Hiram king of Tyre (see 1 Kgs 9:11–13), especially as it follows immediately upon the mention of ארגמן "purple," a term that evokes the Phoenicians.[137]

As we have seen periodically already, both the Targum and Ibn Ezra interpreted certain passages in the Song in the light of Solomon's political history. This approach has been shared by more modern intepreters as well, most prominently Leroy Waterman,[138] who suggested that certain passages in the book carry political overtones. More recently Louis Stadelmann renewed this angle in his treatment of the poem as a political statement of the Persian period.[139] Notwithstanding the common thread of a political reading, these studies nevertheless place the Song in very different interpretive frameworks: the former as a drama, the latter as an early document of liberation theology. Neither work, however, cited Near Eastern analogs in support of their political interpretations. The interpretive framework of our study differs in that it bases its understanding of the Song on known Near Eastern (*tašbīb* and *hijāʾ*) and Mediterranean (Greek) poetic genres, along with the internal evidence. This approach, we submit, permits both the surface reading of the Song of Songs as an erotic love poem and the more subtle reading of the poem as a political invective.

The Importance of Dialect

We conclude this work where we began, with a consideration of the Song's dialect. As we have shown, the poem is an Israelian composition. However, we have not until this point considered the colloquial nature of the language. M. H. Segal, for one, was struck by the presence of colloquial Hebrew features

137. Pope, *Song of Songs*, 630, read the passage similarly, though in inverted fashion. In his view, "the king" in Song 7:6 is the king of Tyre: "The allusion … comes naturally after the mention of the purple which designated the Phoenician coast. The king of Tyre is bound to the tresses of Israel; this expression recalls the alliance which existed between the two nations at the epoch of David and Solomon."

138. Waterman, "דודי in the Song of Songs," 101–10; Waterman, "The Rôle of Solomon in the Song of Songs," 171–87, especially, 182; and idem, *The Song of Songs: Translated and Interpreted as a Dramatic Poem* (Ann Arbor: University of Michigan Press, 1948). Another early work that treated the Song as a drama is G. Pouget and J. Guitton, *The Canticle of Canticles* (trans. J. L. Lilly; New York: Declan X. McMullen, 1934), though we hasten to add that the drama theory first was proposed as early as 1722; see further Gordis, "The Song of Songs," 289–90, repr. in *Poets, Prophets, and Sages*, 359–60.

139. Stadelmann, *Love and Politics*.

in the Song of Songs, especially noticeable in the lines spoken by the female lover.[140] Like the Arabic and Greek invectives, the Song's colloquial elements perhaps added an air of "street talk," which helped to underscore the poem's more vulgar aspects. The Song's Israelian features, meanwhile, add another dimension to the poem. As the representative dialect of the northern tribes, the Song's language can be placed squarely in a discourse of discontent. In sum, the poem's dialect, when coupled with the numerous other features discussed above, allows us to see the Song of Songs as an early form of invective poetry analogous to later Greek and Arabic (*tašbīb* and *hijāʾ*) invective genres.

140. Segal, "Song of Songs," 478–79; repr. in idem, *The Pentateuch*, 229. See more thoroughly Rendsburg, *Diglossia in Ancient Hebrew*, 198.

Conclusion

As indicated in the introduction, the four chapters that constitute the greater part of this study could stand as individual units—that is to say, they could have been published separately as journal articles, for example. That said, however, we here wish to emphasize that the four chapters hinge together to create the unified argument that we now wish to advance.

All who have read the Song of Songs, certainly those who have done so with a literary eye, agree that the poem is a highly sophisticated composition. Its power lies in the tension created between its seductive devices of sound and variation (see chs. 2 and 3), which entice one to listen and to become "captivated by its tresses," and its content (see ch. 4), which forces one to pause and constantly rethink the meaning of its words. Indeed, it is only by listening carefully and rethinking its subtle double entendres that the poem's use of dialect (see ch. 1) reveals its invective punch. In light of this intersection of dialect, literary devices, and genre, we hope to have made clear by now the importance of appreciating the many facets of the Song of Songs in concert.

As the reader is keenly aware by now, there are many issues in the Song of Songs that we have not treated herein. We have not, for example, dealt with such questions as to whether the book is a unified composition or a series of independent songs gathered together on one scroll. Similarly, we have not addressed the issue of how many characters are present in the book: Are there just two characters: the male lover and the female lover? Or are there three characters: the male lover, the female lover, and a royal intruder? In like manner, who is the Solomon figure in the poem? Is he the male lover? the royal intruder? simply someone referred to from time to time? We also have not delved into other aspects of the book, such as the feminist reading of the Song of Songs.

We find all such questions of great interest, but by and large our intention in the present volume was not to enter into the matters enumerated above, electing instead to treat only the specific topics studied herein. Nevertheless, we can address some of these issues briefly, especially as our opinions on these matters do intersect with the topics treated herein. We beg the reader's forbearance, however, if we provide only a basic outline of our arguments. On the matter of the unity of the book, we very much believe that the Song of Songs is a unified composition. In fact, we would argue, since the entire book reflects Israelian Hebrew, with no single (hypothesized) poem lacking IH features, that the book is a unified work. Were it a collection of individual songs from ancient Israel, one might expect certain sections to lack IH elements, but such is not the case. One could argue, of course, that the book remains a collection of shorter poems—all of which were composed in northern Israel—but such a view would carry a high burden of proof.

Similarly, we note that the many cases of alliteration cited in chapter 2 span the borders of poetic units posited by those scholars who see the Song of Songs as a collection of independent compositions.[1] We would argue, by contrast, that these alliterations help establish an overall unity for the entire book. For example, 4:8 often is seen as a short song unto itself or as the final line of a section, with 4:9–11 or 4:9–5:1 representing an independent unit within the Song of Songs.[2] In chapter 2, however, we noted the alliteration created between מענות "dens" in 4:8 and מעיניך "of your eyes" in 4:9, with two of these consonants (*ʿayin* - *nun*) heard again in the rare word ענק "strand," also in 4:9 (see p. 90). In like manner, most scholars who read the book as a compilation of individual songs posit one unit ending at 6:3 and another one beginning at 6:4.[3] Again, however, in chapter 2 we noted how the rare word נדגלות "luminaries" in 6:4 rehearses the sounds found in ירד לגנו "went down to his garden" in 6:2 (see p. 100). When one multiplies such examples, as easily could be done here, one begins to see that a unified reading of the Song of Songs is far preferable.[4]

We further believe that the conclusions forthcoming from chapter 3 on polyprosopon in the poetry also support a unified reading of the Song of Songs. To our mind, the variations inherent in the repeated lines are evidence

1. For a survey of opinions, see White, *A Study of the Language of Love*, 32–33.

2. See, for example, ibid., 163; and M. Falk, *The Song of Songs: A New Translation and Interpretation* (San Francisco: HarperCollins, 1990), xix.

3. Again, see, for example, White, *A Study of the Language of Love*, 32, 163; and Falk, *The Song of Songs*, xix.

4. In like fashion, Edward Greenstein demonstrated how alliterations and wordplays in Exod 18 cross the boundaries of sources postulated by those scholars who see this chapter as emanating from more than one pen (though, to be sure, most scholars, it appears, assign the entire chapter to E). See E. L. Greenstein, "Jethro's Wit: An Interpretation of Wordplay in Exodus 18," in *On the Way to Nineveh: Studies in Honor of George M. Landes* (ed. S. L. Cook and S. C. Winter; ASOR Books 4; Atlanta: Scholars Press, 1999), 167 n. 10.

of a single composition, intentionally created by a single author with the goal of keeping the minds of his readers (listeners) alert as they experience the poetry read aloud.[5] In sum, we see no reason to divide the Song of Songs into separate component parts.

We hold that only two main characters are present in the poem: the male lover and the female lover (with the chorus responsible for some lines as well, of course). We see no evidence for a third main character—be it another (conjectured) male intruding on the relationship between the two lovers or anyone else. We believe that Solomon is simply referred to at various places in the poem—with the reasons therefore now evident, given the approach we have presented in chapter 4.

In addition, we are very much taken by the feminist readings that have been proposed by scholars. By our counting, the female lover speaks 65 verses, and the male lover speaks 36.5 verses (with the remaining 15.5 verses belonging to the chorus, for a total of 117 verses; see the appendix to this conclusion for the raw data). True, individual verses are of varying lengths, but spread over the eight chapters of the book, this factor begins to have a minimal effect on the overall picture. In short, the female voice carries the poem, with her speaking almost twice as many lines as her male counterpart. When one takes into further account that included in the male's lines are two *waṣf* sections, which are more stylized than other parts of the poem (that is, these passages proceed from one body part to the next, thereby providing the male voice a ready-made structure to follow), one sees that the female voice is even more dominant, especially when it comes to the creative expression of emotions. In addition, as previous scholars have noted, two lines in particular reverse the usual order of things (read: the order in a male-dominated world). We refer to Song 2:9, where the male lover views the female lover through the window from the outside (see our brief comment above, p. 156, as well as the translation, n. l), and to 7:11, which turns the tables on the famous passage in Gen 3:16, for now the male's desire is for the female, not vice versa, as per the garden of Eden story (see the translation, n. ae). Finally, we call attention to the fact that the author grants the female lover both the opening and closing lines of the poem (1:2–7, uninterrupted; and 8:5b-12 and 8:14, with the male voice heard briefly in 8:13).[6]

---

5. As noted in chapter 3, Michael Fox used these repetends to argue for the unity of the Song as well, though he approached the material in slightly different fashion. See Fox, *The Song of Songs*, 209–15.

6. See R. Alter, "The Song of Songs: An Ode to Intimacy," *BRev* 18.4 (2002): 24–32, 52, in particular 27.

There is, of course, one further issue that has divided scholars: the date of the Song of Songs. In this case, we will offer more than brief remarks, for this issue demands our detailed attention. As is well known, the range of dates proposed by scholars for the composition of the Song of Songs is considerable. The great majority of scholars, of course, date the book to the Persian period, based mainly on linguistic arguments, most significantly the presence of פרדס "orchard" in 4:13, presumed to be a loanword from Persian.[7] Chaim Rabin, on the other hand, dated the book to the tenth century B.C.E., based mainly on what he perceived to be parallels with Tamil poetry, especially in light of assumed Israelite voyages to India during the reign of Solomon.[8]

On the one hand, the issue of date does not affect our thesis that the subtext of the Song of Songs inveighs against Solomon, since the king's excesses were legendary and could have been exploited by early and later authors alike with equal polemical force. On the other hand, we believe that the invective inherent in the poem, assuming that our comparison to Arabic *hijāʾ* and *tašbīb* poetry is germane, fits the period of the divided kingdom best. Clearly it was during the existence of the northern kingdom (930–721 B.C.E.) that large segments of the population were wroth with Solomon. One could further argue, in fact, that it was during the beginning of this period that anti-Solomonic fervor was strongest. The key passage in Song 6:4, which presents Tirzah and Jerusalem as parallel terms, supports this position, for the former was the capital of the northern kingdom from sometime during the reign of Jeroboam I (see 1 Kgs 14:17) until the sixth year of the reign of Omri (see 1 Kgs 16:23), that is, approximately, 918–876 B.C.E. We would date the Song to specifically this period.

The main argument in favor of a late date for the Song of Songs is one of language. Typically this argument asserts that the large number of Aramaisms and Mishnaisms points to a late date. In chapter 1, however, we have explained these features otherwise.[9] The Aramaisms are not true Ara-

---

7. See, for example, A. Brenner, "Aromatics and Perfumes in the Song of Songs," *JSOT* 25 (1983): 75–81; and M. D. Goulder, *The Song of Fourteen Songs* (JSOTSSup 36; Sheffield: JSOT Press, 1986), 73–74.

8. C. Rabin, "The Song of Songs and Tamil Poetry," *Studies in Religion* 3 (1973–74): 205–19.

9. Note the comment of W. M. Schniedewind, *How the Bible Became a Book* (New York: Cambridge University Press, 2004), 235 n. 4: "Both Ecclesiastes and Song of Songs have several Aramaisms. Although Aramaisms do not definitively make a book late (cf. A. Hurvitz, "The Chronological Significance of 'Aramaisms' in Biblical Hebrew," *IEJ* 18 [1968]: 234–40), one has to come up with a special explanation (e.g., dialect, genre) to account for the peculiarities." We believe that we have done exactly

maisms, that is, borrowings from Aramaic during the postexilic period, but rather lexical and grammatical features shared by Israelian Hebrew and Aramaic during their coexistence over centuries. Similarly, the Mishnaisms are not indications of late date but rather evidence for the northern dialect in which the Song of Songs was composed.[10] The only bona fide signals of a late date, or at least potentially so, are the Persian and Greek loanwords, פרדס "orchard" in 4:13 and אפריון "canopy-bed" in 3:9, respectively. Thus, it is to these words that we now turn our attention.

We begin with the word פרדס "orchard."[11] As noted, most scholars believe that the word derives from Iranian, with Avestan *pairidaeza* "enclosure" the most commonly cited etymon. One must recall, however, the following: (1) Avestan is an eastern Iranian dialect (in contrast to Old Persian and Median, which are western Iranian dialects), and thus it is hard to imagine how an Avestan word would have reached Hebrew; and (2) the term *pairidaeza* is attested but once in Avestan—in a somewhat pejorative manner, in fact, with reference to an enclosure built around a man defiled by corpse contamination.[12] These points are countered by the presence of Akkadian *pardēsu* "enclosed garden," attested from the sixth century B.C.E. onward (that is, in the Neo-Babylonian dialect),[13] which leads one to assume that the Iranian word also was current in Old Persian and/or Median, whence it spread to Akkadian, Hebrew, Aramaic, and Greek (on which see below). Nevertheless, the lack of absolute evidence has led some to seek another source for the word פרדס. Rabin wrote as follows: "The word is generally agreed to be Persian, though the ancient Persian original is not quite clear.... It seems to

---

this, in presenting the language of the Song of Songs as a dialect of northern Israel and in proposing that the genre of the composition matches that of medieval Arabic *hijāʾ* poetry.

10. Alternatively, the Mishnaic features in the Song of Songs could be interpreted as evidence of colloquial Hebrew. See in general Rendsburg, *Diglossia in Ancient Hebrew*. On the Song of Songs in particular, with reference both to the Aramaic-like features as evidence of Israelian Hebrew and to the Mishnaic-like features as evidence of either a regional dialect or the colloquial dialect, see A. Hurvitz, "Ha-Lashon ha-ʿIvrit ba-Tequfa ha-Parsit," in *Shivat Ṣiyyon: Yeme Shilton Paras* (ed. H. Tadmor and I. Ephʿal; Ha-Historiya shel ʿAm Yisraʾel; Jerusalem: Alexander Peli, 1983), 217–18.

11. For basic information, see M. Ellenbogen, *Foreign Words in the Old Testament: Their Origin and Etymology* (London: Luzac, 1962), 136.

12. The evidence is presented in detail by J. P. Brown, *Israel and Hellas* (3 vols.; BZAW 231, 278, 299; Berlin: de Gruyter, 1995–2001), 3:128.

13. Black, George, and Postgate, *A Concise Dictionary of Akkadian*, 266.

me, however, that this word, to which also Greek *paradeisos* belongs, may be of different origin."[14] Oddly, Rabin did not pursue the thought further, though given his overall approach—connections between the Song of Songs and South Asia—one assumes that he had Sanskrit in mind. Indeed, the Sanskrit lexicon includes a vocable with the potential to be the source of Hebrew פרדס, namely, *paradhis* "enclosure, fence, wall, protection."[15]

In theory, given the handful of Sanskrit and Tamil words that reached Israel in antiquity (including one during the tenth century B.C.E.: תכי "peacock," appearing in 1 Kgs 10:22, borrowed from Tamil *tokay* "peacock"[16]), one might wish to countenance the possibility that פרדס derives from Sanskrit *paradhis*. The rules of Sanskrit phonology, however, preclude this option, since the word never would have been pronounced in the manner of *paradhis*, which is, after all, merely the entry form in the dictionary.[17] We return,

---

14. Rabin, "The Song of Songs and Tamil Poetry," 215.

15. M. Monier-Williams, *Sanskrit-English Dictionary* (2nd ed.; Oxford: Clarendon, 1899), 596. Note that in Hindu mythology the word *paridhis* refers to the ocean surrounding the earth.

16. See Rabin, "The Song of Songs and Tamil Poetry," 208. We state "during the tenth century B.C.E.," since we believe that the description of Solomon's commercial and other ventures in 1 Kgs 9–10 derives from authentic records (royal annals and the like) dated to his reign. For a detailed treatment of Indo-Aryan words in Near Eastern languages, see C. Rabin, "Millim ba-ʿIvrit ha-Miqraʾit mi-Leshon ha-ʾIndo-ʾArim she-ba-Mizraḥ ha-Qarov," in *Sefer Shmuel Yeivin: Meḥqarim ba-Miqraʾ, Arkheʾologya, Lashon ve-Toledot Yisraʾel, Mugashim lo be-Hagiʿo le-Seva* (ed. S. Abramsky; Jerusalem: Kiryat Sefer, 1970), 462–97. Some of the words treated by Rabin clearly have alternative explanations, but a good number of them betray Indo-Aryan origins. See also M. P. O'Connor, "Semitic **mgn* and Its Supposed Sanskrit Origin," *JAOS* 109 (1989): 30 n. 30. As the title of this article suggests, O'Connor rejected the view (correctly, in our opinion) of W. von Soden that the root מגן "give, bestow" derives from Sanskrit, but he did not deny the existence of Sanskrit words in Hebrew altogether. In the same spirit, note that, contra the opinion of earlier scholars, the derivation of Hebrew אלמגים/אלגמים "sandalwood" (or some other wood, perhaps) from Sanskrit *valguka* cannot be sustained; see J. C. Greenfield and M. Mayrhofer, "The ʾAlgummim/ʾAlmuggim-Problem Reexamined," in *Hebräische Wortforschung: Festschrift zum 80. Geburtstag von Walter Baumgartner* (ed. B. Hartmann; VTSup 16; Leiden: Brill, 1967), 83–89.

17. Consider the following, for which we are indebted to Michael Weiss of Cornell University (e-mail exchanges, August–September 2005). The Sanskrit form *paridhis* includes the nominative singular morpheme *-s*, but this ending would never surface as [s]. Since it follows an /i/ in this case, the "ruki" rule would take effect, and the final consonant thus would become the retroflex fricative [ṣ]. (The name of

therefore, to the conclusion, with the vast majority of scholars, that פרדס derives from an Iranian source, either Old Persian or Median.[18]

The latter option suggests, by the way, that פרדס could have entered Hebrew in preexilic times. The Medes entered the scene of history at a relatively early time, appearing for the first time on the Black Obelisk of Shalmaneser III, dated to year 24 of his reign, or circa 834 B.C.E.[19] It would not be surprising if the garden tradition of Iran spread westward to Assyria and even to the Levant sometime during the late ninth or early eighth century B.C.E. Of course, this is still too late to accommodate the word פרדס in Hebrew by the tenth century, but the gap closes nonetheless.[20] Indeed, the northern kingdom of Israel was very much in existence during the period of Assyr-

---

this rule is derived from the fact that /s/ > [ṣ] after the segments /r,u,k,i/.) Moreover, the pronunciation with [ṣ] would be retained only in some sandhi settings; before a voiced consonant it would become [r], and in pause it would shift to visarga, that is, an [h] sound. For the Sanskrit origin of Hebrew פרדס still to be countenanced, accordingly, one would have to assume (1) that the word was borrowed as *paridhiṣ*, and (2) that the final consonant would be rendered by Hebrew *samekh*. While the former is possible, the latter is unlikely, though we desist from entering into a discussion here about the actual phonetic values of the different Hebrew sibilants, including *ṣade*. The question of the latter is the subject of an entire monograph: R. C. Steiner, *Affricated* Ṣade *in the Semitic Languages* (AAJRMS 3; New York: American Academy for Jewish Research, 1982).

18. Incidentally, even if the word did occur in Old Persian, which seems very likely, it must have been a borrowing from Median into that language. That is to say, since the palatal /gh/ resolves as [z] and not [d] in the form, as is proper for Old Persian, the term must be a loanword from Median into Old Persian. The Old Persian word, incidentally, is directly continued by Modern Persian *pālez* "garden," and it also serves as the source for Armenian *partez* "garden" (an early loanword, borrowed before the Armenian consonant shift occurred) and Greek παράδεισος. This information also courtesy of Michael Weiss (see previous note).

19. See B. Brentjes, "The History of Elam and Achaemenid Persia: An Overview," in *Civilizations of the Ancient Near East* (ed. J. M. Sasson; New York: Charles Scribner's Sons, 1995), 1011–12.

20. If one accepts the case for an Iranian word entering Hebrew at a relatively early date, a potential parallel may exist in the word פלדה in Nah 2:4, assuming this word does mean "steel" and that it is indeed derived from Iranian (cf. Modern Persian *pūlād*). Of course, Nahum dates to the very end of the Assyrian period, by which point Iranian loans into Semitic are more plausible, even if the conquest of Cyrus the Great was still eighty or so years away.

ian-Median interaction, with several floruits during the eighth and seventh centuries (under the Omrides and under Jeroboam II, respectively).[21]

All of these notions, however, must remain highly speculative and without any real supporting evidence. By contrast, there is considerable evidence pointing to a late appearance of פרדס in Hebrew, especially as it is used in Song 4:13 with the meaning "garden." As noted above, the Akkadian *pardēsu* "enclosed garden" is attested only from the sixth century B.C.E. onward,[22] when a Persian presence is first felt in the most direct manner. The Greek evidence supports this contention. Xenophon uses the term παράδεισος for the pleasure parks used by the Persian kings,[23] though the main emphasis appears to be as large enclosures filled with wild animals for hunting, with a secondary focus on forests as a source of timber.[24] The term is not used to describe the gardens of Pasargadae and Persepolis, for example. Only from the third century B.C.E. onward did the Greek word παράδεισος come to mean "garden, orchard."

The Hebrew word פרדס appears in the Bible twice elsewhere: Qoh 2:5 and Neh 2:8. The latter reference approximates Xenophon's usage, since the context in Nehemiah is a personal forest belonging to the king, with an official called שׁמר הפרדס "the keeper of the enclosure" in charge of the distribution of wood needed for the construction of the city gates and the gates of the temple in Jerusalem. The passages in Song 4:13 and Qoh 2:5, by contrast, refer to gardens and orchards with fruit trees in them. There is no reason to assume a priori that the semantics of Hebrew פרדס exactly parallels that of Greek παράδεισος, but if it does, since the latter comes to mean "garden, orchard" relatively late, then one would date the final form of the two biblical scrolls to a very late period as well.[25] On the other hand, one

21. Of this opinion is also F. Dorseiff, *Antike und alter Orient* (Leipzig: Koehler & Amelang, 1959), 200. We have not been able to consult his work directly, but Oswald Loretz, *Qohelet und der alte Orient: Untersuchungen zu Stil und theologischer Thematik des Buches Qohelet* (Freiburg: Herder, 1964), 23 n. 16, cited his view (not with approval, though) that פרדס may have existed in West Semitic before the Persian period, since Persian-style garden architecture was famous and subject to emulation.

22. See J. Black, A. George, and N. Postgate, *A Concise Dictionary of Akkadian* (Wiesbaden: Harrassowitz, 2000), 266.

23. H. G. Liddell and R. Scott, *A Greek-English Lexicon* (9th ed.; Oxford: Clarendon, 1940), 1308. Note, further, that Pollux (9.13) specifically stated that the Greek term is of Persian origin.

24. For treatment, see Brown, *Hellas and Israel*, 3:121–29.

25. Presumably this was one of the key factors that led H. L. Ginsberg to write as follows: "The language of the Song of Songs shows that in its present form it is late,

could assume that the Hebrew term developed this meaning—quite easily, we might add—independently of its meaning in Greek and at an earlier time. We would not claim, for example, that the appearance of פרדס with the meaning "orchard" in the Song of Songs and in Qohelet means that both books date to the third century B.C.E.

We turn now to אפריון "canopy-bed" in Song 3:9.[26] Though many scholars consider this lexeme to be a borrowing from Greek φορεῖον "litter, sedan-chair," attested from the fourth century B.C.E. onward (Dinarchus, etc.),[27] another potential source is the Sanskrit form *paryanka*, as suggested already by nineteenth-century scholars, including Brown-Driver-Briggs.[28] In contrast to the difficulties encountered with positing a Sanskrit source for פרדס, in this case, such a borrowing is linguistically possible.[29] In addition, one might expect the Hebrew term (the Greek term also?) to have come from the East, since the portable canopy-bed is associated most frequently with that part of the globe.[30] Indeed, our English word *palanquin* derives ultimately from the Sanskrit as well.[31] Furthermore, to cite one scholar who has questioned the presumed Greek origin of אפריון, we refer to Ian Young: "The

---

perhaps as late as the third century B.C.E." (*The Five Megilloth and Jonah* [Philadelphia: Jewish Publication Society, 1969], 3). He returned to this point more explicitly in his discussion of פרדס in Qohelet (52).

26. Oddly, this word is not treated by Ellenbogen, *Foreign Words in the Old Testament.*

27. See, e.g., Fox, *Song of Songs*, 125. For the Greek evidence, see Liddell and Scott, *A Greek-English Lexicon*, 1950.

28. BDB, 68. For the Sanskrit term, technically *pary-anka*, see Monier-Williams, *Sanskrit-English Dictionary*, 607.

29. While there is no ready explanation for the loss of the final syllable *-ka* (assuming a direct borrowing from Sanskrit into Hebrew), we do note that such things do occur when words are borrowed from one language into another. Indeed, Nepali *palaṅ* "luxurious bed," borrowed from Hindi *palang* and derived from Sanskrit *paryanka*, *palyanka*, reflects the same process. See R. L. Turner, *A Comparative and Etymological Dictionary of the Nepali Language* (London: Paul, Trench, Trubner, 1931), 368.

30. Although אפריון is not among the words treated in the article, for the general picture see C. Rabin, "Lexical Borrowings from Indian Languages as Carriers of Ideas and Technical Concepts," in *Between Jerusalem and Benares: Comparative Studies in Judaism and Hinduism* (ed. H. Goodman; Albany: State University of New York Press, 1994), 25–32, 281–82.

31. *Oxford English Dictionary.*

fact that scholars have suggested so many possibilities for the origin of this word should indicate that we do not have enough evidence to decide."[32]

So while the Sanskrit option must remain open, it is far more likely that אפריון comes from Greek.[33] We do not, however, believe that the word automatically needs to be considered a late borrowing. At least three Greek words appear in Hebrew in early texts, namely, לפיד "torch, lightning" (Exod 20:18, etc.), לשכה "(meeting) hall" (1 Sam 9:22, etc.), and מכרה "sword" (Gen 49:5), not to mention words with more complicated origins, most famously, פילגש "concubine," though plainly derived from a Mediterranean source (whether Greek, Italic, or other).[34] True, Greek φορεῖον is not attested until the fourth century B.C.E., as noted above, so the point may not be relevant. But even if φορεῖον "litter, sedan-chair" did occur earlier in Greek, without leaving a trace in the historical record, one could imagine specifically this kind of noun—a *Kulturwort*, as with the three others noted above—passing from Greek to Hebrew at an early time.

We summarize the above treatments of the two relevant lexemes as follows: (1) in line with the majority of scholars, we hold that פרדס is a borrowing from Old Persian, probably during the Persian period itself; (2) we accept that אפריון is borrowed from Greek, but we do not necessarily hold that this occurred during the late period. The word easily may have entered the Hebrew language in preexilic times.

The conclusions above, especially concerning פרדס, yields the finding that the Song of Songs in its present state is a product of the Persian period. Such finds would appear to stand in the way of our argument that beneath the surface meaning of the book lies an invective against Solomon in particular or the Judahite monarchy in general. It is hard to imagine anyone in, let us say, fifth-century Israel still fighting this battle. True, one could envision the Samaritans holding such a view, but there is no evidence linking the Songs of Songs to this group.

The solution to this problem, we believe, lies in the poem's long history of textual transmission and reception. Ancient scribes and the oral performers of literature generally had no sense of canonical or fixed text in the way that later came to exist (at least in theory, since minor variations always exist).

32. Young, *Diversity in Pre-exilic Hebrew*, 162.

33. See the detailed treatment of F. Rundgren, "אפריון 'Tragsessel, Sänfte,'" *ZAW* 74 (1962): 70–72.

34. Basic bibliography for this last word: C. Rabin, "The Origin of the Hebrew Word *Pilegeš*," *JSS* 25 (1974): 353–64; S. Levin, "Hebrew {*pi(y)lέgεš*}, Greek παλλακή, Latin *paelex*: The Origin of Intermarriage among the Early Indo-Europeans and Semites," *General Linguistics* 23 (1983): 191–97; and Brown, *Israel and Hellas*, 1:65–70.

Instead, as scholars know well, texts in antiquity frequently were altered or updated by later scribes or their oral performers. Sometimes large-scale operations were conducted, especially by scribes responsible for the written forms of our texts. Thus, for example, entire passages were rearranged, older sections were omitted, and/or new sections were added. At other times, the changes were minimal, as when a single word or form was changed or updated. All of these changes may be seen when comparing, for example, the books of Kings and Chronicles, the Masoretic Text and the Septuagint, the Masoretic Text and a Qumran manuscript, the various recensions of the Epic of Gilgamesh, and so on.

Readers who are aware of our (that is, both authors') scholarship will know that generally speaking we are reticent to enter into such matters—that is to say, typically we treat only the Masoretic Text in our research. In the current instance, however, given what we perceive to be the prevailing evidence for the origin of the Song of Songs in the kingdom of Israel (while it still existed, that is), we feel the need to follow the lead of scholars who have dealt with the development of biblical books over time.[35] From this vantage point, accordingly, we are not overly concerned with the presence of the single word פרדס in the text of the Song of Songs, since it very well may be the product of linguistic updating. We would posit that the word פרדס was introduced into the text by a later scribe, during the Persian period (or possibly during the Hellenistic period), when this word became current in ancient Israel, presumably replacing a synonym. That is to say, a hypothesized שְׁלחיך X רמונים (with "X" representing our unknown word) was modified to שְׁלחיך פרדס רמונים, as Song 4:13 currently reads.

We are keenly aware that in chapter 2 (pp. 92–93) we noted that the word פרדס is effectively included in the passage in order to enhance the alliteration. We repeat our observation here:

> As is well known, the noun פרדס "orchard" in verse 13 is a rare noun in the Bible. The poet's selection of this word may be explained by the requirements of alliterative exigency. The word begins with *pe* and *reš*, the same two consonants that occur in the words פרי "fruit" and כפרים "henna." Note that these sounds are evenly distributed in the verse, with one set in each stich. Furthermore, the *reš* and *dalet* in פרדס is rehearsed in נרדים "nard"

35. Here we have in mind such works as S. Niditch, *Oral World and Written Word: Ancient Israelite Literature* (Louisville: Westminster John Knox, 1996); and D. M. Carr, *Writing on the Tablet of the Heart: Origins of Scripture and Literature* (New York: Oxford University Press, 2005).

(plural form) later in verse 13 and in נרד "nard" (singular form) in verse 14.[36]

This finding, however, does not necessarily mean that פרדס was original to the text. It could have replaced an earlier word and still serve to augment the alliteration. We present here an apt parallel.

As scholars of the Dead Sea Scrolls noted early on, and as E. Y. Kutscher demonstrated in detail, there are literally hundreds of differences between MT Isaiah and 1QIsa^a.[37] In the opinion of Kutscher, and in his wake everyone else, the latter represents a later text-type than the former. The Qumran manuscript shows clear sign of conscious updating. Occasionally these changes are lexical updatings, with a more current word replacing an older word. An excellent example is the use of יחמול (with *waw* hanging) in 1QIsa^a in place of ישמח in MT Isa 9:16.[38] The latter represents the only case in Biblical Hebrew where the root שמח means "have pity on" (cf. Arabic *smḥ* [even if we expect Arabic *šmḥ*, in light of the Hebrew *śin*]).[39] The individual responsible for the Qumran manuscript either did not understand the word or felt that his readers would not understand the word, and thus he replaced the root שמח with the more common usage חמל "have pity on," a suitable parallel verb to רחם slightly later in the verse.

What has not been noticed until now, though, is the manner in which חמל serves the sounds of this verse in a better way than the root שמח. True, both verbs have *mem* and *ḥet*, so presumably either would work fine in Isa 9:16. But the following is rather striking: the presence of the *lamed* in חמל,

36. Incidentally נרד "nard" in Song 4:13–14 (once in the singular, once in the plural) is a prime example of a Hebrew lexeme borrowed from Sanskrit, where the word is attested as both *nalada* and *narada*. The plant is native to South Asia but not to the Middle East.

37. E. Y. Kutscher, *Ha-Lashon ve-ha-Reqaʿ ha-Leshoni shel Megillat Yeshaʿyahu ha-Shelema mi-Megillot Yam ha-Melaḥ* (Jerusalem: Magnes, 1959).

38. Ibid., 179.

39. This point is treated briefly in ibid., 179 (with n. 38). For additional philological and/or text-critical discussion, see the following: F. Perles, "Notes critiques sur le texte d l'*Ecclésiastique*," *REJ* 35 (1897): 63–64; I. L. Seeligman, "Meḥqarim be-Toledot Nusaḥ ha-Miqraʾ," *Tarbiz* 25 (1956): 130–31, repr. in idem, *Meḥqarim be-Sifrut ha-Miqraʾ* [ed. A. Hurvitz, E. Tov, and S. Japhet; Jerusalem: Magnes, 1992], 308–9); and J. C. Greenfield, "Lexicographical Notes II," *HUCA* 30 (1959): 141–42. For a similar issue arising in Ben Sira, raised already by Seeligman in the aforecited article, see now M. Kister, "Some Notes on Biblical Expressions and Allusions and the Lexicography of Ben Sira," in *Sirach, Scrolls, and Sages* (ed. T. Muraoka and J. F. Elwolde; Leiden: Brill, 1999), 165.

in combination with the *mem* and *ḥet,* enhances the alliteration with a host of words in the verse with either *lamed*, *reš*, or *nun*, namely, אלמנותיו ,בחוריו, ירחם ,חנף ,מרע, and נבלה, in addition to which note מבלעים as the last word in the preceding verse. Note further that there is not a single sibilant in the twenty-one words in this verse from the start through the *ʾatnaḥ* (that is, apart from ישׂמח), and in the eight words that appear after the *ʾatnaḥ* there are only two sibilants (in זאת and in שׁב). Clearly the word יחמול in 1QIsa[a] serves this verse alliteratively far better than ישׂמח of the MT. Now, were we to have only the Qumran manuscript, we would have no reason to assume that the root חמל replaced an older, earlier (and now [presumably] obsolete) שׂמח "have pity on." The root fits nicely as a parallel lexeme to רחם, and it works wonderfully given the other sounds present in the verse. So it is with פרדס in Song 4:13, we submit. In following this course, we readily admit to a procedure not typical of our scholarship. But we also do not feel that we need to corner ourselves and stay totally clear of the "linguistic updating" approach, especially in light of the analog from Isa 9:16 just presented.

We further note that if any book in the Bible would be susceptible to later accretions or replacements of earlier synonyms, it most likely is the Song of Songs. Since this composition is the Bible's singular exemplar of love poetry, which at some point no doubt circulated among the populus at large in ways different from, say, a book of the Torah or a book of the Prophets,[40] we are more open to this approach than we might otherwise be were we treating another biblical book.[41] In the words of H. L. Ginsberg, "No doubt Israel always had such songs, but they were handed down orally and were modified, and old verses or whole songs were replaced by new, as the language changed."[42]

40. We also imagine that, with the passage of time, any recollection of the poem's use as an invective against the Judahite monarchy would have waned, and the Song of Songs would have been read as beautiful love poetry, pure and simple.

41. There is still one other option available: the approach of Robert Gordis (among others), who claimed that the Song of Songs is a compilation of individual love poems, some of which are early and some of which are late. We could follow this line and propose that the composition as a whole is early but that a later individual poetic unit was inserted in this particular place in chapter 4, which included the word פרדס. As noted above, however, we prefer to view the poem as a unified whole, for the reasons expressed. See R. Gordis, *The Song of Songs and Lamentations: A Study, Modern Translation and Commentary* (New York: Ktav, 1974), 24–25; as well as the summary in Young, *Diversity in Pre-exilic Hebrew*, 158.

42. Ginsberg, *The Five Megilloth and Jonah*, 3.

In addition to the above point, we now happily note the recent work of David Carr, who also is not overly concerned with the presence of a single Persian word in the Song of Songs. In his work on the creation of literature in antiquity, Carr notes that scribes would have seen fit to adapt texts from other cultures for their own cultural milieu, and he specifically mentions the Song of Songs (along with Proverbs and others) as biblical books with the greatest degree of similarity to other ancient Near Eastern compositions.[43] Carr posits the era of the divided monarchy as the most productive time for such scribal and literary activity. It was in such settings, with Israel and Judah as independent political entities in their native lands, and with kings sponsoring royal chancelleries, that texts from Egypt and Mesopotamia would have been read, considered, and adapted for Hebrew usage and dissemination. Given the remarkable similarities between the love poetry of New Kingdom Egypt and the Song of Songs from ancient Israel, Carr understands the former exercising considerable influence on the production of the latter during the time of the divided monarchy. We concur with this viewpoint, though we are more specific in our reconstruction, which situates the Song of Songs specifically in the northern kingdom of Israel, for all the reasons that we have explained herein.

We conclude with our summary position: the Song of Songs was written circa 900 B.C.E.,[44] in the northern dialect of ancient Hebrew, by an author of unsurpassed literary ability, adept at the techniques of alliteration and polyprosopon, able to create the most sensual and erotic poetry of his day, and all the while incorporating into his work a subtext critical of the Judahite monarchy in general and Solomon in particular.

---

43. D. M. Carr, "Method in Dating Biblical Texts," paper delivered at the joint meeting of the National Association of Professors of Hebrew and the Society of Biblical Literature, Washington, D.C., 20 November 2006. We thank Professor Carr for his profitable discussion with us on this issue.

44. One final linguistic point can be made here, even though it is not definitive. We refer to the usage המלך שלמה in 3:9, which follows SBH word order (28 times in Kings; see also Jer 52:20), as opposed to שלמה המלך, the LBH equivalent (for this specific collocation, see 1 Chr 29:24; 2 Chr 10:2; in addition to which there are eight instances of דויד המלך in Chronicles). This point is not definitive, however, since the standard form המלך שלמה continues into postexilic times (witness five attestations in Chronicles) and the "late" usage דוד המלך can be found in 2 Sam 13:39 (though many scholars, noting the difficulties inherent in this verse, consider it to be a late addition).

Appendix to Conclusion

Distribution of Verses in the Song of Songs: Male, Female, Chorus

1:1–1:7	Female	7	
1:8–1:11	Male		4
1:12–14	Female	3	
1:15	Male		1
1:16–2:1	Female	3	
2:2	Male		1
2:3–13	Female	11	
2:14	Male		1
2:15–3:5	Female	8	
3:6–10	Chorus		
4:1–16a	Male		15.5
4:16b	Female	0.5	
5:1	Male		1
5:2–5:8	Female	7	
5:9	Chorus		
5:10–5:16	Female	7	
6:1	Chorus		
6:2–6:3	Female	2	
6:4–6:9	Male		6
6:10	Chorus		
6:11–6:12	Male		2
7:1–7:6	Chorus		
7:7–7:10	Male		4
7:11–8:4	Female	8	
8:5a	Chorus		
8:5b–8:12	Female	7.5	
8:13	Male		1
8:14	Female	1	

Total number of verses: 65 (female); 36.5 (male)
(remaining 15.5 verses are of the chorus, for a total of 117 verses)

The Song of Songs: Translation and Notes

Our translation of the Song of Songs attempts to adhere as closely as possible to the Hebrew text. As such, we follow the lead set by Everett Fox, most prominently, in his approach to translation.

In addition, we have attempted to utilize common English words to render common Hebrew words and rare English words to render rare Hebrew words (see notes h and ac, for example).

We also follow Fox's lead in our representation of proper names. Throughout this volume we have used standard English forms for proper names (Gilead, Lebanon, Solomon, etc.). In our translation, however, we have opted for a closer representation of the Hebrew (i.e., Masoretic) forms (Gilʿad, Levanon, Shelomo, etc.).

We further believe that the Masoretic paragraphing should be indicated in an English translation, and thus we have done so in our presentation of the text. While we consider (with most scholars) the Aleppo Codex to be the most authoritative witness to the biblical text, in this case we are encumbered by the fact that only Song 1:1–3:11 is preserved in the extant part of the Aleppo Codex. Accordingly, we have elected to follow the paragraphing system of the Leningrad Codex. *Setuma* breaks are indicated by an extra blank line. The sole *petuḥa* break in the book, after 8:10, is indicated by two blank lines. The Aleppo Codex, as preserved, has *petuḥa* breaks after 1:4 and 1:8, whereas the Leningrad Codex has *setuma* breaks in these two places. As for the remaining part of the Song of Songs in the "Aleppo tradition," we note a difference of opinions by the editors responsible for the two major publications of the Aleppo Codex at one place. Mordecai Breuer (*Torah, Neviʾim, Ketuvim* [Jerusalem: Mosad Ha-Rav Kook, 1989], שג) indicates a *setuma* break after 4:11, which is also reflected in the Leningrad Codex; the *Keter Yerushalayim* volume (notwithstanding its nod to Breuer on the title page) has no break of any sort at this juncture (737/תשלז).

We also have introduced different fonts in our translation to reflect the different characters present in the Song of Songs, as follows:

- Minion Pro is used for the two principal characters, with the more flowing italic *Minion Pro* used for the dominant female voice and the regular Minion Pro used for the responsive male voice.
- The superscription in 1:1 is indicated by Garamond.
- **The lines spoken by the chorus are produced in Gill Sans.**
- The few lines spoken by the brothers, 8:8–9, in the mouth of the female, are indicated by Skia.

Note that one cannot be absolutely certain about the attribution of all the spoken lines to a particular character (male lover, female lover) or group (chorus, brothers). Such uncertainty, however, probably is germane for only about 10 percent of the lines. In most cases, when the second-person masculine singular forms (verbs, pronouns, etc.) are used, we assume that the female lover is speaking, addressing her beloved. Conversely, when the second-person feminine singular forms are used, we assume that the male lover is speaking.

Finally, observe that there are two sets of notes accompanying our translation. The lettered notes (a, b, c) refer to general literary uses, while the numbered notes (1, 2, 3) refer specifically to issues relevant to the *hijāʾ* and *tašbīb* genres raised in chapter 4.

The Song of Songs

1:1 The song of songs, which is Shelomo's.[1]
1:2 *May he kiss me with the kisses of his mouth,*
For your love is better than wine.[a 2]
1:3 *To the scent of your good oils,*
"Turaq oil"[b] *is your name;*
Therefore the maidens love you.[3]
1:4 *Draw me, after you let us run;*
The king has brought me to his chambers,
Let us be glad and let us rejoice in you,
Let us recall[c] *your love more than wine,*
(More than) smooth-wine, they love you.

1:5 *Black am I, and comely,*
O daughters of Yerushalayim;
Like the tents of Qedar,
Like the curtains of Shelomo.[5]

---

a. The shift from third person in the first stich to second person in the second stich sounds odd to English ears, but this is common in Hebrew poetry.

b. The Hebrew word *turaq* remains an enigma. Presumably it describes a particularly fine type of oil.

c. The Hebrew root *zkr* typically means "remember," thus our rendering "recall." But a homonymous root, which serves as the basis for the common word *zākār* "male," bears a sexual connotation. Accordingly, a second meaning is evident as well, something like "let us make-love your love."

---

1. Or, in light of the object of the invective, "the song of songs concerning Shelomo." See also the references to this wealthiest of kings in 1:5; 3:7, 9, 11; 8:11, 12.

2. The poet begins immediately with the wine imagery that will flow throughout the poem, a feature that the Song of Songs shares with Arabic *hijāʾ* poetry.

3. The female lover notes that other women love the male protagonist as well, both here and in the final stich of the next verse. See also 6:9, though in this passage we learn that other women acclaim the female lover. The praise by others, external to the main characters, is another feature of *hijāʾ* poetry, on which see chapter 4, pp. 152–53.

4. Given the *hijāʾ* quality of the poem, we opt to retain MT here (see ch. 4, p. 141) and thereby reject the oft-proposed emendation to "Salma."

5. "The sons of my mother," of course, is a poetic way of stating "brothers" (who would have to be full brothers, not half-brothers). Given that "brothers" can refer to political allies in Biblical Hebrew (see ch. 4, pp. 157–58), we suggest that a political reading may be inherent here, as befitting the overall charges within *hijāʾ*

1:6 *Do not look at me, that I am dark,*
That the sun has glared at me;
The sons of my mother were angry at me,
They set me as keeper of the vineyards,
(But) my own vineyard I have not kept.[6]
1:7 *Tell me, O whom my inner-being*[d] *loves,*[7]
Where do you desire/shepherd?[e] [8]
Where do you cause-(them)-to-lie-down at noon?
Lest I become like one-who-veils,[f]
Beside the flocks of your friends.
1:8 If you do not know, yourself,
O most beautiful among women;
Go out, yourself, by the footprints of the flock,
And shepherd your kids,
At the dwellings of the shepherds.

1:9 To a mare in Pharaoh's chariotry,[9]

---

d. Here and throughout the translation we render *nepeš* with "inner-being," which captures the essence of the ancient Hebrew understanding of the word better than English "soul" or other alternatives.

e. Note the Janus parallelism (see ch. 1, §1.1.2, pp. 13–14), with the pivot word *tirʿeʰ* meaning both "desire" (paralleling what precedes) and "shepherd" (anticipating what follows).

f. The notoriously difficult Hebrew term *ʿôṭyāʰ*, on which see also chapter 4, p. 154 n. 84.

---

poetry. Among other relevant passages in the Song of Songs, see, for example, 8:1 with "brother" meaning "ally."

6. The first of numerous references to vineyards, orchards, and gardens within the Song of Songs, which is also characteristic of *hijāʾ* poetry in the Arabic tradition (see ch. 4, pp. 147–49). See also 1:14; 2:13, 15; 4:12, 13, 15, 16; 5:1, 13; 6:2, 11; 7:13; 8:11–12, 13.

7. The Hebrew root *ʾhb* "love" is used for "fealty" in a political sense throughout the Bible, and we suggest that this undertone is present in the Song of Songs as well (see ch. 4, p. 157).

8. The double meaning in this word and the Janus parallelism inherent in this verse is treated in note e (see also §1.1.2, pp. 13–14). Yet a third connotation is present, however. The verbal root *rʿy* can bear both humans as the subject, in which case the sense is "shepherd," and animals as the subject, in which case the sense is "graze." With the latter sense, however, the meaning can be extended to "devastate" (< "overgraze"), and thus this passage also contains a veiled critique of the king; see chapter 4, p. 153.

9. One does not necessarily expect military terminology within love poetry, but

I liken you, my darling.[10]
1:10 Your cheeks are lovely with circlets,
Your neck with strings-of-beads.
1:11 Circlets of gold we will make for you.
With spangles of silver.
1:12 *While[g] the king is on his divan,*[h 11]
My nard gives forth its scent
1:13 *A sachet of myrrh is my beloved to me,*
Between my breasts may he lodge.
1:14 *A cluster of henna is my beloved to me,*
From the vineyards of ʿEn Gedi.

1:15 Behold you are beautiful, my darling,
Behold you are beautiful, your eyes are doves.
1:16 *Behold you are beautiful, my beloved, indeed pleasant,*
Indeed our bed is verdant.
1:17 *The rafters of our house are cedars,*
Our runners are cypresses.
2:1 *I am a daffodil of the Sharon,*
A lily of the valleys.
2:2 Like a lily among the brambles,
So is my darling among the daughters.[12]

---

g. Hebrew *ʿad še-*, rendered "until" throughout the Song of Songs, though we opt for "while" here for better sense.

h. Hebrew *mesab*, a rare noun, rendered here with "divan," a relatively rare English word. In addition, "divan" conveys a sense of royalty, aristocracy, and officialdom and thus befits the mention of the king here.

---

the parallel with *hijaʾ* poetry (on which see ch. 4, p. 149–50) accounts for the presence of such language in the Song of Songs. For other relevant passages, see 3:7-8; 4:4; 6:4, 12, 7:5; 8:9–10.

10. This is the first of many passages in the poem that extol the female lover but that, in light of *hijāʾ* technique, are to be understood as satririal praise. In addition, the term *raʿyāh* "darling" is the feminine form of *rēaʿ* "friend," which elsewhere bears the political connotation of "ally" (see ch. 4, p. 158).

11. Possibly the allusion here is to the laziness of the king (see also 3:7 and 9, with other furniture terms, where Shelomo is mentioned specifically by name). This would be a very direct critique of royal behavior, needless to say; see further chapter 4, p. 167.

12. Once the undertone of *raʿyāh* "darling" as "ally" is established (see n. 10), it is easy to sense the secondary meaning of *bānôt* "daughters" as "vassals" (see ch. 4, p. 158–59).

2:3 *Like an apricot-tree among the trees of the forest,*
So is my beloved among the sons;
In his shade I delight and I sit,[i]
And his fruit is sweet to my palate.[13]
2:4 *He brought me to the house of wine,*
And his glance[j] *toward me is love.*[14]
2:5 *Support me with raisin-cakes,*
Spread me among the apricots;
For I am sick with love.
2:6 *His left-hand is beneath my head,*
And his right-hand embraces me.
2:7 *I adjure you, O daughters of Yerushalayim,*
By the gazelles, or by the hinds of the field;[15]
Do not rouse, and do not arouse love,
Until it desires.

2:8 *Hark, my beloved,*
Behold he comes,
Bounding over the mountains,
Leaping over the hills.
2:9 *My beloved is-like*[k] *a gazelle,*

---

i. The Hebrew construction collocates two suffix-conjugation verbs, separated by the conjunctive "and." A more idiomatic rendering would be "I delight to sit."

j. If taken from the Hebrew noun *degel*, then "his banner." But we have chosen to relate the word here to the Akkadian verb *dagālu* "see." Of course, both meanings could be inherent, given the thread of polysemy that permeates the book.

k. The hyphenated form "is-like" is used here to render the verbal root *d-m-h*, in contrast to "is like" and "are like" in a number of other passages, where the Hebrew includes the unexpressed copula followed by the preposition *kə-*. In four other passages (1:9; 2:17; 7:8; 8:14), we are able to avail ourselves of the verb "liken" to render verbal forms of *d-m-h*.

---

13. The erotic imagery here is part and parcel of the *hijā*ʾ style.

14. The noun ʾ*ahăbā*ʰ "love" indicates "alliance," once the political reading of the Song of Songs within the context of invective poetry is recognized. See also 2:5; 5:8 and the refrains in 2:7; 3:5; 8:4.

15. Here and in the parallel passage (3:5) the words *ṣəbā*ʾ*ôt* and ʾ*aylôt* can be understood as terms for "rulers, nobles," in addition to which the first word carries the meaning of "armies." Such political language shines through in the *hijā*ʾ genre; see chapter 4, p. 163.

Or a fawn of the hinds;[16]
Behold, he stands behind our wall,
Gazing through the windows,
Peering through the lattices.[l] [17]
2:10 *My beloved speaks, and he says to me:*
"Arise,[m] *my darling, my beautiful, and go forth.*
2:11 *For behold, the winter has passed,*
The rain has departed, gone.
2:12 *The blossoms appear in the land,*
The time of pruning/singing[n] *has arrived;*
The voice of the turtledove is heard in our land.
2:13 *The fig-tree perfumes its young-fruit,*

---

l. Typically in biblical literature, we gain the male perspective, and thus we witness "the woman in the window" motif through a man's eyes; that is, the "reader" is outside, and he or she views Rahab, Sisera's mother, Michal, Jezebel, and Lady Wisdom looking out *beʿad haḥallôn* "through the window" (see ch. 4, p. 156, for references). Here, by contrast, we gain the female perspective. True, she remains inside the house, which is the woman's domain, but the "camera" is there with her as she looks out to see her male lover approaching and peering *min haḥallônôt* "through the window" (lit. "windows') from without.

m. The actual expression is *qûmî lāk*, with an additional element "you, yourself" after the verb, as also occurs at the end of this stich in *ləkî lāk*. While we have managed to capture the latter with "go forth," instead of simple "go," we have not attempted to capture the former, but rather content ourselves with simple "arise." The same wording occurs at 2:13.

n. In one of the most brilliant of all passages in the Song—indeed, in the entire Bible—we are treated here to a dazzling display of the poet's talent with this Janus parallelism. The Hebrew word *zāmîr*, placed in the middle stich, means both "pruning" and "singing"; with the first meaning it looks back to the first stich and the key word "blossoms," while with the second meaning it looks forward to the third stich with the key phrase "voice of the turtledove." See C. H. Gordon, "New Directions," *BASP* 15 (1978): 59–66.

---

16. The first refrain above (2:7 = 3:5) introduces fauna (especially deer imagery) into the poem, the effect of which is heightened here by the female lover's comparing her beloved to a gazelle or a fawn. This too is an element of *hijaʾ* poetry, as discussed in chapter 4, p. 149. Many other passages also refer to animals: 2:15, 17; 4:1–2 (≈ 6:5-6); 4:5 (≈ 7:4); 4:8; 5:11, 12; 6:9; 8:14.

17. On the level of reading the Song of Songs as *hijāʾ* poetry, we note that gender reversal (see n. l) can serve to enhance the invective (see ch. 4, pp. 156–57).

And the vines in bud, they give forth fragrance;
Arise, my darling, my beautiful, and go forth."[o]

2:14 O my dove, in the crannies of the rock,
In the covert of the cliff,
Show me your visage,
Let me hear your voice;[18]
For your voice is sweet,
And your visage is lovely.

2:15 *Catch us the foxes,*
The little foxes,
Ruining the vineyards,
And our vineyards in bud.[19]
2:16 *My beloved is mine, and I am his,*
Grazing among the lilies.[20]
2:17 *Until the day(-wind) blows,*
And the shadows flee;
Turn, liken yourself, my beloved, to a gazelle,
Or to a fawn of the hinds,
Upon the mountains of cleavage.[p]

3:1 *On my couch at night,*
I sought whom my inner-being loves,

---

o. Note that identical lines (2:10b, 13c) bracket the male lover's speech to the female lover in her imagined 3.5-verse representation of his words.

p. Hebrew *beter* (here in pausal form *bāter*) has elicited much discussion. We prefer to derive the word from the verbal root *b-t-r* "cleave," thus our rendering "cleavage," and to see here a reference to the female lover's breasts, imagined as mountains. That is to say, she invites her beloved to her breasts, echoing the sentiment expressed in 1:13.

---

18. While the physical distance between the two lovers has been intimated from the outset (see 1:7), here we gain a reminder that the two lovers are apart. This point comprises an important component of *hijā'* poetry (see ch. 4, pp. 145–46)—and see further below, especially 3:1; 5:6; 6:1.

19. Since viticultural terms are used metaphorically for Israel in the Bible, quite possibly the "foxes" here allude to Israel's (sc. the vineyard's) enemies attacking her. See chapter 4, p. 164.

20. The reference to "grazing," both here and in the parallel verse in 6:3, once more suggests an invective against the king (see above, n. 8 on 1:7).

I sought him, but I did not find him.[21]

3:2 *Let me arise, please, and let me roam the city,*
In the streets and in the piazzas,
Let me seek whom my inner-being loves;
I sought him, but I did not find him.

3:3 *The watchmen found me,*
They who go-about the city;
"He whom my inner-being loves, did you see (him)?"

3:4 *Scarcely had I passed them,*
When I found him whom my inner-being loves;
I grabbed hold of him, and I would not let him loose,
Until I brought him to the house of my mother,
And to the chamber of she-who-conceived-me.

3:5 *I adjure you, O daughters of Yerushalayim,*
By the gazelles, or by the hinds of the field;
Do not rouse, and do not arouse love,
Until it desires.

3:6 Who is this coming up from the wilderness,
Like columns of smoke;
Redolent with myrrh and frankincense,
With every powder of the merchant.

3:7 Behold the litter of Shelomo,
Sixty heroes surround it, from among the heroes of Yisra᾿el.

3:8 All of them, grasping the sword,
Trained in battle,
Each-man, his sword on his thigh,
For fear of the night.

3:9 The king Shelomo made himself a palanquin,
From the trees of the Levanon.

3:10 Its pillars he made of silver,
Its support of gold;
Its riding-seat of purple,

21. The poet here increases our awareness, in very direct wording, of the distance between the two lovers.

Its interior arranged/burning with leather/love,[q] [22]
From the daughters of Yerushalayim.
3:11 *Go out and see, O daughters of Ziyyon,*
The king Shelomo;
With the crown (with) which his mother crowned him,
On the day of his wedding,
And on the day of the happiness of his heart.

4:1 Behold you are beautiful, my darling,[23]
Behold you are beautiful,
Your eyes are doves,
Behind your braids;
Your hair is like a flock of goats,
That flow down from Mount Gilʿad.
4:2 Your teeth are like a flock of shorn-ones,
Who come up from the washing;
All of whom are twinned,
And none of them bereaved.
4:3 Like a thread of scarlet are your lips,
And your mouth[r] is lovely;
Like a slice of pomegranate is your cheek,
Behind your braids.
4:4 Like the tower of David is your neck,
Built to the heights;
A thousand shields hang upon it,
All the weapons of the heroes.

---

q. A double polysemy is present here. Hebrew *rāṣûp* means both "arranged" and "burning," while the common noun *ʾahăbaʰ* "love" bears the rarer meaning of "leather" (cf. Arabic *ʾihāb*).

r. Not the usual Hebrew for "mouth," namely, *peʰ*, but rather a unique word *midbār*, literally "speaking-organ," evoked here for the purposes of alliteration, as explained in chapter 2.

---

22. While we have lined up the translation options respectively, "arranged with leather" and "burning with love," the political reading of the poem suggests a cross-over to allow for the reading "arranged with love," i.e., "arranged in an alliance" as well. One can only marvel at this kind of poetic virtuosity. The political overtones continue in the next verse with reference to the king's crown.

23. This is the first of the *waṣf* poems (4:1–7) describing the female lover, which describes her beauty in great detail and which at the same time is to be seen as ironic praise.

4:5 Your two breasts are like two fawns,
Twins of a doe,
Grazing among the lilies.
4:6 Until the day(-wind) blows,
And the shadows flee;
I will go to the mountain of myrrh,
And to the hills of frankincense.
4:7 All of you is beautiful, my darling,
And there is no blemish in you.

4:8 With me, from Levanon, (my) bride,[24]
With me, from Levanon, come;
Bound from the summit of ʾAmana,
From the summit of Senir and Ḥermon,
From the dens of lions,
From the mountains of leopards.
4:9 You entice me, my sister, (my) bride,[25]
You entice me with but one of your eyes.
With but one strand from your necklace.
4:10 How beautiful is your love,
My sister, (my) bride;
How better than wine is your love,
And the scent of your oils, than all spices.
4:11 Your lips drip honey, (my) bride;
Honey and milk under your tongue,
And the scent of your clothes is like the scent of Levanon.

4:12 A locked garden is my sister, (my) bride;
A locked fountain, a sealed spring.
4:13 Your shoots are an orchard of pomegranates
With fruit of choice-fruits;
Henna with nard.[26]

---

24. Another term that suggests a political arrangement is introduced here, since *kallāʰ* "bride" can mean "nation" (see ch. 4, p. 158).

25. The first of a series of occurrences of the word "sister" as the epithet by which the male lover calls his female lover, all in very close proximity to each other at the middle of the composition (see also 4:10, 12; 5:1, 2). The term naturally raises the issue of incest, which also is present in *hijāʾ* poetry (see ch. 4, pp. 153–55). For "brother," see 8:1.

26. The poet spices his or her language with references to sweet-smelling aromatics in the central section of the composition (4:13, 16; 5:1, 13). This feature is found in *hijāʾ* poetry as well, on which see chapter 4, pp. 151–52.

4:14 Nard and saffron,
Cane and cinnamon,
With all trees of frankincense;
Myrrh and aloes,
With all heads of spices.
4:15 A spring of the gardens,
A well of living water,
And streams from Levanon.
4:16 Awake, north(-wind), and come, south(-wind),
Blow upon my garden,
May its spices stream;
May my beloved come to his garden,
And may he eat of the fruit of its choice-fruits.[27]
5:1 I have come to my garden, my sister, (my) bride,
I have plucked my myrrh with my spice,
I have eaten my honeycomb with my honey,
I have drunk my wine with my milk;
Eat, friends! Drink! And be-drunk with love!

5:2 *I am asleep, but my heart is awake,*[28]
Hark, my beloved knocks,[s]
"Open for me, my sister, my darling,
My dove, my perfect-one,
For my head is filled with dew,
My locks with droplets of the night."
5:3 *I have removed my tunic,*
How shall I put it on?
I have washed my feet,
How shall I soil them?
5:4 *My beloved sent forth his hand through the hole,*
And my innards emoted for him.
5:5 *I arose to open for my beloved,*

---

s. In the lines that follow, the female lover envisions the male lover addressing her, and thus we have placed these words in quotation marks. On the string of epithets "my sister, my darling, my dove, my perfect-one," see chapter 3, p. 123–24.

---

27. Another erotic image, characteristic of *hijā*ʾ, as explained in chapter 4, pp. 147–49.

28. This passage introduces the dream scene, which is paralleled in *hijā*ʾ poetry, as noted in chapter 4, pp. 146–47.

And my hands dripped myrrh,
And my fingers, flowing myrrh,
On the handles of the lock.[29]
5:6 *I opened for my beloved,*
And my beloved, turned-away, passed;
My inner-being went out when he spoke,
I sought him, but I did not find him,
I called him, but he did not answer me.[30]
5:7 *The watchmen found me,*
They who go-about the city,
They struck me, they wounded me;[t]
They lifted my shawl from upon me,
The watchmen of the city-walls.
5:8 *I adjure you, O daughters of Yerushalayim,*
If you find my beloved,[31]
What will you tell him?[u]
That I am sick with love?
5:9 How is your beloved more so than other beloveds,
O most beautiful of women?
How is your beloved more so than other beloveds,
That you adjure us so?
5:10 *My beloved is radiant and red,*[32]

---

t. Note that the first encounter with the night watchmen of the city, described in 3:3, was perfectly normal, whether friendly or neutral. The reader expects such an encounter here as well but is astonished and shocked to see that the female lover was mistreated by them. In short, the poet has set the reader up via the first meeting but now pulls a surprise with the second meeting.

u. Alternatively, one could read this stich as "Do not tell him," understanding מה as the negative particle "not," though this seems less likely in light of our discussion in chapter 3, pp. 115–16.

---

29. Undoubtedly the most erotic line in the poem, in the female lover's imagined encounter with her lover—which again serves the *hijā'* nature of the composition.

30. The unrequited love, which is noted in 2:14 and 3:1, here gains its ultimate expression. As noted above and in chapter 4, pp. 145–46, this is an important feature of *hijā'* poetry as well.

31. As with similar terminology in the Song of Songs, *dôd* "beloved" also evokes the sense of "ally"; this sense is evident, perhaps not throughout the poem, where it occurs repeatedly (in the romantic sense of "beloved'), but within the present context.

32. The description of the male lover (5:10–15) parallels the three *waṣf* poems concerning the female lover and further adds to the sarcastic nature of the poem.

More dazzling than a myriad.
5:11 *His head is gold bullion,*
His locks are curled,
Black as the raven.
5:12 *His eyes are like doves,*
At the rivulets of water;
Washed in milk,
Sitting by the pool.
5:13 *His cheeks are like a bed of spices,*
Towers of perfumes;
His lips are lilies,
Dripping (with) flowing myrrh.
5:14 *His hands are bracelets of gold,*
Inlaid with beryl;
His loins are a block of ivory,
Studded with sapphires.[33]
5:15 *His calves are pillars of marble,*
Supported on pedestals of bullion;
His form is like Levanon,
Choice as the cedars.
5:16 *His palate is sweets,*
All of him is delights;
This is my beloved,
And this is my friend,
O daughters of Yerushalayim.
6:1 **To where has your beloved gone?**
O most beautiful among women.
To where has your beloved turned?[34]
Let us seek him with you.
6:2 *My beloved went down to his garden,*
To the beds of spices;[v]

---

v. Note that in 5:13 the Hebrew is *ʿărûgat habbośem* "bed of spices," with the former noun in the singular, whereas in 6:2 the expression is *ʿărûgôt habbośem* "beds

---

33. These two verses (5:14–15) present a series of precious stones and metals to describe the male lover's body. On the parallel use of such imagery in *hijāʾ* poetry, see chapter 4, pp. 151–52.

34. Now not only the female lover, but her female friends as well, make reference to the distance that separates the two lovers.

To graze in the gardens,
And to gather lilies.[35]
6:3 *I am my beloved's, and my beloved is mine,*
Grazing among the lilies.

6:4 You are beautiful, my darling, like Tirza,[36]
Comely as Yerushalayim;
Awesome as the luminaries.
6:5 Turn your eyes from before me,
For they dazzle me;
Your hair is like a flock of goats,
That flow down from the Gilʿad.
6:6 Your teeth are like a flock of ewes,
Who come up from the washing;
All of whom are twinned,
And none of them bereaved.
6:7 Like a slice of pomegranate is your cheek,
Behind your braids.
6:8 There are sixty queens, and eighty concubines;
And maidens without number.
6:9 One is my dove, my perfect-one,
One is she unto her mother,
Pure is she to she-who-bore-her;
Daughters see her, and they extol her,
Queens and concubines, and they praise her.[37]

6:10 **Who is this who comes-into-sight like the dawn;**
Beautiful as the moon;
Pure as the sun,
Awesome as the luminaries.

---

of spices," with the former noun in the plural. On this kind of variation in the Song of Songs, see chapter 3.

---

35. On the passage's political overtones, see chapter 4, pp. 153–54.

36. The second of the *waṣf* poems (6:4–7) describing the beauty of the female lover, with many of the lines repeating (though not in verbatim fashion, as per ch. 3). As noted above, while these poems may look praiseworthy on the surface, the exaggerated flattery reveals a sarcastic tone.

37. See n. 3 above.

6:11 To the walnut garden I went down,
To see the produce of the palm tree;[w]
To see whether the vine blooms,
Whether the pomegranates blossom.
6:12 I do not know, my inner-being sets me,
The chariots of ʿAmminadav.[x]
7:1 Return, return, O Shulammite,
Return, return, that we may gaze at you,[38]
How you gaze at the Shulammite,
Like a dance of the two-camps.
7:2 How beautiful are your feet in sandals,[39]
O daughter of the noble;[40]
The curves of your thighs are like ornaments,
The work of the hands of an artisan.
7:3 Your vulva[y] is a bowl of the crescent,
Let it not lack mixed-wine;[41]
Your "stomach" is a heap of wheat,[z]

---

w. Hebrew *naḥal* means both "wadi, stream" (its common meaning) and "palm tree" (a rare usage). Both senses are appropriate here—thus polysemy is evident—though we elect the latter in our translation since the context is that of fruit trees.

x. The three phrases of this verse provide no difficulties (save, perhaps, for the sense of ʿAmminadav)—and thus our rendering proceeds quite literally—yet the overall meaning is rather obscure.

y. The word *šōr* (its usual form), *šōrer* (its form here), normally means "navel," as in Ezek 16:4 and in postbiblical Hebrew and Aramaic. In Prov 3:8 the word stands for the entire body via synecdoche. In Song 7:3, however, we take the word as a euphemism for "vulva," especially since the b-line refers to its serving as a container of moisture, indeed, the most delectable of liquids, mixed-wine.

z. To a modern reader, comparison of the lover's stomach to a stack of wheat may seem inapt. We understand Hebrew *beṭen*, normally "stomach," at times "womb," to refer to the female genitals here. The parallelism with *šōrer* "vulva" (on which see the previous note) bears this out. The wheat and the lilies then would refer to pubic hair.

---

38. While on the surface this line may not look very erotic, the reader is directed to the reference in chapter 4 (p. 154 n. 64) for further elucidation.

39. The third of the *waṣf* poems (7:2-10) extolling the beauty of the female lover, which once more, given the elaborate language, bears a sardonic tone.

40. Whatever the exact sense of *bat nādîb* "daughter of the noble," we sense here another political term, not only with "daughter" as "vassal" (see above, n. 12), but with "noble, nobleman" as well.

41. The erotic language is clear and once more serves the author's invective mode.

Bordered with lilies.
7:4 Your two breasts are like two fawns,
Twins of a doe.
7:5 Your neck is like the tower of ivory;
Your eyes are pools in Heshbon,
By the gate of Bat-Rabbim,
Your nose is like the tower of Levanon,
Looking towards Damesseq.
7:6 Your head upon you is like Karmel/crimson,[aa]
The strands[ab] of your head are like purple;
A king is captured by (your) tresses.[ac]
7:7 How beautiful are you,
And how pleasant are you,
Love among enjoyments.
7:8 This your stature is likened to a palm tree,
And your breasts, to clusters.
7:9 I said, "I will ascend the palm tree,
I shall grasp its fronds";
And may your breasts be like clusters of the vine,[42]
And the scent of your nose like apricots.

Finally, note that the word ʿ*ărēmā*ʰ "heap, stack" may bear sexual connotation, as in Ruth 3:6; compare the English expression "rolling around in the hay."

aa. Hebrew *karmel*, the name of the large mountain at modern-day Haifa, but evoking *karmîl* "crimson, carmine" as well. The term is a classic example of a Janus word: as the name of a mountain, it points back to the toponyms "Levanon" and "Damesseq" in the previous verse (especially "Levanon," another high mountain); with the meaning "crimson, carmine," it points ahead to ʾ*argāmān* "purple" in the b-line. See S. M. Paul, "Polysemous Pivotal Punctuation: More Janus Double Entendres," in *Texts, Temples, and Traditions: A Tribute to Menahem Haran* (ed. M. V. Fox et al.; Winona Lake, Ind.: Eisenbrauns, 1996), 373–74; repr. in *Divrei Shalom: Collected Studies of Shalom M. Paul on the Bible and the Ancient Near East, 1967–2005* (Culture and History of the Ancient Near East 23; Leiden: Brill, 2005), 481–83.

ab. Hebrew *dallā*ʰ, elsewhere used as "thrum, thread," but here used for "hair"—and thus English "strand" works beautifully in both contexts.

ac. Hebrew *rəhāṭîm*, from the same root as *rahîṭîm* in Song 1:17. In the latter instance, it means "runners" in the sense of "beams"; in our present verse "runners" means "long tresses of hair," as the context makes clear.

---

42. A final example of highly sexual imagery characteristic of *hijā*ʾ poetry. We note an accumulation of such passages here in chapter 7, as the Song of Songs reaches its climax.

7:10 And your palate is like good wine,
Coursing to my beloved as smooth-wine;
Fluxing (on) the lips of those-who-sleep.[ad]
7:11 *I am my beloved's,*
And toward me is his urge.[ae]

7:12 *Go, my beloved, let us go out to the field,*
Let us lodge among the villages/henna-plants.
7:13 *Let us arise-early to the vineyards,*
Let us see if the vine has bloomed,
(If) the bud has opened,
(If) the pomegranates have blossomed;
There I will give my love to you.
7:14 *The mandrakes give forth scent,*
And over our openings are all choice-fruits,
New-ones, also old-ones;
My beloved, I have hidden (them) for you.
8:1 *Who would give you as a brother to me,*
One-who-sucked the breasts of my mother;[43]
I would find you in the street, I would kiss you,
And they would not mock me.
8:2 *I would lead him, I would bring him to the house of my mother,*
She who teaches me;
I would ply you with spiced wine,
With the juice of my pomegranate.
8:3 *His left-hand is under my head,*[af]

---

ad. A notoriously difficult passage, with the obscure reference to *yəšēnîm* "those-who-sleep." We have chosen the unusual verb "flux" to render the unusual (and dialectal [see ch. 1, §1.1.4, pp. 14–15]) participial form *dôbēb*.

ae. Note how the feminine major tone is demonstrated in a passage such as this. In the garden of Eden story, a woman's urge is toward her husband's (Gen 3:16). In the Song of Songs, by contrast, the tables are turned, and the male's urge is toward the female lover.

af. We take note of the variation in wording, to avoid verbatim repetition: in 2:6 the phrase occurs with the preposition *taḥat lə-*, rendered as "beneath"; here the phrase occurs with the simple preposition *taḥat*, which we render with the slightly shorter English equivalent "under." See further chapter 3.

---

43. Here we get the sole instance of "brother," as the female lover addresses her male lover. On the matter of incest and its place in invective poetry, see above, n. 25 (on 4:9).

And his right-hand embraces me.
8:4 *I adjure you, O daughters of Yerushalayim,*
Do not rouse, and do not arouse love,
Until it desires.

8:5 Who is this coming up from the wilderness,
Leaning on her beloved;
Under the apricot-tree I aroused you,
There your mother birth-panged you,
There she-who-bore you birth-panged.
8:6 *Set me as a seal upon your heart,*
As a seal upon your arm,
For love is as strong as death,
Passion as fierce as She'ol[ag]*;*
Its darts are darts of fire,
The intensest-flame.[ah]
8:7 *Great waters cannot quench love,*
And rivers cannot swill it away;
If one would give all the wealth of his house for love,
They would surely mock him.

8:8 We have a sister, a little-one,
And she has no breasts;
What shall we do for our sister,
On the day when she is spoken for?
8:9 If she is a wall,
Will we build upon her a silver turret?
And if she is a door,
Will we confine her (with) a board of cedar?
8:10 *I am a wall,*
And my breasts are like towers;

---

ag. The ancient Israelite concept of the netherworld, to which all dead people descended beneath the earth.

ah. Hebrew *šalhebetyā*^{h} (or *šalhebetyāh*, depending on the manuscript) clearly derives from the word for "flame." This specific form is difficult; the suffix *-yā*^{h} (or *-yāh*) may be the shortened form of Yahweh (certainly if the latter reading is accepted), which at times may serve as the superlative. We have attempted to capture the unusual aspect of this form with our rendering "intensest-flame."

Thus I have become in his eyes,
As one who finds goodwill.[ai]

8:11 *Shelomo had a vineyard in Baʿal-Hamon,*[44]
He gave the vineyard to the keepers;
Each brings for his fruit,
A thousand (pieces of) silver.
8:12 *My own vineyard is before me;*
The thousand is for you, Shelomo,
And two-hundred to keepers of his fruit.
8:13 O you who sits in the gardens,
Friends attend to your voice,[45]
Let me hear you.
8:14 *Flee, my beloved,*
And liken yourself to a gazelle,
Or to a fawn of the hinds,
Upon the mountains of spices.[aj]

---

ai. Hebrew *šālôm*, continuing the pun on this root (and on like-sounding words); see further Shelomo in the next verse.

aj. The phrase "mountains of cleavage" from 2:17 has been altered to "mountains of spices" here in 8:14. The reader is to understand these passages in connection with 1:13–14, where the female lover imagines her male lover as a sachet of myrrh and a cluster of henna lodging between her breasts. This imagery, of course, reflects the well-known practice of women wearing sachets of spices between their breasts.

---

44. The excesses of Shelomo are self-evident in this verse and the next; see chapter 4, p. 167.

45. Here the word for "friends" is *ḥăbērîm* (see above, n. 10, for the [relatively?] synonymous term *rēaʿ* "friend'), which also can be taken as "allies."

Bibliography

Abramsky, S. "Ha-ʾIsha ha-Nishqefet baʿad ha-Ḥalon," *Beth Mikra* 25 (5740/1980): 114–24.

Abū Tammām (Ḥabīb ibn Aws al-Tāʾī). *Dīwān al-Ḥamāsah*. Clāhūr: Al-Maktabah al-Salafiyah, 1979.

Abū-Lughod, L. "Shifting Politics in Bedouin Love Poetry." Pages 24–45 in *Language and the Politics of Emotion*. Edited by C. A. Lutz and L. Abū-Lughod. Cambridge: Cambridge University Press, 1990.

Abusch, T. "Gilgamesh's Request and Siduri's Denial." Pages 1–14 in *The Tablet and the Scroll: Near Eastern Studies in Honor of William W. Hallo*. Edited by M. E. Cohen, D. C. Snell, and D. B. Weisberg. Bethesda, Md.: CDL, 1993.

Academy of the Hebrew Language. *The Historical Dictionary of the Hebrew Language: Materials for the Dictionary, Series I, 200 B.C.E.–300 C.E.* Jerusalem: Academy of the Hebrew Language, 1988.

———. *Maʾagarim: The Hebrew Language Historical Dictionary Project*. CD-ROM version. Jerusalem: Academy of the Hebrew Language, 1998.

Adams, P. G. "Alliteration." Pages 36–38 in *The New Princeton Encyclopedia of Poetry and Poetics*. Edited by A. Preminger and T. V. F. Brogan. Princeton: Princeton University Press, 1993.

———. "Assonance." Pages 102–4 in *The New Princeton Encyclopedia of Poetry and Poetics*. Edited by A. Preminger and T. V. F. Brogan. Princeton: Princeton University Press, 1993.

Ahituv, S. *Ha-Ketav ve-ha-Miktav*. Jerusalem: Bialik, 2005.

———. "Sharon, Sharoni." *ʾEnṣiqlopedya Miqraʾit* 8 (1982): cols. 263–64.

Albright, W. F. "Archaic Survivals in the Text of Canticles." Pages 1–7 in *Hebrew and Semitic Studies Presented to Godfrey Rolles Driver*. Edited by D. W. Thomas and W. D. McHardy. Oxford: Clarendon, 1963.

———. *Yahweh and the Gods of Canaan*. London: School of Oriental and African Studies, 1968.

Alexander, P. S. "The Song of Songs as Historical Allegory: Notes on the Development of an Exegetical Tradition." Pages 14–29 in *Targumic and Cognate Studies: Essays in Honour of Martin McNamara*. Edited by K.

J. Cathcart and M. Maher. JSOTSup 230. Sheffield: Sheffield Academic Press, 1996.

Altbauer, M. "ʿOd ʿal Semadar she-ʿal Qanqan me-Ḥaṣor." Pages 64–66 in *Zalman Shazar Volume = Eretz Israel* 10. Jerusalem: Israel Exploration Society, 1971.

Alter, R. *The Art of Biblical Narrative*. New York: Basic Books, 1981.

———. "The Song of Songs: An Ode to Intimacy." *BRev* 18.4 (2002): 24–32, 52.

Andersen, F. I., and D. N. Freedman. *Micah*. AB 24E. New York: Doubleday, 2000.

Andrzejewski, B. W., and I. M. Lewis. *Somali Poetry: An Introduction*. Oxford: Clarendon, 1964.

Astell, A. W. *The Song of Songs in the Middle Ages*. Ithaca, N.Y.: Cornell University Press, 1990.

Audet, J.-P. "The Meaning of the Canticle of Canticles." *TD* 5 (1957): 88–92.

Avishur, Y. "Le-Ziqa ha-Signonit ben Shir ha-Shirim ve-Sifrut ʾUgarit." *Beth Mikra* 59 (1974): 508–25.

———. *Stylistic Studies of Word-Pairs in Biblical and Ancient Semitic Literatures*. AOAT 210. Neukirchen-Vluyn: Neukirchener, 1984.

Badawi, M. M. "The Function of Rhetoric in Medieval Arabic Poetry: Abū Tammām's Ode on Amorium." *JAL* 9 (1978): 43–56.

Bakon, S. "Song of Songs." *JBQ* 22 (1994): 211–20.

Bar-Asher, M. "ʾAḥduta ha-Hisṭorit shel ha-Lashon ha-ʿIvrit u-Meḥqar Leshon Ḥakhamim." *Meḥqarim ba-Lashon* 1 (1985): 75–99.

Bauer, H., and P. Leander. *Historische Grammatik der hebräischen Sprache*. Halle: Niemeyer, 1922.

Bausani, A. "*Ghazal*." *EncIsl* 2:1028–36.

Beeston, A. F. L., et al., eds. *Arabic Literature to the End of the Umayyad Period*. Cambridge: Cambridge University Press, 1983.

Beeston, A. F. L., M. A. Ghul, W. W. Müller, and J. Ryckmans. *Sabaic Dictionary/Dictionnaire Sabéen*. Leuven: Peeters, 1982.

Bellis, A. O. "The New Exodus in Jeremiah 50:33–38." Pages 157–68 in *Imagery and Imagination in Biblical Literature: Essays in Honor of Aloysius Fitzgerald, F.S.C.* Edited by L. Boadt and M. S. Smith. CBQMS 32. Washington, D.C.: Catholic Biblical Association of America, 2001.

Benz, F. L. *Personal Names in the Phoenician and Punic Inscriptions*. Rome: Biblical Institute Press, 1972.

Benzinger, I., and S. Ochser. "Sharon." *JE* 11:233–34.

Bergant, D. "'My Beloved is Mine and I Am His' (Song 2:16)." *Semeia* 68 (1996): 23–40.

Berlin, A. *The Dynamics of Biblical Parallelism*. Bloomington: Indiana University Press, 1985.

———. "On the Interpretation of Psalm 133." Pages 141–47 in *Directions in Biblical Hebrew Poetry*. Edited by E. Follis. Sheffield: JSOT Press, 1987.
———. *Poetics and Interpretation of Biblical Narrative*. Sheffield: Almond, 1983.
Beyer, K. *Die aramäischen Texte vom Toten Meer*. Göttingen: Vandenhoeck & Ruprecht, 1984.
Biale, D. "The God with Breasts: El Shaddai in the Bible." *History of Religions* 21 (1982): 240–55.
Biella, J. C. *Dictionary of Old South Arabic: Sabaean Dialect*. HSS 25. Chico, Calif.: Scholars Press, 1982.
Black, J., A. George, and N. Postgate. *A Concise Dictionary of Akkadian*. Wiesbaden: Harrassowitz, 2000.
Blau, J. "Benoni Paʿul be-Horaʾa ʾAqtivit." *Leshonenu* 18 (5713/1953): 67–81.
———. *On Polyphony in Biblical Hebrew*. Proceedings of the Israel Academy of Sciences and Humanities 6/2. Jerusalem: Israel Academy of Sciences and Humanities, 1982.
———. *On Pseudo-Corrections in Some Semitic Languages*. Jerusalem: Israel Academy of Sciences and Humanities, 1970.
Bloch, A., and C. Bloch. *The Song of Songs*. New York: Random House, 1995.
Boadt, L. "Intentional Alliteration in Second Isaiah." *CBQ* 45 (1983): 353–63.
Bonebakker, S. A. "Religious Prejudice against Poetry in Early Islam." *Medievalia et Humanistica: Studies in Medieval & Renaissance Culture* 7 (1976): 77–99.
Brenner, A. "Aromatics and Perfumes in the Song of Songs." *JSOT* 25 (1983): 75–81.
———. *Colour Terms in the Old Testament*. JSOTSup 21. Sheffield: JSOT Press, 1982.
———. "'Come Back, Come Back the Shulammite' (Song of Songs 7.1–10): A Parody of the *Waṣf* Genre." Pages 251–75 in *On Humor and the Comic in the Hebrew Bible*. Edited by Y. T. Radday and A. Brenner. JSOTSup 92. Bible and Literature Series 23. Sheffield: Almond, 1990.
———. "My Song of Songs." Pages 567–79 in *A Feminist Companion to Reading the Bible: Approaches, Methods, and Strategies*. Edited by A. Brenner and C. Fontaine. Sheffield: Sheffield Academic Press, 1997.
———. "A Note on *Bat-Rabbîm* (Song of Songs VII 5)." *VT* 42 (1992): 113–15.
———. *The Song of Songs*. Sheffield: JSOT Press, 1989.
Brentjes, B. "The History of Elam and Achaemenid Persia: An Overview." Pages 1001–21 in *Civilizations of the Ancient Near East*. Edited by J. M. Sasson. New York: Charles Scribner's Sons, 1995.
Breuer, M. *Torah, Neviʾim, Ketuvim*. Jerusalem: Mosad Ha-Rav Kook, 1989.
Broadribb, D. "Thoughts on the Song of Solomon." *Abr-Nahrain* 3 (1961–62): 10–36.

Brockelmann, C. *Lexicon Syriacum*. Halle: Niemeyer, 1928.
———. *Syrische Grammatik*. Berlin: Reuther & Reichard, 1899.
Brogan, T. V. F. "Polyptoton." Pages 967–68 in *The New Princeton Encyclopedia of Poetry and Poetics*. Edited by A. Preminger and T. V. F. Brogan. Princeton: Princeton University Press, 1993.
———. "Variation." Page 1341 in *The New Princeton Encyclopedia of Poetry and Poetics*. Edited by A. Preminger and T. V. F. Brogan. Princeton: Princeton University Press, 1993.
Brown, C. S. "Theme and Variations as a Literary Form." *Yearbook of Comparative and General Literature* 27 (1978): 35–43.
Brown, F., S. R. Driver, and C. A. Briggs. *A Hebrew and English Lexicon of the Old Testament*. Oxford: Clarendon, 1906.
Brown, J. P. *Israel and Hellas*. 3 vols. BZAW 231, 276, 299. Berlin: de Gruyter, 1995–2001.
———. "The Mediterranean Vocabulary of the Vine." *VT* 19 (1969): 146–70.
Bryson, B. *The Mother Tongue*. New York: William Morrow, 1990.
Burkert, W. *The Orientalizing Revolution: Near Eastern Influence on Greek Culture in the Early Archaic Age*. Cambridge: Harvard University Press, 1992.
Burney, C. F. *Notes on the Hebrew Text of the Books of Kings*. Oxford: Clarendon, 1903.
Buss, M. J. "The Psalms of Asaph and Korah." *JBL* 82 (1963): 382–92.
Carr, D. M. "Gender and the Shaping of Desire in the Song of Songs." *JBL* 119 (2000): 233–48.
———. "Method in Dating Biblical Texts." Paper delivered at the joint meeting of the National Association of Professors of Hebrew and the Society of Biblical Literature, Washington, D.C., 20 November 2006.
———. *Writing on the Tablet of the Heart: Origins of Scripture and Literature*. New York: Oxford University Press, 2005.
Casanowicz, I. M. "Paronomasia in the Old Testament." Ph.D. diss. Johns Hopkins University, 1892.
Ceresko, A. R. "The Function of Antanaclasis (*mṣ*ʾ 'to Find' // *mṣ*ʾ 'to Reach, Overtake, Grasp') in Hebrew Poetry, Especially in the Book of Qoheleth." *CBQ* 44 (1982): 551–69.
Černy, J. "Consanguineous Marriages in Pharaonic Egypt." *JEA* 40 (1954): 23–29.
Chance, J. K. "The Anthropology of Honor and Shame: Culture, Values and Practice." *Semeia* 68 (1996): 139–51.
Chen, Y. "Israelian Hebrew in the Book of Proverbs." Ph.D. diss. Cornell University, 2000.
Chomsky, W. *David Kimḥi's Hebrew Grammar (Mikhlol)*. New York: Bloch, 1952.

Clines, D. J. A., ed. *Dictionary of Classical Hebrew*. 8 vols. Sheffield: Sheffield Academic Press, 1993–.

Cogan, M. *1 Kings*. AB 10. New York: Doubleday, 2000.

———. "… From the Peak of Amanah." *IEJ* 34 (1984): 255–59.

Cohen, A. *The Psalms*. London: Soncino, 1945.

Cooper, A., and B. R. Goldstein. "Exodus and *maṣṣôt* in History and Tradition." *Maarav* 8 (1992): 15–37.

Cooper, J. S. "New Cuneiform Parallels to the Song of Songs." *JBL* 90 (1971): 157–62.

Cowley, A. E. *Aramaic Papyri of the Fifth Century B.C.* Oxford: Clarendon, 1923.

Dalman, G. "Die Blume *ḥabaṣṣelet* der Bibel." Pages 62–68 in *Vom Alten Testament: Karl Marti zum siebzigsten Geburtstage gewidmet*. Edited by K. Budde. BZAW 41. Giessen: Töpelmann, 1925.

Davenport, G. *Archilochus, Sappho, Alkman: Three Lyric Poets of the Late Greek Bronze Age*. Berekley: University of California Press, 1980.

Davidson, R. M. "Theology and Sexuality in the Song of Songs: Return to Eden." *Andrews University Seminary Studies* 27 (1989): 1–19.

Dietrich, M., O. Loretz, and J. Sanmartín. *The Cuneiform Alphabetic Texts from Ugarit, Ras Ibn Hani and Other Places*. Münster: Ugarit-Verlag, 1995.

Dirksen, P. B. "Canticles." Pages 11–24, 8*–13*, 26*–28*, 38*–40*, 56*–64* in *General Introduction and Megilloth*. Vol. 18 of *Biblia Hebraica Quinta*. Edited by A. Schenker. Stuttgart: Deutsche Bibelgesellschaft, 2004.

———. "Song of Songs III 6–7." *VT* 39 (1989): 219–24.

Donner, H., and W. Röllig. *Kanaanäische und aramäische Inschriften*. 3 vols. Wiesbaden: Harrassowitz, 1971–76.

Dorseiff, F. *Antike und alter Orient*. Leipzig: Koehler & Amelang, 1959.

Driver, G. R. "Hebrew Notes on 'Song of Songs' and 'Lamentations.'" Pages 134–46 in *Festschrift, Alfred Bertholet zum 80. Geburtstag gewidmet von Kollegen und Freunden*. Edited by W. Baumgartner. Tübingen: Mohr Siebeck, 1950.

———. "Hebrew Poetic Diction." Pages 26–39 in *Congress Volume: Copenhagen, 1953*. VTSup 1. Leiden: Brill, 1953.

Driver, S. R. *An Introduction to the Literature of the Old Testament*. New York: Charles Scribner's Sons, 1920.

Edzard, D. O. "Zur Ritualtafel der sog. 'Love Lyrics.'" Pages 57–69 in *Language, Literature, and History: Philological and Historical Studies Presented to Erica Reiner*. Edited by F. Rochberg-Halton. New Haven: American Oriental Society, 1987.

Eissfeldt, O. "Psalm 80." Pages 65–78 in *Geschichte und Altes Testament: Albrecht Alt zum 70. Geburtstag dargebracht*. Edited by W. Zimmerli. BHT

16. Tübingen: Mohr Siebeck, 1953. Repr. as pages 221–32 in vol. 3 of O. Eissfeldt, *Kleine Schriften*. 6 vols. Tübingen: Mohr Siebeck, 1962–79.

———. "Psalm 80 und Psalm 89." *WO* 3 (1964–66): 27–31. Repr. as pages 132–36 in vol. 4 of O. Eissfeldt, *Kleine Schriften*. 6 vols. Tübingen: Mohr Siebeck, 1962–79.

Eitan, I. "Biblical Studies." *HUCA* 14 (1939): 1–32.

Elitzur, Y. *Ancient Place Names in the Holy Land*. Jerusalem: Magnes; Winona Lake, Ind.: Eisenbrauns, 2004.

Ellenbogen, M. *Foreign Words in the Old Testament: Their Origin and Etymology*. London: Luzac, 1962.

Elliott, J. H. "The Evil Eye in the First Testament: The Ecology and Culture of a Pervasive Belief." Pages 147–59 in *The Bible and the Politics of Exegesis: Essays in Honour of Norman K. Gottwald on His Sixty-Fifth Birthday*. Edited by D. Jobling et al. Cleveland: Pilgrim, 1991.

Emerton, J. A. "Lice or a Veil in the Song of Songs 1:7." Pages 127–40 in *Understanding Poets and Prophets: Essays in Honour of George Wishart Anderson*. Edited by A. G. Auld. JSOTSup 152. Sheffield: JSOT Press, 1993.

Even-Shoshan, A. *Qonqordanṣya Ḥadasha*. Jerusalem: Kiryat Sefer, 1992.

Falk, M. *The Song of Songs: A New Translation and Interpretation*. San Francisco: HarperCollins, 1990.

———. "The *waṣf*." Pages 225–33 in *A Feminist Companion to the Song of Songs*. Edited by A. Brenner. Sheffield: JSOT Press, 1993.

Faulkner, R. O. *The Ancient Egyptian Pyramid Texts*. Oxford: Clarendon, 1969.

Fishbane, M. "Orally Write Therefore Aurally Right." Pages 531–46 in *The Quest for Contrext and Meaning: Studies in Biblical Intertextuality in Honor of James A. Sanders*. Edited by C. A. Evans and S. Talmon. Leiden: Brill, 1997.

Fitzgerald, A. "BTWLT and BT as Titles for Capital Cities." *CBQ* 37 (1975): 167–83.

Fitzmyer, J. A. *The Genesis Apocryphon of Qumran Cave I*. Rome: Biblical Institute Press, 1971.

Fokkelman, J. P. "Genesis 37 and 38 at the Interface of Structural Analysis and Hermeneutics." Pages 152–87 in *Literary Structures and Rhetorical Strategies in the Hebrew Bible*. Edited by L. J. de Regt, J. de Waard, and J. P. Fokkelman. Assen: Van Gorcum, 1996.

Folmer, M. L. *The Aramaic Language in the Achaemenid Period: A Study in Linguistic Variation*. Leuven: Peeters, 1995.

Foster, B. R. *Before the Muses: An Anthology of Akkadian Literature*. Bethesda, Md.: CDL, 1993.

Fox, M. V. "*ʾamon* Again," *JBL* 115 (1996): 699–702.

———. *The Song of Songs and the Ancient Egyptian Love Songs*. Madison: University of Wisconsin Press, 1985.

Frahm, Eckart. "Humor in assyrischen Königsinschriften." Pages 147–62 in *Intellectual Life in the Ancient Near East: Papers Presented at the 43rd Rencontre assyriologique internationale, Prague, July 1–5, 1996*. Edited by J. Prosecky. Prague: Academy of Sciences of the Czech Republic, Oriental Institute, 1998.

Friedrich, J., and W. Röllig. *Phönizisch-punische Grammatik*. Rome: Pontifical Biblical Institute, 1970.

Gábor, I. *Der hebräische Urrhythmus*. Giessen: Töpelmann, 1929.

Garr, W. R. *Dialect Geography of Syria-Palestine, 1000–586 B.C.E.* Philadelphia: University of Pennsylvania Press, 1985.

———. "On the Alternation between Construct and *DĪ* Phrases in Biblical Aramaic." *JSS* 35 (1980): 213–31.

Garsiel, M. *Biblical Names: A Literary Study of Midrashic Derivations*. Ramat-Gan: Bar-Ilan University Press, 1991.

Gaudefroy-Demombynes, M. *Le monde musulman et byzantin jusqu'aux Croisades*. Paris: de Baccard, 1931.

Gelder, G. J. van. "Against Women, and Other Pleasantries." *JAL* 16 (1985): 61–72.

———. *The Bad and The Ugly: Attitudes towards Invective Poetry (Hija') in Classical Arabic Literature*. Leiden: Brill, 1988.

Gevirtz, S. "Asher in the Blessing of Jacob (Genesis xlix 20)." *VT* 37 (1987): 154–63.

———. "Of Syntax and Style in the 'Late Biblical Hebrew'—'Old Canaanite' Connection." *JANES* 18 (1986): 25–29.

Ginsberg, H. L. *The Five Megilloth and Jonah: A New Translation*. Philadelphia: Jewish Publication Society, 1969.

———. *The Israelian Heritage of Judaism*. New York: Jewish Theological Seminary, 1982.

———. "The Northwest Semitic Languages." Pages 102–24, 293 in *Patriarchs*. Edited by B. Mazar. WHJP. New Brunswick, N.J.: Rutgers University Press, 1970.

Ginsburg, C. D. *The Song of Songs and Qoheleth*. New York: Ktav, 1970.

Giovannini, M. J. "Female Chastity Code in the Circum-Mediterranean: Comparative Perspectives." Pages 61–74 in *Honor and Shame and the Unity of the Mediterranean*. Edited by D. D. Gilmore. Washington, D.C.: American Anthropological Society, 1987.

Goitein, S. D. "Ayumma Kannidgalot (Song of Songs VI.10) 'Splendid Like the Brilliant Stars.'" *JSS* 10 (1965): 220–21.

———. "The Song of Songs: A Female Composition" [Hebrew original, 1957]. Pages 58–66 in *A Feminist Companion to the Song of Songs*. Edited by A. Brenner. Sheffield: JSOT Press, 1993.

Goldziher, I. *Abhandlungen zur arabischen Philologie*. 2 vols. Leiden: Brill, 1896.

Golomb, D. M. *A Grammar of Targum Neofiti*. Chico, Calif.: Scholars Press, 1985.

Gordis, R. *The Book of Job: Commentary, New Translation, and Special Studies*. New York: Jewish Theological Seminary, 1978.

———. "The Root דגל in the Song of Songs." *JBL* 88 (1969): 203–4.

———. "The Song of Songs." Pages 281–325 in *Mordecai M. Kaplan: Jubilee Volume on the Occasion of His Seventieth Birthday*. Edited by M. Davis. New York: Jewish Theological Seminary of America, 1953. Repr. as pages 351–98 in Gordis, *Poets, Prophets, and Sages: Essays in Biblical Interpretation*. Bloomington: Indiana University Press, 1971.

———. *The Song of Songs and Lamentations: A Study, Modern Translation and Commentary*. New York: Ktav, 1974.

———. "A Wedding Song for Solomon." *JBL* 63 (1944): 263–70.

Gordon, C. H. "New Directions." *BASP* 15 (1978): 59–66.

———. "North Israelite Influence on Postexilic Hebrew." *IEJ* 5 (1955): 85–88.

———. *Ugaritic Textbook*. AnOr 38. Rome: Pontifical Biblical Institute, 1967.

Gottlieb, I. B. "The Jewish Allegory of Love: Change and Consistency." *Journal of Jewish Thought and Philosophy* 2 (1992): 1–17.

Goulder, M. D. *The Song of Fourteen Songs*. JSOTSup 36. Sheffield: JSOT Press, 1986.

Greenberg, J. H. "Internal *a*-Plurals in Afroasiatic (Hamito-Semitic)." Pages 198–204 in *Afrikanistische Studien*. Edited by J. Lukas. Berlin: Akademie Verlag, 1955.

Greenfield, J. C. "Aramaic Studies and the Bible." Pages 110–30 in *Congress Volume: Vienna, 1980*. Edited by J. A. Emerton. VTSup 32. Leiden: Brill, 1981.

———. "Lexicographical Notes II." *HUCA* 30 (1959): 141–51.

Greenfield, J. C., and M. Mayrhofer. "The ʾAlgummim/ʾAlmuggim-Problem Reexamined." Pages 83–89 in *Hebräische Wortforschung: Festschrift zum 80. Geburtstag von Walter Baumgartner*. Edited by B. Hartmann. VTSup 16. Leiden: Brill, 1967.

Greenspahn, F. E. *Hapax Legomena in Biblical Hebrew*. SBLDS 74; Chico, Calif.: Scholars Press, 1984.

Greenstein, E. L. "Jethro's Wit: An Interpretation of Wordplay in Exodus 18." Pages 155–71 in *On the Way to Nineveh: Studies in Honor of George M. Landes*. Edited by S. L. Cook and S. C. Winter. ASOR Books 4. Atlanta: Scholars Press, 1999.

———. "Kirta." Pages 9–48 in *Ugaritic Narrative Poetry*. Edited by S. B. Parker. SBLWAW 9. Atlanta: Society of Biblical Literature, 1997.

———. "Wordplay, Hebrew." *ABD* 6:968–71.

Grossberg, D. "Canticles 3:10 in the Light of a Homeric Analog and Biblical Poetics." *BTB* 11 (1981): 124–32.

Guidi, I. *L'Arabie antéislamique: quatre conférences donneés à l'université égyptienne du Caire en 1909*. Paris: Geuthner, 1921.

Gunkel, H. *Die Psalmen*. HKAT 2/2. Göttingen: Vandenhoeck & Ruprecht, 1926.

Halkin, A., and D. Hartman. *Crisis and Leadership: Epistles of Maimonides*. Philadelphia: Jewish Publication Society, 1985.

Hamori, A. "Love Poetry (*Ghazal*)." Pages 202–18 in *ʿAbbasid Belles-Lettres: Arabic Literature 750–1258*. Edited by J. Ashtiany, T. M. Johnstone, J. D. Latham, and R. B. Serjeant. Cambridge History of Arabic Literature. Cambridge: Cambridge University Press, 1990.

Harris, Z. S. *Development of the Canaanite Dialects*. New Haven: American Oriental Society, 1939.

Hayward, J. A. "*Madiḥ, madḥ*." *EncIsl* 5:958–959.

Hillers, D. R., and E. Cussini. *Palmyrene Aramaic Texts*. Baltimore: Johns Hopkins University Press, 1996.

Hodge, C. T. "Ritual and Writing: An Inquiry into the Origin of the Egyptian Script." Pages 3–22 in *Linguistics and Anthropology: In Honor of C. F. Voegelin*. Edited by M. D. Kinkade, K. L. Hale, and O. Werner. Lisse: Peter de Ridder Press, 1975. Repr. as pages 199–220 in *Afroasiatic Linguistics, Semitics, and Egyptology: Selected Writings of Carleton T. Hodge*. Edited by S. B. Noegel and A. S. Kaye. Bethesda, Md.: CDL, 2004.

Hoftijzer, J., and K. Jongeling. *Dictionary of the North-West Semitic Inscriptions*. 2 vols. Leiden: Brill, 1995.

Hurowitz, V. A. "Nursling, Advisor, Architect? אמון and the Role of Wisdom in Proverbs 8, 22–31." *Bib* 80 (1999): 391–400.

Hurvitz, A. *Beyn Lashon le-Lashon*. Jerusalem: Bialik, 1972.

———. "The Chronological Significance of 'Aramaisms' in Biblical Hebrew." *IEJ* 18 (1968): 234–40.

———. "Ha-Lashon ha-ʿIvrit ba-Tequfa ha-Parsit." Pages 210–309 in *Shivat Ṣiyyon: Yeme Shilton Paras*. Edited by H. Tadmor and I. Ephʿal. Ha-Historiya shel ʿAm Yisraʾel. Jerusalem: Alexander Peli, 1983.

———. "Le-Diyyuqo shel ha-Munaḥ אמון be-Sefer Mishle 8:30." Pages 647–50 in *Ha-Miqraʾ bi-Reʾi Mefarshav: Sefer Zikkaron le-Sarah Qamin* (*The Bible in the Light of Its Interpreters: Sarah Kamin Memorial Volume*). Edited by S. Japhet. Jerusalem: Magnes, 1994.

Hüttenmeister, F. G. *Übersetzung des Talmud Yerushalmi: Sheqalim–Scheqelsteuer.* Tübingen: Mohr Siebeck, 1990.

Israelit-Groll, S. "Ostracon Nash 12 and Chapter 5 of Song of Songs." Pages 131–35 in *Proceedings of the Tenth World Congress of Jewish Studies: Jerusalem, August 16–24, 1989: Division A: The Bible and Its World*. Jerusalem: World Union of Jewish Studies, 1990.

Izre'el, S. *Amurru Akkadian: A Linguistic Study*. 2 vols. Atlanta: Scholars Press, 1991.

Jacobi, R. "*nasīb*." *EncIsl* 7:978–83.

Jastrow, M. *A Dictionary of the Targumim, the Talmud Babli and Yerushalmi, and the Midrashic Literature*. 2 vols. London: Luzac, 1903.

Javadi, H. *Satire in Persian Literature*. Rutherford: Fairleigh Dickinson University Press, 1988.

Jongeling, B., C. J. Labuschagne, and A. S. van der Woude. *Aramaic Texts from Qumran*. Leiden: Brill, 1976.

Joosten, J. "The Syntax of *zeh Mošeh* (Ex 32,1.23)." *ZAW* 103 (1991): 412–15.

Joüon, P. "Notes de critique textuelle (AT) 2 Rois 6,8–10." *MUSJ* 5 (1911–12): 477–78.

Kaufman, S. A. "The Classification of the North West Semitic Dialects of the Biblical Period and Some Implications Thereof." Pages 41–57 in *Proceedings of the Ninth World Congress of Jewish Studies: Panel Sessions: Hebrew and Aramaic Languages*. Jerusalem: World Congress of Jewish Studies, 1988.

Kaufman, S. A., and M. Sokoloff. *A Key-Word-in-Context Concordance to Targum Neofiti*. Baltimore: Johns Hopkins University Press, 1993.

Keel, O. *Das Hohelied*. ZBK, AT 18. Zürich: Theologischer Verlag Zürich, 1986.

Kessler, R. *Some Poetical and Structural Features of the Song of Songs*. Leeds University Oriental Society Monograph Series 8. Leeds: Leeds University, 1957.

Keter Yerushalayim. Jerusalem: N. Ben-Zvi Printing, 2000.

Kimelman, R. "Rabbi Yohanan and Origen on the Song of Songs: A Third-Century Jewish Disputation." *HTR* 73 (1980): 567–95.

Kister, M. "Some Notes on Biblical Expressions and Allusions and the Lexicography of Ben Sira." Pages 160–87 in *Sirach, Scrolls, and Sages*. Edited by T. Muraoka and J. F. Elwolde. Leiden: Brill, 1999.

Knoppers, G. N. "'Yhwh Is Not with Israel': Alliances as a *Topos* in Chronicles." *CBQ* 58 (1996): 601–26.

Koehler, L., and W. Baumgartner, eds. *Lexicon in Veteris Testamenti libros*. Leiden: Brill, 1953.

König, E. *Historisch-kritisches Lehrgebäude der hebräischen Sprache*. 2 vols. Leipzig: Hinrichs, 1895.

Kraeling, E. G. *The Brooklyn Museum Aramaic Papyri*. New Haven: Yale University Press, 1953.

Krahmalkov, C. R. *Phoenician-Punic Dictionary*. Leuven: Peeters, 2000.

Krauss, S. *Griechische und Lateinische Lehnwörter im Talmud, Midrasch und Targum*. 2 vols. Berlin: S. Calvary, 1898–99.

Kressel, G. M. "An Anthropologist's Response to the Use of Social Science Models in Biblical Studies." *Semeia* 68 (1996): 153–60.

Kutscher, E. Y. *Ha-Lashon ve-ha-Reqaʿ ha-Leshoni shel Megillat Yeshaʿyahu ha-Shelema mi-Megillot Yam ha-Melaḥ*. Jerusalem: Magnes, 1959.

———. *A History of the Hebrew Language*. Leiden: Brill, 1982.

———. *The Language and Linguistic Background of the Isaiah Scroll (1QIsa[a])*. Leiden: Brill, 1974.

———. *Meḥqarim ba-ʾAramit ha-Gelilit*. Jerusalem: Hebrew University, 1969.

———. *Studies in Galilean Aramaic*. Ramat-Gan: Bar Ilan University Press, 1976.

Landsberger, F. "Poetic Units within the Song of Songs." *JBL* 73 (1954): 203–16.

Leander, P. *Laut- und Formenlehre des Ägyptisch-aramäischen*. Göteborg: Elanders, 1928.

Lefkovits, J. K. *The Copper Scroll (3Q15): A Reevaluation*. STDJ 25. Leiden: Brill, 2000.

Leick, G. *Sex and Eroticism in Mesopotamian Literature*. London: Routledge, 1994.

Lesky, A. *A History of Greek Literature*. New York: Crowell, 1966.

Levenson, J. D., and B. Halpern. "The Political Import of David's Marriages." *JBL* 99 (1980): 507–18.

Levin, S. "Hebrew {*pi(y)lέḡεš*}, Greek παλλακή, Latin *paelex*: The Origin of Intermarriage among the Early Indo-Europeans and Semites." *General Linguistics* 23 (1983): 191–97.

———. "The 'Qeri' as the Primary Text of the Hebrew Bible." *General Linguistics* 35 (1995): 181–223.

———. *Semitic and Indo-European I: The Principal Etymologies*. Current Issues in Linguistic Theory 129. Amsterdam: Benjamins, 1995.

———. *Semitic and Indo-European II: Comparative Morphology, Syntax and Phonetics*. Current Issues in Linguistic Theory 226. Amsterdam: Benjamins, 2002.

Lewalski, B. *Paradise Lost and the Rhetoric of Literary Forms*. Princeton: Princeton University Press, 1987.

Liddell, H. G., and R. Scott. *A Greek-English Lexicon*. 9th ed. Oxford: Clarendon, 1940.

Lipiński, E. *Semitic Languages: Outline of a Comparative Grammar*. Leuven: Peeters, 1997.

Long, G. A. "A Lover, Cities, and Heavenly Bodies: Co-Text and the Translation of Two Similes in Canticles (6:4c; 6:10d)." *JBL* 115 (1996): 703–9.

Loretz, O. *Qohelet und der alte Orient: Untersuchungen zu Stil und theologischer Thematik des Buches Qohelet*. Freiburg: Herder, 1964.

Lys, D. "Notes sur le Cantique." Pages 170–78 in *Congress Volume: Rome, 1968*. Edited by G. W. Anderson et al. VTSup 17. Leiden: Brill, 1969.

Macuch, R. *Handbook of Classical and Modern Mandaic*. Berlin: de Gruyter, 1965.

Malone, J. L. "Wave Theory, Rule Ordering and Hebrew-Aramaic Segolation." *JAOS* 91 (1971): 44–66.

Margalit, B. "Alliteration in Ugaritic Poetry: Its Role in Composition and Analysis." *UF* 11 (1979): 537–57.

———. "Alliteration in Ugaritic Poetry: Its Role in Composition and Analysis (Part II)." *JNSL* 8 (1980): 57–80.

Margolis, M. L. *A Manual of the Aramaic Language of the Babylonian Talmud*. Munich: Beck, 1910.

Mariaselvan, A. *The Song of Songs and Ancient Tamil Love Poems: Poetry and Symbolism*. Rome: Pontifical Biblical Institute, 1988.

Martin, G. D. "Textual Histories of Early Jewish Writings: Multivalencies vs. the Quest for 'The Original.'" Ph.D. diss. University of Washington, 2007.

May, H. G. "Some Cosmic Connotations of *Mayim Rabbîm*, 'Many Waters.'" *JBL* 74 (1955): 9–21.

Mazurel, J. W. "De Vraag naar de Verloren Broeder: Terugkeer en herstel in de boeken Jeremia en Ezechiel." Ph.D. diss. Universiteit van Amsterdam, 1992.

McCreesh, T. P. *Biblical Sound and Sense: Poetic Sound Patterns in Proverbs 10–29*. JSOTSup 128. Sheffield: Sheffield Academic Press, 1991.

Meek, T. J. "Babylonian Parallels to the Song of Songs." *JBL* 43 (1924): 245–52.

———. "Canticles and the Tammuz Cult." *AJSL* 39 (1922): 1–14.

———. *The Song of Songs and the Fertility Cult: Symposium of the Oriental Club of Philadelphia*. Philadelphia: n.p., 1924.

Meyers, C. L. "Gender Imagery in the Song of Songs." *HAR* 19 (1986): 209–23.

Michel, W. L. *Job in the Light of Northwest Semitic*. 2 vols. BibOr 42. Rome: Biblical Institute Press, 1987.

Miralles, C., and J. Pórtulas. *Archilocus and the Iambic Poetry*. Rome: Ateneo, 1983.

Monier-Williams, M. *Sanskrit-English Dictionary*. 2nd ed. Oxford: Clarendon, 1899.

Monroe, J. T. "The Strip-Tease That Was Blamed on Abū Bakr's Naughty Son: Was Father Being Shamed, or Was the Poet Having Fun? (Ibn Quzmān's *Zajal* No. 133)." Pages 94–139 in *Homoeroticism in Classical Arabic Literature*. Edited by J. W. Wright and E. K. Rowson. New York: Columbia University Press, 1997.

Montgomery, J. A., and H. S. Gehman. *A Critical and Exegetical Commentary on the Book of Kings*. ICC. Edinburgh: T&T Clark, 1950.

Morag, S. "On the Historical Validity of the Vocalization of the Hebrew Bible." *JAOS* 94 (1974): 307–15.

———. "Rovede Qadmut: ʿIyyunim Leshoniyim be-Mishle Bilʿam." *Tarbiz* 50 (1980–81): 1–24.

Moran, W. L. "The Ancient Near Eastern Background of the Love of God in Deuteronomy." *CBQ* 25 (1963): 77–87. Repr. as pages 170–81 in Moran, *The Most Magic Word: Essays on Babylonian and Biblical Literature.* CBQMS 35. Washington, D.C.: Catholic Biblical Association, 2002.

———. "An Assyriological Gloss on the New Archilochos Fragment." *HSPh* 82 (1978): 17–19.

Muecke, D. C. *The Compass of Irony*. London: Methuen, 1969.

Murphy, R. E. *The Song of Songs*. Minneapolis: Fortress, 1990.

———. "The Unity of the Song of Songs." *VT* 29 (1979): 436–43.

Na'aman, N. "Two Notes on the Monolith Inscription of Shalmaneser III from Kurkh." *Tel-Aviv* 3 (1976): 89–106.

Nasuti, H. P. *Tradition History and the Psalms of Asaph*. SBLDS 88. Atlanta: Scholars Press, 1988.

Niditch, S. *Oral World and Written Word: Ancient Israelite Literature*. Louisville: Westminster John Knox, 1996.

Nissinen, M. "Love Lyrics of Nabû and Tašmetu: An Assyrian Song of Songs?" Pages 585–634 in *"Und Mose schrieb dieses Lied auf": Studien zum Alten Testament und zum Alten Orient: Festschrift für Oswald Loretz zur Vollendung seines 70. Lebensjahres*. Edited by M. Dietrich and I. Kottsieper. AOAT 250. Münster: Ugarit-Verlag, 1998.

Noegel, S. B. "Dialect and Politics in Isaiah 24–27." *AuOr* 12 (1994): 177–92.

———. "Drinking Feasts and Deceptive Feats: Jacob and Laban's Double Talk." Pages 163–79 in *Puns and Pundits: Word Play in the Hebrew Bible and Ancient Near Eastern Literature*. Edited by S. B. Noegel. Bethesda, Md.: CDL, 2000.

———. *Janus Parallelism in the Book of Job*. JSOTSup 223. Sheffield: Sheffield Academic Press, 1996.

———. "'Word Play' in Qohelet." *JHS* 7 (2007): 1–28.

Nöldeke, T. *Compendious Syriac Grammar*. London: Williams & Norgate, 1904.

———. *Kurzgefasste Syrische Grammatik*. Leipzig: Tauchnitz, 1898.

O'Connor, M. P. "Semitic **mgn* and Its Supposed Sanskrit Origin." *JAOS* 109 (1989): 25–32.

———. "Women in the Book of Judges." *HAR* 10 (1987): 277–93.

Olmo Lete, G. del, and J. Sanmartín. *Diccionario de la Lengua Ugarítica*. 2 vols. Barcelona: Editorial AUSA, 1996–2000.

———. *A Dictionary of the Ugaritic Language*. Edited and translated by W. G. E. Watson. 2 vols. Leiden: Brill, 2004.

Olyan, S. M. "Honor, Shame, and Covenant Relations." *JBL* 115 (1996): 201–18.

Omlin, J. A. *Der Papyrus 55001 und seine satirische-erotischen Zeichnungen und Inschriften*. Catalogo del Museo Egizio di Torino 3. Turin: Edizioni d'Arte Fratelli Pozo, 1973.

Orton, H., S. Sanderson, and J. Widdowson. *The Linguistic Atlas of England.* London: Croom Helm, 1978.

Osimo, B. "Nabokov's Selftranslations: Interpretation Problems and Solutions in Lolita's Russian Version." *Sign Systems Studies* 27 (1999): 215–33. Online: http://www.ut.ee/SOSE/sss/articles/osimo_27.htm.

Pardes, I. *Countertraditions in the Bible: A Feminist Approach.* Cambridge: Harvard University Press, 1992.

Parpola, S. *Assyrian Prophecies.* SAA 9. Helsinki: Helsinki University Press, 1997.

———. *Neo-Assyrian Toponyms.* Neukirchen-Vluyn: Kevelaer, Butzon & Bercker, 1970.

Paul, S. M. "A Lover's Garden of Verse: Literal and Metaphorical Imagery in Ancient Near Eastern Love Poetry." Pages 99–110 in *Tehillah le-Moshe: Biblical and Judaic Studies in Honor of Moshe Greenberg.* Edited by M. Cogan, B. L. Eichler, and J. H. Tigay. Winona Lake, Ind.: Eisenbrauns, 1997.

———. "Polysemous Pivotal Punctuation: More Janus Double Entendres." Pages 369–74 in *Texts, Temples, and Traditions: A Tribute to Menahem Haran.* Edited by M. V. Fox et al. Winona Lake, Ind.: Eisenbrauns, 1996. Repr. as pages 477–83 in *Divrei Shalom: Collected Studies of Shalom M. Paul on the Bible and the Ancient Near East, 1967–2005.* Culture and History of the Ancient Near East 23. Leiden: Brill, 2005.

Payne Smith, J. *A Compendious Syriac Dictionary.* Oxford: Clarendon, 1903.

Pellat, C. "*Hidja.*" *EncIsl* 3:352–55.

Pérez Fernández, M. *An Introductory Grammar of Rabbinic Hebrew.* Leiden: Brill, 1999.

Perles, F. "Notes critiques sure le texte d l'*Ecclésiastique.*" *REJ* 35 (1897): 48–64.

Polzin, R. *Late Biblical Hebrew: Toward an Historical Typology of Biblical Hebrew Prose.* HSM 12. Missoula, Mont.: Scholars Press, 1976.

Pope, M. H. *Song of Songs.* AB 7C. Garden City, N.Y.: Doubleday, 1977.

Pouget, G., and J. Guitton. *The Canticle of Canticles.* New York: Declan X. McMullen, 1934.

Provan, I. W. *1 and 2 Kings.* NIBC. Peabody, Mass.: Hendrickson, 1995.

Rabin, C. "The Emergence of Classical Hebrew." Pages 71–78, 293–95 in *The Age of the Monarchies: Culture and Society.* Edited by A. Malamat and I. Ephʿal. WHJP. Jerusalem: Masada, 1979.

———. "Leshonam shel ʿAmos ve-Hosheaʿ." Pages 117–36 in *ʿIyyunim be-Sefer Tre-ʿAsar.* Edited by B. Z. Luria. Jerusalem: Kiryath Sepher, 1981.

———. "Lexical Borrowings from Indian Languages as Carriers of Ideas and Technical Concepts." Pages 25–32, 281–82 in *Between Jerusalem and Benares: Comparative Studies in Judaism and Hinduism.* Edited by H. Goodman. Albany: State University of New York Press, 1994.

———. "Millim ba-ʿIvrit ha-Miqraʾit mi-Leshon ha-ʾIndo-ʾArim she-ba-Mizraḥ ha-Qarov." Pages 462–97 in *Sefer Shmuel Yeivin: Meḥqarim ba-Miqraʾ, ʾArkheʾologiya, Lashon ve-Toledot Yisraʾel, Mugashim lo be-Hagiʿo le-Sevaʿ*. Edited by S. Abramsky. Jerusalem: Kiryat Sefer, 1970.

———. "The Origin of the Hebrew Word *Pilegeš*." *JSS* 25 (1974): 353–64.

———. *A Short History of the Hebrew Language*. Jerusalem: Jewish Agency, 1973.

———. "The Song of Songs and Tamil Poetry." *Sciences religieuses/Studies in Religion* 3 (1973/74): 205–19.

Rankin, H. D. *Archilochus of Paros*. Park Ridge, N.J.: Noyes, 1977.

Rankin, O. S. "Alliteration in Hebrew Poetry." *JTS* 31 (1930): 285–91.

Ratcliffe, R. R. "Defining Morphological Isoglosses: The 'Broken' Plural and Semitic Subclassification." *JNES* 57 (1998): 81–123.

Ratner, R. J. "Morphological Variation in Biblical Hebrew Rhetoric." Pages 143–59 in *Let Your Colleagues Praise You: Studies in Memory of Stanley Gevirtz 2 = Maarav* 8 (1992). Edited by R. J. Ratner, L. M. Barth, M. L. Gevirtz, and B. Zuckerman. Rolling Hills Estates, Calif.: Western Academic Press, 1993.

Rendsburg, G. A. "Additional Notes on 'The Last Words of David' (2 Sam 23,1–7)." *Bib* 70 (1989): 403–8.

———. "Alliteration in the Exodus Narrative." Pages 83–100 in *Birkat Shalom: Studies in the Bible, Ancient Near Eastern Literature, and Postbiblical Judaism Presented to Shalom M. Paul on the Occasion of His Seventieth Birthday*. Edited by C. Cohen, A. V. Hurowitz, A. Hurvitz, Y. Muffs, B. J. Schwartz, and J. H. Tigay. Winona Lake, Ind.: Eisenbrauns, 2008.

———. "The Ammonite Phoneme /Ṯ/." *BASOR* 269 (1988): 73–79.

———. "Ancient Hebrew Phonology." Pages 65–83 in vol. 1 of *Phonologies of Asia and Africa*. Edited by A. S. Kaye. 2 vols. Winona Lake, Ind.: Eisenbrauns, 1997.

———. "Aramaic-Like Features in the Pentateuch." *HS* 47 (2006): 163–76.

———. "Baasha of Ammon." *JANES* 20 (1991): 58–59.

———. "Biblical Literature as Politics: The Case of Genesis." Pages 47–70 in *Religion and Politics in the Ancient Near East*. Edited by A. Berlin. Bethesda, Md.: University Press of Maryland, 1996.

———. "A Comprehensive Guide to Israelian Hebrew: Grammar and Lexicon." *Orient* 38 (2003): 5–35.

———. "The Dialect of the Deir ʿAlla Inscription." *BO* 50 (1993): 314–15.

———. *Diglossia in Ancient Hebrew*. AOS 72. New Haven: American Oriental Society, 1990.

———. "The Galilean Background of Mishnaic Hebrew." Pages 225–40 in *The Galilee in Late Antiquity*. Edited by L. I. Levine. New York: Jewish Theological Seminary, 1992.

———. "The Geographical and Historical Background of the Mishnaic Hebrew Lexicon." *Orient* 38 (2003): 105–15.

———. "Hebrew Philological Notes (II)." *HS* 42 (2001): 187–95.

———. "Israelian Hebrew Features in Genesis 49." Pages 161–70 in *Let Your Colleagues Praise You: Studies in Memory of Stanley Gevirtz 2 = Maarav* 8 (1992). Edited by R. J. Ratner, L. M. Barth, M. L. Gevirtz, and B. Zuckerman. Rolling Hills Estates, Calif.: Western Academic Press, 1993.

———. *Israelian Hebrew in the Book of Kings.* Bethesda, Md.: CDL, 2002.

———. "Israelian Hebrew in the Song of Songs." Pages 315–23 in *Biblical Hebrew in Its Northwest Semitic Setting: Typological and Historical Perspectives.* Edited by S. E. Fassberg and A. Hurvitz. ScrHier 39. Jerusalem: Magnes, 2005.

———. "Late Biblical Hebrew and the Date of 'P.'" *JANES* 12 (1980): 65–80.

———. *Linguistic Evidence for the Northern Origin of Selected Psalms.* SBLMS 43. Atlanta: Scholars Press, 1990.

———. "Linguistic Variation and the 'Foreign Factor' in the Hebrew Bible." *IOS* 15 (1996): 177–90.

———. "More on Hebrew *Šibbōlet*." *JSS* 33 (1988): 255–58.

———. "Morphological Evidence for Regional Dialects in Ancient Hebrew." Pages 84–85 in *Linguistics and Biblical Hebrew.* Edited by W. R. Bodine. Winona Lake, Ind.: Eisenbrauns, 1992.

———. "The Northern Origin of Nehemiah 9." *Bib* 72 (1991): 348–66.

———. *The Redaction of Genesis.* Winona Lake, Ind.: Eisenbrauns, 1986.

———. "Shimush Bilti Ragil shel Kinnuy ha-Remez ba-Miqra᾽: ʿEdut Nosefet le-᾽Ivrit Ṣefonit bi-Tqufat ha-Miqra᾽." *Shnaton* 12 (2000): 83–88.

———. "Some False Leads in the Identification of Late Biblical Hebrew Texts: The Cases of Genesis 24 and 1 Samuel 2:27–36." *JBL* 121 (2002): 23–46.

———. "*Talpiyyôt* (Song 4:4)." *JNSL* 20 (1994): 13–19.

———. "*UT* 68 and the Tell Asmar Seal." *Or* 53 (1984): 448–52.

Rendsburg, G. A., and S. L. Rendsburg. "Physiological and Philological Notes to Psalm 137." *JQR* 83 (1993): 385–99.

Robert, A., and R. Tournay. *Le Cantique des cantiques: Traduction et commentaire.* Paris: Librarie Lecoffre, 1963.

Rofé, A. "Ephraimite Versus Deuteronomistic History." Pages 221–35 in *Storia e tradizioni di Israele: Scritti in onore di J. Alberto Soggin.* Edited by D. Garrone and F. Israel. Brescia: Paideia, 1992.

Rosenbaum, S. N. *Amos of Israel: A New Interpretation.* Macon, Ga.: Mercer University Press, 1990.

Rossell, W. H. *A Handbook of Aramaic Magical Texts.* Ringwood Borough, N.J.: Shelton College, 1953.

Rundgren, F. "אפריון 'Tragsessel, Sänfte.'" *ZAW* 74 (1962): 70–72.

Sæbø, M. "On the Canonicity of the Song of Songs." Pages 267–77 in *Texts, Temples, and Traditions: A Tribute to Menahem Haran*. Edited by Michael V. Fox et al. Winona Lake, Ind.: Eisenbrauns, 1996.

Sáenz-Badillos, A. "Hebrew Invective Poetry: The Debate Between Todros Abulafia and Phinehas Halevi." *Prooftexts* 16 (1996): 49–73.

Sasson, J. M. "The Blood of Grapes: Viticulture and Intoxication in the Hebrew Bible." Pages 399–419 in *Drinking in Ancient Societies: History and Culture of Drinks in the Ancient Near East*. Edited by L. Milano. Padua: Sargon, 1994.

———. "A Further Cuneiform Parallel to the Song of Songs?" *ZAW* 85 (1973): 359–60.

———. "On M. H. Pope's *Song of Songs* [AB 7c]." *Maarav* 1 (1978–79): 177–96.

———. "Word Play in the O.T." *IDBSup*, 968–70.

Sasson, V. "King Solomon and the Dark Lady in the Song of Songs." *VT* 39 (1989), 407–14.

Schniedewind, W. M. *How the Bible Became a Book*. New York: Cambridge University Press, 2004.

Schoeler, G. "Bashshār b. Burd, Abū ʾl-ʿAtāhiyah, Abū Nūwās." Pages 280–99 in *ʿAbbasid Belles-Lettres: Arabic Literature 750–1258*. Edited by J. Ashtiany, T. M. Johnstone, J. D. Latham, and R. B. Serjeant. Cambridge History of Arabic Literature. Cambridge: Cambridge University Press, 1990.

Schoville, K. N. "The Impact of the Ras Shamra Texts on the Study of the Song of Songs." Ph.D. diss. University of Wisconsin, 1969.

Schwartz, B. J., and A. Focht. "אמון—Constantly." *ZAH* 14 (2001): 43–49.

Seeligman, I. L. "Meḥqarim be-Toledot Nusaḥ ha-Miqraʾ." *Tarbiz* 25 (1956): 118–39. Repr. as pages 295–318 in Seeligman, *Meḥqarim be-Sifrut ha-Miqraʾ*. Edited by A. Hurvitz, E. Tov, and S. Japhet. Jerusalem: Magnes, 1992.

Seeman, D. "The Watcher at the Window: Cultural Poetics of a Biblical Motif." *Prooftexts* 24 (2004): 1–50.

Segal, M. H. *Diqduq Leshon ha-Mishna*. Tel-Aviv: Devir, 1936.

———. *A Grammar of Mishnaic Hebrew*. Oxford: Clarendon, 1927.

———. "Song of Songs." *VT* 12 (1962): 470–90. Repr. as pages 221–41 in idem, *The Pentateuch, Its Composition, and Its Authorship and Other Biblical Studies*. Jerusalem: Magnes, 1967.

Segert, S. *Altaramäische Grammatik*. Leipzig: VEB Verlag, 1975.

———. *A Grammar of Phoenician and Punic*. Munich: Beck, 1976.

———. "Old Aramaic Phonology." Pages 115–25 in vol. 1 of *Phonologies of Asia and Africa*. Edited by A. S. Kaye. 2 vols. Winona Lake, Ind.: Eisenbrauns, 1997.

Sells, M. A. "Guises of the *Ghūl*: Dissembling Simile and Semantic Overflow in the Classical *Nasīb*." Pages 130–64 in *Reorientations: Arabic and Per-*

sian Poetry. Edited by S. P. Stetkevych. Bloomington: Indiana University Press, 1994.

Shapiro, M. "Repetition." Pages 1035–37 in *The New Princeton Encyclopedia of Poetry and Poetics*. Edited by A. Preminger and T. V. F. Brogan. Princeton: Princeton University Press, 1993.

Smith, C. "'With an Iron Pen and a Diamond Tip': Linguistic Peculiarities in the Book of Jeremiah." Ph.D. diss. Cornell University, 2003.

Smith, M. "The Baal Cycle." Pages 81–180 in *Ugaritic Narrative Poetry*. Edited by S. B. Parker. SBLWAW 9. Atlanta: Scholars Press, 1997.

Sokoloff, M. *A Dictionary of Jewish Babylonian Aramaic*. Ramat-Gan: Bar Ilan University Press, 2002.

———. *A Dictionary of Jewish Palestinian Aramaic*. Ramat-Gan: Bar Ilan University Press, 1990.

Soulen, R. N. "The *waṣfs* of the Song of Songs and Hermeneutic." Pages 214–24 in *A Feminist Companion to the Song of Songs*. Edited by A. Brenner. Sheffield: JSOT Press, 1993.

Sperl, S. "Islamic Kingship and Arabic Panegyric Poetry in the Early 9th Century." *JAL* 8 (1977): 20–35.

Spiegel, J. *Die Erzählung von Streite des Horus und Seth in Pap. Beatty I als Literaturwerk*. Leipziger Ägyptologische Studien 9. Glückstadt: Augustin, 1937.

Stadelmann, L. *Love and Politics: A New Commentary on the Song of Songs*. New York: Paulist, 1992.

Steiner, R. C. *Affricated* Ṣade *in the Semitic Languages*. AAJRMS 3. New York: American Academy for Jewish Reseaerch, 1982.

Stetkevych, J. "Name and Epithet: The Philology and Semiotics of Animal Nomenclature in Early Arabic Poetry." *JNES* 45 (1986): 89–124.

Stetkevych, S. P. *Abū Tammām and the Poetics of the ʿAbbasid Age*. Studies in Arabic Literature 13. Leiden: Brill, 1991.

———. "Intoxication and Immorality: Wine and Associated Imagery in Al-Maʿarri's Garden." Pages 29–48 in *Literature East and West, Critical Pilgrimages: Studies in the Arabic Literary Tradition*. Edited by J. W. Wright and E. K. Rowson. Austin: University of Texas Press, 1989.

Stinespring, W. F. "Daughter of Zion." *IDBSup*, 985.

Tal, A. *A Dictionary of Samaritan Aramaic*. 2 vols. Leiden: Brill, 2000.

Tayib, Abdulla el. "Pre-Islamic Poetry." Pages 27–113 in *Arabic Literature to the End of the Umayyad Period*. Edited by A. F. L. Beeston et al. Cambridge: Cambridge University Press, 1983.

Toporov, V. N. "Die Urspringe der indoeuropäischen Poetik." *Poetica* 13 (1981): 189–251.

Tov, E. "Canticles." Pages 195–220 in *Qumran Cave 4.XI: Psalms to Chronicles*. Edited by E. Ulrich et al. DJD XVI. Oxford: Clarendon, 2000.

——. “Three Manuscripts (Abbreviated Texts?) of Canticles from Qumran Cave 4.” *JSS* 46 (1995): 88–111.

Trible, P. “Depatriarchalizing in Biblical Interpretation.” *JAAR* 41 (1973): 42–45.

Troupeau, G. “*Naʿt*.” *EncIsl* 7:1034.

Tuell, S. S. “A Riddle Resolved by an Enigma: Hebrew גלש and Ugaritic *gl<u>t</u>*.” *JBL* 112 (1993): 99–104.

Turner, R. L. *A Comparative and Etymological Dictionary of the Nepali Language*. London: Paul, Trench, Trubner, 1931.

Tyloch, W. “Ugaritic Poems and the Song of Songs.” Pages 295–301 in *Šulmu IV: Everyday Life in the Ancient Near East: Papers Presented at the International Conferance Poznan, 19–22 September, 1989*. Edited by J. Zablocka and S. Zawadski. Historia 182. Poznan: Uniwersytet im Adama Mickiewicza w Poznaniu, 1993.

Ullendorff, Edward. “The Bawdy Bible.” *BSOAS* 42 (1979): 425–56.

Wagner, M. *Die lexikalischen und grammatikalischen Aramäismen im alttestamentlichen Hebräisch*. BZAW 96. Berlin: Töpelmann, 1966.

Wallace, C. V. (= C. W. Gordon). “Broken and Double Plural Formations in the Hebrew Bible.” Ph.D. diss. New York University, 1988.

Wanner, E. “The Parser’s Window.” Pages 211–23 in *The Cognitive Representation of Speech*. Edited by T. Myers, J. Laver, and J. Anderson. Amsterdam: North-Holland, 1981.

Waterman, L. “דודי in the Song of Songs.” *AJSL* 35 (1919): 101–10.

——. “The Rôle of Solomon in the Song of Songs.” *JBL* 44 (1925): 171–87.

——. *The Song of Songs: Translated and Interpreted as a Dramatic Poem*. Ann Arbor: University of Michigan Press, 1948.

Watkins, C. *How to Kill a Dragon: Aspects of Indo-European Poetics*. Oxford: Oxford University Press, 1995.

Watson, W. G. E. *Classical Hebrew Poetry: A Guide to Its Techniques*. JSOTSup 26. Sheffield: JSOT Press, 1986.

——. “Puns Ugaritic Newly Surveyed.” Pages 117–34 in *Puns and Pundits: Word Play in the Hebrew Bible and Ancient Near Eastern Literature*. Edited by S. B. Noegel. Bethesda, Md.: CDL, 2000.

——. “Some Ancient Near Eastern Parallels to the Song of Songs.” Pages 253–71 in *Words Remembered, Texts Renewed: Essays in Honour of John F. A. Sawyer*. Edited by J. Davies, G. Harvey, and W. G. E. Watson. JSOTSup 195. Sheffield: Sheffield Academic Press 1995.

Webber, E. J. “Comedy and Satire in Hispano-Arabic Spain.” *Hispanic Review* 26 (1958): 1–11.

West, M. L. “Some Oriental Motifs in Archilochus.” *ZPE* 102 (1994): 1–5.

Westenholz, J. G. “Metaphorical Language in the Poetry of Love in the Ancient Near East.” Pages 381–87 in *La Circulation des Biens, des Per-*

sonnes et des Idées dans le Proche-Orient ancien: Actes de la XXXVIIIe Rencontre Assyriologique Internationale (Paris, 8–10 juillet 1991). Edited by D. Charpin and F. Joannès. Paris: Editions Recherche sur les Civilisations, 1992.

Westenholz, J. G., and A. Westenholz. "Help for Rejected Suitors: The Old Akkadian Love Incantation: MAD V 8." *Or* 46 (1977): 198–219.

Westermarck, E. *Ritual and Belief in Morocco*. 2 vols. London: Macmillan, 1926.

Wetztein, J. G. "Die syrische Dreschtafel," *Zeitschrift für Ethnologie* 5 (1873): 270–302.

Whedbee, J. W. "Paradox and Parody in the Song of Solomon: Towards a Comic Reading of the Most Sublime Song." Pages 266–78 in *A Feminist Companion to the Song of Songs*. Edited by A. Brenner. Sheffield: JSOT Press, 1993.

White, J. B. *A Study of the Language of Love in the Song of Songs and Ancient Egyptian Poetry*. SBLDS 38. Missoula, Mont.: Scholars Press, 1978.

Wimsatt, W. K. *The Verbal Icon: Studies in the Meaning of Poetry*. Lexington: University of Kentucky Press, 1954.

Wortley, W. V. "Some Rabelaisian Satiric Techniques." *Satire News Letter* 5.1 (1967): 8–15.

Yoo, Y. J. "Israelian Hebrew in the Book of Hosea." Ph.D. diss. Cornell University, 1999.

Young, I. *Diversity in Pre-exilic Hebrew*. FAT 5. Tübingen: Mohr Siebeck, 1993.

———. "The 'Northernisms' of the Israelite Narratives in Kings." *ZAH* 8 (1995): 63–70.

———. "Notes on the Language of 4QCant^{b}." *JJS* 52 (2001): 122–31.

Zaborski, A. "Archaic Semitic in the Light of Hamito-Semitic." *ZAH* 7 (1994): 234–44.

Zevit, Z. "Cognitive Theory and the Memorability of Biblical Poetry." Pages 199–212 in *Let Your Colleagues Praise You: Studies in Memory of Stanley Gevirtz 2 = Maarav* 8 (1992). Edited by R. J. Ratner et al. Rolling Hills Estates, Calif.: Western Academic Press, 1993.

Ziadeh, F. "Prosody and the Initial Formation of Classical Arabic." *JAOS* 106 (1986): 333–38.

Zohary, M. *Plants of the Bible*. Cambridge: Cambridge University Press, 1982.

Index of Primary Texts

Hebrew Bible

Genesis
1:2 70
1:7 113
3:16 173, 204 n. ae
22:21–22 30
23:3 25
25:24 123 n. 24
26:8 156 n. 94
29:10–11 105
30:38, 41 52 (2x), 52 n. 226
31:21, 23, 25 121
32:3 102 n. 51
32:31 82
33:4 71
34:19 164
37:2 65 n. 9
37:15 65 n. 9
38 165 n. 129
38:14 99, 99 n. 48
38:27 123 n. 24
49 5
49:5 180
49:8–12 165 n. 129
49:15 32

Exodus
2:10 70
2:16 52 (2x), 52 n. 226
7:28 33
15:15 163
18 172 n. 4
20:18 180
21:19 38
22:1 36
26:1 49
28:11 49
30:23 93 n. 44
32:1 29 (2x)
32:27 82

Leviticus
19:18 12

Numbers
1 107
1:22 108
1:42 108
7 107
7:18–19 108
16:30 17
21:18 24
21:25 158
22:24 164 n. 126
23:7 22, 28
24:6 47
29 107
29:19 108, 109
29:31 108, 109
32:42 158 n. 103

Deuteronomy
3:9 60 n. 10
3:11 32
3:12 121
8:9 23, 23 n. 90
21:14 164

Deuteronomy (*cont.*)
32 5, 11 n. 30
33 5
33:11 28 n. 107
33:13–16 42
33:15 22

Joshua
2:15 156
9:12 29
9:12–13 30
9:13 29 (2x)
15:45, 47 158 n. 103
19:18 161

Judges
3:3 30
5 22
5:7 15, 19
5:10 59
5:11 14
5:14 22
5:15 22
5:16 17
5:20 28
5:28 156
5:31 157
6:17 15
7:3 121
7:12 15
7:23 28
8:6 163
8:25 15
8:26 90
10:11 28
11:40 14
18:2 25
19:1 18
19:16 28
20:3 18 (2x)
20:4 18

1 Samuel
2:22 163 n. 123
2:33 68 n. 18
9:22 180
10:1 71
13:21 17
19:12 156
20:20 12 (2x)
28:4 161
28:16 13, 13 n. 40

2 Samuel
1:16, 26 32
1:18 25
1:19 163
6:5 14, 76
6:16 156
11:2 167 n. 136
12:25 162
13 154 n. 87
13:6, 8 89 n. 40
13:39 184 n. 44
15:37 158 n. 102
16:16 158 n. 102
23:1 32
23:1–7 5

1 Kings
1:3 161
1:15 9
4:5 158 n. 102
5:15 157
5:27–30 167
5:27–32 167
6:1, 37–38 40
6:25 40
6–8 40
7:37 40
8:2 40
9:11–13 168
9:13 157
9:15–19 162 n. 120
9:19 167
9–10 176 n. 16
10:21–22 167
10:22 176
11:1–3 167
11:33 59

14:14 29
14:17 174
15:2 154 n. 87
16:23 174
19:6 84
19:8 17

2 Kings
4:2, 3, 7 (K) 20
4:8 161
4:12 9, 161
5 31
6:6 40
6:9 26
6:11 15, 16 (2x)
6:13 18 (2x), 18 n. 60
6:33 29
9:30 156
11:33 59
14:9 34
14:25 17
15:25 25
15:28 28
16:17 84
19:23 48
19:24 48
23:7 24
24:14 49

Isaiah
3:18–21 90
3:23 95
5:1–10 148 n. 71, 164
5:22 51 (2x)
6:6 84
7:9 70
8:2, 7 28 n. 107
9:16 182 (2x), 183
13:14 153
13:20 74
14:31 48
16:8 91
17:10 32
17:11 51 n. 222
18:5 23, 37 (2x), 53
18:6 36
19:14 50, 51
23:13 29, 30
24:23 44
24–27 5, 44, 48
26:6 48 (2x)
29:18 67 n. 13
30:26 44, 45, 46
34:2 163
34:13 23, 34
35:1 77
37:24 48
37:25 48
41:24 69 (2x)
46:1 26 n. 100, 158 n. 103
49:18 158
63:11 153
65:11 50

Jeremiah
1:13 48
3:5 12
3:7 157
4:23 70
5:7–9 162
6:3 153
6:4 22
6:20 38 n. 154
6:22 48
7:7 28
11:15 21
13:27 162
16:13 17
17:5 28
18:16 17
25:3, 5 28
31:22 102
31:26 38 n. 154
32:2 12
33:12 74
39:8 25
44:18, 28 28
48:15 70
50:19 153
50:33–38 69 n. 22

Jeremiah (*cont.*)
50:34 69 n. 22
50:36 69 n. 22
50:37 69 n. 22 (2x)
50:38 69 n. 22
51:12 25
51:58 25
52:15 48, 49
52:20 184 n. 44

Ezekiel
1:4 48
4:12 22
4:15 22
10:3 113
13:4 164 n. 127
16:4 202 n. y
16:27 158 n. 103
16:37 38 n. 154
16:45 157
17:13 163
23:1–6 158
23:17–21 163
26:4 25
26:7 48
26:18 59
26:61 158
27 23
27:5 27
27:19 99
32:9 32
33:32 38
34:2 153
34:14 153
34:15 74
34:17 163
34:23 164
36:38 153
38:20 80
44:20 43
46:14 43

Hosea
2:2 25
2:15 53 n. 227, 102
4:14 158
9:4 38 n. 154
9:6 23, 34
13:2 72
13:7 41, 89

Joel
3:3 81

Amos
3:12 32
6:4 32 (2x)
6:11 44 n. 185

Jonah
1:7 15, 16 (2x)
1:12 15, 16 (2x)
2:7 41 n. 169
3:2 17

Micah
1:10–16 64 n. 7
1:14 70
5:5 153
6–7 5
7:14 153

Nahum
1:2 12
2:4 177 n. 20
3:18 153

Habakkuk
3:6 23

Zechariah
11:1–3 32
11:7, 10 32

Malachi
3:4 38 n. 154

Psalms
2:12 71
6:7 32 (2x)

9:7 13
16:6, 11 31
19 45, 46
19:2–7 45
19:3 45
19:5 45
19:7 45
19:8–15 45
19:11 41, 42, 91
20:6 98
21:6 70
23:2 74
29 11 n. 30
29:1 25
29:6 60 n. 10
36:7 22
41:4 32 (2x)
45:9 28
45:10 25
47:10 24, 25
50:10 22
55:9 65, 66
58:11 48
73:19 28
74:13 24, 25
74:14 24 (2x)
75:9 50
76:5 22
77:6 25
77:18 22
78:49 25
80 7, 7 n. 17
80:2 7, 164
80:2–3 42
80:3 7
80:11 42
80:13 42
81:3 31
87:1 22
102:10 50
103 21, 21 n. 81
103:3, 4, 5 21
103:9 12
104:25 29 (2x)
104:34 38 n. 154
107:41 153
113:8 24
116:7, 19 20
116:8 28
116:9 24, 25
118:20 29
123:2 19 (3x)
130:4 17
132:2 32
133 15, 15 n. 49, 157
133:1 31
133:2 15
133:3 15, 22
135 21, 21 n. 81
135:9 21
137:6 21 (2x)
139 14
139:2, 17 14
139:20 13
140:5 48
141:4, 6 31

Job
7:13 32
8:12 46
11:12 88 n. 40
15:33 23
16:12 12
17:13 53 n. 2
20:9 73
28:7 73
30:5 28
30:28 45
31:27 71
31:40 34
36:11 31
37:1 35
40:6 28
40:17 164, 164 n. 124 (4x)
41:10 17
41:22 53 n. 2

Proverbs
1:9 90
3:8 202 n. y

Proverbs (*cont.*)
3:24 38 n. 154
5:3 41
7:6 156
7:8 38, 81
7:13 71
7:16 32
8:30 48, 48 n. 207 (2x)
9:2, 5 50
12:27 35 n. 138
13:19 38 n. 154
16:24 41
20:17 38
23:30 50
24:13 41 (2x), 91
24:26 72
24:31 23
25:12 53 n. 2, 102
25:16, 17 41
26:9 34
27:6 17
27:7 41
27:8 28
29:12 22
31:3 59

Ruth
3:6 203 n. z

Song of Songs
1:1 9, 15, 70–71, 140, 161
1:1–3:11 187
1:1–7 185
1:2 16, 17, 71–72, 72, 151
1:2–7 173
1:3 72
1:3–4 72–73, 153
1:4 72 (2x), 151, 162, 187
1:4, 6 71
1:5 84, 141 (2x), 161, 189 n. 1
1:6 12, 16, 58, 73, 148, 155, 159, 167
1:7 13, 14, 18 (3x), 18 n. 60, 25, 73–74, 74, 106, 154, 159, 161, 194 n. 18, 194 n. 20
1:7–8 74 (2x)
1:8 25, 74 (2x), 125 n. 28, 187
1:8–11 185
1:9 74, 143, 150, 159, 162, 162 n. 120, 192 n. k
1:9, 15 123
1:10 75
1:10–11 74–75
1:11 75
1:12 19 (2x), 75, 167
1:12–14 185
1:13 194 n. p
1:13–14 206 n. aj
1:14 148, 190 n. 6
1:15 76, 112 (3x), 185
1:15–16 75–76
1:16 31, 32 (2x), 76 (2x)
1:16–2:1 185
1:17 13, 14, 25, 33 (2x), 58, 76, 76–77, 203 n. ac
1–2 83
2 109
2:1 9
2:1–3 77
2:2 34, 77 (2x), 123, 159, 185
2:3 145
2:3–13 185
2:4 78, 151, 159
2:4, 8 78
2:5 52 n. 227, 113, 159, 192 n. 14
2:5–7 78
2:6 113 (2x), 204 n. af
2:7 19, 71, 84, 108 n. 5, 114 (2x), 115 (2x), 115 n. 17, 116, 149, 159, 163 (2x), 192 n. 14, 203 n. 16
2:7, 17 19
2:8 34, 78
2:9 35 (3x), 36, 78–79, 116, 117, 126, 149, 156 (2x), 173
2:9, 17 162
2:9–3:2 57
2:10 125, 126 (3x)
2:10, 13 123 (2x)
2:10b, 13c 194 n. o
2:11 36, 36 n. 144
2:12 23 (2x), 24

2:13 20 (2x), 37, 79, 80, 125, 126 (4x), 148, 162, 193 n. m
2:13, 15 37, 79, 79–80, 190 n. 6
2:14 38 (2x), 80 n. 33, 123, 124, 146, 185, 199 n. 30
2:15 80, 148, 149, 164
2:15, 17 193 n. 16
2:15–3:5 185
2:16 74, 111, 117 (2x), 154
2:17 19, 21, 25, 58 (4x), 59, 109, 116, 117 (4x), 125, 125 n. 29, 126 (3x), 149, 192 n. k, 206 n. aj
3:1 80, 81, 118, 119 (2x), 146, 159, 194 n. 18, 199 n. 30
3:2 38, 81, 118, 119 (2x)
3:3 119 (2x), 199 n. t
3:4 156
3:4, 5 19
3:4–5 125 n. 30
3:5 19, 71, 108 n. 5, 114 (2x), 115 (2x), 115 n. 17, 116, 149, 159, 163 (2x), 192 n. 14, 192 n. 15, 193 n. 16
3:5, 9–11 57
3:5, 10 84
3:6 81–82, 83, 87, 125, 125 n. 30 (3x), 126 (2x)
3:6, 8 82
3:6, 9 83, 93
3:6–8 125 n. 30
3:6–10 185
3:7 16, 25, 167
3:7, 9 191 n. 11
3:7, 9, 11 141, 189 n. 1
3:7–8 125 n. 30, 150, 191 n. 9
3:7–4:6 125 n. 30
3:8 26, 26 n. 98, 82, 83 (2x)
3:9 83, 93, 167 (2x), 175, 179, 184 n. 44
3:9–10 83–84
3:9–11 84–85, 159
3:10 52 n. 227, 85
3:11 85 (2x), 94 n. 45, 167
4 109, 123, 183 n. 41
4:1 39 (2x), 85, 85–86, 112 (2x), 113, 120 (2x), 120 n. 22, 121 (2x), 143
4:1, 7 123
4:1–16a 185
4:1–2 86–87, 101, 149, 193 n. 16
4:1–5 120
4:1–7 130, 144, 196 n. 23
4:1b–3, 8–11a, 14–5:1 57
4:2 40, 86, 121 (2x)
4:2–3 87
4:3 87–88, 125, 125 n. 29, 126, 127
4:4 88, 121, 122, 131, 143, 150, 191 n. 9
4:5 74, 120, 122 (2x), 143, 149, 193 n. 16
4:6 19 (2x), 21, 58 (2x), 125, 125 n. 29, 126 (2x), 167
4:7–8 160
4:8 21, 25, 27 (2x), 41 (3x), 58 (9x), 59, 60, 62, 89, 89–90, 90, 125 n. 29, 149, 158, 172 (2x), 193 n. 16
4:8–9 88–89, 90
4:9 27, 58, 88, 90, 123, 155, 172 (2x), 204 n. 43
4:9–11 172
4:9–12 158
4:9–5:1 172
4:10 58 (2x), 92, 123, 151, 155
4:10, 12 197 n. 25
4:11 41 (2x), 91, 187
4:11, 13 91–92
4:12 92 (2x), 123, 148, 155, 162, 190 n. 6
4:13 42, 55, 92, 93, 148, 174, 175, 178 (2x), 181, 183, 190 n. 6, 197 n. 26
4:13–14 75, 92–93, 152, 182 n. 36
4:14 78 n. 32, 93 (2x)
4:14–15 83, 93–94
4:15 27 (2x), 28, 57, 149, 190 n. 6
4:16 42, 58, 116, 145, 149, 152, 190 n. 6, 197 n. 26
4:16b 185
5 123
5:1 41, 42, 123, 149, 151, 152, 155, 158, 185

Song of Songs (*cont.*)
5:1, 13 190 n. 6, 197 n. 26
5:1, 2 197 n. 25
5:1–2 94
5:2 43, 95, 116, 123 (3x), 124 (2x), 146, 155
5:2, 11 43 (2x)
5:2–6 94–95, 124
5:2–8 185
5:3 44, 95 (2x), 155
5:4 96
5:4–6 96
5:4–10 96
5:5 95 (2x), 96, 145
5:6 95 (2x), 102, 118, 119 (2x), 146, 194 n. 18
5:7 25, 95, 119 (2x), 155
5:7–8 160
5:7–10 95–96
5:8 71, 95, 108 n. 5, 113, 114, 115 (5x), 116 (2x), 157, 159, 192 n. 14
5:8, 16 84
5:8–10 96
5:9 185
5:10, 13–14 97–98
5:10–15 144, 199 n. 32
5:10–16 130, 185
5:11 149
5:11, 12 193 n. 16
5:11, 13 96–97, 97
5:12 44 (2x), 96, 149
5:12, 14 78, 98
5:13 96, 124 (2x), 149, 152, 200 n. v
5:14 98–99, 99
5:14–15 99, 152 (3x), 200 n. 33
6 83
6:1 125 n. 28, 146, 185, 194 n. 18
6:2 74, 100, 124 (2x), 149, 164, 172, 190 n. 6, 200 n. v
6:2, 4–5 100
6:2–3 185
6:3 74, 100, 111, 117 (2x), 154, 172, 194 n. 20
6:4 100, 123, 150, 172 (2x), 174
6:4, 12 191 n. 9
6:4–7 130, 144, 201 n. 36
6:4–9 185
6:5 39, 100, 120, 121 (2x), 152, 164 n. 128
6:5–6 101, 149, 193 n. 16
6:5–6, 8–9 39, 101
6:5–7 120
6:6 121 (2x)
6:7 101, 120, 125, 126, 126 n. 31, 127
6:8 28 (3x), 101, 167
6:9 101, 123, 124 (2x), 149, 153, 160, 189 n. 3, 193 n. 16
6:10 44 (2x), 101, 185
6:10–11 101
6:11 46, 149
6:11–12 185
6:12 150
7 109, 203 n. 42
7:1 9, 145, 161, 162
7:1–2 102
7:1–6 162, 185
7:2 47 (2x), 53 n. 227, 140, 160
7:2–6 120
7:2–8 130
7:2–10 144, 202 n. 39
7:3 50, 51 (2x), 102–103, 145, 202 n. y
7:4 122 (2x), 149, 193 n. 16
7:5 121, 122, 131, 143, 150, 191 n. 9
7:6 13, 52, 58, 156, 167, 168 n. 137
7:7 31
7:7–10 185
7:8 29 (2x), 30, 143, 192 n. k
7:8–9 103, 120
7:8–10 120, 145
7:9 53
7:9–10 120
7:10 14, 15, 25, 151
7:11 105, 117, 173
7:11–8:4 185
7:12 152
7:13 37, 79, 104, 149, 190 n. 6
7:13–14 104
8 83, 109
8:1 72, 155, 160, 190 n. 5, 197 n. 25

8:1–2 105
8:1–2 (7:11) 104–105
8:2 151, 156
8:3 113 (2x)
8:4 19 (2x), 71, 84, 108 n. 5, 114, 115 (2x), 116 (3x), 159, 163, 192 n. 14
8:5 87 n. 38, 105, 116, 125, 125 n. 30, 126 (3x)
8:5a 185
8:5b–12 173
8:5b–8:12 185
8:6–7 160
8:8 160, 160 n. 105
8:8–9 188
8:9 150
8:9–10 191 n. 9
8:10 143, 150, 161 (2x), 187
8:11 161
8:11, 12 12, 58, 141, 189 n. 1
8:11–12 149
8:11–12, 13 190 n. 6
8:12 16
8:13 149, 158, 160, 173, 185
8:13–14 105–106
8:14 25, 58, 109, 116, 117 (4x), 126, 149, 173, 185, 192 n. k, 193 n. 16, 206 n. aj

Qohelet
1:14 14
1:17 14
2:5 178 (2x)
8:17 16
12:4, 5 38, 81
12:12 17

Lamentations
1:2 158
2:15, 16 15
3:12 12 (2x)
4:9 15
5:18 15

Esther
2:14 164

Daniel
1:12 23
1:16 23
2:9 19
4:15 30
6:5 19
8:3 163
9:9 17

Ezra
3:7 93
5:4 30
8:20 15

Nehemiah
2:8 178
3:15 91
3:25 12
4:12 26 n. 100
9 5, 17, 22, 54 (2x)
9:17 17
9:22 22
9:24 22
12:39 12

1 Chronicles
5:20 15
27:27 15
27:33 158 n. 102
29:24 184 n. 44

2 Chronicles
2:7 27, 93
4:3 113
10:2 184 n. 44
25:18 34
30:17 17

Extracanonical Works

Ben Sira
7:22 49
49:1 23 n. 91

Tobit
3:11 156 n. 95

4 Ezra
7:101 28

New Testament

Luke
13:14 28

Targumim

Targum Onqelos
Gen 4:3 46
Exod 7:28 33
Exod 26:1 49
Deut 32:2 43

Targum Pseudo-Jonathan
Exod 22:1 36
Num 6:4 37
Num 22:25 51
Num 35:33 44
Deut 21:23 44

Targum Neofiti
Gen 4:22 49
Gen 7:11 36
Gen 8:6 33
Gen 8:7 19
Gen 8:22 36
Gen 26:8 36
Gen 34:31 44
Gen 39:12, 15, 18 38
Gen 50:1 33
Exod 21:19 38
Exod 26:1 49
Lev 11:21 34
Num 22:24 51
Deut 22:8 51
Deut 24:11 38
Deut 32:2 43

Fragment Targum
Deut 33:2 43

Samaritan Targum
Gen 15:10 40
Deut 27:15 49
Deut 32:2 43

Targum Jonathan
Josh 2:15, 18, 21 36
Judg 5:28 36
1 Sam 19:12 36
2 Sam 3:31 33
2 Sam 6:16 36
2 Sam 22:43 38
1 Kgs 20:34 38
2 Kgs 19:29 46
Isa 18:5 37
Isa 18:6 36
Jer 3:3 43
Jer 14:22 43

Targum to Job
Job 31:12 46

Targum to Proverbs
Prov 3:20 43
Prov 7:12 38
Prov 7:17 43

Targum to Lamentations
Lam 4:14 44

Other Versions

LXX
Gen 32:3 102 n. 51
Josh 13:26 102
Judg 7:25 96
Song 2:7 163 n. 123

Song 3:5 163 n. 123
Song 8:4 163 n. 123

Peshitta
Gen 3:9 18
Gen 4:22 49
Exod 28:11 49
Exod 44:20 43
Song 4:8 41, 59
Song 5:2, 11 43
Song 8:14 25

Dead Sea Scrolls

CD 12:17 35
1QIsa[a] 61, 182–183
3Q15:i:5 (Copper Scroll) 99
4QCant[a] 125 n. 30
4QCant[b] 1, 57–62, 57 n. 1, 78 n. 32, 125 nn. 29–30, 126 n. 31, 126 n. 32
4:8 59
4QCant[c] 125 n. 30
11QT 3:10 23 n. 91
Genesis Apocryphon 19:19, 20 20

Rabbinic Literature

Mishnah
m. ʿArak. 2:3 38
m. B. Bat. 6:2 44
m. Demai 1:3 38
m. Git. 3:8 37
m. Ketub. 4:6 30
m. Mak. 3:5 34 n. 131
m. Makš. 4:5 44
m. Naz. 3:2 30
m. Naz. 7:2 30
m. Nid. 2:7 9
m. ʾOhal. 8:2 22
m. ʿOr. 1:7 37
m. Roš Haš. 1:1 28
m. Šabb. 20:4 22
m. Šeb. 1:2 43
m. Ter. 11:2 36
m. Yad. 3:5 1, 129

Tosefta
t. B. Bat. 4:9 43
t. B. Qam. 11:15 34 n. 131
t. Menaḥ. 9:3 10 n. 24
t. Naz. 4:7 43
t. Šabb. 5:11 34
t. Šabb. 16:19 44
t. ʿUq. 2:11 46

Sifra
Qedošim 4:1 37

Sifre Bemidbar
22 43

Talmud Yerushalmi
y. Pesaḥ. 31a [50] 39
y. Sanh. 20b [16] 35
y. Šeqal. 47a 15
y. Yoma 5:2 9, 10 n. 24

Talmud Bavli
b. Ber. 40a 162
b. Ketub. 111a 163
b. Nid. 21a 9
b. Pesaḥ. 37b 39
b. Šabb. 77a 9, 10 n. 24
b. Sanh. 99b 139 n. 46
b. Yebam. 97a 15

Bereshit Rabba
15:17 162
95 44

Shemot Rabba
23b [28] 39

Vayyiqraʾ Rabba
105:5 33

Qohelet Rabba
2b (10) 38

Pesiqta de Rab Kahana
392:11 34

Ancient Near Eastern Texts

Ugaritic Texts
CAT 1.4:V:7 39
CAT 1.6:1 141 n. 50
CAT 1.8:II:13 39
CAT 1.14:1 141 n. 50
CAT 1.14:I:10–11 67
CAT 1.14:I:21–23 68
CAT 1.15:IV:7 163 n. 121
CAT 1.16:1 140 n. 50
CAT 1.19:I:31 47, 47 n. 199
CAT 1.24:1 47
CAT 1.24:17–18 47
CAT 1.92:5 39
CAT 1.101:7 39

KAI
2:93–94 42 n. 175
76B:8 42
145:9 40
178:2–3 49

Lachish Letters
4:5 53 n. 227

Cowley, *Aramaic Papyri*
8 20

Pyramid Texts
Utterance 253, §275 66 n. 11

Shishak List
Shishak List no. 22 102

State Archives of Assyria
9 158 n. 103

Arabic Texts

Ibn al-Muʿtazz, *Kitāb al-Badīʿ* 136, 160
Ibn Duhayd, *Risalāt at-Tawābiʿ wal-zawābiʿ* 142

Miscellaneous

Aristotle, *Poetics* 139
Eusebius, *Onomasticon* 162.4–5 9
Domingo González, *De divisione philosophiae* 139
Maimonides, *Epistle to Yemen* 163

Index of Authors and Reference Works

Abramsky, S., 176 n. 16
Abu-Lughod, L., 135 n. 28
Abusch, T., 162 n. 119
Academy of the Hebrew Language, 6 n. 14, 18 n. 64, 23 n. 91, 33 nn. 127–29, 34 nn. 131 and 134, 35 nn. 137–38, 36 nn. 142–43, 37 nn. 145 and 150, 38 n. 155, 40 nn. 164–65, 43 nn. 180–81, 44 nn. 185 and 187, 45 nn. 191–92, 46 nn. 195–96, 49 nn. 209–10, 50 n. 215, 52 n. 224
Adams, P. G., 64 nn. 6 and 8
Ahituv, S., 10 n. 24, 53 n. 2
Albright, W. F., 11 n. 29, 31 n. 121
Alexander, P. S., 130 n. 3
Altbauer, M., 37 n. 148
Alter, R., 107 n. 1, 109 n. 10, 173 n. 6
Andersen, F. I., 64 n. 7
Andrzejewski, B. W., 64 n. 3, 110, 111, 111 nn. 13–14
Audet, J. P., 129 n. 2
Avishur, Y., 10, 10 n. 29, 11 n. 30
Badawi, M. M., 136 n. 29, 157 n. 98, 160 n. 107, 161 n. 111
Bakon, S., 132 n. 17
Bar-Asher, M., 49 n. 208
Bauer, H., 17 n. 56, 122 n. 23
Baumgartner, W., 84 n. 34; *see also* KB; *HALOT*
Bausani, A., 134 nn. 23–24
BDB, 12 n. 35, 18, 18 n. 60, 34 n. 133, 35 n. 138, 38 n. 153, 46 n. 198, 49 n. 212, 51 n. 22, 86 n. 36, 164 n. 124, 179 n. 28
Beeston, A. F. L., 90 n. 42
Bellis, A. O., 69 n. 22
Benz, F. L., 31 n. 120
Benzinger, I., 10 n. 24
Bergant, D., 132 n. 14, 165, 165 nn. 130–32, 166 n. 133
Berlin, A., 64 n. 7, 86 n. 37, 157 n. 100
Beyer, K., 22 n. 84, 33 n. 126, 35 n. 136, 50 n. 216, 51 n. 223
Biale, D., 165 n. 129
Biella, J. C., 90 n. 42
Black, J., 122 n. 23, 175 n. 13, 178 n. 22
Blau, J., 26 n. 100, 37 n. 144, 65 n. 10, 96 n. 46, 102 n. 51
Bloch, A., 2, 116 n. 19
Bloch, C., 2, 116 n. 19
Boadt, L., 67, 69, 69 nn. 20–22
Bonebakker, S. A., 136 n. 29
Brenner, A., 73 n. 28, 123 n. 25, 129 n. 1, 131 nn. 9 and 11, 156 n. 90, 158, 159 n. 104, 162 n. 115, 174 n. 7
Brentjes, B., 177 n. 19
Breuer, M., 187
Briggs, C. A. *See* BDB.
Brockelmann, C., 18 n. 63, 21 n. 78, 42 n. 177, 43 n. 182, 49 n. 212
Brogan, T. V. F., 108, 108 nn. 4 and 6, 109 n. 8, 115 n. 18
Brown, C. S., 108 n. 4
Brown, F. *See* BDB.
Brown, J. P., 50 n. 218, 51 n. 221, 175 n. 12, 178 n. 24, 180 n. 34
Bryson, B., 31 n. 117
Burkert, W., 138, 138 n. 42
Burney, C. F., 15 n. 47, 18, 18 n. 60, 20 n. 73

Buss, M. J., 43 n. 179
Carr, D. M., 132 n. 14, 166 n. 132, 181 n. 35, 184, 184 n. 43
Casanowicz, I. M., 70 n. 24
Ceresko, A. R., 115 n. 18
Černy, J., 155 n. 87
Chance, J. K., 132 n. 14, 166 nn. 132–33
Chen, Y., 5 n. 10, 38 nn. 154 and 158, 42 n. 176, 53 n. 2
Chomsky, W., 26 n. 99
Cogan, M., 60 n. 8, 154 n. 87
Cohen, A., 21 n. 81
Cooper, A., 162 n. 120
Cooper, J. S., 131 n. 7
Cowley, A. E., 20 n. 76
Cussini, E., 41 n. 167
Dalman, G., 77 n. 30
Davenport, G., 143 n. 56
Dietrich, M., 47 n. 199
Dirksen, P. B., 59 n. 5, 94 n. 45
DNWSI, 31 n. 118, 40 n. 166, 42 n. 175, 45 n. 193, 46 n. 196, 47 n. 204, 49 n. 211
Donner, H., 49 n. 213
Dorseiff, F., 178 n. 21
Driver, G. R., 32 n. 124, 51 n. 219, 54, 54 n. 229, 84 n. 34
Driver, S. R., 9, 9 n. 22, 10, 49 n. 212; *see also* BDB
Eissfeldt, O., 7 n. 17
Eitan, I., 41 n. 172
Elitzur, Y., 161 n. 113
Ellenbogen, M., 175 n. 11, 179 n. 26
Emerton, J. A., 154 n. 84
Even-Shoshan, A., 12 n. 37
Falk, M., 131 n. 11, 172 nn. 2–3
Faulkner, R. O., 66 n. 11
Fishbane, M., 139 n. 46
Fitzmyer, J. A., 20 n. 76
Focht, A., 48 n. 207
Fokkelman, J. P., 20 n. 72, 65 n. 9
Folmer, M. L., 26 n. 96
Fox, E., 187
Fox, M.V., 1, 2, 9 n. 23, 10, 10 n. 27, 14 n. 44, 18 n. 66, 26 n. 98, 28 n. 108, 41 n. 170, 48 n. 207, 54 n. 228, 73 nn. 27 and 29, 90 n. 41, 91 n. 43, 112 n. 15, 130 n. 6, 154 nn. 84 and 87, 173 n. 5, 179 n. 27
Frahm, Eckart, 139 n. 43
Freedman, D. N., 64 n. 7
Friedrich, J., 21 n. 79
Gábor, I., 64 n. 3
Garr, W. R., 15 n. 48, 26 n. 96
Garsiel, M., 17 n. 57, 64 n. 7, 161, 161 n. 111, 162 n. 116
Gehman, H. S., 16, 16 n. 52
Gelder, G. J. van, 133 n. 20, 134, 134 nn. 21–22, 135 nn. 26–27, 136 nn. 30–32, 144, 144 nn. 59–60, 160 n. 106
George, A., 122 n. 23, 175 n. 13, 178 n. 22
Gevirtz, S., 24, 24 nn. 92–93
Ghul, M. A., 90 n. 42
Ginsberg, H. L., 7 n. 17, 8 n. 21, 23 n. 90, 47, 48 n. 205, 178 n. 25, 183, 183 n. 42
Giovannini, M. J., 165 n. 130
Goitein, S. D., 100 n. 50, 150 n. 72, 156, 156 n. 90
Goldstein, B. R., 162 n. 120
Goldziher, I., 137, 138 n. 39
Golomb, D. M., 21 n. 77
Gordis, R., 100 n. 50, 129 n. 1, 130 n. 4, 150 n. 72, 162 n. 117, 168 n. 138, 183 n. 41
Gordon, C. H., 7, 8 n. 18, 20 n. 74, 31 n. 119, 33 n. 125, 42 n. 174, 45 n. 193, 46 n. 196, 47 nn. 200 and 204, 50 n. 217
Goulder, M. D., 174 n. 7
Greenberg, J. H., 21 n. 83, 22 n. 83
Greenfield, J. C., 5 n. 11, 52 n. 225, 176 n. 16, 182 n. 39
Greenspahn, F. E., 44 n. 186, 68 n. 18, 70 n. 23, 105 n. 53
Greenstein, E. L., 68 n. 18, 115 n. 18, 172 n. 4
Grossberg, D., 84 n. 34
Guitton, J., 168 n. 138
Gunkel, H., 7 n. 17

Halkin, A., 163 n. 122
HALOT, 12 n. 35, 34 n. 133, 38 n. 153, 46 n. 198, 51 n. 222, 164 n. 124
Halpern, B., 154 n. 87
Hamori, A., 134 n. 23, 135 n. 28, 136 n. 34
Harris, Z. S., 29 n. 113
Hartman, D., 163 n. 122
Hayward, J. A., 134 n. 23
Hillers, D. R., 41 n. 167
Hodge, C. T., 66 n. 11
Hoftijzer, J. *See DNWSI.*
Hurowitz, V. A., 48 n. 207
Hurvitz, A., 4, 11, 11 n. 31, 15 n. 49, 16, 16 n. 53, 18 n. 66, 21 n. 81, 48 n. 207, 54, 175 n. 10
Hüttenmeister, F. G., 15 n. 45
Israelit-Groll, S., 130 n. 6
Izre'el, S., 26 n. 97
Jacobi, R., 134 n. 25, 146 n. 67
Jastrow, M., 7 n. 14, 14 n. 45, 18 nn. 62 and 64, 33 n. 126, 34 nn. 130, 132 and 135, 35 nn. 136 and 139–42, 37 nn. 146 and 150–51, 38 nn. 154–55, 40 nn. 164–65 and 167, 42 n. 177, 43 nn. 183–84, 44 n.n 185 and 187–88, 46 nn. 197–98, 49 nn. 209–11, 50 n. 216, 51 n. 223, 89 n. 40
Javadi, H., 134 n. 21
Jongeling, B., 20 n. 76; *see also DNWSI*
Joosten, J., 28 n. 109, 29 n. 112
Joüon, P., 26 n. 99
Kaufman, S. A., 6 n. 12, 36 n. 141, 59 n. 4
KB, 12 n. 36, 34 n. 133, 35 n. 138, 38 n. 153, 46 n. 198, 51 n. 222, 86 n. 36, 164 n. 124
Keel, O., 77 n. 30
Kessler, R., 112 n. 15
Kimelman, R., 129 n. 3
Kister, M., 182 n. 39
Knoppers, G. N., 158 n. 100
Koehler, L. *See* KB; *HALOT.*
König, E., 27 n. 105
Kraeling, E. G., 20 n. 76
Krahmalkov, C. R., 31 n. 118, 42 n. 175, 45 n. 193, 46 n. 196, 47 n. 204, 49 n. 213
Krauss, S., 34 n. 131
Kressel, G. M., 166 n. 133
Kutscher, E. Y., 8 n. 18, 15, 15 n. 47, 20 n. 77, 44, 44 n. 189, 61, 61 n. 13, 182, 182 nn. 37–39
Labuschagne, C. J., 20 n. 76
Landsberger, F., 132 n. 12
Leander, P., 17 n. 56, 20 n. 75, 122 n. 23
Lefkovits, J. K., 99 n. 49
Leick, G., 131 n. 7
Lesky, A., 142 n. 55
Levenson, J. D., 154 n. 87
Levin, S., 51, 51 n. 220, 120 n. 21, 180 n. 34
Lewalski, B., 139 n. 45
Lewis, I. M., 64 n. 3, 110, 111, 111 nn. 13–14
Liddell, H. G., 178 n. 23, 179 n. 27
Lipiński, E., 36 n. 144, 71 n. 26
Loretz, O., 47 n. 199, 178 n. 21
Lys, D., 145 n. 63
Macuch, R., 30 n. 114
Malone, J. L., 42 n. 173
Margalit, B., 67–70, 67 nn. 14–16
Margolis, M. L., 27 n. 101
Mariaselvan, A., 131 n. 6
Martin, G. D., 132 n. 17
May, H. G., 130 n. 6
Mayrhofer, M., 176 n. 16
Mazurel, J. W., 8 n. 18
McCreesh, T. P., 63 n. 2, 64 n. 5
Meek, T. J., 130 n. 6
Meyers, C. L., 156, 156 n. 97
Michel, W. L., 47 n. 199
Miralles, C., 161 n. 108
Monier-Williams, M., 176 n. 15, 179 n. 28
Monroe, J. T., 129 n. *, 134 n. 21, 138, 138 n. 40, 142, 142 nn. 52 and 54, 146 n. 66, 147 n. 68, 148 n. 70, 151 n. 73, 152, 152 nn. 76–78
Montgomery, J. A., 16, 16 n. 52
Morag, S., 10, 10 n. 28, 47, 47 n. 201

Moran, W. L., 138 n. 42, 157 n. 99
Muecke, D. C., 144 n. 58
Müller, W. W., 90 n. 42
Murphy, R. E., 2, 8 n. 20, 19 n. 67, 132 n. 12
Na'aman, N., 60 n. 8
Nasuti, H. P., 43 n. 179
Niditch, S., 181 n. 35
Nissinen, M., 131 n. 7, 139 n. 43, 156 n. 95
Noegel, S. B., 2, 13 nn. 41–42, 45 nn. 190 and 194, 48 n. 206, 63 n. 2, 66 n. 11, 105 n. 52, 115 n. 18, 124 n. 26, 154 nn. 85–86, 161 n. 110
Nöldeke, T., 21 n. 78, 26 n. 101
O'Connor, M. P., 176 n. 16
Ochser, S., 10 n. 24
Olmo Lete, G. del, 31 n. 119, 33 n. 125, 45 n. 193, 46 n. 196, 47 nn. 200 and 204, 50 n. 217, 68 n. 19
Olyan, S. M., 166, 166 n. 134
Omlin, J. A., 138 n. 43
Orton, H., 31 n. 117
Osimo, B., 118 n. 20
Pardes, I., 131 n. 11
Parpola, S., 60 n. 8, 158 n. 103
Paul, S. M., 2, 145 n. 63, 148 n. 71, 151 n. 74, 155, 155 n. 88, 162 n. 119
Payne Smith, J., 18 n. 62, 41 n. 171, 42 n. 177, 43 nn. 182–83, 49 n. 211
Pellat, C., 133 n. 19
Pérez Fernández, M., 15 n. 50, 16 n. 51, 16 n. 54, 18 n. 58, 19 n. 68, 22 n. 85, 26 nn. 95 and 100, 30 n. 116
Perles, F., 182 n. 39
Polzin, R., 27 n. 106
Pope, M. H., 2, 10, 10 n. 26, 14 n. 44, 112 n. 15, 130 n. 6, 131, 131 nn. 7–8, 140 n. 48, 141 n. 51, 145 n. 63, 156, 156 n. 92, 168 n. 137
Pórtulas, J., 161 n. 108
Postgate, N., 122 n. 23, 175 n. 13, 178 n. 22
Pouget, G., 168 n. 138
Provan, I. W., 154 n. 87
Rabin, C., 3 n. 1, 4 n. 6, 18, 18 nn. 61 and 65, 174–76, 174 n. 8, 176 nn. 14 and 16, 179 n. 30, 180 n. 34
Rankin, H. D., 135 n. 27, 138 n. 41, 142 n. 55, 143 n. 56, 144, 145 n. 62, 161, 161 n. 109, 162 n. 118
Rankin, O. S., 64 n. 3
Ratcliffe, R. R., 22 n. 83
Ratner, R. J., 27 n. 103, 109, 109 n. 9
Rendsburg, G. A., 2, 3 nn. 2–3, 4 nn. 4–5 and 7, 6 nn. 12–13, 11 n. 34, 13 n. 39, 14 n. 43, 15 nn. 46 and 49, 16 nn. 53 and 55, 18 n. 59, 20 nn. 71–72, 21 nn. 80 and 82, 22 nn. 86–89, 23 n. 90, 24 nn. 92 and 94, 26 n. 99, 27 n. 104, 28 n. 107, 29 n. 110, 31 n. 122, 32 n. 123, 40 n. 163, 43 n. 178, 45 n. 194, 47 n. 203, 52 nn. 225 and 227, 54 n. 231, 59 n. 3, 60 nn. 8 and 10, 63 n. 2, 64 n. 4, 65 n. 10, 66 n. 12, 88, 88 n. 39, 124 n. 27, 154 n. 87, 165 n. 129, 169 n. 140, 175 n. 10
Rendsburg, S. L., 21 n. 80
Richardson, M. E. J. *See HALOT.*
Robert, A., 8 n. 20, 19 n. 67, 164 n. 126
Rofé, A., 7 n. 16
Röllig, W., 21 n. 79, 49 n. 213
Rosenbaum, S. N., 4 n. 6
Rossell, W. H., 30 n. 114
Rundgren, F., 180 n. 33
Ryckmans, J., 90 n. 42
Saebø, M., 132, 132 n. 18
Sáenz-Badillos, A., 139 n. 47
Sanderson, S., 31 n. 117
Sanmartín, J., 31 n. 119, 33 n. 125, 45 n. 193, 46 n. 196, 47 nn. 199–200, 48 n. 204, 50 n. 217, 68 n. 19
Sasson, J. M., 37 n. 152, 115 n. 18, 131 n. 7
Schniedewind, W. M., 174 n. 9
Schoeler, G., 133 n. 20
Schoville, K. N., 130 n. 6
Schwartz, B. J., 48 n. 207
Scott, R., 178 n. 23, 179 n. 27
Seeligman, I. L., 182 n. 39

Segal, M. H., 15 n. 50, 16 nn. 51 and 54, 18 n. 58, 19 n. 68, 22 n. 85, 26 nn. 95 and 100, 30 n. 116, 131 nn. 9–10, 140 n. 49, 168, 169 n. 140
Segert, S., 13 n. 38, 20 n. 75, 21 n. 79, 22 n. 84, 30 n. 115
Sells, M. A., 134 n. 25, 137, 137 nn. 35–37
Shapiro, M., 108, 108 n. 3
Smith, C., 7 n. 15
Smith, M., 39 n. 160
Sokoloff, M., 19 n. 70, 27 n. 102, 30 n. 114, 33 n. 126, 34 n. 135, 35 n. 136, 36 nn. 140–41, 37 n. 147, 38 nn. 154 and 156, 38 n. 157, 39 n. 161, 40 n. 167, 42 n. 177, 43 nn. 183–84, 45 n. 193, 46 n. 198, 49 n. 211, 51 n. 223
Sperl, S., 137 n. 38
Spiegel, J., 138 n. 43
Stadelmann, L., 157 n. 99, 168, 168 n. 139
Steiner, R. C., 177 n. 17
Stetkevych, S. P., 129 n. *, 133 n. 19, 138 n. 40, 153, 153 nn. 79–83, 155, 155 n. 89
Tal, A., 41 n. 168, 49 n. 211
Tayib, Abdulla el, 133 nn. 19–20, 134 n. 23
Toporov, V. N., 63 n. 3
Tournay, R., 8 n. 20, 19 n. 67, 164 n. 126
Tov, E., 57 n. 1, 59, 62, 125 nn. 29–30, 126 nn. 31–32
Trible, P., 131 n. 11, 156, 156 n. 91
Troupeau, G., 136 n. 33
Tuell, S. S., 39, 39 nn. 159 and 162
Turner, R. L., 179 n. 29
Tyloch, W., 130 n. 6
Ullendorff, E., 145 nn. 63–65, 161 n. 112, 164 n. 125
Wagner, M., 8 n. 19
Wallace, C. V., 22 n. 83
Wanner, E., 110, 110 n. 12
Waterman, L., 132 n. 17, 143 n. 57, 161 n. 111, 168, 168 n. 138
Watkins, C., 64 n. 3
Watson, W. G. E., 31 n. 119, 63 n. 1, 67 n. 17, 107 n. 2, 130 n. 6, 132 n. 15
Webber, E. J., 139 n. 44
West, M. L., 138 n. 42
Westenholz, A., 139 n. 43
Westenholz, J. G., 139 n. 43, 144 n. 61
Westermarck, E., 152 n. 77
Whedbee, J. W., 129, 129 n. 1, 131 n. 9, 132, 132 nn. 13 and 16, 156, 156 n. 93, 167, 167 n. 135
White, J. B., 112 n. 15, 172 nn. 1–3
Widdowson, J., 31 n. 117
Wimsatt, W. K., 112 n. 16
Wortley, W. V., 147 n. 69
Woude, A. S. van der, 20 n. 76
Yoo, Y. J., 4 n. 6, 5 n. 10, 53 n. 2
Young, I., 11, 11 n. 32, 15 n. 46, 16 n. 53, 36 n. 144, 57, 57 n. 1, 58, 58 n. 2, 59, 59 n. 6, 60, 60 nn. 7 and 9, 61, 61 nn. 11–12 and 14, 179, 180 n. 32, 183 n. 41
Zaborski, A., 22 n. 83
Zevit, Z., 109, 110, 110 nn. 11–12
Ziadeh, F., 129 n. *, 160 n. 107
Zohary, M., 10 n. 25

Index of Premodern Authors

ʿAbdallāh ibn ʿUmar Al-ʿArjī, 145, 147, 149, 152
Abī ʿĀmir Ibn Šuhayd, 141, 147
Abraham Ibn Ezra, 146, 152, 154, 158, 160 n. 105, 162 n. 114, 164 n. 128, 167–68
Abū Nuwās, 150
Aqiba, 1, 129–30
Archilochus, 135 n. 27, 138, 142, 144, 160–62
Aristotle, 139
Averroes, 139
Dinarchus, 179
Domingo González, 139
Eusebius, 9, 161 n. 113
Ibn al-Muʿtazz, 136, 160
Ibn al-Rīmī, 136
Ibn Duhayd, 142, 149
Ibn Quzmān, 135 n. 27, 151
Jawwās al-Ḍabbīʾ, 153
Maimonides, 163, 163 n. 122
Nicolas de Lyra, 130 n. 3
Rashi, 130 n. 3
Todros Abulafia, 139
Ubaydallāh ibn Qays Ar-Ruqayyāt, 144, 146, 150
Xenophon, 178

Index of Words and Phrases

Hebrew

א

אב (fruit) 46, 47 n. 202
אב (father) 108
אבירם 17
אבק 82
אבקה 82 (3x)
אדב 68 n. 18
אהב 157 (3x), 157 n. 99, 158, 158 n. 102, 190 n. 7
אהבה 84, 192 n. 14, 196 n. q
אומנון 60 (3x), 60 n. 9
אח 157 (2x), 158
אחד 27 n. 102
אחד ענק 27
אחות 157, 158 (2x)
אחזי חרב 26
אחתי כלה 123 (2x)
אחתי רעיתי יונתי תמתי 123 (2x)
אי 59
איב 157, 158 n. 102
איכה 18 (2x)
איל 163 (2x), 192 n. 15
אילה 163
אין 69
אכילה 17
אל 101
אלמגים/אלגמים 176 n. 16
אלמנה 183
אלף 88
אם 115 (4x)
אמון 48, 48 n. 207 (2x), 49 (4x)
אמונות 49
אמן 48, 49, 50, 50 n. 214
אמנה 60 (2x)
אמר 103
אני לדודי 117–18
אני לדודי ודודי לי 117
אני לו 117
אסר 26 n. 100
אפס 69
אפע 69 (2x)
אפריון 84 (2x), 85, 175, 179 (2x), 179 n. 30, 180 (2x)
ארבות 36
ארגמן 168, 203 n. aa
ארה 42, 43, 54
ארז 76
ארפד 53 n. 227
ארץ 13, 25 (2x)
אשר 15, 70 (2x)
את 59 (3x), 61, 62, 71
אתה 59

ב

בוא 41
בוש 33
בחון 49
בחור 183
בחר 69
בטן 202 n. z
ביצה 13
בית 76
בית האצל 64 n. 7
בלע 183
בנות ירושלם 84
בנות ציון 85
בעד 86, 88, 113
בקש 80 (2x), 81 (4x)

בקשתיו ולא מצאתיו 119
ברושים 14, 76
ברותים 14, 76 (2x)
ברח 106, 117
בריאה 17
בשׂם 59, 100
בת 158, 191 n. 12
בת נדיב 202 n. 40
בתינו קרות 25
בתר 40, 41, 194 n. p

ג

גאל 44 (2x)
גבור 69 n. 22
גדר 51, 52
גובה 103
גל 22, 92 (4x)
גל נעול 162
גלעד 39, 86 (3x), 87, 113, 121 (2x)
גלשׁ 39 (4x), 40, 54 (2x), 86, 87 (3x), 101
גמל 37 (2x), 53
גן 92 (2x), 100 (3x), 101 (2x)
גן נעול 162
גפן 79 (2x)

ד

דבב 14, 14 nn. 44–45, 204 n. ad
דבשׁ 41 (3x), 41 n. 173, 42 (2x), 91 (2x)
דגול 98 (2x)
דגל (banner) 78, 192 n. j
דגל (glance) 78 (2x)
דובב 14
דובב שׂפתי ישׁנים 14
דוד 95 (3x), 96 (4x), 104 (2x), 115, 117 (3x), 157, 162 (2x), 199 n. 31
דודי 104 (3x)
דודי לי 118
דודי לי ואני לו 117
דלג 78 (2x), 78 n. 32
דלה 203 n. ab
דמה 74, 103, 117 (2x), 192 n. k

ה

הגה 138 n. 39
היכן 18
היפה בנשׁים 125 n. 28
הליכה 17
הלך 14, 126 (3x), 126 n. 32 (2x)
המון 49
המלך שׁלמה 184 n. 44 (2x)
הנה 76
הר 21 (3x), 22 (7x), 23 (2x), 58 (6x), 90, 121 (2x)
הר גלעד 120
הרי בשׂמים 25
הרי בתר 25
הרעה בשׁושׁנים 74
הררי נמרים 25

ז

זאת 183
זאת קומתך 29–30
זג 37
זהב 75 (2x)
זוב 14 (2x)
זכר 189 n. c
זמיר 193 n. n
זרע 23 (3x)

ח

חבצלת 10 n. 25 (2x), 77 (2x)
חבצלת השׁרון 10
חבר 106, 158, 206 n. 45
חוה 45
חוח 34 (4x)
חוץ 38 (2x)
חזה 145 n. 64, 161 n. 112
חטה 103
חי 24
חלאים 53 n. 227 (3x)
חלב 97
חלון 36
חלי 102 (5x)
חליפה 17
חמה 45, 46 (7x), 46 n. 195, 54
חמוק 102 (2x)
חמל 182 (4x), 183 (2x)
חנט 79 (2x)
חנינה 17

חנף 44 (2x), 183
חסר 103
חפץ 164, 164 n. 124 (3x)
חץ 22
חק 22
חרב 69 n. 22
חרה 73 (2x)
חרוז 75 (4x)
חרך 35 n. 138 (3x)
חרכים 35, 36, 79
חרף 36 (4x)
חרש 49 (6x), 49 n. 209
חשב 49

ט

טלל 58–59, 125 n. 29
טמא 44 (2x)
טנף 44 (2x), 95
טנפת 44

י

יגיעה 17
יד 96 (2x)
ידידיה 162
ידיו גלילי 98
יונה 85, 123, 124
יונתי תמתי 123–24
יין 72
ים 24
יער 94
יצא 85 (4x), 64 n. 7
ירד 100, 164
ירד לגנו 172
ירח 40, 44, 45 (3x)
ירך 82
ישב 14
ישן 204 n. ad
יתום 183

כ

כ- 81, 192 n. k
כוכב 100
כי 113
כל 82, 83, 86, 87
כלה 92 (2x), 158, 197 n. 27
כעדר הקצובות 40
כף 95
כפר 93 (3x)
כרכם 93
כרם 104
כרמיל 203 n. aa
כרמל 203 n. aa
כתל 35 (4x), 35 n. 137
כתנת 95

ל

ל- 71 (3x), 71 n. 25, 113, 140
לא עני 119
לב 88
לבב 88 (2x), 89 (2x)
לבבה 89 n. 40
לבונה 83 (3x), 93, 94
לבנה 44, 45 (5x), 45 n. 190, 46, 54
לבנון 27 (3x), 83 (4x), 89 (2x), 93
לויתן 24
לחי 97
לכי־לך 193 n. m
לכיש 64 n. 7
למד 83
לפיד 180
לשכה 180

מ

מבעד לצמתך 112–13, 126 n. 31
מגד 42 (2x)
מגדל 98
מגדל דויד 122
מגדל השן 122
מגן 176 n. 16
מד 59
מדבר 82, 87 (3x), 87 n. 38, 88, 105, 196 n. r
מדרגה 78 n. 32, 80 (3x)
מה 115 (4x), 116, 196 n. u
מה תחזו 102
מהר גלעד 120
מור 82, 93
מזג 50 (3x), 51 (2x), 103 (3x)
מזיגה 50
מחלה 102 (2x)

מחנה 102 (3x)
מחנים 102 n. 51
מחתרת 36
מטה 32, 33 (3x)
מטרא 12
מטרה 12 (4x)
מטתו שלשלמה 25
מישר 72, 73 (2x)
מכרה 180
מלא 78, 98 (2x), 99
מלאת 44 (2x), 98
מלה 45
מלחמה 83
מלך 59
ממסך 50 (2x)
מן 27 (4x), 28 (2x), 28 n. 107, 57 (2x), 121 (2x)
מן הגלעד 121
מן־החלנות 193 n. l
מן לבנון 27 (4x)
מסב 191 n. h
מסך 50 (2x), 51 (4x)
מספר 108
מעה 99
מעון 58, 90
מעין חתום 162
מענה 90 (2x), 172
מענות אריות 25
מעקה 51
מראה 80 n. 33 (2x)
מרקח 97
משועל 164 n. 126
משך 72, 73
משכב 80 (2x)
משכנות הרעים 25

נ

נבלה 183
נגד 100
נגינה 17
נדגלות 100 (3x), 101 (2x), 172
נוף 43
נחל 47 (2x), 202 n. w
נחת 26, 26 n. 99
נטישה 17
נטף 91 (2x), 95
נטר 12 (7x), 58
נסך 108 (2x), 109 (2x)
נעים 76, 112
נעל 92
נעם 31 (3x), 32, 54
נפש 95, 190 n. d
נפת 41 (2x), 42 (2x), 54, 91 (4x)
נצה 23 (4x), 24
נצר 11, 12
נרד 75 (3x), 93 (3x), 182 n. 36
נשיקה 16, 17, 71 (2x)
נשק 71 (5x), 72, 105
נשׂא 26 n. 100
נתן 24, 75 (2x), 79
נתר 34, 35 (2x)

ס

סבב 117
סהר 103
סוג I 51
סוג II 51, 51 n. 222, 52, 103 (4x)
סוסה 74
סליכה 17
סם 23 (3x), 23 n. 91
סמדר 37 (2x), 53, 79, 80 (4x), 104
סנסנים 53
סעה 65, 66 (3x)
סער 65 (2x), 66 (2x)
סתו 36 (4x), 36 n. 144
סתונית 36
סתר 80 (2x)

ע

עבר 96
עד שׁ- 19 (3x), 191 n. g
עד שתחפץ 163 (2x)
עדר 85 (2x), 86 (5x), 113
עדרי חבריך 25
עור 94, 116 (6x)
עורב 96 (3x), 97 (2x)
עז 85, 86
עזב 23
עטה 154 n. 84, 190 n. f
עין 58, 76, 86 (2x), 90 (2x), 112, 172

עיר 119 (2x)
על 78, 105
על הרי בשׂמים 117
על הרי בתר 117
עלה 105
עלי תשוקתו 118 (2x)
עלף 99 (7x), 99 n. 48
עם 21 (2x), 22 (3x)
ענק 90 (2x), 172
עץ 94
עצי לבונה 94
עצי (ה)לבנון 93
ערב 38 (2x), 38 n. 154 (3x), 69 n. 22, 96
ערוגה 97 (2x), 100 (3x)
ערוגות הבשׂם 124, 200 n. v
ערוגת הבשׂם 124, 200 n. v
עריסה 33
ערמה 203 n. z
ערס 33
ערף 43
ערר 13 (3x), 13 n. 40
ערשׂ 32 (3x), 32 n. 123, 33 (5x), 76 (3x), 112
עשוק 49
עשת 99 (4x)

פ

פג 37, 53, 79 (2x), 162
פה 196 n. r
פלגש 101 (2x), 180
פלדה 177 n. 20
פעל 69
פעם 47, 48 (4x), 48 n. 206, 54
פצירה 17
פקד 108
פרי 93
פרדס 55, 92, 93, 174, 175 (3x), 176 (2x), 177 (3x), 177 n. 17, 178 (3x), 178 n. 21, 179 (2x), 179 n. 25, 180 (2x), 181 (4x), 182, 183, 183 n. 41
פרח 51 n. 222
פרי 46, 47 n. 202
פרע 43
פשט 95
פתח 95 (3x)

צ

צאנן 64 n. 7
צבא 163
צבי 163 (2x), 163 n. 123 (2x), 192 n. 15
צד 22
צדני 59
צהרים 74 (3x)
צור 11
ציד 35 n. 138
ציון 85 (3x)
צל 11, 21, 22, 58 (2x), 77
צעיף 99 n. 48
צרר 13

ק

קולך ערב 38
קומה 103 (3x)
קומי לך 20, 193 n. m
קוץ 34
קוצות 43 (2x)
קורה 76
קטר 81 (2x), 82 (2x), 126
קיר 35 (4x), 35 n. 137, 51
קמוש 23 (2x)
קפץ 34, 35
קצב 40 (4x), 41, 121
קרא 67 n. 13
קראתיו ולא ענני 119
קרב 108
קריאה 17
קרע 13 n. 40

ר

ראה 80 n. 33 (2x), 85 (2x), 104
ראש 41, 89 (2x)
רביבים 43, 44
רבץ 73, 74
רגל 47, 48
רדיד 95 (2x), 96
רהב 164 n. 128
רהט 13, 34, 52 (5x), 58, 203 n. ac
רהיט 13, 33 (3x), 52, 58, 76 (2x), 203 n. ac
רהיטני 34 n. 131
רוח 65, 66

רוץ 13, 33, 59
רחל 121
רחם 182, 183 (2x)
רחץ 97
רטן 34
ריח 75
ריח שלמתיך 92
רכב 69 n. 22
רכל 82 (4x)
רכש 64 n. 7
רמון 88, 93, 104
רסיסים 43, 44, 44 n. 185
רסס 44 n. 185
רע II 13 n. 40, 94, 158, 191 n. 10, 206 n. 45
רע III 14
רעה 13 (2x), 14 (2x), 65 n. 9, 74 (4x), 100 (2x), 153 (3x), 154 (2x), 157, 190 n. e, 190 n. 8
רעיה 74, 86 (2x), 94, 123, 158, 191 n. 10, 191 n. 12
רעיתי תפתי 123 (2x)
רענן 76 (2x), 112
רעע 13 n. 41, 183
רעף 43
רפד 52 n. 227, 53 n. 227 (2x), 84
רפידה 52 n. 227, 84
רפידים 53 n. 227
רפק 87 n. 38, 105 (2x), 126
רצה 13
רצף 84, 196 n. q
רצפה 84 (3x)
רצפת 84
רצפים 84
רצץ 13 n. 41

ש

-ש 11 n. 33, 15 (7x), 16 (3x), 54, 70, 113
שׁוב 14, 183
שׁולמית 161 (3x)
שׁונם 161 n. 113
שׁונמי 161
שׁועל 164 n. 126
שׁוק 38 (3x), 81 (4x)
שׁור 41 (5x), 89 (3x)
שׁושן/שׁושנה 10 n. 25
שׁזף 73
שׁחיטה 17
שׁחר 73 (2x), 97
שׁיר 71
שׁכול 86, 87
-שׁל 11 n. 33, 16 (5x)
שׁלהבתיה 205 n. ah
שׁלום 161, 206 n. ai
שׁלט 88
שׁלח 91
שֶׁלַח 91
שׁלחה 91 (3x), 92
שׁלמה (Solomon) 16, 71
שׁלמה (lest) 18, 161
שׁם 72
שׁמן 72 (2x), 73
שׁמר 119
שׁמרי החמות 25
שׁמשׁ 45, 46 (3x), 46 n. 195
שׁן 87
שׁנה 14
שׁני 87
שׁנן 22
שׁפיר 64 n. 7
שׁקה 105
שׁר 202 n. y, 202 n. z
שׁריקה 17
שׁשׁים המה מלכות 28, 54
שׁתה 51

שׂ

שׂלמה 141
שׂמח 72, 73, 182 (4x), 183 (3x)
שׂניר 89
שׂער 85, 86 (4x)
שׂערך כעדר העזים 85
שׂפה 72, 91
שׂפתי ישׁנים 25

ת

תאנה 79, 162
תבואה 46
תואם 122 (2x), 122 n. 23 (2x)

תועבה 69
תור 75 (2x)
תורק 72, 189 n. b
תחת 113 (2x), 204 n. af
תחת התפוח עוררתיך 116
תחת ל- 113 (5x), 204 n. af
תימרה 81, 82, 126
תירוש 73
תך 22
תכי 176
תלה 88
תלפיות 88 (4x)
תם 123, 124
תמר 103 (2x)
תעה 65 n. 9
תשוקה 105
תשורי מראש אמנה 41

AKKADIAN

kur*am-ma-na-nu* 60
ummiānu 50 n. 214
dagālu 98, 192 n. j
ḫabaṣillatu 77 n. 30
pardēsu 175, 178
sinsinnu/*sissinnu* 53
tuʾāmu 122 n. 23
tūʾamu 122 n. 23
tuʾīmu 122 n. 23
tuʾû 122 n. 23

ARABIC

ʾihāb 196 n. q
ʿaraǧa 97
ʿunq 90
ġaraba 96
ġarb 96
ġdr 85
ġurāb 96
ḫafaḍa 164 n. 124
ḫafiẓa 164 n. 124
ḥaly 102
laḥy 97
mā 115
mʿn 90
maġrib 96
rhṭ 52
smḥ 182
šaḥara 97
šitāʾ 36 n. 144
šuḥḥār 97

ARAMAIC

אבא 46
אומן 49 (2x)
איכא 18
אנבא 46
ארעא 13
בהת 33
ביעה 13
גלש 39
ד- 19
דוב 14
די 19
דיל 16 (2x)
דילמא 18
היכא 18
זיל 16 (2x)
חד 27 n. 102 (2x)
חוחא 34
חרך 36 (2x)
טור 12
טלל 12, 22, 58, 59
טנף 44
יתב 14
כד 22
כתל 35
מגד 42, 42 n. 177
מזג 50
מירת 73 n. 27
נטר 12, 33
נסק 13
סיג 51
סמדר 37
עד 19
עם 22
עריב 38
ערס 33

ערר 13
פגא 37
פגג 47, 53
קפץ 35
קצב 40 (2x)
קצוב 41
רהט 13, 33
רסיסין 43
רסס 43 (2x), 44 n. 185
רעה 13
שמש 46
תוב 14
תני 14

ARMENIAN

partez 177 n. 18

AVESTAN

pairidaeza 175 (2x)

BERBER

agellīd 151 n. 75

CUSHITE

bo:r 22 n. 83
il 22 n. 83

EGYPTIAN

m 115
ma-ḥa$_2$–n-ma$_4$ 102

ENGLISH

asphodel 77 n. 30
palanquin 179

GREEK

asphodelos 77 n. 30
κωμωδέω 139
Μαανάιμ 102
Μανάιμ 102
misge 51
paradeisos (παραδεισος) 176, 177 n. 18, 178 (3x)
Σουλήμ 161 n. 113
φορειον 179, 180 (2x)
Ωρηβ 96

HINDI

palang 179 n. 29

LATIN

asphodelus/asphodilus 77 n. 30
misce 51

NEPALI

palaṅ 179 n. 29

PERSIAN (MODERN)

pālez 177 n. 18
pūlād 177 n. 20

PHOENICIAN

אלנם 23
נעם 31 (2x)
נעמן 31
נפת 42
עקצב 40 n. 166
קצב 40
שמש 46

SANSKRIT

nalada/narada 182 n. 36
paradhis 176 (3x), 176 n. 15, 176 n. 17
paryanka (*pary-anka*) 179, 179 nn. 28–29
valguka 176 n. 16

Syriac

איכא 18 (2x)
היכא 18
מגדא 42 n. 177
עבר 41
רסס 43
שׂור 41

Ugaritic

ib 47 (5x), 47 n. 199, 47 n. 200
ʾbd 68, 68 n. 18
itdb 68 n. 18 (2x)
ʿrb 96 (2x)
ʿrš 32, 76
bʿl 141 n. 50
brḥ 106
glṯ 39 (2x)
grdš 68 (5x)
ḥbr 106
ḥdy 102
ḥlb 97
ḥtk 68 (4x)
ḫrb 68 n. 19
kly 68
krmm 47
krt 68 (4x), 140 n. 50 (2x)
lḥm 97
mḫṣ 68
mknt 68 (3x)
mrṯ 73 n. 27
msk 50
nʿm 31, 76
nbt 42
nkl 47
nkl wib 47
pʿn 47
rḥ 92
rḥṣ 97
rqḥ 97
rš 68
ṣmt 68
šlḥ 92
špš 46
tbt 68

Index of Languages

Afar-Saho, 22 n. 83
Akkadian, 50 n. 214, 53, 60, 77 n. 30, 98, 122 n. 23, 156 n. 95, 175, 178, 192 n. j; *see also* Amurru Akkadian; Neo-Assyrian; Neo-Babylonian; Old Akkadian.
Ammonite, 14 n. 43, 15
Amurru Akkadian, 26
Arabic, 29, 35 n. 138, 36 n. 144, 47, 52, 66, 76, 85, 90, 96, 97, 102, 102 n. 51, 115, 130, 133, 134 n. 25, 137, 145, 153, 164 n. 124, 165, 182, 196 n. q
Aramaic (general), 4, 6, 8–9, 11–14, 16, 18–24, 19 n. 70, 26–30, 32–40, 32 n. 124, 36 n. 144, 38 n. 154, 41 n. 173, 42–46, 42 n. 177, 44 n. 185, 49–54, 57–61, 57 n. 1, 73 n. 27, 175, 175 n. 10, 202 n. y; *see also* Mandaic; Palmyrene; Syriac; and the following entries.
Aramaic, Biblical, 30, 46 n. 198
Aramaic, Imperial, 13, 20
Aramaic, Jewish Babylonian, 46 n. 198
Aramaic, Jewish Palestinian, 39
Aramaic, Middle, 13
Aramaic, Nabatean, 49
Aramaic, Official, 49
Aramaic, Old, 13
Aramaic, Postbiblical, 202 n. y
Aramaic, Qumran, 20
Aramaic, Samaritan, 20 n. 70
Armenian, 177 n. 18
Avestan, 175
Berber, 151 n. 75
Canaanite, 8 n. 21, 23, 60
Cushitic. *See* Afar-Saho; Somali.
Deir ʿAlla dialect, 27–28, 57, 59
Egyptian, 102, 115, 130
English, 5 n. 9, 12, 19, 26 n. 100, 31 n. 117, 53, 77, 77 n. 30, 84, 90, 93, 164, 179, 190 n. d, 191 n. h, 203 nn. z and ab, 204 n. af
French, 5 n. 9
German, 5 n. 9, 90
Greek, 34 n. 131, 51, 67 n. 30, 102, 139, 143 n. 56, 165, 175–76, 177 n. 18, 178–80, 178 n. 23, 179 n. 27, 180 n. 34
Hebrew, Amoraic (MH^2), 6, 6 n. 14, 14, 35, 36, 38 n. 154, 39, 40
Hebrew, Benjaminite, 7, 12, 22, 28, 38 n. 154
Hebrew, Ephraimite, 3
Hebrew, Galilean, 3
Hebrew, Jerusalemite, 41 n. 173
Hebrew, Late Biblical (LBH), 4, 7, 12, 17, 27–28, 53–54, 184 n. 44
Hebrew, Mishnaic (MH), 6, 6 n. 14, 9, 14–16, 16 n. 54, 18–20, 22–23, 26, 28, 30, 33–38, 35 n. 138, 40, 43–46, 44 n. 185, 49–50, 49 n. 208, 52–54, 59, 91, 99
Hebrew, Postbiblical, 35, 39, 45, 46, 202 n. y
Hebrew, Standard Biblical (SBH), 3, 9, 12, 13 n. 41, 21, 54, 58, 59, 62, 184 n. 44
Hebrew, Tannaitic (MH^1), 6, 6 n. 14, 34, 35, 38 n. 154
Hebrew, Transjordanian, 3
Hindi, 179 n. 29
Indo-Aryan, 176 n. 16
Indo-European (IE), 51, 63 n. 3, 180 n. 34

Iranian, 175, 177, 177 n. 20; *see also* Avestan; Median; Old Persian; Persian; Persian, Modern
Italian, 5 n. 9
Latin, 51, 53, 67, 77 n. 30
Magyar (Old Hungarian), 63, 64 n. 3
Mandaic, 30
Median, 175, 177, 177 n. 18
Moabite, 59
Neo-Assyrian, 122 n. 23
Neo-Babylonian, 175
Nepali, 179 n. 29
Old Akkadian, 139 n. 43
Old English, 63–65, 63 n. 3
Old German, 63–64, 63 n. 3
Old Hungarian. *See* Magyar.
Palmyrene, 40 n. 167, 49
Persian, 55, 174–178, 177 n. 18, 178 n. 23, 180, 184.
Persian, Modern, 177 n. 18, 177 n. 20
Phoenician, 4, 6, 8, 8 n. 21, 15, 20–21, 23–24, 30, 31, 40, 42, 45–46, 47, 47 n. 204, 48, 49, 50, 51, 54, 54 n. 229, 59, 60 n. 10
Punic, 21, 40, 42, 51
Sanskrit, 176, 176 nn. 16–17, 177 n. 17, 179–80, 179 nn. 28–29, 182 n. 36
Somali, 63, 64 n. 3, 65
Syriac, 18, 20 n. 70, 21, 26, 28, 28 n. 109, 30, 41, 42 n. 177, 43, 49
Tamil, 176
Ugaritic, 4, 6, 8, 8 n. 21, 11 n. 30, 20, 24, 31, 32, 39–40, 39 n. 159, 42, 45, 46–47, 47 n. 204, 48, 50, 54, 66–68, 68 nn. 18–19, 70, 73 n. 27, 76, 92, 96–97, 102, 106, 130

Index of Subjects

A-line, 68, 91, 117, 119, 120
absolute, 17 n. 56, 74, 75, 122 n. 23
accent mark, 114, 114 n. 17, 115 n. 17, 120, 121
  Masoretic marks, 124 n. 27, 125
addressee-switching, 6, 6 n. 12, 28 n. 107, 30, 45, 50
Afroasiatic (Hamo-Semitic), 21 n. 83, 71 n. 26, 115
Akkadian literature, 139 n. 43
Akkadianism, 53
Aleppo Codex, 18 n. 60, 94 n. 45, 187
allegory (allegorical), 129, 129–30 n. 3, 133, 154,
alliterationis causa (alliterative exigency), 67, 72, 76, 86, 87, 88, 92, 93, 98, 99 n. 48
allusion, 136, 160–62, 165, 167, 191 n. 11
ally (allies), 157–62, 158 n. 102, 190 nn. 5 and 10, 191 n. 12, 199 n. 31, 206 n. 45
ambiguity (ambiguous), 71 n. 25, 136, 141, 160
Ammonites, 159
Amoraic, 6, 14, 34
Amorities, 159
Amos, book of, 4–5, 4 n. 6
Amurru Akkadian, 26
anagram (anagrammatic), 72, 74, 81, 82, 95, 96, 98, 100, 101
Analogiebildung, 22 n. 83, 23, 122 n. 23
anaphoric, 29
anarthrous noun, 27–28, 57
Anglo-Saxon poetry, 63 n. 3, 64
antanaclasis, 115 n. 18
antonym(ic), 157
Aqhat story, 32
Aramaic segholate, 41 n. 173
Aramaism, 8, 12, 19, 26 n. 100, 43, 54 n. 229, 57, 57 n. 1, 61, 174–75, 174 n. 9
Aramaizing, 5
Arameans, 30, 60
archaic absolute. *See* absolute
Asaph, 5, 7, 22, 43, 43 n. 179, 50
assimilated *nun*, 58
assonance, 64–65, 82, 85, 97
Assyrian king, 48
Assyrian-Median interaction, 177–78
Assyrian period, 177 n. 20
Assyrians, 30, 158
asyndetic parataxis, 117
ʾ*atnaḥ*, 119, 126–27, 183
B-line, 68, 91, 117, 119, 120, 202 n. y, 203 n. aa
B-word, 32, 32 n. 124, 41, 51
Baal cycle, 39
Babylonians, 163
Balaam story, 5, 28
baṣta, 136
bed, 32–33, 100, 179 n. 29, 191
  beds of ivory, 33
  bed of sickness, 32
  bed of spices, 97, 124, 149, 152, 164, 200, 200–201 n. v
  canopy-bed, 175, 179
  deathbed, 33
  garden bed, 97
bedouin, 130, 132
beloved, 39, 75, 94, 95–96, 104, 115, 117–18, 119, 120, 123, 131, 144–46, 148–49, 151–52, 154–55, 157, 160,

beloved (*cont.*)
162, 164, 188, 191, 192, 193, 193 n. 16, 194, 194 n. p, 198, 199, 199 n. 31, 200, 201, 204, 205, 206
Ben Sira, 23 n. 91, 35, 43, 45, 46, 182 n. 39
Benjaminite(s), 12, 17, 32
Berber customs, 152
black, 75, 97
Black Obelisk of Shalmaneser III, 177
breasts, 120, 122, 143, 145, 149, 150, 155, 160–61, 162 n. 115, 191, 194 n. p, 197, 203, 204, 205, 206 n. aj
bride, 60, 92, 123, 154, 158, 161, 197 n. 24
brother, 154 n. 87, 157, 158 n. 100, 161, 189–90 n. 5, 197 n. 25, 204 n. 43
brother-sister, 155 n. 87
brothers, 188, 189 n. 5
Bul, 40
calque, 16, 18–19
Canaanite solar hymn, 45–46
casus pendens, 68
cedar, 34, 76, 164, 191, 200, 205
cedars of God, 42
cedars of Lebanon, 42, 48
Chaldeans, 30
chastity, 155, 162, 165, 165 n. 132
Chronicles, books of, 27, 158 n. 100, 181, 184 n. 44
cinnamon, 93, 152, 198
cognate accusative, 70
colloquial language, 168–69
colloquial dialect, 6, 135, 138, 175 n. 10
colloquial English, 164
colloquial Hebrew, 168, 175 n. 10
comic, 2, 131, 139 n. 45, 162 n. 115
concubine, 18, 101, 153, 160, 167, 180, 201
construct, 21–23, 24, 47, 58, 75, 80, 82, 101, 103, 122
couch, 76, 80, 112, 146, 159, 167 n. 136, 194
divan, 25, 167, 191, 191 n. h
cult(ic), 132 n. 17, 133
cultic hymn, 131
cult(ic) (*cont.*)
cults of Gad and Meni, 50
daffodil (*asphodel*), 77, 77 n. 30, 191
dance, 102, 162 n. 115
dance of the two camps, 102, 161, 202
dancer, 120, 162 n. 115
Daniel, book of, 24, 27
Danites, 25
darling, 74, 85–86, 94, 112, 123, 125, 143, 150, 155, 191, 191 n. 10, 193, 194, 196, 197, 198, 198 n. s, 201
darling (ally), 158–60, 162, 191 n. 12
Dead Sea Scrolls, 23 n. 91, 26, 43, 46, 57 n. 1, 61, 125 n. 29, 182
dental, 79, 82, 91
dental liquid, 71
dental plosive, 80
emphatic dental, 76
interdental, 14
voiced dental, 75, 82, 99
voiceless dental, 76, 99
Deuteronomy, book of, 23 n. 90
dishonor. *See* honor
divan. *See* couch
double entendres, 2, 48 n. 207, 148 n. 71, 171
double plural, 24-25, 54
pseudo-double plural, 24-25
dove, 75, 85, 112, 123–24, 146, 149, 155, 191, 194, 196, 198, 198 n. s, 200, 201
drama, 168, 168 n. 138
dream, 95, 123, 136, 146, 146 n. 67, 198 n. 28
Egyptian poetry, 138 n. 43, 184
Elisha cycle, 15–16, 18, 20, 30, 40
erotic, 133–34, 136–37, 147, 199 n. 29, 202 n. 38
de-eroticize, 129 n. 2
erotic imagery, 144–45, 192 n. 13, 198 n. 27
erotic language, 144 n. 61, 202 n. 41
erotic poem (poetry), 133, 138 n. 43, 168, 184
erotic prelude, 134, 136
homoerotic, 151

Ethanim, 40
etymology (etymological), 84, 86, 102, 138 n. 39
etymon (etyma), 76, 97, 102 n. 51, 175
euphemism (euphemistic), 144, 144 n. 61, 202 n. y
exodus, the, 162 n. 120
explicit language, 144
eye, 22 n. 83, 75–76, 85–86, 88, 90, 100, 112, 139, 143, 149, 152, 155, 161, 164 n. 128, 172, 191, 193 n. l, 196, 197, 200, 201, 203, 206
evil eye, 152
fawn(s), 116–17, 122, 143, 147, 149, 162 n. 115, 193, 193 n. 16, 194, 197, 203, 206
female lover, 77, 95, 96, 117–18, 119–20, 122, 123–24, 130, 154 n. 87, 169, 171, 173, 185, 188, 189 n. 3, 191 n. 10, 193 n. 16, 194 nn. o–p, 196 n. 23, 197 n. 25, 198 n. s, 199 nn. t, 29 and 32, 200 n. 34, 201 n. 36, 202 n. 39, 204 nn. ae and 43, 206 n. aj
female voice, 117–18, 123, 173, 188
feminine (gramatical), 17 n. 56, 20–21, 21 n. 81, 23, 40, 59, 82, 85, 90, 101, 116, 158, 161, 188, 191 n. 10
feminine tone, 204 n. ae
feminist, 171, 173
fig, 79, 162
fig-tree, 37, 79, 148, 162, 193
unripe fig, 37, 53
fire, darts of, 160, 205
flattery, 133
double-edged flattery, 142, 165 n. 129
exaggerated flattery, 141, 143 n. 57, 201 n. 36
sarcastic flattery, 133, 141
flock(s), 25, 39, 40, 52 n. 226, 74, 85–86, 87, 113, 120–21, 143, 149, 153–54, 159, 161, 190, 196, 201
fortification(s), 135, 147
fountain, 92, 148, 162, 197
foxes, 148–49, 164, 164 nn. 126–27, 194, 194 n. 19
frankincense, 81, 83, 93–94, 152, 195, 197, 198
friend(s), 25, 94, 105–6, 151, 154, 161, 190, 198, 199 n. t, 200, 200 n. 34, 206
friends (allies), 158–60, 158 n. 102, 191 n. 10, 206 n. 45
garden, 92, 100, 101, 124, 135, 142, 145, 148–49, 152, 160, 162, 164, 172, 177, 177 n. 18, 178, 178 n. 21, 190 n. 6, 197, 198, 200, 201, 206
enclosed garden, 175, 178
garden bed, 97
garden of Eden, 173, 204 n. ae
pleasure garden, 55
walnut garden, 101, 149, 202
gazelle, 114–15, 116–17, 135, 141, 147, 149, 159, 192, 193 n. 16, 194, 195, 206
gazelles (rulers/nobles), 163, 163 nn. 121 and 123
geminate, 21, 22 n. 83, 23, 58
Genesis, book of, 5, 7, 52
gender, 156–57, 165, 166 n. 132, 193 n. 17
gender roles, 156–57, 163 n. 123
genitive ending, 74
ghazal, 134, 134 nn. 24–25
ʿUdhrī *ghazal*, 135 n. 28
Gibeonites, 30
Gideon cycle, 15, 28
Gilgamesh, Epic of, 181
grapes, 37, 53
graze, 100, 149, 153, 157, 161, 164, 190 n. 8, 201
hair, 39, 43, 52, 85–86, 96, 120, 136, 143, 149, 196, 201, 202 n. z, 203 nn. ab and ac
hairlocks, 43
hairstyling, 34 n. 131
ḫalq, 134, 144
hapax legomenon, 35, 36, 37, 44, 50, 53, 66, 69, 70, 70 n. 23, 79, 84, 85, 86, 88, 95, 105
Hazor epigraph, 37, 53
henna, 92–93, 148, 152, 181, 191, 197, 204, 206 n. aj
hijāʾ, 2, 71 n. 25, 133–37, 133 n. 19, 134

n. 21, 138–40, 141, 142 n. 53, 144, 145, 150, 152, 153, 155, 165, 168, 169, 174, 175 n. 9, 188, 189 nn. 2–5, 190 n. 6, 191 nn. 9–10, 192 nn. 13 and 15, 193 nn. 16,–17, 194 n. 18, 197 nn. 25–26, 198 nn. 27–28, 199 nn. 29–30, 200 n. 33, 203 n. 42
hind, 114–15, 116–17, 149, 159, 163, 192, 193, 194, 195, 196, 206
Hindu mythology, 176 n. 15
Hipʿil, 73, 116
Hitpaʿel, 105
Hittites, 25
Hivites, 30
honey, 41–42, 54, 91, 94, 151, 197, 198
  honeycomb, 94, 151, 198
honor, 153, 155, 165, 165 n. 132, 166, 166 n. 132
  dishonor, 142, 169
homoerotic. *See* Erotic
homonym, 44 n. 185, 52, 87
  homonymous, 12, 189 n. c
horse(s), 135, 162; *see also* mare and stallions
Hosea, book of, 4–5, 4 n. 6, 5 n. 10, 11 n. 36
ḫuluq, 136
humor, 133
hyperbole, 139
Iambic, 161
imperative, 74, 85, 116, 117
incest, 135, 153–54, 154 n. 87, 155 n. 87, 158, 197 n. 25, 204 n. 43
Indo-Europeans, 180 n. 34
innuendo, 145, 162–64
interdental. *See* dental
invective, 133–34, 136, 139, 139 n. 46, 140–41, 155 n. 87, 157, 161, 163–64, 165–66, 166 n. 132, 169, 171, 174, 180, 183 n. 40, 189 n. 1, 193 n. 17, 194 n. 20, 202 n. 41
  Arabic invective, 135, 137, 139, 139 n. 43, 140, 144, 146, 152, 154, 157, 169
  Egyptian mythology and erotic poetry as invective, 138 n. 43
invective (*cont.*)
  Greek invective, 138, 140, 144, 152, 154, 161, 169
  invective genre of praise, 138
  invective poetry, 2, 135–37, 139, 140, 160, 192 n. 14, 204 n. 43
    political invective, 133, 138 n. 43, 168
Iranians, 111
irony, 144 n. 58
  ironic praise, 144, 196 n. 23
Isaiah, book of, 44, 61, 182
isogloss, 6, 8, 12, 13, 14, 21, 27, 33, 36, 60
ʾItpaʿal, 44
ivory, 99, 136, 151, 152
  beds of ivory,33
  block of ivory, 98–99, 152, 200
  tower of ivory, 121–22, 143, 150, 203
Jacob and Laban story, 52
jamāl, 136
Janus parallel, 13–14, 48 n. 207, 190 nn. e and 8, 193 n. n, 203 n. aa
Jeremiah, book of, 12, 21, 22, 38 n. 154
Job, book of, 5, 12, 45–46, 59, 124 n. 26
Jonah, book of, 16-17
Judah, tribe of, 141, 165 n. 129
Judahite(s), 25, 47, 54 n. 230, 164
Judges, book of, 4–5
judges, northern, 4
Ketiv, 18 n. 60, 126
king(s), 25, 59, 157, 158 n. 102, 167, 168 n. 137, 184, 189, 190 n. 8, 191, 191 n. h, 194 n. 20, 195, 196, 196 n. 22, 203
  Aramean king, 16
  Assyrian king, 48
  Judahite king, 34
  king of Israel, 26, 28, 34
  king of Tyre, 168, 168 n. 137
  King Solomon. *See* Solomon
  Persian king, 178
Kings, book of, 4–5, 17, 30, 181, 184 n. 44
kingship, 167
Korah, 5, 22
Kret Story (Epic), 32, 67
Kulturwort, 180

labial, 60 n. 9, 80, 81, 82, 99
Lamentations, book of, 12
laryngeal, 75, 77
Leningrad Codex, 18 n. 60, 94 n. 45, 187
Leviathan, 24
lions, 18, 135, 141
  dens of lions, 25, 89–90, 149, 197
liquids, 66
  liquid dental, 71
luminaries, 100–101, 150, 172, 201
Maʿalot, 19
male lover, 72, 75, 77, 80, 123–24, 130–31, 154, 154 n. 87, 156, 171, 173, 185, 188, 189 n. 3, 193 n. l, 194 n. o, 197 n. 25, 198 n. s, 199 n. 31, 200 n. 33, 204 nn. ae and 43, 206 n. aj
male voice, 123, 173, 188
mandrake, 104, 204
maqqef, 102
mare, 74, 143, 150, 153, 159, 162, 162 n. 120, 190
Masora, 115 n. 17, 124
Masoretes, 120
Masoretic, 59, 91, 187
Masoretic marks. *See* accent marks
Masoretic Text, 57–62, 78 n. 32, 181–83, 189 n. 4
mater lectionis, 115 n. 17
Medes, 177
Mesopotamian poetry, 138 n. 43
metaphor(ical), 145, 147, 148 n. 71, 149–50, 151 n. 74, 157–58, 161, 162 n. 115, 164, 164 n. 127, 194 n. 19
  viticultural metaphors, 161, 194 n. 19
metaplastic root, 85
metathesis, 73 n. 27, 77 n. 30
metonym(ic)/(y), 137
military, 135–36, 147, 149, 156, 161, 163, 190–91 n. 9
Miqraʾ, 120
Mishnaic, 28, 175 n. 10
Mishnaisms, 174-175
Moabites, 159
monarchy
  divided monarchy, 184
monarchy (*cont.*)
  Judahite monarchy, 2, 180, 184 n. 40, 185
  united monarchy, 157
morpheme, 18, 20, 23, 176 n. 17
morphology(ical), 1, 109, 119, 120, 122, 123 n. 24, 124, 126, 160 n. 107
motif, 132 n. 17, 135, 137, 147, 156, 193 n. l
mujūn, 142, 142 n. 53
munaḥ, 124
myrrh, 81–83, 92–93, 95–96, 145, 151–52, 191, 195, 197, 198, 199, 200, 206 n. aj
mythopoetic symbols, 138 n. 40
Nabokov, 118, 118 n. 20
Nahum, book of, 177 n. 20
nard, 75, 92–93, 148, 152, 181–82, 182 n. 36, 191, 197, 198
nasals, 66, 77, 79
nasīb, 133 n. 20, 134, 134 n. 24, 134–35 n. 25, 136–37, 144, 155, 157
naʿt, 136
Nehemiah, book of, 12, 27, 178
Neo-Babylonians, 30
Nipʿal, 34, 73, 88 n. 40
Nitpaʿel, 44
nomen actionis, 16-18
nomen rectum, 24–25
nomen regens, 24–25
Numbers, book of, 109
Omrides, 178
oneupmanship , 124 n. 26
onomatopoetic effect, 66
orchard, 91–92, 135, 147–48, 174–75, 178–79, 181, 190 n. 6, 197
Paʿel, 34, 44
palanquin, 83–85, 159, 167, 179, 195
palatal, 177 n. 18
palm tree, 46–47, 47 n. 202, 103, 135, 143, 145, 147, 149, 202, 202 n. w, 203
parallelism, 32 n. 124, 41, 51, 64 n. 7, 69, 110, 202 n. z
paronomasia, 70 n. 24, 71, 80 n. 33, 93, 98, 161, 161 n. 109

partial alliteration, 68
penis, 164
perfect-one, 123–24, 155, 198, 198 n. s, 199 n. t, 201
perfume, 79, 97–98, 126, 148, 152, 162, 193, 200
periphrastic fenitive, 25
Persian period, 8, 15, 168, 174, 178 n. 23, 180–81
Persian-style garden architecture, 178 n. 21
Pharaoh, 74
Pharaoh's chariotry, 74, 143, 150, 159, 189
Pharaoh's mares, 162, 162 n. 120
pharyngeal , 75
pharyngeal fricative, 66, 79, 86, 90
Phoenician city-states, 51
Phoenicianisms, 40, 50
Phoenicianizing, 50
Phoenicians, 168
Piʿel, 34, 40, 44, 89 n. 40
Pilpel, 51 n. 222
plene spelling, 49
ploce, 109
plosive. *See* dental plosive or velar plosive, respectively
poets/reciters, 110, 111
Polel, 116
political invective. *See* invective
polyprosopon, 108–9, 117, 120, 126–27, 172, 184
polyptoton, 108-109, 123 n. 24
polysemy, 91, 192 n. j, 202 n. w
pomegranate, 87–88, 91–93, 104, 126, 148–49, 151, 196, 197, 201, 202, 204
postbiblical, 15, 33, 43
postbiblical texts, 33, 99, 129, 202 n. y
postexilic, 15, 21 n. 81, 26 n. 100
postexilic compositions, 21
postexilic dating, 9, 19
postexilic period, 15, 50, 54, 175, 184 n. 44
precious metals, 136, 152, 200 n. 33
preexilic biblical texts, 15
preexilic times, 177, 180
prefix conjugation (PC), 71, 74, 119
pre-Islamic poetry, 133 n. 20, 137 n. 38
pronominal suffix, 20, 21, 21 nn. 79 and 81, 23, 42, 68, 71–72, 76, 79, 89, 90, 119
prophets, 4-6, 164 n. 127, 183
propinquity, 84
Proto-Semitic, 11, 13, 14, 20, 102 n. 51
Proverbs, book of, 5, 5 n. 10, 31, 35 n. 138, 41, 50, 184
Psalms, book of, 4–5, 7, 15, 25, 28, 31, 48
pseudo-double plural. *See* double plural
Puʿal, 81, 99
pubic hair, 202 n. z
puns (punning), 136, 157, 160–61, 161 n. 111, 163
puns on Solomon, 161–62
purple, 159, 168, 168 n. 137, 195, 203, 203 n. aa
Qal, 34, 40, 116
qasīda, 133 n. 20, 134 n. 25
Qeri, 18 n. 60, 20, 76, 126
qətāl, 36
qətaltōl, 73
*qətîlā*ʰ, 16–18, 16 nn. 54 and 56
Qohelet, book of, 5, 14, 15, 179, 179 n. 25
raven, 96–97, 149, 200
reduplicatory plurals, 21–23, 21 n. 83, 22 n. 83, 90
refrain, 19, 71, 96, 108, 108 n. 5, 114–16, 127, 192 n. 14, 193 n. 16
royal intruder, 171
runners, 33–34, 52, 76, 167, 191, 203 n. ac
saffron, 92-93, 152, 198
1 Samuel, book of, 7
sandhi setting, 177 n. 17
sarcasm, 131
  sarcastic flattery, 133, 141
  sarcastic humor, 133
  sarcastic nature, 199 n. 32
  sarcastic tone, 132, 201 n. 36
scatological reference, 139 n. 43
seasons, 147
  winter, 36, 36 n. 144, 148, 193

segholate. *See* Aramaic segholate
Semitic, 50 n. 214, 51, 65, 71 n. 26, 76, 88, 115, 176 n. 16, 177 n. 20
  Northwest Semitic, 14, 20, 42, 45, 47, 50 n. 214, 51, 178 n. 21
  Semitic family, 50 n. 214
  West Semitic, 77 n. 30
Septuagint (LXX), 59, 96, 181
sex, 142, 146, 162, 163 n. 123
  inverted sex role, 153
  sexual connotation, 189 n. c, 199 n. 7
  sexual innuendo, 145, 162, 164
  sexual metaphors, 151 n. 74, 161
  sexual overtones, 162, 164
shame, 134, 138, 162, 165–67, 165 n. 132, 166 n. 132, 166 n. 133
Sheol, 160, 205
shepherd (verb and noun)
Shulammite, 9–10, 102, 145, 159, 161–62, 162 n. 114, 202
sibilants, 36 n. 144, 66, 72, 77, 86, 103, 177 n. 17, 183
Sidonians, 59
simile, 39, 122, 137
sister, 88, 92, 94, 123, 133, 148, 149, 154, 154 n. 87, 155, 161, 197, 198, 198 n. s, 205
  brother-sister marriages, 154–55 n. 87, 197 n. 25; *see also* incest
  sister (ally), 157–58, 160, 160 n. 105, 163
  sister of Neobule, 142
skin, 136
Solar hymn. *See* Canaanite solar hymn
Somali poetry, 110
Song of Deborah, 14, 15, 17, 19, 22, 28, 59
sons of Heth. *See* Hittites
spice, 23, 59, 100, 136, 145, 151–52, 197, 197 n. 26, 198, 206 n. aj
  bed of spices, 97, 100, 124, 149, 152, 164, 200, 200 n. v
  mountains of spices, 25, 116–17, 206, 206 n. aj
spice (*cont.*)
  spiced wine. *See* wine
spring (water), 92, 148–49, 162, 197, 198
stallions, 153, 163
stative participle, 116
style-switching, 6, 6 n. 12, 16, 30, 32, 45, 48, 51, 59, 169
subjunctive/future, 119
suffix conjugation (SC), 119, 192 n. h
sukkot, 108
synecdoche, 137, 202 n. y
Talmud Yerushalmi, 35
Tamil poetry, 174
Tannaitic sources/texts, 6, 34, 36, 38, 46
Tannin, 24
Targum(im), 27 n. 102, 33, 35, 36, 38, 43, 44, 51, 167–68
tašbib, 2, 133–38, 140–41, 144, 145, 150–51, 165, 168–69, 174
teeth, 87, 121, 136, 149, 151, 196, 201
tipḥa, 119
toponym, 9–10, 25, 53 n. 227, 60 n. 10, 83, 85–86, 89, 93, 121, 203 n. aa
Torah, 45, 67, 111, 183
tower, 98, 122, 135, 143, 147, 150, 161, 205
  tower of David, 121–22, 131, 143, 150, 196
  tower of ivory, 121–22, 143, 150, 203
  tower of Lebanon, 131, 143, 150, 203
  tower of perfumes, 97–98, 152, 200
Transjordanian dialects, 4, 31
Transjordanian setting, 5, 46–47
Turaq oil, 72, 189, 189 n. b
turtledove, 193, 193 n. n
ʿUdhrī *ghazal*. *See ghazal*
Ugaritic poetry, 10, 47, 67, 67 n. 17, 140 n. 50
united monarchy. *See* monarchy
unrequited love, 135, 135 n. 28, 145–46, 199 n. 30
vacat, 125 n. 29
variant spelling, 116
velar fricative, 66, 86
velar plosive, 80, 81, 82, 87

verbatim repetition, 115 n. 17, 123, 125–26, 204 n. af
verbs
  I-*y*, 85
  III-ʾ, 85
  III-*y*, 85
verdant, 76, 112, 191
vine(s), 79, 104, 145, 148–49, 162, 164, 194, 202, 203, 204
vineyard(s), 47, 79, 104, 135, 140 n. 49, 147–49, 148 n. 71, 155, 159, 164, 164 n. 126, 167, 190, 190 n. 6, 191, 194, 194 n. 19, 204, 206
visarga, 177 n. 17
voiced, 14, 50–51, 66, 68, 69, 75, 80, 82, 87, 90, 92, 99, 103, 105, 177 n. 17
voiceless, 14, 50–51, 66, 68, 69, 76, 80, 81–82, 87, 92, 99, 103, 105
Vulgate, 59
vulva, 103, 145, 202, 202 nn. y–z
wall(s), 35, 42, 78–79, 135, 142–44, 147, 150, 161, 176, 193, 205
  city walls, 25, 155, 160, 199
waṣf, 130–33, 136–37, 143, 157, 159, 173
wind, 65–66, 92, 125, 145, 147–48, 194, 197, 198
window, 36, 78, 117, 156, 156 nn. 94–95, 173, 193, 193 n. l
wine, 9, 14, 37, 72, 73 n. 27, 135–36, 145, 147, 150–51, 159, 189, 189 n. 2, 197, 198, 204
  house of wine, 151, 159, 192
  mixed wine, 50–51, 103, 145, 202, 202 n. y
  new wine, 73
  smooth-wine, 72, 72 n. 27, 151, 153, 189, 204
  spiced wine, 105, 151, 204
wine-hall, 180
wineskins, 29
word pairs, 11 n. 30, 111
Yemenite Jews, 111
zaqef qaton, 119, 124
Ziv, 40

Index of Names

ʿAbd al-Malik, 144
Abigail, 154 n. 87
Abijam, 154 n. 87
Abimelech, 156 n. 94
Abraham, 24, 154 n. 87
Absalom, 154 n. 87
Adonis (divine), 31
Ahijah, 59
Amaziah, 34
Amnon, 154 n. 87
Amos, 4, 4 n. 6
Asa, 154 n. 87
Athaliah, 59
Baal (divine), 39, 141 n. 50
Balaam, 5, 22, 47
Benjamin, 7, 42
David, 32, 154 n. 87, 157, 157 n. 99, 158 n. 102, 161 n. 171, 167 n. 136, 168 n. 137
Deborah, 4
Dinah, 44
Eli's sons, 163 n. 123
Elijah, 17
Elisha, 26
Ephraim, 7, 42
Gad (divine), 50
Gideon, 4
Hezekiah, 17
Hiram, 157, 168
Hosea, 4, 4 n. 6, 158
Isaiah, 30, 48, 51, 158
Ishtar (divine), 139 n. 43
Issachar, 32
Jabra al-Maxzūmīya, 147
Jacob (Israel), 7, 32, 33
Jehoash, 34
Jephthah, 4, 14
Jeremiah, 7, 48
Jeroboam I, 30, 167, 174
Jeroboam II, 178
Jezebel, 156, 193 n. l
Jonah, 16
Jonathan, 7, 12, 32
Joseph, 7, 42, 65 n. 9
Judah, 165 n. 129, 167
Kret, 67–68, 140 n. 50, 141 n. 50
Lady Wisdom, 156, 193 n. l
Lycambes, 138, 142
Maacah, 154 n. 87
Manasseh, 7, 42
Marduk (divine), 139 n. 43
Meni (divine), 50
Michal, 156, 193 n. l
Moses, 29
Muhammad Ibn Hišām, 147
Naaman, 31
Nebat, 167
Nehemiah, 26 n. 100
Neobulé, 138, 142
Nikkal-and-Ib (divine), 47
Oholibah, 163
Omri, 174
Pekah, 28
Rachel, 7
Rahab, 156, 193 n. l
Rebekah, 123 n. 24
Sarah, 154 n. 87
Saul, 7, 17, 32
Samuel, 13
Sennacherib, 48, 139 n. 43

Shu (divine), 66 n. 11
Sisera's Mother, 156, 193 n. l
Solomon (Shelomo), 16, 25, 40, 70–71, 83–84, 132 n. 17, 140–41, 149–50, 159, 161–63, 161 n. 111, 162 n. 120, 167–68, 168 n. 137, 171, 173–74, 176 n. 16, 180, 184, 187, 189, 189 n. 1, 191 n. 11, 195, 196, 206, 206 nn. ai and 44
Tamar (of Genesis), 123 n. 24
Tamar (of 2 Samuel), 154 n. 87
Umm al-Banīn, 144
witch of Endor (necromancer), 13
Yahweh (divine), 45, 157, 205 n. ah
Zarpanitum (divine), 139 n. 43

Index of Toponyms

Amana, 9, 41, 60, 89, 197
Anathoth, 7, 12, 17, 21
Aram, 5, 19, 31, 51, 52
Arslan Tash, 59
Baal Hamon (Baʿal-Hamon), 149, 167, 206
Baal Hermon, 30
Babylon, 25, 139
Bashan, 32
Bat-Rabbim, 203
Benjamin, 7, 12, 18, 28, 167
Byblos (Amarna), 24, 50
Canaan, 11, 30, 46
Carmel (Karmel), 9–10, 203, 203 n. aa
Cush, 28 n. 107
Damascus (Damesseq), 9, 19, 32, 131, 143, 150, 203, 203 n. aa
Dan, 25
Egypt, 32, 50, 130 n. 6, 155 n. 87, 162 n. 120, 163, 184
Ein-Gedi, 10, 148, 191
Ephraim, 13, 18, 59
Galilee, 9–10
Gath-hepher, 17
Gibeah, 18, 28
Gibeon, 30
Gilboa, 32
Gilead (Gilʿad), 9, 25, 28, 39, 85–87, 101, 113, 120–21, 143, 149, 187, 196, 201
Hazor, 37
Hermon (Ḥermon), 9, 22, 30, 60 n. 10, 89, 197
Heshbon, 9, 158–59, 203
Iran, 177
Israel (Yisraʾel), 3, 4, 9, 21, 26, 28, 31, 34, 45, 51, 54, 60, 106, 111, 132 n. 14, 140, 148 n. 71, 150, 150 n. 72, 157, 158, 160 n. 105, 164–67, 168 n. 137, 172, 175 n. 9, 176, 177, 180, 181, 183, 184, 194 n. 19, 195
Jerusalem (Yerushalayim), 3, 10, 25, 45, 84, 114, 149–50, 158, 159–60, 162, 162 n. 114, 163–64, 174, 178, 189, 192, 195, 196, 199, 200, 201, 205
Jezreel, 9
Judah, 3, 7, 9, 25, 37, 46, 51, 59, 150 n. 72, 167, 184
Kedar, 141
Khirbet Saruna, 10
Lebanon (Levanon), 9, 27, 30, 32, 34, 42, 48, 57, 60, 83, 88–89, 91, 93–94, 131, 143, 149, 150, 158–60, 167, 187, 195, 197, 198, 200, 203, 203 n. aa
Lebo-hamath, 30
Leptis Magna, 49
Mahanaim, 9, 102, 102 n. 51
Manasseh, 13
Massa, 59
Mesopotamia, 8, 50, 130 n. 6, 184
Midian, 52
Mizpah, 18
Pasargadae, 178
Persepolis, 178
Phoenicia, 50, 68 n. 137
Qedar, 189
Rabbah, 158-159
Samaria, 158, 163
Senir, 9, 89, 197
Sharon, 9–10, 10 n. 24, 77, 191
Shiloh, 59

Shunem, 9–10, 161
Solem/Solam, 161 n. 113
Tabor (Mount), 9
Tiberias, 9–10
Tirzah (Tirza), 9, 150, 174, 201
Tripolitana, 49
Tyre, 23, 25, 30, 59, 157, 168, 168 n. 137
Ugarit, 51, 130 n. 6
Yavneʾel Valley, 10
Zion, 45, 84–85, 158, 159

LaVergne, TN USA
10 November 2009
163656LV00001B/57/P

9 781589 834224